INSTITUTIONAL INVESTORS AND CORPORATE STOCK—A BACKGROUND STUDY

NATIONAL BUREAU OF ECONOMIC RESEARCH

STUDIES IN CAPITAL FORMATION AND FINANCING

1. *Capital Formation in Residential Real Estate: Trends and Prospects*
   Leo Grebler, David M. Blank, and Louis Winnick
2. *Capital in Agriculture: Its Formation and Financing since 1870*
   Alvin S. Tostlebe
3. *Financial Intermediaries in the American Economy since 1900*
   Raymond W. Goldsmith
4. *Capital in Transportation, Communications, and Public Utilities: Its Formation and Financing*
   Melville J. Ulmer
5. *Postwar Market for State and Local Government Securities*
   Roland I. Robinson
6. *Capital in Manufacturing and Mining: Its Formation and Financing*
   Daniel Creamer, Sergei P. Dobrovolsky, and Israel Borenstein
7. *Trends in Government Financing*
   Morris A. Copeland
8. *The Postwar Residential Mortgage Market*
   Saul B. Klaman
9. *Capital in the American Economy: Its Formation and Financing*
   Simon Kuznets
10. *The National Wealth of the United States in the Postwar Period*
    Raymond W. Goldsmith
11. *Studies in the National Balance Sheet of the United States*
    Volume I, Raymond W. Goldsmith and Robert E. Lipsey
    Volume II, Raymond W. Goldsmith, Robert E. Lipsey, and Morris Mendelson
12. *The Flow of Capital Funds in the Postwar Economy*
    Raymond W. Goldsmith
13. *Institutional Investors and Corporate Stock—A Background Study*
    Raymond W. Goldsmith, Editor

Institutional Investors and Corporate Stock — A Background Study

RAYMOND W. GOLDSMITH, *Editor*

YALE UNIVERSITY

Published by

NATIONAL BUREAU OF ECONOMIC RESEARCH

1973

Distributed by COLUMBIA UNIVERSITY PRESS

NEW YORK AND LONDON

This is a revision of the Institutional Investor Study Report of the Securities and Exchange
Commission, Supplementary Volumes I and II, originally published by the United States
Government Printing Office, Washington, D.C., 1971.

Library of Congress no.: 73-171574

ISBN: 0-87014-237-2

Printed in the United States of America

Relation of the Directors to the Work and Publications
of the National Bureau of Economic Research

1. The object of the National Bureau of Economic Research is to ascertain and to present to the public important economic facts and their interpretation in a scientific and impartial manner. The Board of Directors is charged with the responsibility of ensuring that the work of the National Bureau is carried on in strict conformity with this object.

2. The President of the National Bureau shall submit to the Board of Directors, or to its Executive Committee, for their formal adoption all specific proposals for research to be instituted.

3. No research report shall be published until the President shall have submitted to each member of the Board the manuscript proposed for publication, and such information as will, in his opinion and in the opinion of the author, serve to determine the suitability of the report for publication in accordance with the principles of the National Bureau. Each manuscript shall contain a summary drawing attention to the nature and treatment of the problem studied, the character of the data and their utilization in the report, and the main conclusions reached.

4. For each manuscript so submitted, a special committee of the Board shall be appointed by majority agreement of the President and Vice Presidents (or by the Executive Committee in case of inability to decide on the part of the President and Vice-Presidents), consisting of three directors selected as nearly as may be one from each general division of the Board. The names of the special manuscript committee shall be stated to each Director when the manuscript is submitted to him. It shall be the duty of each member of the special manuscript committee to read the manuscript. If each member of the manuscript committee signifies his approval within thirty days of the transmittal of the manuscript, the report may be published. If at the end of that period any member of the manuscript committee withholds his approval, the President shall then notify each member of the Board, requesting approval or disapproval of publication, and thirty days additional shall be granted for this purpose. The manuscript shall then not be published unless at least a majority of the entire Board who shall have voted on the proposal within the time fixed for the receipt of votes shall have approved.

5. No manuscript may be published, though approved by each member of the special manuscript committee, until forty-five days have elapsed from the transmittal of the report in manuscript form. The interval is allowed for the receipt of any memorandum of dissent or reservation, together with a brief statement of his reasons, that any member may wish to express; and such memorandum of dissent or reservation shall be published with the manuscript if he so desires. Publication does not, however, imply that each member of the Board has read the manuscript, or that either members of the Board in general or the special committee have passed on its validity in every detail.

6. Publications of the National Bureau issued for informational purposes concerning the work of the Bureau and its staff, or issued to inform the public of activities of Bureau staff, and volumes issued as a result of various conferences involving the National Bureau shall contain a specific disclaimer noting that such publication has not passed through the normal review procedures required in this resolution. The Executive Committee of the Board is charged with review of all such publications from time to time to ensure that they do not take on the character of formal research reports of the National Bureau, requiring formal Board approval.

7. Unless otherwise determined by the Board or exempted by the terms of paragraph 6, a copy of this resolution shall be printed in each National Bureau publication.

(Resolution adopted October 25, 1926, and revised February 8, 1933,
February 24, 1941, and April 20, 1968)

LETTER OF TRANSMITTAL

NATIONAL BUREAU OF ECONOMIC RESEARCH, INC.

NEW YORK, N.Y., *December 30, 1970*

HON. HAMER BUDGE,
Chairman, U.S. Securities and Exchange Commission,
Washington, D.C.

DEAR JUDGE BUDGE: I am herewith submitting the National Bureau's report on *Institutional Investors and Corporate Stock* in accordance with our contract of June, 1969. A preliminary version of this report was sent to you in June of this year; the present report differs from that preliminary report mainly in details, not in substance. The enclosed report has been reviewed by a committee of our board and has been accepted as an official National Bureau report.

Nevertheless, this report should still be regarded as preliminary in some senses. The work undertaken by the National Bureau in the preparation of the report had limited objectives. We have assembled and updated statistical materials which provide background and underlying information which could be utilized by the Commission in its comprehensive study of the impact of the activities of institutional investors upon the national economy. We have revised and extended earlier National Bureau work on the national balance sheet for the United States and also made some additions to the Federal Reserve Board's flow-of-funds statistics.

We understand that the Commission wishes to publish the report prepared by the National Bureau without significant modification and we are pleased to have this done with the recognition that the report is designed to serve the limited objectives of providing the underlying data requested by the Commission.

As a result of the conflict between the immovable deadline for the submission of your Commission's report to the Congress and the unexpected difficulties and delays which almost unavoidably arise in extensive statistical projects of the type represented by this report, I regret that we have not been able as of this date to edit the text of the report as thoroughly or to check the data as carefully as we would have liked to do and as we do in projects where we can continue to work until we are entirely satisfied with the results. We have, however, checked and rechecked the figures to the extent that time has permitted and have completed at least a preliminary editing of the contents.

We have not had, moreover, the time required to complete all of the analyses that the data, or the complex problems of the financial industry, would suggest. I am sure that in this regard we share a common experience with your staff that has been in charge of the institutional investors study. I would add that as part of the Bureau's long-term and ongoing commitment to financial research we hope to involve ourselves in some of these analyses in the future as time and resources permit.

Meanwhile, we believe that no errors remain in the present version that would substantially affect the facts and figures or the conclusions that can be drawn from them.

Very sincerely yours,

JOHN R. MEYER,

President.

Contents

INSTITUTIONAL INVESTORS AND CORPORATE STOCK—A BACKGROUND STUDY

1

Basic Considerations

RAYMOND W. GOLDSMITH

YALE UNIVERSITY

1. PURPOSE, SCOPE, AND LIMITATIONS OF REPORT

The purpose of this report is to provide a comprehensive, quantitative basis for appraising the position of, the holdings of, and transactions in corporate stock by institutional investors.[1] Such an appraisal was needed by the Securities and Exchange Commission as a background for its Institutional Investors' Study. That study concentrates on the activities of financial institutions in the stock market during the latter part of the 1960's and deals with the subject in much greater detail than was required of the background study. It is based on extensive new primary statistical data which were not available for this report.

The holdings of corporate stock by financial institutions are viewed in this report in terms of their roles: (a) as part of the assets of financial institutions and (b) as an element in the equity of corporations. These aspects can be examined most satisfactorily within the framework of a sectorized national balance sheet. Transactions are regarded as a component of the flows—new issues of and trading in—corporate shares; in that guise, they are best seen within the structure of a flow of funds account.[2] The choice of the analytic framework for holdings and transactions is explained briefly in section 4.

The first task of the study, therefore, is to establish within this framework, in as much detail and as accurately as this can be done on the basis of the available statistical data and for as long a period as is possible and relevant, the facts concerning holdings of and the trading in corporate stock by the main types of financial institutions. More specifically, it is

---

[1] For a list of the types of institutions included, see section 5a.
[2] A brief description will be found in section 4.

necessary to determine two sets of ratios: (1) the share of corporate stock in the total assets of, and in the acquisition of financial assets by the different types of financial institutions; and (2) the relation of the stockholdings and stock transactions of financial institutions to the total value of corporate stock outstanding or traded.

It would be desirable to determine these ratios separately for the main types of corporate stock, for instance, for common and preferred stock, and for the stock of the main groups of financial and nonfinancial corporations. Generally, however, we must be content with ratios for all corporate stock together. It is desirable to make these calculations on at least an annual basis, but this is possible only for the period beginning with the 1950's.

On the basis of these figures and ratios we must try to determine whether definite trends have existed in the institutional holdings of, and in the transactions in, corporate stock in relation to the assets of financial institutions and to the volume of corporate stock outstanding or traded; and we must study how these movements have changed since corporations and financial institutions became important features in the American economic and financial scene during the third quarter of the nineteenth century. Finally, we must try to explain such significant movements as may be found, at least to the extent of ascertaining the immediate economic and institutional determinants. It will not be possible in this report to go beyond this first stage of causal analysis since this would require an analysis of the entire process of American economic and financial development during the last century.

This report, therefore, is primarily fact-finding and descriptive in nature and procceds on a fairly high level of aggregation. It does not deal with the desirability, from the point of view of whatever standards the analyst may want to apply, of the developments observed. Nor does it consider, except in section 2, policies that might have led to different trends from those actually observed or that might affect their continuation or modification. Because of lack of data, time, and resources, no attention is paid to the experience of individual financial institutions or of subgroups within the fairly broad categories distinguished by available statistics, or to developments during periods shorter than a single year.

Technically the core of this report is a set of sectoral annual balance sheets and sources-and-uses-of-funds statements for the years 1953 through 1968, and the equivalent but much rougher statistics for spans of seven to twenty years during earlier periods that are presented in Chapter 2. These statistics generally distinguish four nonfinancial sectors (households, including or separating agriculture and other unincorporated business enterprises; nonfinancial corporations; state and local governments; and the federal government). The financial sector is divided into about a dozen institutional subsectors. The main contributions of the report from the statistical point of view for the postwar period are:

1. Estimates of national wealth—structures, equipment, inventories, and land—by sectors for the period 1959–68 and the revision of previous estimates for the years 1952–58.

2. The separation of personal trust funds administered by commercial banks (to be included with financial institutions) and of two groups of nonprofit institutions (foundations and universities and colleges) from the household sector, which thus becomes considerably more homogeneous.

3. A rough breakdown of the now more narrowly defined household sector into half-a-dozen subsectors classified by wealth (Appendix V).

4. The inclusion of several relatively small groups of financial institutions which formerly were omitted from the flow of funds statistics: fraternal insurance organizations, mortgage companies (formerly included with finance companies), closed-end investment companies, and common trust funds.

The main statistical limitations of this material are briefly discussed in section 5.

2. THE ROLE OF CORPORATE STOCK AND OF FINANCIAL INSTITUTIONS IN THE AMERICAN ECONOMY

There can be no doubt about the importance of either corporate stock or financial institutions for the size and character of the financial superstructure of the American economy. After all, in 1968 corporate stock having a total value of fully $1,000 billion (excluding intercorporate holdings) represented about one-fourth of the value of all financial assets outstanding in the United States, while the assets of financial institutions, including personal trust departments, came to approximately $1,600 billion, equal to another two-fifths of the total. Eliminating the duplication involved in the corporate holdings of stock by financial institutions of about $250 billion, financial institutions and corporate stock together represented more than one-half of the financial superstructure of the United States. The question, however, is to what extent and how the operations of financial institutions on the one hand and the issuance of and transactions in corporate stock on the other have contributed to the growth of the American economy in the past 100 to 120 years, a period during which both of them acquired substantial importance. The same question, of course, can be asked for the postwar period. In what direction have these phenomena influenced the present organization and efficiency of the American economy, as well as the distribution of its ownership and control?

Answers to these questions are not as evident as it may appear. For it is not sufficient to argue that the modern American economy, as the economy of any other developed noncommunist country, could · not operate without the process of indirect saving and investment through financial institutions or without the widespread ownership of large business enterprises that is made possible through marketable corporate stock. Following the method of counterfactual hypotheses dear to some contemporary economic historians, one may visualize a modern economy organized predominantly in privately owned large enterprises, without financial institutions other than a monetary system and without use of corporate stock, or at least wihout a stock market, in which case participation in the ownership of corporations would be nonmarketable and similar to equity in partnerships. In such an economy, enterprises would be financed by a combination of retained earnings and the issuance of different types of claims sold directly to savers. It is even easier to visualize a modern economy without nonmonetary financial institutions (and thus still having a banking system issuing paper currency and check deposits, though not accepting time and saving deposits), in which both corporate stock and all types of claims against nonfinancial borrowers are held directly by savers and are traded among them on organized exchanges or elsewhere. If the American economy had thus been limited to internal and external direct financing, through the sale of securities to the non-financial scctor (excluding external indirect financing by financial institutions except in the form of money), could it have grown as it actually has and could it have reached the present level of production and consumption?

The main difference between this hypothetical economy, lacking nonmonetary financial institutions and marketable corporate stock, and the actual one that exists today in the United States lies in the structure of the portfolio of households. At the present time, fully one-tenth of household portfolios consist of direct claims aganst nonfinancial sectors; fully two-fifths consist of equities in corporate and unincorporated business enterprises, and another two-fifths are claims against and stock of financial nonmonetary intermediaries (the remaining one-tenth represents money held by individuals). In the hypothetical economy, household portfolios would be divided exclusively—apart from money—among the first two types of financial instruments. (It may be well to recall how much closer the actual situation was to this hypothesis as late as 1900. At that time individuals' portfolios consisted of approximately one-fourth of non-monetary claims against and stock in financial institutions, while claims against and stock in nonfinancial sectors accounted for over two-thirds of total household financial assets, money making up the remaining 5 percent).[3]

What are the preconditions regarding investors' habits, the operations of the investment banking machinery, and the level and structure of yields of financial instruments that would make it possible to operate the present American economy without nonmonetary financial institutions and without marketable corporate stock? Or, phrased differently, in what respects would an American economy, having basically the present structure of production, differ in the absence of nonmonetary financial institutions and of marketable corporate stock, assuming the existence of a monetary system in the form of a central bank that issued both currency and check money and had as assets monetary metals, foreign exchange, and claims against nonfinancial sectors, the Treasury, and business and state and local governments?

1. Almost certainly the value of household saving and investment would be lower than it actually is and was, although we cannot say by how much. This can be deduced from the fact that households have actually preferred indirect nonmonetary to direct saving for a large part of their total accumulated financial assets, and that the elasticity of substitution between direct and indirect nonmonetary financial saving of households is very unlikely to be perfect. Hence, we could not expect a reduction in indirect nonmonetary household saving to have been fully compensated for by an identical increase in their direct financial saving. As a result, reproducible tangible wealth would almost certainly be lower than it actually is today. The question is, which forms of capital formation or real assets would be more important and which less important than they actually are?

2. The absence of nonmonetary financial institutions would mean the absence of deposit claims against banks and thrift institutions and of contractual claims against insurance companies and pension and social security funds (i.e., policyholders' and beneficiaries' equity), and of

[3] See R. W. Goldsmith, R. E. Lipsey, and M. Mendelson, *Studies in the National Balance Sheet of the United States*, Vol. 2, Princeton, Princeton University Press for National Bureau of Economic Research, 1963, pp. 72–73. Personal trust funds are treated as nonmonetary claims against financial institutions while equity in unincorporated business is regarded as part of direct financial assets.

shares in investment companies and other financial institutions. The consequences are not quite as radical as it might appear. Insurance and pension organizations could operate on a pay-as-you-go principle—life insurance companies selling only short-term insurance—thus avoiding the accumulation of assets except for a small working fund in the form of money. There is little doubt, however, that the taxes or equivalent levies necessary to operate this regime of provision for retirement income would have reduced individual consumption less than the voluntary, contractual, and compulsory saving under the present system. Instead of holding claims against thrift institutions, households would have acquired short-, medium-, and long-term obligations directly from the nonfinancial sectors that certainly would have been issued in much larger amounts, and probably also in smaller denominations, than under the present system, if only because governments and business enterprises would have had to find substitutes for the funds now supplied by financial institutions. It is unlikely, though not impossible, that the additional sales would be as large as the foregone saving in the form of thrift deposits and insurance contracts.

3. If liquidity preference (including preference for not only money but also other nearly riskless claims encashable in practice on demand) had been the same as it has been, it is very likely that households or business enterprises would hold more money than they do now. This means that part of the external financing of the nonfinancial sectors now provided by nonmonetary financial institutions would have been furnished by the monetary system. This would not necessarily have led to a sharper rise in prices as the income velocity of circulation would have been lower.

4. Concentration among business enterprises probably would be considerably more pronounced, one of the important probable consequences of the absence of nonmonetary financial institutions and of marketable corporate stock. The reason is that under such a regime the need to raise a much larger proportion of external financing by sale of obligations directly to households (and to a limited extent to other business enterprises with surplus funds) would have given an advantage to enterprises widely known to the general public and able to sell large homogeneous debt issues in small denominations.

5. For the same reasons long-, medium-, and short-term obligations of business enterprises and governments would be much more extensively distributed than they are now, or have been in the past. Similarly the secondary market, on exchanges or over the counter, for these obligations would be much broader and more active. In other words, there would

have occurred a large-scale replacement of "debtor substitution," which is the essence of financial intermediation by "brokerage." Brokers' offices—dealing in obligations rather than in stocks—would functionally and physically have taken the place of the edifices of commercial banks, savings and loan associations, and credit unions, and the treasurers of large nonfinancial enterprises and government units would deal with investment banks and brokers instead of with commercial banks and thrift and insurance organizations.

6. In the absence of banks and finance companies, all consumer credit would be extended by the business enterprises producing or selling the commodity or service. These enterprises would have to raise the necessary funds by either income retention or by sale of their own obligations to the general public. This would most likely lead to a much more pronounced concentration in retail trade.

7. Trade credit (accounts receivable and payable) would almost certainly be more important because of the absence of commercial banks as suppliers of short-term funds. This would have given another advantage to large units able to sell their own obligations on a nationwide or at least a regional market. It also is possible that the difficulty of securing short-term funds would have led to earlier or more intensive economizing on inventories, with the consequence of a more restricted assortment (less choice for consumers) and longer delays in filling orders.

8. Security credit would be insignificant, if it is assumed that brokers and dealers in securities would be prevented from becoming financial institutions by accepting deposits from customers, even in the form of temporary credit balances.

9. Among the main sectors of real capital formation, the one probably most seriously affected by the absence of financial institutions would be owner-occupied homes. It obviously would be much more difficult for the prospective owners of such structures to find mortgage lenders among other individuals, or possibly among builders using their accumulated savings, than it is now where these loans are made routinely in large numbers by financial institutions. Assuming the same total demand for shelter, multifamily structures owned by large real estate corporations able to sell their bonds to the general public would probably have taken the place of a substantial fraction of present one-family owner-occupied homes and of small apartment houses owned by individuals. Thus the absence of financial institutions would have resulted in a quite different distribution of housing between owner-occupied and rented quarters.

10. For similar reasons, farmers would probably have found it more

difficult to secure long-term and even short-term funds. Hence, it is likely that large agricultural enterprises, well enough known to sell their obligations to the general public through the investment banking and brokerage machinery, though probably on a local and regional rather than on a national basis, would have grown more rapidly than they have. On the other hand, concentration among owner-operated farms probably would have made less progress, the farmers being hampered by fewer sources of funds to acquire additional acreage, with the consequence of less inequality among farmers.

11. The absence of marketable corporate stock and financial institutions, of course, would have very great influence on the financial structure of nonfinancial business enterprises. In particular, the need to rely exclusively on debt financing might have led to substantially less venturesome attitudes by entrepreneurs. That rapid economic growth is possible with a much higher debt-to-equity ratio than prevails in the United States is, however, indicated by the cases of Japan and Italy in the postwar period; and it is possible that nonfinancial enterprises would have adapted themselves fully to the need of relying much more on debt financing. The absence of substantial net worth would have made investment in the debt securities of nonfinancial enterprises more risky and thus would have acted as another incentive to greater concentration, since it may be assumed that giant enterprises would have been better able to reduce the danger of inability to meet their obligations by spreading of risk and, ultimately, by reliance on the central government.

12. Regional differences in interest rates, saving, and investment probably would be larger than observed, if the American economy had operated without nonmonetary financial institutions and without a market for corporate stock. While it is possible that a substantial degree of equalization in the availability and terms of direct external finance would have been brought about by the operation of a more highly developed net of investment banking facilities and a much broader secondary market in the obligations of governments and business enterprises, it is very unlikely that this could have been done as efficiently as is possible through the activities of financial institutions operating on a nationwide scale directly or indirectly, e.g., through a system of correspondents.

13. The probable effects of the absence of financial institutions and of a stock market on the level of interest rates, on the differentials among rates, and on the fluctuations in rates are very difficult to assess. It seems likely, however, that under such conditions the level of interest rates on obligations of nonfinancial issuers would have been somewhat higher than

it actually has been, because savers, who, as history shows, have preferred to hold claims against nonmonetary financial institutions, would have to be offered higher rates to hold claims against nonfinancial issuers. It is not certain that this differential would have been substantially larger than the interest margin inherent in the operation of nonmonetary financial institutions. Of the main rates, that for home mortgages probably would have been raised most. The yield on Treasury securities probably would have been lowered relative to other rates because they would have become, even more than in actuality, the haven of risk-averting savers. In the absence of the generally smoothing influence of financial institutions, variations in rates, both over full business cycles and for shorter periods, as well as seasonally, most likely would have been more pronounced; so would interregional differences in interest rates.

14. One important argument remains to be met. Would not the absence of commercial banks as we know them have slowed down the growth of the American economy gravely, given the crucial importance assigned to expansionary bank credit in many theories of economic development (starting with that of Joseph Schumpeter),[4] an importance backed by the concrete examples of Germany before World War I and of Japan after World War II? It is hard to deny the likelihood of some influence in this direction, but it should be realized that, in the counterfactual hypothetical situation envisaged here, the expansion of check money by the central bank would have taken the place of the expansion of the credit of commercial banks, reflecting the creation of check deposits which has been observed in the actual development of the American economy.

The question then comes down to whether the assets likely to have been acquired by the central bank in issuing check money would have differed sufficiently from those actually acquired by commercial banks to retard economic growth substantially. The answer depends on the assumption made about the methods of operation of the central bank. If it had limited itself to international assets and to Treasury securities, the growth-reducing influence of its operations, which replaced those of commercial banks, probably would have been substantial. If, on the other hand, the central bank had acquired short- and long-term obligations of business enterprises as part cover for its currency and check money issues, as is entirely compatible with the essence of the counterfactual hypothesis, the retarding effect might have been very small. One important difference

---

[4] *Theorie der Wirtschaftlichen Entwicklung*, Duncker and Humblot, 1912; translated by R. Opie as *The Theory of Economic Development*, Cambridge, Mass., Harvard University Press, 1934.

between the two regimes, however, would have remained: In the absence of the numerous individual commercial banks, mostly of local character, that have constituted the American banking system, concentration of the creation of money in the hands of one central bank would have provided the possibility of a much more conscious allocation of expansionary credit among industries, regions, borrowers of different size, businesses of different degree of risk, and other characteristics. This allocation might well have differed considerably from that which actually took place in a system combining competition and oligopoly and essentially guided by considerations of risk and profitability. Thus, a considerable difference in the allocation of expansionary bank credit between the two regimes is a possibility, but is not a necessity, particularly if the operations of the central bank had been decentralized to regional and possibly local levels.

We may conclude from this imaginary picture of a mid-twentieth century America without financial institutions and without marketable corporate stock (and hence without a stock market) that the rate of household and total national saving and investment would have been somewhat lower, the rate of growth of output somewhat smaller, and the stock of reproducible tangible assets somewhat smaller than they actually turned out to be. Whether the difference would have been large enough substantially to affect the standard of living of the American people is uncertain. However, it would have considerably affected the distribution of wealth—though not necessarily the distribution of earned income—by sharply reducing realized and unrealized capital gains on corporate stocks, which are the main source of modern large fortunes. This might have had great influence on the social structure of the United States in the direction of lessening inequality. Thus the absence of marketable corporate stock probably would have been more important in making the economy different from what it now is than the absence of nonmonetary financial institutions.

These speculations at the same time indicate the effect of the introduction and spread of a market in corporate stock and of nonmonetary financial institutions on the country's economic growth. In brief these two developments are likely to have slightly increased the volume of national saving and investment and hence the rate of growth of the economy and its stock of tangible assets; to have reduced the level, variability, and regional differences of interest rates; to have retarded the trend towards concentration among business enterprises; but to have accelerated the accumulation of large fortunes. Among the main nonfinancial sectors of the economy the operation of nonmonetary financial

institutions has probably been most helpful to the market for home and
farm mortgages, and thus to the spread of home ownership, in the face of
rapid urbanization of the country, to the maintenance of the family farm
system, and even more to the concentration of farm operations in a
declining number of family farms.

We may now turn to a much weaker counterfactual hypothesis, but one
that may be more directly relevant to this study. This is the assumption
that, in the face of the existence of nonmonetary financial institutions and
of a stock market, financial institutions would have been prevented, by
statute, tradition, or otherwise, from owning or administering corporate
stock portfolios.

This assumption is counterfactual essentially only for the period since
World War I, and in a significant sense only for the last two decades. For
the half-century before World War I, the actual situation was so close to
this weaker counterfactual hypothesis that its investigation is without
much interest. The main exception to the hypothesis—the administration
of substantial blocks of stock by personal trust departments of banks and
trust companies—certainly is not a sufficient basis for a claim that anything
of importance in the American economy would have been different if these
blocks had been administered directly by the beneficiaries or by nonfinancial trustees.

For the period since World War I, or at least for the last twenty years,
however, the absence of financial institutions as buyers of corporate stock
might have had substantial influence on the character of the market for
corporate stock, for stock prices, for individual portfolios, and possibly
even for some more basic factors, like the levels of interest rates, saving,
and investment. Until well into the 1950's, actual purchases of corporate
stock by financial institutions were so small that the effects could only
have been minor. It is only during the last dozen years, and particularly
since 1965, that the absorption of corporate stock by financial institutions
has been large enough for its absence to have possibly led to substantial
differences in the market for corporate stock, and with less likelihood in the
basic economic situation of the country.

It is doubtful that the funds available to thrift and insurance organizations would have been smaller if they had not bought any corporate stock.
The only difference would have been the acquisition of about $50 billion
of government, corporate, or foreign bonds and of mortgages in lieu of an
equal amount of corporate stock. Investment companies, of course, would
have been of much smaller size if they had been limited to fixed interest
bearing securities, reducing the demand for stock by less than $15 billion.

This however would not have been a net reduction in the demand for stocks of all types, but only a substitution of the demand for stocks of industrial, etc., corporations for that of investment companies.

As we do not know enough about the nature of the stocks bought by financial institutions, it is difficult to say how the retention of these stocks in individual portfolios—not necessarily those owning them at the beginning of the period—would have affected any basic economic factor such as interest rates, saving, investment, and corporate financing. In view of the very low volume of net issues of corporate stock (discussed in Chapter 4) it is, however, unlikely that the absence of financial institutions as buyers would have made much difference in the total volume of stock issued by nonfinancial corporations, except in the cases of a few corporations favored much more by financial institutions than by individual holders.

There are only two aspects of the market for corporate stock in which we may be certain that the absence of financial institutions as buyers would have had a substantial effect: the price of common stock and the volume of stock trading. It is very likely that the observed rise in stock prices would have been smaller, particularly during the 1960's, if financial institutions had not bid away fully $60 billion of stock, or something like one-eighth of their total portfolios, from the previous individual holders. It is even more certain that the volume of trading on exchanges and in the over-the-counter market would have been smaller, since individual shareholders are unlikely to have indulged as much in in-and-out trading in the late 1960's as the adherents of the performance cult among financial institutions. Because of our limited information on the distribution of stock purchases by institutional investors among individual issues and groups of them it is again very difficult to say how their absence would have affected relative stock prices. Obviously, the relative prices of the favorites of financial institutions would have risen less in comparison with other stocks, but unless we know much more about the character of these favorites such a statement is not very meaningful. Since stock prices reached their peak near the end of 1968 and have been declining sharply in 1969 and the first half of 1970, it becomes even more doubtful what net effect, if any, the substitutions of about $60 billion of purchases of common stock by institutions (excluding their personal trust departments) has had in the long run on the level of stock prices in general and on relative stock prices, let alone on basic factors of the economy.

Thus, the tentative conclusion regarding the weaker counterfactual hypothesis is that it would not have made very much of a difference for the basic factors of the American economy—though it would have substantially affected employment and profits in the securities business—if financial institutions had been prevented from acquiring corporate stock.

3. THE DETERMINANTS OF THE SHARE OF FINANCIAL INSTITUTIONS IN CORPORATE STOCK

a. *The Factors Involved*

An understanding of the level and the movements of the share of financial institutions in the total amount of corporate stock issued during a given period or outstanding at one point in time requires an analysis of the factors which determine the level and movements of the numerator and the denominator of the appropriate ratio, i.e., (a) the value of the net purchases and the holdings of corporate stock by financial institutions; and (b) the volume of total net issues and the market value of outstandings of corporate stock.

Beginning with the numerator of these ratios, net acquisition of corporate stock by financial institutions during a given period may be decomposed into two parts.

1. The increase or decrease in total assets of financial institutions during the period, excluding valuation changes which reflect changes in the price of corporate stock and secondarily in the price of other assets. This increase or decrease, in turn, is dependent on several important economic factors which cannot be followed and explained here, such as the degree of monetization of the economy, the share of indirect saving (i.e., saving through financial institutions) in total saving, and the degree of layering among financial institutions (i.e., the extent to which some financial institutions hold claims against or shares of other financial institutions).

2. The proportion of the net acquisition of assets by financial institutions which are allocated to corporate stock; or the statistically more easily ascertainable proportion of the change in assets other than claims against other financial institutions, which takes the form of corporate stock.

The volume of net new issues of corporate stock, the denominator of the ratio, in turn, depends on two factors:

3. The volume of securities issued by domestic corporations, which may be regarded as closely connected with the volume of capital expenditures that is financed externally, i.e., through borrowing or the issuance of equity securities.

4. The proportion of total net issues by corporations that takes the form of stock. This ratio is affected by numerous factors, such as differences

among yield rates for debt and equity securities, the costs of issuing different types of securities, asset price changes, variability of issuer's income, the issuer's capital structure, tax considerations, and many other factors studied by the theory of finance.

Chart 1-1 illustrates schematically the relations between these four factors, indicates the ratios which link them, and shows a few important related relationships. According to the approach taken here, the share of financial institutions in the issues of corporate stock (β)—the figure in

CHART 1-1

The Derivation of the Ratio of Net Purchases of Nonfinancial Corporations by Financial Institutions

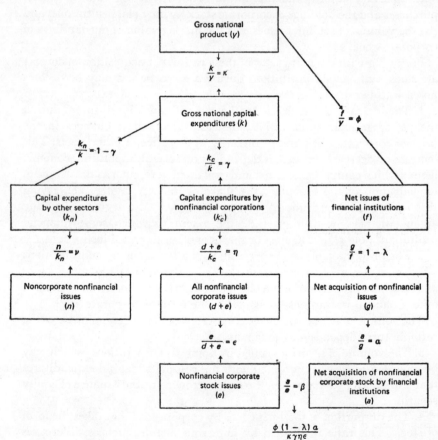

$$\frac{\phi(1-\lambda)a}{\kappa\gamma\eta\epsilon}$$

which this report is primarily interested—is thus seen to be the result of seven ratios:

a. The new-issue ratio of financial institutions, i.e., the ratio of total net new issues by financial institutions to gross national product (ϕ);

b. The layering ratio (λ), which measures the extent to which net issues by financial institutions consist of issues to other financial institutions and which in accounting terms can be defined as the ratio of the combined to the consolidated issues of all financial institutions;

c. The share of corporate stock in total net acquisition of assets by financial institutions other than claims against (and stock of) other financial institutions (α);

d. The national capital formation ratio, i.e., the ratio of total gross capital expenditures to gross national product (κ);

e. The share of nonfinancial corporations in total gross capital expenditures (γ);

f. The external financing ratio of nonfinancial corporations (η), i.e., the ratio of total capital expenditures of nonfinancial corporations to the net issuance of debt and equity securities by them;

g. The share of stock in total net new issues by nonfinancial corporations (ϵ).

The seven ratios then combine in the expression,

$$\beta = \frac{\phi(1 - \lambda)\alpha}{\kappa\gamma\eta\epsilon},$$

the three ratios of the numerator referring to financial institutions, the four ratios of the denominator to nonfinancial corporations.[5] The absolute value of gross national product, of course, does not influence the value of this ratio, a desirable feature since it makes the ratios for different periods of time or for different countries directly comparable.

---

[5] It will be seen that the expression's numerator,

$$\phi(1 - \lambda)\alpha = \frac{\text{increase in combined assets of financial institutions}}{\text{gross national product}}$$

$$\times \frac{\text{increase in consolidated assets of financial institutions}}{\text{increase in combined assets}}$$

$$\times \frac{\text{institutional net purchases of corporate stock}}{\text{total uses of funds of financial institutions}},$$

simplifies (approximately) to express net institutional acquisitions of stock in nonfinancial corporations as a fraction of gross national product; and its denominator,

(continued)

These relations may be illustrated by an example which is not too different from the figures observed for the United States during the post-war period. With a net new-issue ratio of financial institutions of $\phi = 0.10$; a layering ratio λ of 0.10, so that $1 - \lambda = 0.90$; a share of corporate stock in total net acquisition of assets by financial institutions of $\alpha = 0.05$; a national capital formation ratio (including consumer and government durables) of $\kappa = 0.25$; a share of corporations in total national capital expenditures of $\gamma = 0.30$; an external financing ratio of nonfinancial corporations of $\eta = 0.35$; and a proportion of stock in external financing of $\epsilon = 0.05$, the value of the ratio of financial institutions to total net new issues of stocks by nonfinancial corporations emerges as equal to about $3\frac{1}{2}$.[6] Thus the net acquisition of stock of nonfinancial corporations by financial institutions would on these assumptions be about three and one-half times as large as the total issuance of such stock (the excess, of course, being offset by net sales by nonfinancial sectors), a figure which is corroborated by flow of funds statistics.

Relationships equivalent to these flow magnitudes and ratios, of course, exist between the values of the holdings of corporate stock by financial institutions and the value of corporate stock outstanding at a given point of time, since these magnitudes may be regarded as the result of (1) the accumulation of net issues of corporate stock and of net asset acquisitions by financial institutions in the past, and (2) realized and

---

(*Note 5, continued*)

$$\kappa\gamma\eta\epsilon = \frac{\text{total gross capital expenditures}}{\text{gross national product}}$$

$$\times \frac{\text{capital expenditures by nonfinancial corporations}}{\text{total gross capital expenditures}}$$

$$\times \frac{\text{external financing by nonfinancial corporations}}{\text{capital expenditures by nonfinancial corporations}}$$

$$\times \frac{\text{net new issues of corporate stock by nonfinancial corporations}}{\text{external financing by nonfinancial corporations}},$$

simplifies (exactly) to express total net new issues of stock by nonfinancial corporations as a fraction of gross national product. The quotient, of course, provides the desired fraction of nonfinancial corporate stock acquired during a particular period of time by all financial institutions together.

[6] In figures:

$$\frac{(.10)\ (.90)\ (.05)}{(.25)\ (.30)\ (.35)\ (.05)} = 3.43$$

unrealized valuation changes on corporate stock and other price-sensitive assets since the time of issuance or acquisition by financial institutions. As these relationships are more complex algebraically than those existing among the flows illustrated in Chart 1-1, which disregard valuation changes during the relatively short periods to which they refer, their derivation is not given here.[7]

b. Total Resources of Financial Institutions

Before assessing the share of corporate stockholdings in the assets of financial institutions, it is necessary to identify the determinants of the growth of total assets of these institutions. From the economic point of view, the resources of financial institutions—in accounting, equal to sources of funds, i.e., liabilities and net worth—may be regarded as representing essentially five components, each of which has its own determinants and often follows its own path.

The first component is money, in the form of (a) bank notes issued in the United States primarily by commercial banks (state banks before 1864, national banks from 1864 to 1935) and by the Federal Reserve banks (since 1914); and (b) demand deposits with commercial banks.[8]

The second component consists of (a) thrift deposits of households with commercial and savings banks, saving and loan associations, and credit unions, and (b) household claims against insurance organizations, including life insurance companies and private and government pension funds. These constitute an important part of an individual's financial and total saving. For this reason this component also includes, where statistically feasible, individual holdings of investment company shares.

The third component is of a mixed nature, comprising time and savings deposits and insurance claims of nonfinancial sectors other than households, i.e., mainly those of business, government, nonprofit institutions, and foreigners.

The fourth component consists of the equity of financial institutions in corporate form. The equity in mutual financial institutions, such as most life insurance companies, saving and loan associations and mutual savings banks, may be regarded as a form of claim of the depositors or policyholders, which is held predominantly by households.

---

[7] For such a derivation, see R. W. Goldsmith, *Financial Structure and Development*, New Haven, Yale University Press, 1969, p. 80 ff.

[8] As is well known, some economists prefer a broader definition of money, which includes the time and savings deposits with commercial banks and sometimes even deposits with a few other financial institutions. If such a definition is accepted, the second and third components are reduced correspondingly.

The fifth and last component is made up of claims and debts among financial institutions and of equity securities of one financial institution held by another, and thus constitutes a duplication eliminated in a consolidated balance sheet of the financial sector.

The changes in these items are, of course, matched by equivalent changes in assets on the other side of the balance sheet, if capital gains and other valuation changes are excluded on both sides.

Since economic interest is not primarily directed to the absolute dollar values involved but to their relation to economic magnitudes characteristic of the size of an economy, it is preferable to express the figures as percentages of gross national product in the case of issues of financial instruments and of national wealth in the case of financial assets and liabilities. We may then express the net issues by financial institutions in a simple equation. On the left-hand side of this equation we find the magnitude we want to explain, namely, the ratio of all issues[9] of financial institutions to gross national product, a ratio which has been designated by ϕ. On the right side we encounter five components of ϕ, four of which are expressed as ratios to national product.

The first component is the ratio of net issues of money (m), i.e., the net change in the money stock, to gross national product. This ratio depends on numerous factors which have been analyzed for decades by monetary theory. Among them are the factors which determine the income and transactions velocity of money, such as the degree of division of labor in the economy; payment habits, particularly the extent to which payments are synchronized; and the propensity to use money for purposes other than as the medium of exchange, e.g., the propensity to hoard it or to hold it as a temporary investment.

The second component depends on total personal saving and on the share of claims against thrift institutions and insurance organizations (and possibly of purchases of stock of open-end investment companies) in total personal saving. Total personal saving, again, may be regarded as the product of, first, the personal saving ratio (s), i.e., the ratio of total saving to personal disposable income; and, second, the share of personal disposable income in GNP (p). The definition and the determinants of total personal saving have been subject to long debates among economists and statisticians, debates which are far from being settled. In the United States the personal saving ratio, if defined to include saving through

---

[9] The term "issues" it may be recalled, refers not only to stocks and bonds, but also to the net increase in all other forms of short- and long-term liabilities and equity (such as increases in earned net worth). (Issues may, of course, be negative.)

consumer durables, as well as the ratio of personal disposable income to gross national product have shown substantial cyclical variations and have suffered a few marked disturbances over short periods, for instance during the two world wars and during the Great Depression. During this century and probably since the middle of the nineteenth century, however, the ratios do not seem to have shown a continuous pronounced trend. For this investigation the personal saving ratio is defined as the share of personal saving that is in the form of household·claims against thrift institutions and insurance organizations. This ratio must be compared with its competitors for individuals' saving, such as the purchases of government and corporate securities and of mortgages and saving through tangible assets, primarily homes and consumer durables, as is done in Chapter 5, and may be treated as exogenous. The latter ratio may, in turn, be regarded as the product of two other relations: the share of gross financial saving (i.e., the accumulation of financial assets excluding valuation changes) in total personal saving (c), and the share of household claims against thrift institutions and insurance organizations in total financial saving (t).

The third component (x) is a residual. Time and saving deposits of nonfinancial sectors, other than households, and business claims against property insurance companies are its largest single elements. It may be regarded here as exogenous.

While a small part of the equity of financial institutions in corporate form is held by nonfinancial business and by government, it may be justified to make the simplifying assumption that all equity securities of financial corporations are held by households except those in the hands of other financial institutions. Hence we may use the share of equity (net issues of corporate stock plus retained earnings) in total issues of financial institutions as the determining factor and may designate it by e.

Claims and holdings of equity securities among financial institutions are best measured by the layering ratio (λ), i.e., the share of the issues of financial institutions absorbed by other financial institutions.

We then have

$$\phi = [m + (s \cdot p \cdot c \cdot t) + x + (e\phi)](1 - \lambda)$$
$$= \frac{[m + (s \cdot p \cdot c \cdot t) + x](1 - \lambda)}{1 - e(1 - \lambda)}.$$

For purposes of illustration we may assume the following period averages for the components of ϕ:

$m = 2$ percent of GNP;

s = 10 percent of personal disposable income;
p = 80 percent of GNP;
c = 75 percent of total personal saving;
t = 60 percent of total personal financial saving;
x = 1 percent of GNP;
e = 5 percent of total issues by financial institutions;
λ = 10 percent.

This yields, if ϕ is expressed as a percentage of gross national product,

$$\phi = \frac{[2 + (10 \times .80 \times .75 \times .60) + 1](1.00 - .10)}{1.00 - .05(1.00 - .10)} = 6.20.$$

On these assumptions, therefore, the issues of financial institutions—and hence, in the absence of valuation changes, the change in the assets of financial institutions—equal 6.2 percent of GNP.

If this ratio had, on the average, prevailed over a very long period, and if GNP had increased, again on the average for the same long period, by g percent a year, then the ratio of the assets of financial institutions to national product (F), which in the absence of valuation changes is equal to their cumulated past net issues, to the final period's gross national product (y), would be approximately $F/y = \phi/g$. If, for instance, gross national product had been increasing at an average of 5 percent per year, and if ϕ had had the value of 6.2 percent assumed in the illustration above, then F would be equal to $6.20/.05 = 124$ percent of current gross national product. Further, assuming a ratio between net national wealth and gross national product (sometimes called the capital-output ratio) of 4, F would be equal to $124/4 = 31$ percent of national wealth.[10]

The formula thus shows how the components distinguished here influence the relative size of financial institutions in an economy's capital flows and wealth holdings. It shows, for instance, that (in the absence of valuation changes) the assets of financial institutions (F) are positively related to m, s, p, c, t, x, and e, but negatively related to g and k. A discussion of the factors which, in turn, affect the level and movements of these components is beyond the scope of this report, though an idea will be given, as

[10] The derivation of these relations is somewhat more difficult, if the period for which data are available is shorter, if the component ratios have during parts of the period deviated considerably from their average for the entire period, and if part of the assets of financial institutions (primarily their holdings of corporate stock) have undergone valuation changes (see Goldsmith, *Financial Structure and Development*, Chapter 2). The essential relationships are, however, not affected by such complications.

far as the data are available, of how the observed values of each have moved over the last century in the United States.

c. The Share of Corporate Stock in the Assets of Financial Institutions

There are at least half a dozen factors that must be considered in looking behind the share of corporate stock in the assets of financial institutions and the makeup of their stock portfolios. One of these, of course, is the set of regulations, by statute or less formal means, which limit or even prohibit the holding of stock for most types of financial institutions, and which, in addition, make provisions regarding the character of the stocks that may be held, thus affecting the size and composition of the institutions' portfolios. Such regulations are most rigid for banks, but they also are fairly strict for life insurance companies and public pension funds. They are more lenient, i.e., allowing a larger proportion of stocks to be held and imposing fewer conditions on the types of stock held, in the case of property insurance companies. They are almost absent for investment companies, private pension funds, common trust funds, and, apart from the provisions in individual trust instruments, for personal trust funds. On the other hand, the holding of certain stocks is required for a few types of financial institutions, such as the holdings of stock in the Federal Reserve banks by member commercial banks and the holdings of stock in the Federal Home Loan Banks by member saving and loan associations.

Traditions, partly stemming from possible adverse publicity, are an additional factor that often have kept actual stock holdings below legally permitted levels. The effect of such traditions has been particularly evident in the case of state and local pension funds and in the case of life insurance companies, from the time of the Armstrong-Hughes investigation early in this century[11] to fairly recent years.

Given regulations and traditions, relative yields, taking account not only of stipulated or expected regular income but also of the chance of capital losses or gains and of the extent of price fluctuations, probably have been a determining factor in the total size of an institution's stock portfolio and even more in its makeup. Until World War I, and probably even until World War II, expected current yields were probably the most important single factor. In the postwar period, however, chances of capital gains (and risk of capital loss) have come to play a more important role, together with tax considerations and protection against inflation, in determining the size and the structure of institutional stock portfolios.

---

[11] *Report of the Joint Committee of the Senate and Assembly of the State of New York Appointed to Investigate the Affairs of Life Insurance Companies*, 1906.

Liquidity, i.e., the chance of being able to sell blocks of stock rapidly and without substantially influencing their price, has been an important factor for those types of financial institutions that keep a substantial part of their total assets in corporate stock, particularly in common stock, and may have to face substantial withdrawals or other needs for funds. Thus, liquidity is likely to have played the relatively greatest role in determining the size and makeup of the stock portfolio in the case of investment companies and of non-life-insurance companies.

A minor factor accounting for a small proportion of total stock held by financial institutions is convenience. This is responsible for the relatively moderate holdings of stocks in real estate corporations that own the building in which the institution conducts its business and of service corporations, like safe-deposit corporations, owned by commercial banks.

Another minor factor is the involuntary acquisition of stock, particularly the exchange of stock for bonds or loans issued by debtors forced to reorganize their capital structure.

A final factor, which at times has been of importance, is control of either financial institutions of the same type as the holder or of other financial or nonfinancial corporations. Because such holdings usually have been prohibited by regulations, particularly during the last half century, they have constituted only a relatively small proportion of the total stock holdings of financial institutions. There are two exceptions, however: the holdings of stocks of operating non-life-insurance companies by other companies of this type, and the holdings of commercial bank stocks by life insurance companies in the two decades or so before the Armstrong-Hughes investigation.

These different types of stockholdings are rarely, if ever, specifically distinguished in the balance sheets or other accounting records of financial institutions. The character of a specific stockholding generally can only be inferred from the nature of the holding itself.

In view of the multiplicity, variety, and, in some cases, nonquantitative nature of the factors apparently influencing the share of corporate stock in the asset holdings and acquisitions of financial institutions it is not surprising that efforts at an econometric determination of the shares have so far been unsuccessful.[12]

d. The Supply of Corporate Stock

The supply of corporate stock from which the holdings of financial

[12] See Chapter 5, section 2.

institutions are drawn may be divided into three categories whose levels and movements often differ considerably.

The first, and in practice by far the most important, component consists of the stock of domestic nonfinancial corporations. Issues of such stock (net of retirements) during any given period (e_c) may be regarded as the product of (1) total issues of securities by domestic nonfinancial corporations including all forms of debt (i_c) and (2) the share of stocks in total issues (a_c). The first component, in turn, can be resolved into total gross capital expenditures by nonfinancial corporations (k_c) and their external financing ratio ($g_c = i_c/k_c$), a formulation based on the assumption that a substantial part of the stock issues of nonfinancial corporations are connected with their capital expenditures, defined more or less broadly. Total capital expenditures of nonfinancial corporations, finally, may be expressed as the product of total national capital formation (k) and the share of nonfinancial corporations in national capital formation ($b_c = k_c/k$). Again expressing the supply of corporate stock in terms of gross national product rather than as an absolute figure, we obtain the following expression for the supply of stock by nonfinancial domestic corporations:

$$\frac{e_c}{y} = \frac{k}{y} \times b_c \times g_c \times a_c,$$

where k/y is the national capital formation ratio. The left-hand ratio e_c/y may be regarded and interpreted as a weighted average of corresponding ratios for the main groups of nonfinancial corporations which differ considerably in the relevant values of b, g, and a.

To illustrate, using values not too far from those observed in the United States during the postwar period (and including consumer and government durables in capital formation), we obtain

$$\frac{e_c}{y} = 0.25 \times 0.50 \times 0.30 \times 0.10 = 0.00375.$$

Thus, the indicated volume of net new issues of stock by domestic nonfinancial corporations is slightly less than 0.4 percent of gross national product.

The value of an expression of this type, which must be regarded as reflecting definitional and functional interrelationships rather than unidirectional causal connections, is that it shows the relative contribution of four relevant economic magnitudes (the national capital formation ratio, the share of nonfinancial corporations in national capital formation, the share of external in total financing of nonfinancial corporations, and the share of stock in these corporations' external financing) to the stock issue ratio of nonfinancial corporations. It also permits us to see whether and how the ratio and its components have changed over time. This is not the place to attempt an explanation of the factors which are responsible for the level and movements of these four magnitudes.

The value of the stock of nonfinancial corporations outstanding at any one date (E_c) of course equals (1) the sum of past issues of such stock (Σe_c) and (2) the differences between the original issue price and the market price at balance sheet valuation of all previously issued stock $(E_c - \Sigma e_c)$, a figure which, of course, depends on the movements of stock prices, so that $E_c = \Sigma e_c + (E_c - \Sigma e_c)$. In practice it is usually possible to estimate E_c and Σe_c directly with a fair degree of accuracy. Aggregate capital gains $(E_c - \Sigma e_c)$ must be obtained as their difference rather than directly as $\Sigma (E_c - e_c)$.

The second and third components of the holdings of corporate stock that are relevant for financial institutions—the stock of domestic financial corporations and the stock of foreign corporations—are of sufficiently small importance for this study to be regarded as exogenous.

However, domestic financial stock issues could be explained by linking them to the total issues of financial institutions or, more appropriately, to the ratio of total issues to gross national product (ϕ). Designating the share of the issues of those financial institutions that operate in corporate (rather than mutual) form by h, and the proportion of stock in total issues of corporate financial institutions by a_f, we obtain the following expression for the ratio of net new issues of stock by financial institutions to gross national product,

$$\frac{e_f}{y} = \phi h a_f,$$

an expression in which a_f may be regarded as the weighted average of the a ratio for the various groups of financial institutions that issue stock, i.e., primarily commercial banks, property insurance companies, finance companies, and investment companies.

4. THE USE OF NATIONAL BALANCE SHEETS AND FLOW OF FUNDS ACCOUNTS IN THE ANALYSIS OF INSTITUTIONAL STOCKHOLDINGS

It would be possible to analyze the level and movements of corporate stockholdings by financial institutions on a piecemeal basis, using only

332.6   In 7s

C. 1

such statistics as happen to be at hand and as are needed in the calculation of the two crucial ratios: the holdings of corporate stock to total assets of the different types of financial institutions, and the stockholdings by financial institutions to the total amount of stock of different types outstanding. To do so, however, while it would considerably reduce the volume of data needed, would not permit us to show the interrelationships between the holdings of stock and of other uses and sources of funds for the different types of financial institutions; between stocks held by financial institutions and those held by other sectors; and between the issuance of stock and other sources and uses of funds of corporations. In other words, such a limited scope of investigation would not provide sufficient material for a satisfactory analysis of the demand for the supply of corporate stock by important sectors of the economy.

Since the Securities and Exchange Commission felt that it needed a comprehensive and consistent picture of stocks and flows of corporate shares in the postwar American economy for its detailed study of financial institutions and the stock market in recent years, use was made of an organized body of statistical data for that period, developed as a part of a comprehensive system of national accounts. This material is known as the Flow of Funds System, although it actually has a broader scope, including integrated information on both stocks of assets and liabilities in existence at a point of time (balance sheet dates) and flows during a period between balance sheet dates (the flow of funds in a narrow sense).

The system of national accounts includes balance sheets and flow of funds statements for as many separate sectors of the economy as are important for the analysis and as can be derived on the basis of the statistical material in existence. Such a system automatically not only provides the two desired sets of ratios of stock holdings to total assets of financial institutions and of such holdings to total stock outstanding, but also permits for each sector (1) an analysis of the structure of assets held and hence of portfolio policies, and (2) of methods of financing and thus of the role of corporate stock as a source of funds. It also makes it possible—provided some additional statistical material is available—to set up a stock and a flow matrix for corporate stock, showing, respectively, interrelations between issuing and holding sectors of corporate stock at a given point of time, or the purchases and sales of stock among sectors during a period of time.

As a starting point in building up sectoral balance sheets and flow of funds accounts for the period 1952–68 on which the investigation centered, there were available the flow of funds accounts of the Federal Reserve

Board, limited to financial assets and liabilities,[13] and complete annual sectoral balance sheets for the years 1952–58 in *Studies in the National Balance Sheet of the United States*.[14]

Owing to the considerable amounts of basic statistical data that have become available during the 1960's, it became necessary to recalculate the estimates of stocks and flows of tangible assets for the entire period 1952–68, with only limited recourse to the earlier estimates for the first few years of the period. While the Federal Reserve Board estimates of stocks and flows of financial assets could be accepted with only minor changes, it was found essential for the present study to supplement these figures in several directions, mainly by breaking down the household sector into about half-a-dozen subsectors, by separately estimating the assets and transactions of personal trust departments of commercial banks and their transfer to the financial institution sector, and by including several minor types of financial institutions. The statistical problems arising in these estimates are described in the appendix and are briefly summarized in the following section.

5. STATISTICAL PROBLEMS

Information on the sources of data and the methods of estimation of the stock and flow data used in the study are provided in Appendix I. At this point it will suffice to discuss three statistical problems of general importance: first, the grouping of the more than 70 million economic units now operating in the United States (households, business enterprises, and governments) into sectors for which separate balance sheets and sources and uses of funds statements are constructed; second, the classification of the very large number of types of assets and liabilities into a few reasonably homogeneous categories; and third, the methods used in valuing assets, liabilities, and equity in balance sheets and in deriving estimates of fund flows from balance sheet data.

a. Sectorization

Sectorization should theoretically be guided by the principle that the units included in a sector are as homogeneous as possible in their economic behavior (in this study, in their portfolio and stock trading policies). Actual sectoring is a compromise between this principle and available

---

[13] The results obtained are published in Board of Governors of the Federal Reserve System, *Flow of Funds Accounts 1945–1968*, May 1970. The study, however, used somewhat more detailed and occasionally revised worksheets.

[14] Goldsmith, Lipsey, and Mendelson (see note 3, above).

statistical data, particularly because of the need to adapt to the existing flow of funds statistics and national balance sheet estimates.

For purposes of this study the essential separation is between financial institutions and nonfinancial sectors. Financial institutions have been defined as organizations that keep most of their assets in the form of claims against, or equity securities of, numerous issuers which they do not control through stock ownership, and that obtain most of their funds from the public rather than from a very narrow group of stockholders or creditors. The grouping of the many organizations meeting this definition follows the traditional pattern, the only one for which extensive statistics are available.[15] The sectoral balance sheets and flow of funds statements for the period 1952–68 thus distinguish the following groups of domestic financial institutions:

1. Federal Reserve banks
2. Commercial banks
3. Mutual savings banks
4. Savings and loan associations
5. Credit unions
6. Federal lending agencies
7. Mortgage companies
8. Finance companies
9. Life insurance companies
10. Fraternal insurance organizations
11. Non-life insurance companies
12. Private (noninsured) pension funds
13. State and local pension funds
14. Open-end investment companies
15. Closed-end investment companies
16. Personal trust departments of commercial banks
17. Common trust funds of commercial banks
18. Security brokers and dealers.

[15] As in practically all such classifications, not every unit belonging to each of the groups defined as financial institutions completely meets the tests laid down above. Thus, captive finance companies may receive all their funds from their parent as undoubtedly do some units in some of the other groups. On the other hand, federal pension funds, as well as the social security system, do not have a diversified portfolio of securities but are limited to obligations of the U.S. Treasury. In such borderline cases the inclusion in or exclusion from the group of financial institutions is to some extent arbitrary. In most such cases the breakdown of a group of institutions into those which belong to the class of financial institutions under strict interpretation of the definition and those that do not is not feasible statistically.

For the period before 1952 a few of the smaller groups are omitted because of lack of data. Some other groups (e.g., 6, 12–15, and 17) enter the statistics only when they become of substantial size, usually in the 1920's or 1930's.

Among the nonfinancial sectors three do not present substantial conceptual or statistical difficulties: nonfinancial corporations, state and local governments, and the rest of the world. All three sectors constitute reasonably well-defined groups for which comprehensive statistics are available—for nonfinancial corporations from the Internal Revenue Service, for state and local governments from the Bureau of the Census, and for the rest of the world from balance of payments statistics— although not in as much detail as would be desirable for the present study.

For nonfinancial corporations a problem arises due to the absence of subsectoring in previous estimates of national balance sheets in flow of funds statistics, notwithstanding very considerable differences in the economic character and in the financial behavior of such subgroups. An attempt was therefore made to break down the total figures for nonfinancial corporations into four subsectors (manufacturing and mining, transportation, communication, and the necessarily heterogeneous remainder), but the difficulties encountered in this attempt were such that no usable estimates could be produced within the confines of this study.

The state and local government sector excludes pension funds of state and local government employees, which are treated as one subgroup of financial institutions. The general funds of state and local governments, however, remain in the sector. So do the relatively small public utility and similar business-type activities of state and local governments.

The estimates for the federal government sector do not include government lending agencies (the most important are in the fields of housing, farm credit, and foreign trade), which are regarded as a subgroup (6) of the financial institutions sector. On the other hand, the funds accumulated for federal employees' pension funds, as well as for the social security system, which could well be regarded as another subgroup, have in accordance with past practice been left in the federal government sector. Occasionally, however, it is indicated how a shift of these organizations to the financial institutions sector would affect the figures.

It has been common practice, due to statistical necessity, to obtain most estimates for the "household" sector as a residual, i.e., by subtracting from the national total aggregate, figures for all other domestic sectors and for the rest of the world. As a result, the so-called household sector has included nonprofit institutions and the assets owned by households but administered by trustees (mostly financial organizations), as well as households proper, unattached individuals, and the statistical errors inherent in this procedure. This sector, therefore, has lacked homogeneity, particularly from the point of view of the management of its financial assets.

In this study two steps have been taken to make the household sector data more homogeneous, particularly for financial analysis. Unfortunately both steps, although important, cannot in the present state of the statistical material go as far as could be desired.

The first step is the separation of funds held by the personal trust departments of commercial banks, which have been made an independent subsector (16) of the financial institutions sector. Logically trust funds administered by nonbank trustees as well as funds effectively administered, although not legally held under trustee arrangements, by investment advisers should be treated similarly. This is not yet possible. For investment advisers, however, at least the present order of magnitude of the funds managed is known.

A second step is the separation of foundations and private educational institutions, the two largest components of nonprofit institutions from the point of view of their financial assets. It also has been possible to estimate the financial assets of labor unions (see Appendix IV), but they have not been eliminated from the "household" sector because of their moderate size and the unavailability of sufficient asset breakdown for part of the period. It has not been feasible to treat other nonprofit institutions, particularly churches and hospitals, in the same way, but the fragmentary currently available information indicates that their financial assets, and particularly their stockholdings, are relatively small compared with those of foundations and private educational institutions.

The household sector so purified still is of a quite heterogeneous character. An attempt has been made, therefore, to allocate the estimated total of financial assets of the sector among half a dozen subsectors of households having different amounts of total wealth. These estimates are necessarily of a very rough character and could be made only for a few recent years. Their derivation and limitations are described in Appendix V.

b. Classification of Assets and Liabilities

Given the very large number of types of tangible assets and of financial instruments and the often vague distinction among them, an integrated system of sectoral balance sheets and flow of funds statements requires a standardized classification of assets and liabilities into a manageable number of reasonably homogeneous types, a classification that can be implemented for all sectors that are distinguished. Such a system obviously cannot provide for separate presentation of all types of assets or of all types of liabilities that may be important for one or for a few sectors or subsectors. It must be limited to those types that are significant for most sectors; that differ substantially in their economic character; and that can be estimated without an excessive margin of error.

The standard classification adopted for this study, set forth in Table 1-1, is, like most such classifications, a result of compromise. It provides a minimum of seven types of tangible assets and five types of financial instruments (money, short-term claims, long-term claims, corporate shares, and equity in unincorporated business enterprises) while net worth is obtained as the difference between total assets and total liabilities.[16] However, the classification also permits a finer breakdown of financial instruments—the three-digit categories in Table 1-1 and the more detailed four-digit categories which may be added—for sectors where the data are available and where these classifications are sufficiently important in the sectors' portfolio structure. Actually it has been possible to implement the three-digit classification for most financial subsectors and for some nonfinancial sectors.

Because of the limitation of the basic statistical data the separation of long-term and short-term claims (categories 220, 330, 420, and 430) requires for a few sectors rather rough methods of allocation. This is unlikely to introduce errors that are significant in the over-all picture. More serious is the fact that the content of long- and particularly of short-term claims is not identical in the documents on which estimates for individual sectors are based. This applies particularly to the treatment of accrued claims and liabilities and of reserves for losses. Such discrepancies are one of the reasons why the national total of claims and liabilities are not equal. Differences in valuation of the same instrument by the holder and issuer and in timing of identical transactions in the accounts of the buyer and seller provide other reasons.

It should be noted that a few types of tangible assets (consumers' inventories of semidurable and perishable commodities; military equipment; subsoil assets; monuments; collectors' items) that are sometimes included in national wealth have been omitted, mainly because of the impossibility or extreme difficulty of obtaining estimates that are more than guesses or (in the case of military equipment and monuments) because of doubts

[16] Details about the definition of these categories and their statistical implementation will be found in Appendix I.

TABLE 1-1

Stock and Flow Categories

100 Tangible assets	300 Total assets
110 Land[a]	400 Liabilities
120 Reproducible tangible assets	410 Domestic money[b]
121 Residential structures	420 Other short-term liabilities
122 Nonresidential structures	421 Bank debt
123 Producer durable equip-	422 Trade debt
ment	423 Other
124 Consumer durables	430 Long-term liabilities
125 Inventories	431 Bonds
126 Monetary metals	432 Mortgages
200 Financial assets	433 Other
210 Domestic money[b]	500 Net worth (300 − 400)
220 Other short-term claims	
221 Against financial institu-	
tions[c]	
222 Treasury securities	
223 Other	
230 Long-term claims[d]	
231 Bonds	
232 Mortgages	
233 Other	
240 Corporate shares	
250 Equity in unincorporated	
businesses	600 Total liabilities and net worth

[a] Does not include subsoil assets.

[b] Currency and check deposits.

[c] Further breakdowns in statements of individual sectors and subsectors would be designated as 2211 and so on. Categories 221–223, 231–233, 421–423, and 431–433 may have to be omitted in some sectors.

[d] Does not include claims against financial institutions; intermediate-term claims included where possible.

about their economic significance.[17] Similarly some financial assets (such as goodwill and patents) are included only to the very incomplete and unsystematic extent to which they happen to appear in the balance sheets of nonfinancial corporations. In this case elimination of these items would be the conceptually indicated procedure.

[17] For estimates of subsoil assets, see R. W. Goldsmith in *Studies in Income and Wealth*, Vol. 14, New York, NBER, 1951, p. 48 ff.; and for those of military equipment in 1952–58, see R. W. Goldsmith, *The National Wealth of the United States in the Postwar Period*, Princeton, Princeton University Press for NBER, 1962, p. 118.

c. Valuation

In principle all items in a balance sheet should be valued at the market price, or at the nearest approximation to it, in order to obtain figures comparable among sectors and among assets and liabilities, while all entries in flow of funds statements should be made at actual transactions values. Limitations in the basic statistical data, as well as some conceptual difficulties, do not permit a consistent application of these principles in actual statistical work to all sectors and to all types of assets and liabilities.

Among tangible assets no market values exist for most categories of nonresidential structures, such as large industrial installations and government structures, and for most types of producer equipment. Here estimated replacement cost, appropriately depreciated for the age of the structure or equipment, must be used as a substitute. Figures of this type can be obtained by applying to the estimated original cost price indexes that are not always adequate and that generally do not take into account quality improvement, particularly in the case of equipment, and hence probably overstate the increase in prices. These difficulties are discussed in Appendix I. Estimates of the value of land present some conceptual and statistical problems of their own that are described in Appendix II.

Among financial assets the most important deviation from the general principle of valuation at "market" is the valuation of long-term debt at face or book value, both where the instruments are traded and where there is no actual market. This defect is not inherent in the method used in compiling sectorial balance sheets, but is due to the limitations of time and resources under which the study was conducted. In a period of generally rising interest rates such as 1952–68, particularly during the later part of the period, the use of book or face values instead of market overstates the actual or hypothetical market value of long-term debt. Insofar as the figures are intended to reflect the values that determine the behavior of holders and issuers, however, it is doubtful that an unequivocal application of market values, or their hypothetical equivalent, would be appropriate. Possibly some figures between face or book value and market value may be preferable, although actual calculation is hardly practicable.[18]

[18] Since there was no possibility to adjust the face or book value of long-term debt to market or equivalent values we did not have to face the difficult and disputed question whether the adjustment should be applied, if at all, only to holders' balance sheets while such debt should be carried in issuers' balance sheets at redemption value irrespective of its market value. The entries in the flow of funds statements are not affected by the adjustment since it reflects an unrealized capital gain or loss which, of course, is not taken into account in the flow of funds estimates.

In the case of corporate stock a specific valuation is needed only for holders, and here market value, or a value which in the case of unlisted securities approximates it, is the indicated standard. While the margin of error in such an estimate is undoubtedly substantial for unlisted stocks, they fortunately constitute only a small portion of total outstanding corporate stock so that even a substantial error would not decisively affect estimates for all corporate stock outstanding. In the case of sectors issuing corporate stock, i.e., nonfinancial corporations and most of the subsectors of the finance sector, no use is made of the market value of the stock because net worth is estimated as the difference between the market value of total assets and the value (essentially the face value) of liabilities.

Difficulties in the case of the flow of funds statements arise from the fact that virtually all estimates for claims are derived as the first difference between the values of the stock of claims at the beginning and at the end of a period. Since these are essentially face or book values, the difference between them includes realized capital gains and losses as well as other revaluations. To correct the first differences for these items detailed income statements are needed, but are not available for most of the nonfinancial sectors and for part of the subsectors of the financial sector. Even where some data of this type are available resources were lacking to carefully investigate the material and to blow up the fragmentary data to cover an entire sector or subsector. The only exceptions are realized capital gains and losses by commercial banks in their transactions in U.S. government securities, which already are allowed for in flow of funds figures published by the Federal Reserve Board. In the period covered by the study, which has been characterized by rising interest rates and falling bond prices, omission of this adjustment leads to an overstatement of net purchases, or an understatement of net sales of bonds by the trading sectors. It is unlikely, however, that the adjustment would be large enough to affect any of the major trends disclosed by the figures except for a few years, a few types of long-term claims, and a few subsectors of the finance sector.

2

The Historical Background: Financial Institutions as Investors in Corporate Stock Before 1952

RAYMOND W. GOLDSMITH

1. SOURCES AND LIMITATIONS OF DATA

The statistical material for the analysis of the holdings of corporate stock by financial institutions before 1952 within a framework of national accounts is naturally much thinner and less reliable than that available for the postwar period on which the report concentrates and with which Chapters 3 to 5 deal. No flow of funds statements exist for the period before the mid–1930's, and for the first decade for which they are available they are not fully comparable to the present system. No national or sectoral balance sheets have been prepared for any date during the nineteenth century, and for the first half of the current century they are available only for a few benchmark years. Similarly the elements from which flow of funds statements and the financial part of the national and sectoral balance sheets are now built up—essentially the balance sheets of groups of financial and nonfinancial sectors published by or reported to government agencies—are less copious, less reliable, and less detailed as we go back in time, particularly to the period before World War I. The statistical evidence used in this chapter therefore is more piecemeal than that utilized for the postwar period. The main source, in addition to the national balance sheets for the benchmark years 1900, 1912, 1922, 1929, 1939, and 1945,[1] are the balance sheets of the main groups of financial institutions.[2] Since no material of this type is available for some important

[1] R. W. Goldsmith, R. E. Lipsey, and M. Mendelson, *Studies in the National Balance Sheet of the United States*, Princeton, Princeton University Press for National Bureau of Economic Research, 2 vols., 1963.
[2] For figures back to 1900 see R. W. Goldsmith, *Financial Intermediaries in the American Economy since 1900*, Princeton, Princeton University Press for NBER, 1958.

groups for the period before 1900 it was necessary to develop estimates based on a small number of companies for property insurance companies and to use figures derived from reports of supervisory agencies in the most important states for mutual savings banks for 1870, 1880, and 1890. Even rougher estimates had to be used for some other figures needed for benchmark dates before 1900.

The nonstatistical historical statements made throughout this chapter are not specifically documented, as they are taken from standard sources and do not claim to represent the results of original research.

The arrangement of this chapter follows the approach outlined in Chapter 1, and uses magnitudes and ratios explained and to some extent justified there.

2. THE SUPPLY OF CORPORATE STOCK, 1850–1952

a. The Growth of Nonfinancial Corporations

Until the railway age, i.e., the beginning of the second third of the nineteenth century, corporations played only a negligible role in the nonfinancial sectors of the American economy, with the exception of canal transportation. In 1850 the share of nonfinancial corporations in national wealth, which is probably as good an indicator of their importance in the economy as can be obtained, is estimated to have been in the neighborhood of only about 7 percent (Table 2-1). Primarily as a result of the rapid expansion of the railroad system, both the absolute value of tangible assets of nonfinancial corporations and their share in national wealth increased sharply. By 1880 nonfinancial corporations owned and operated slightly more than one-fourth of the total tangible assets in the United States. No definite trend can be detected in this ratio during the following eighty years. Thus, the tangible assets of nonfinancial corporations seem to have expanded at approximately the same pace as total national wealth from 1880 to the 1950's, disregarding relatively short and narrow fluctuations.

During this period there occurred, of course, considerable shifts in the industrial distribution of capital expenditures and of tangible assets, but they were not of a nature to lead to substantial changes in the relation of external financing and of stock issues to capital formation for the corporate structure. During the second half of the nineteenth century the share of railroads and public utilities in total tangible assets of nonfinancial corporations apparently remained close to one-half, and the share declined but slowly, to about two-fifths between the 1920's and the late 1940's.

TABLE 2-1

Share of Nonfinancial Corporations in National Wealth and Assets, 1850–1952

	National Assets			Tangible Assets			Financial Assets		
	Total ($billion)	Non-financial Corpora-tions	Share (per-cent)	Total ($billion)	Non-financial Corpora-tions	Share (per-cent)	Total ($billion)	Non-financial Corpora-tions	Share (per-cent)
	(1)	(2)	(3)	(4)	(5)	(6)	(7)	(8)	(9)
1850	9.8	[.7]	[7]	7.2	[.5]	[7]	2.6	[.2]	[8]
1880	66.3	—	—	40.0	[11.0]	[28]	26.3	—	—
1900	156.8	35.0	22	89.8	21.1	23	67.0	13.9	21
1912	306.2	66.4	22	167.2	41.0	25	139.0	25.3	18
1922	644.8	152.3	24	326.1	92.1	28	318.7	60.2	19
1929	973.4	228.1	23	427.1	121.4	28	546.3	106.7	20
1939	863.3	153.5	18	396.5	101.7	26	466.9	51.8	11
1945	1,532.9	251.0	16	578.5	142.9	25	954.5	108.1	11
1952	2,570.5	508.2	20	1,199.3	338.4	28	1,371.2	169.7	12

NOTE: In this and other tables, components may not add exactly to totals because of rounding.

SOURCES:

1900–52: R. W. Goldsmith, R. E. Lipsey, and M. Mendelson, *Studies in the National Balance Sheet of the United States*, Princeton, Princeton University Press for National Bureau of Economic Research, 1963, Vol. II, p. 42 ff.

Col. 4. 1850, 1880: R. W. Goldsmith in *Income and Wealth*, Series II, New York, NBER, 1938, pp. 306, 310, 317.

Col. 7. 1850, 1880: E. S. Shaw and J. G. Gurley, "The Growth of Debt and Money in the United States, 1800–1950: A Suggested Interpretation," *Review of Economics and Statistics*, 1957, p. 256. Figures in brackets are very rough estimates.

Within the regulated industries the steam railroads' share, however, declined sharply, from about seven-eighths in 1870, and a probably equally high percentage in the preceding twenty years—to about 70 percent at the turn of the century, and to not much over 50 percent in 1929 and 1945.[3] Most of the remaining tangible assets of nonfinancial corporations, i.e., from nearly one-half in the mid-nineteenth century to

[3] M. J. Ulmer, *Capital in Transportation, Communications and Public Utilities: Its Formation and Financing*, Princeton, Princeton University Press for NBER, 1960, p. 235 ff.

about three-fifths from the 1920's on, were in the hands of manufacturing and mining corporations.

The stability of the share of nonfinancial corporations in national wealth is the result of several offsetting tendencies. The increasing share of corporations in the total business sector tended to increase the proportion, but the expansion of the tangible assets of government and of consumer durables, well in excess of the growth of total national wealth, worked in the opposite direction.

The supply of corporate stock and the value of stock outstanding, however, are not dependent only on the growth of tangible assets (i.e., structures, equipment, inventories, and land) owned by nonfinancial corporations. At least three other factors influence the absolute volume of the supply of stock of nonfinancial corporations and its relation to aggregate magnitudes such as national wealth or national product.

1. The extent to which additions to the tangible assets of nonfinancial corporations excluding valuation changes, i.e., their capital expenditures, are financed by the issuance of corporate securities in the widest sense (stocks, bonds, mortgages, bank loans, trade credit, and other borrowings) rather than defrayed out of retained earnings, whether earned depreciation allowances or net corporate saving;

2. The share of common and preferred stock in the total external financing of nonfinancial corporations;

3. The discrepancies in the price movements of tangible assets held by nonfinancial corporations and of corporate stock, discrepancies which lead to changes in the ratio of the replacement value of tangible assets of nonfinancial corporations to the market value of their outstanding issues.

b. Total Issues of Nonfinancial Corporations

In the United States, as in all other countries that now possess a developed financial structure, the only important financial instruments in existence were, until well into the nineteenth century, money (in the form of coins and bank notes), short-term trade credit, long-term farm and urban mortgages, and government securities; the only important financial institutions were banks of issue and commercial banks. A few other financial instruments and institutions existed, but they are of interest more as harbingers of things to come than because of their contemporary importance in the economic process.

By 1840, which may be regarded as close to the starting point of the modern financial development of the United States, all financial assets were equal to less than one-half of national wealth and to nearly one and

TABLE 2-2

The Supply of Stock of Nonfinancial Corporations, 1840–1952

(figures in columns 1–8 are in billions of dollars; figures in columns 9–12 are percentages of GNP)

	Issues Outstanding[a]				Net Issues[b]				Issues Outstanding		Net Issues	
	Total (1)	Stocks (2)	Bonds (3)	Other Debt (4)	Total (5)	Stocks (6)	Bonds (7)	Other Debt (8)	Total (9)	Stocks (10)	Total (11)	Stocks (12)
1840	0.3	0.1	0.1	0.1					18	6		
1860	1.5	0.7	0.5	0.3	1.1	0.5	0.4	0.2	39	18	2.0	0.9
1880	9.0	4.0	3.0	2.0	7.2	3.0	2.5	1.8	86	38	5.0	2.0
1900	26.2	11.2	7.1	7.9	15.0	5.0	4.1	5.9	132	56	5.6	1.9
1912	65.2	32.0	18.1	15.1	23.0	4.8	11.0	7.2	182	89	7.0	1.5
1922	129.5	65.1	24.5	39.9	37.6	6.4	6.4	24.8	175	88	6.0	1.0
1929	261.0	164.7	36.3	60.0	42.5	10.6	11.8	20.1	253	160	6.4	1.6
1939	155.2	89.2	31.4	34.6	−26.4	3.8	−4.9	−25.4	171	100	−3.4	0.5
1945	218.4	130.2	23.6	64.6	24.0	1.8	−7.8	30.0	103	61	2.0	0.2
1952	361.8	193.1	44.1	124.6	90.7	10.2	20.5	60.0	105	56	4.7	0.5

Notes to Table 2-2

SOURCES:
Cols. 2–4. 1840, 1860: Based on data on *Hunt's Merchants Magazine*, 1863, p. 354 (for columns 2 and 3).
   1880:   Rough estimate.
   1900–52:   *Studies in the National Balance Sheet*, Vol. II, pp. 42 ff.; after deduction of value of stock of financial institutions (Table 5).
Col. 6.   1860–1900:   Rough estimates.
   1900–45:   R. W. Goldsmith, *A Study of Saving*, Vol. III, Princeton, Princeton University Press, 1956, p. 496 ff.
   1946–52:   Board of Governors of the Federal Reserve System, *Flow of Funds Accounts 1945–1967*, 1968, p. 35.
Cols. 7, 8. 1840–1952: First differences of outstandings.

ᵃ Market value for stock; face value for debt.
ᵇ Period ending with year indicated.

one-half times GNP, while the share of financial institutions in total financial assets outstanding was in the neighborhood of one-fifth (Table 2-2). At that time nonfinancial corporate issues probably accounted for less than one-fifth of all financial instruments outstanding. These low ratios—low compared with similar measures for later dates—reflect the then predominant identity between savers and investors, particularly in the private sector of the economy; and the consequent relatively small importance of external financing outside of the governmental sphere. The low ratios for private external financing indicate the predominance of interfamily and neighborhood transactions over financing by institutions or through the open capital market.

The great changes in the position of corporate securities in the American economy came in two spurts. The first occurred in the 1840's and 1850's when the railroads for the first time generated a large supply of corporate bonds and stocks because of their reliance on external financing through security issues, which in turn was connected with their substantial requirements for long-term funds. The second spurt took place in the period from 1880 to World War I. Incorporation now became predominant in the rapidly expanding manufacturing and mining and the new electric power and communication sectors, again sharply increasing the supply of corporate bonds and stock. As a result, the value of all nonfinancial corporate issues (stocks, bonds, and other debt) increased from an almost insignificant amount in 1840 (apparently of the order of $200 million to $300 million) to over $8 billion in 1880, over $25 billion in 1900, and about $65 billion in 1912. Nonfinancial corporate issues outstanding thus accounted for approximately two-thirds of all financial instruments issued by nonfinancial sectors in 1912. They had become, since the third quarter of the nineteenth century, the largest single group of nonfinancial issues, ahead of the government, financial institutions, and households.

Corporate stock issues (both of nonfinancial and of financial corporations and including intercorporate holdings), which are of particular interest here, increased equally rapidly, from less than $1 billion in 1860 to approximately $4 billion in 1880, $14 billion in 1900, and $38 billion in 1912. Stocks listed on the New York Stock Exchange meanwhile increased from less than $1.5 billion in 1880[4] to nearly $5 billion in 1900, and $13.5 billion in 1912.[5] These figures indicate a share of listed to total stock of fully one-third without substantial changes over the period.[6]

The sharp upward trend in the supply of nonfinancial corporate issues continued until 1929. Total value doubled between 1912 and 1922 and again doubled in the seven years 1923 to 1929. About two-fifths of the increase in the first period (as in 1901–12), but two-thirds in the second period, represented stock price increases rather than net issues. During the 1930's the value of corporate issues outstanding actually decreased sharply by nearly 50 percent. In the case of stock, the result reflects chiefly the fall in prices, but for debt issues, it represents mainly net retirements, which amounted to about one-third of the outstandings of 1929. The increase in the value of corporate securities outstanding resumed in the 1940's and accelerated in the 1950's as the result of sharp increases in stock prices in the face of a very low volume of net issues and of very heavy net new issues of debt.

These movements are more usefully followed in terms of national product than in absolute numbers. It is then found that the ratio of the value of issues of all types by nonfinancial corporations to national product increased very rapidly between 1840 and 1880, more than doubling every twenty years, and exceeded 85 percent of GNP in 1880. The upward trend continued, though at a slower pace, for the next forty years, bringing the ratio to 180 percent of GNP in 1912, equally divided between equity and debt issues. (By comparison, the share of stocks had moved from one-third to two-fifths between 1840 and 1900.) A sharp increase followed in the late 1920's and an even sharper decline

[4] Read off from chart in A. Cowles 3rd and Associates, *Common Stock Indexes 1871–1937*, p. 54.

[5] Goldsmith, *Financial Intermediaries*, Appendix Table F–4 (mimeographed).

[6] At the end of 1929 the value of stock listed on the New York Stock Exchange, $65 billion (R. Meeker, *The Work of the Stock Exchange*, New York, Ronald Press, 1930, p. 546), was equal to 35 percent of all corporate stock, including intercorporate holdings, and 45 percent excluding intercorporate holdings.

in the 1930's and during World War II, both, until the end of the 1930's, reflecting mainly stock price movements. As a result, nonfinancial corporations' securities in 1945 were equal to only one year's GNP, a level they had crossed as far back as 1890. For stocks alone the ratio was slightly above 60 percent, the level of the early 1900's, while the bond ratio, at less than 40 percent, was back to the 1880 level. (The relations were still approximately the same in 1952.) Thus far had the process of nonfinancial corporate debt shrinkage gone as the result of both the debt reductions of the 1930's and the economic expansion and repressed inflation of World War II.

More relevant to an evaluation of the importance of the supply of corporate issues is the ratio over a period of net issues to national product because it takes account of the growing size of the American economy and is not affected directly by stock price movements. This ratio rose sharply during the second half of the nineteenth century—from only 2 percent in 1841–60 to an average of 7 percent during the first three decades of this century, of which slightly less than 1½ percent represented stock of nonfinancial corporations. The latter level has never been equaled since.

These are the facts. What is the explanation? The explanation must be sought, along the lines of the formula of section 3b of Chapter 1, in three factors: (1) the movement of the national capital formation ratio; (2) the share of nonfinancial corporations in national capital expenditures; and (3) the share of external in total financing by corporations, the last two factors being linked by (4) the ratio of total (external and internal) financing to capital expenditures.

Very little is known reliably about these relations for the nineteenth century, and the estimates available for later periods are far from satisfactory until the 1930's or even the 1940's. There is little doubt, however, that between 1840 and 1900 both the national capital formation ratio, and particularly the share of corporations in it, rose substantially. These two movements explain part, and possibly a large part, of the rise in the observed ratio of the issues of nonfinancial corporation to national product, from a level of about 2 percent in the middle of the nineteenth century to over 6 percent at its end. Apparently neither of these two ratios had a substantial upward trend during the current century, or even since the 1880's, nor has the ratio of nonfinancial corporate issues to gross national product (valuation changes excluded). Indeed, the ratio has been lower since 1930 than in the preceding thirty or even seventy years. We must, therefore, turn for further explanation to the ratio of external financing, and of equity financing in particular, to capital expenditures of nonfinancial corporations.

It is not possible without some degree of arbitrariness to match capital expenditures with specific forms of issuance of debt and equity securities or even with total external financing in the statistics of sources and uses of funds, particularly if the accounts are as highly aggregated as to cover all nonfinancial corporations. Therefore, the measure of the importance of external financing and of stock financing in particular must be the share of total external financing and its components in total sources of funds.

TABLE 2-3

Sources of Funds of Nonfinancial Corporations, 1901–52

Sources	1901 to 1912 (1)	1913 to 1922 (2)	1923 to 1929 (3)	1930 to 1939 (4)	1940 to 1945 (5)	1946 to 1952 (6)	1901 to 1952 (7)
I. Total sources of funds (billions of dollars)							
1. Period total	40.0	76.1	86.1	28.3	75.4	201.8	507.7
2. Annual average	3.3	7.6	12.3	2.8	12.6	28.8	9.8
II. Individual sources (percent)	100	100	100	100	100	100	100
1. Internal sources	55	60	55	114	80	58	64
a. Retained profits	22	27	17	−71	32	31	22
b. Capital consumption allowances	34	34	37	184	49	27	42
2. External sources	45	40	45	−14	20	42	36
a. Borrowing[a]	10	20	12	−32	20	27	18
b. Bonds and notes	21	9	14	−1	−5	10	9
c. Stock	14	11	19	19	5	5	10
III. Gross capital expenditures (billions of dollars)	26.1	49.4	51.1	31.2	40.9	149.1	347.8
Percent of I	65	65	59	110	54	74	69

SOURCES:
1901–45: R. W. Goldsmith, *Financial Intermediaries in the American Economy Since 1900*, Princeton, Princeton University Press for NBER, 1958, p. 222.
1946–52: *Flow of Funds Accounts 1945–1967*, p. 35.

[a] Excluding 2b.

The essential figures for the period from 1900 to 1952 are shown in Table 2-3. It is there seen that gross capital formation for the period as a whole absorbed fully two-thirds of total funds of all nonfinancial corporations taken together, the ratio deviating substantially from this level only during the 1930's. The remaining funds were utilized to acquire financial assets, primarily cash, trade receivables, and securities held for liquidity, yield, or control.

Of the total funds raised by nonfinancial corporations during this half-century, fully three-fifths came from internal sources, primarily earned depreciation allowances and secondarily retained earnings. It is the remaining third—a total of more than $180 billion from 1901 through 1952—representing external financing, that may be regarded as the matrix of the volume of issues of stock by nonfinancial corporations. The ratio of external to total financing was close to two fifths in the three periods distinguished between 1901 and 1929 although, of course, there were substantial short-term fluctuations. The ratio, which had been very low between 1930 and 1945, returned to the earlier level after World War II.

There are, unfortunately, no comprehensive data available on the financing of nonfinancial corporations before 1900. For the then most important single industry, the railroads,[7] the share of external financing apparently was considerably higher, at least from 1880 on, than it was after the turn of the century for all nonfinancial corporations. Thus, from 1880 to 1907 the retained earnings of railroads accounted for only 5 percent of their total sources of funds, and no contribution was made by capital consumption allowances.[8]

Data are lacking to calculate the ratios separately for the main industries even for most of this century. The ratios for large corporations in manufacturing and mining[9] seem to have been close to the overall ratio for all nonfinancial corporations. Among the other industries it is fairly certain that the external financing ratios were higher than the average for public utility and real estate corporations and lower than the average for corporations in trade and service. For the end of the period, the years

---

[7] Both in 1870 and in 1890 railroads accounted for approximately one-fifth of the dividends paid by all nonfinancial corporations, which may give a reasonable idea of their relative importance, although it is very likely that the railroad's share of external financing was considerably higher than this ratio. (See A. J. Schwartz, "Gross Dividend and Interest Payments by Corporations at Selected Dates in the 19th Century," in *Trends in the American Economy in the Nineteenth Century*, Studies in Income and Wealth, Vol. 24, Princeton, Princeton University Press for NBER, 1960, pp. 417–18.)

[8] See Ulmer, *op. cit.*, p. 502.

[9] See S. Kuznets, *Capital in the American Economy: Its Formation and Financing*, Princeton, Princeton University Press for NBER, 1961, p. 251.

1945–52, when some relevant data are available, the external financing ratio was about 55 percent for large corporations in the public utility and railroad industries compared with 30 percent for large manufacturing corporations.[10]

c. The Share of Stock Issues in External Financing of Nonfinancial Corporations

The crucial fact here is how far total external financing needs, which were determined by expansion of activities and possibilities of internal financing—and, of course, were also influenced by the ease or difficulty of external financing—were met by the sale of corporate stock rather than by short- or long-term borrowing. In this case there is a definite break between the experience of the first four decades of this century, during which the sale of corporate stock contributed on the average one-sixth of total external financing (Table 2-3), with a range from one-ninth to almost one-fifth for the four periods, and that of the 1940–52 period, when the contribution was as low as 5 percent. No overall figures are available for the nineteenth century, but it is likely that the share of corporate stock in external financing by nonfinancial corporations during the second half of the century was at least as high as the 1900–40 level and may have been considerably higher. In the case of the railroads, stock outstanding constituted about 55 percent of total external financing in 1855, 50 percent in 1880, and 40 percent in 1900.[11]

While comprehensive information on the total volume of external financing and the issuance of stock by the different industries is lacking, it is possible to obtain a rough idea of the distribution of the stock outstanding among the main industries at several benchmark dates between 1835 and 1952. These ratios, of course, are not identical with the distribution of funds raised through the sale of stocks because they are influenced by differentials in stock price movements among industries. Furthermore, for the last decades of the nineteenth century the distribution of dividends paid by different industries must be used rather than the market value of their stock outstanding, and the two distributions again are not identical because the price-dividend ratio differs for the stock of different industries. The main trends appearing in Tables 2-4 and 2-5 should nevertheless roughly reflect the distribution of stock financing among the main industries, even though the three sources used for different parts of the period are far from being fully comparable.

[10] See Goldsmith, *Financial Intermediaries*, p. 229 ff.
[11] See Bureau of the Census, *Historial Statistics of the United States, Colonial Times to 1957*, 1960, pp. 428, 433.

TABLE 2-4

Industrial Distribution of Corporate Stock Outstanding 1835–1949

(percent)

Industry	1835 (1)	1859[a] (2)	1871 (3)	1890 (4)	1900 (5)	1912 (6)	1922 (7)	1929 (8)	1939 (9)	1949 (10)
1. Railroads	2	15	19	20	39	26	10	6	4	3
2. Other transportation	7	8	5	3	7[b]	7[b]	5[b]	11[b]	12[b]	10[b]
3. Gas and electricity	0	5	4	8						
4. Banks and insurance	64	39	26	21	20	15	16	11	9	8
5. Manufacturing and mining	18	24	38	39	34	52	69	72	75	79
6. Other	9	9	8	9						
7. Total	100	100	100	100	100	100	100	100	100	100

SOURCES:

Cols. 1–4. Based on distribution of dividends as estimated by A. J. Schwartz, "Gross Dividend and Interest Payments by Corporations at Selected Dates in the 19th Century," in *Trends in the American Economy in the Nineteenth Century*, Studies in Income and Wealth, Vol. 24, Princeton, Princeton University Press for NBER, 1960.

Cols. 5–10. Based on estimated market value in *Financial Intermediaries*, Appendix F.

[a] 1860 alternate, and for some groups substantially different, estimates of the value of corporate stock (rather than dividends), may be derived from *Hunt's Merchants Magazine*, 1863, p. 23. According to these estimates, railroads accounted for 45 percent of the total, public utilities for 13 percent, and banks and insurance companies for 44 percent, no entries being shown for corporations in manufacturing, mining, trade, and service.

[b] All public utilities except railroads.

TABLE 2-5

The Supply of Stock of Financial Institutions, 1840–1952

(*$billion*)

	Total (1)	Federal Reserve Banks[a] (2)	Commercial Banks[b] (3)	Property Insurance Companies[b] (4)	Federal Home Loan Banks[a] (5)	Investment Companies[c] Open End (6)	Investment Companies[c] Other (7)	Total Percent of Stock of Nonfinancial Corporations[b] (8)
1840	$0.33	—	$0.29	$0.04	—	—	—	330%
1860	0.49	—	0.42	0.07	—	—	—	70
1880	1.00	—	0.90	0.10	—	—	—	25
1900	2.70	—	2.40	0.30	—	—	—	24
1912	6.00	—	5.00		—	—	—	19
1922	11.00	$.33	9.20		—	—	—	17
1929	22.00	.45	15.80	3.10	—	$0.13	$2.52	13
1939	10.90	.35	6.10	2.80	$.17	0.53	0.95	12
1945	16.47	.59	9.30	3.80	.20	1.30	1.28	13
1949	17.69	.83	8.20	4.20	.23	3.10	1.13	13
1952	26.36	.97	13.00	6.00	.32	3.90	2.17	14

SOURCES:

Col. 1. Sum of columns 2 to 7 supplemented by rough estimates for groups for which no figures were available for some dates.

Col. 2. *Federal Reserve Bulletin.*

Col. 3. 1840–60: *Hunt's Merchants Magazine*, 1863, p. 23 (also for column 4).
        1880: Rough estimates.
        1900–49: *Financial Intermediaries*, Appendix Table F-29.

Col. 4. 1900, 1929, 1949: *Ibid.*, Appendix Tables F-5 to F-7.
        1939, 1945, 1949: Rough estimates, based mainly on movements in Standard and Poor's index of fire insurance stocks. (The 1952 estimate in columns 3 and 4 is substantially above an alternative, and probably more reliable, figure in an annual series used in Chapter III for the period 1952–1968, the derivation of which is described in Appendix VI. This alternative estimate has not been used here in order not to destroy the continuity and comparability of the estimates for the earlier period.)

Col. 5. 1939–52: United States Savings and Loan League, *Savings and Loan Fact Book*, various issues.

Notes to Table 2-5 (concluded)

| Col. 6. | 1929, 1939:
1945–52: | *Study of Saving*, Vol. I, p. 559.
Flow of Funds Accounts 1945–1968, 1970, p. 64. |
| Col. 7. | 1929–52: | Net worth of all investment companies (*Financial Intermediaries*, p. 396) less column 6. |

ᵃ Book value.
ᵇ Market value.
ᶜ Assets or net worth of companies.

The main structural change in the distribution of corporate stock among industries, and hence in the volume of stock of nonfinancial corporations available for acquisition by financial institutions, is the declining share of banks and property insurance companies in the total of all corporate stock issued and outstanding (see the discussion in the following section). This movement reflects not a decline or even a stagnation in the volume of stock of financial corporations issued or outstanding, but rather, an increase in the use of the corporate form in almost all other sectors of business and the more rapid rate of growth of the equity of some important nonfinancial sectors, particularly manufacturing and public utilities.

Among nonfinancial corporations an outstanding movement is the rapid rise in the share of railroads from about 1840 to the end of the century.[12] The share of all public utilities other than railroads did not show a long-term trend, although it varied between a low of 5 percent (1922) and a high of around 12.5 percent (1859, 1939). Within this category, however, distribution among industries changed radically. The figures were dominated in the nineteenth century first by the shares of canal companies and then by those of gas companies. Since World War I, on the other hand, most of the share has been accounted for by electric power and telephone companies. The result is that the "other" category, which in the twentieth century is represented mostly by shares of manufacturing (including oil) companies, accounted for about four-fifths of the total in 1949 compared with three-tenths to three-fifths before World War I.

---

[12] The increase in the share of railroads between 1890 and 1900 shown in Table 2-4 is overstated because the estimate for the first date is based on the railroads' share in total dividends paid while that for the second date is derived from estimates of the market value of the shares of different industries. The price-dividend ratio probably was higher for railroads than for all other nonfinancial industries taken together.

d. The Supply of Stock of Financial Corporations

Financial institutions may, of course, also invest in the shares of other financial institutions, of their own or of a different type. Indeed, in the latter case, the advantage of control may be an important added incentive for holding. These securities have widened the supply of corporate stock available to financial institutions, though not to a decisive extent since World War I. During the nineteenth century, however, the situation was different. Thus in 1840 the value of the stock of banks and insurance companies was estimated at three times that on nonfinancial corporations, and the ratio seems to have been in the neighborhood of two-thirds in 1860.[13] By the turn of the century the ratio had declined to below 30 percent, and in 1912 it had fallen to about 20 percent. After a further slow decline during the following quarter century, the ratio stabilized at around one-eighth of the value of the stock of nonfinancial corporations; the increasing ratio for open-end investment company stock approximately offset the continuing decline in the ratio for bank and insurance company stock. The relevant figures are shown in Table 2-5.

This secular decline in the proportion of the total supply of corporate stock that consists of shares of financial institutions is due primarily to the downward trend in the ratio of net worth to liabilities in virtually all types of financial institutions other than investment companies. In commercial banks, for example, net worth was equal to fully 50 percent of liabilities in 1860, less than 20 percent in 1900, less than 15 percent in 1929, and only 7 percent in 1952.

e. Foreign Stocks

Shares in financial or nonfinancial foreign companies have played a negligible role in the portfolios of financial institutions as a whole, and in that of each type except investment companies. Even for these companies the proportion probably never exceeded one-tenth of the total stock portfolio and consisted mostly of stocks in Canadian companies. In 1952 the ratio was down to less than 4 percent for open-end companies, almost exclusively in Canadian stocks. This has been due both to statutory limitations against foreign investment except in Canada and to the then prevailing unpopularity of foreign securities. Foreign stocks may, therefore, be excluded when considering the supply of corporate stock on which financial institutions could draw. In 1952 they probably constituted only about 1 percent of the stock portfolio of all financial institutions excluding

---

[13] *Hunt's Merchants Magazine*, 1863, p. 313 ff.

personal trust funds, and less than one-half of 1 percent including them.

3. THE SOURCES OF FUNDS OF FINANCIAL INSTITUTIONS

Before looking at the movements of the main determinants and their contribution to the value of the new-issue ratio of financial institutions (the ϕ ratio of Chapter 1, which is approximated by the change in the assets of financial institutions divided by the period's total gross national product), it is well to recall the path which that ratio has taken from 1840 to 1952, particularly its fairly regular upward trend, which has carried it from not much more than 1 percent of GNP, in the period 1841 to 1860, to 2.3 percent in the following two decades, 4.2 percent from 1881 to 1900, and to 5.2 percent in the period 1901–12. Since then the ratio has been at a considerably higher level, except during the 1930's, when it fell back to 4.3 percent. For the periods 1913–22 and 1923–29 the ratio averaged close to 8 percent. The peak was reached during World War II, with nearly 20 percent. This was followed by a sharp decline to 7 percent in 1946–52 (Table 2-6).

a. The Issuance of Money

The first main component of ϕ (the ratio, m, of the change in money in circulation—i.e., currency and check deposits—to the period's gross national product) increased from less than 0.5 percent of GNP in the 1840's and 1850's to 0.7 percent in the following two decades. This advance continued, the average for 1881–1900 rising to 1.2 percent and further advancing to a peak level of 2 percent for 1913–22. These forty years are the period of the most rapid development of the commercial banking system and of check payments, influenced near the end by the inflation of World War I. There followed a sharp decline to one-half of 1 percent in the period 1923–29, i.e., below the level of 1861–80, probably representing in part absorption of excess liquidity created during World War I. The value of m again rose sharply during the 1930's to an average of 1.2 percent, reflecting the only partly successful efforts of the government at reflation and the public's hoarding that accompanied the very low level of interest rates during the mid- and late 1930's. World War II led to an extraordinary increase in m—to an average of more than $6\frac{1}{2}$ percent for 1940–45, a result in part of the repressed inflation of that period which was backed by price and wage controls. As after World War I, m declined sharply to 1.3 percent for the period 1946–52, reflecting the accumulation of excess liquid assets in preceding years.

TABLE 2-6

Determinants of Growth of Assets of All Financial Institutions in the United States, 1861–1952

(percent of gross national product)

		Net Issues of:			Change in Assets of All Financial Institutions[c] (5)	Ratio: Col. 4 to Col. 5 (6)
	Money[a] (1)	Commercial Bank Time Deposits (2)	Thrift and Insurance Organiza- tions[b] (3)	Total (4)		
1861–1880	0.7	0.1	0.9	1.7	2.3	.74
1881–1900	1.4	0.4	1.3	3.1	4.2	.74
1901–1912	1.4	1.1	1.7	4.2	5.2	.81
1913–1922	1.9	1.4	1.7	11.0	7.5	.67
1923–1929	0.5	1.0	3.2	4.7	8.0	.59
1930–1939	1.3	−0.5	2.5	3.2	4.3	.74
1940–1945	6.7	1.5	5.1	13.3	19.4	.69
1946–1952	1.3	0.5	4.7	6.5	7.0	.93

[a] Bank notes held by public plus adjusted demand deposits (from 1880, M. Friedman and A. J. Schwartz, *A Monetary History of the United States, 1867–1960*, Princeton, Princeton University Press for NBER, 1963, p. 704 ff.); rough estimates for 1860.

[b] Increase in total assets of mutual savings banks, postal savings system, saving and loan associations, credit unions, and all insurance and pension organizations (*Financial Intermediaries*, pp. 73–74, and rough estimates for 1861–1900).

[c] *Ibid.* Excludes personal trust departments and investment holding companies.

The share of the issuance of money in total issues of financial institutions, i.e., the ratio m/ϕ, followed the same general pattern, but with fewer fluctuations during the nineteenth century. For all the four periods between 1860 and 1922 m constituted approximately three-tenths of ϕ and thus was one of the two most important single components of the ratio. During this period, which extends from the beginning of the railroad age through World War I, the provision of the medium of exchange was still one of the most important, if not the most important, single function of the country's financial system, as it still is in many less developed countries. The share of m in ϕ was considerably lower from 1923 to 1929. The repressed inflation of World War II raised the share of m in ϕ to an all-time peak of fully one-third. The share then declined sharply to about one-fifth in 1946–52.

b. Household Thrift Claims

The most important single component of the ϕ ratio in all periods except during World War II were thrift deposits (including time and saving deposits with commercial banks) and insurance and pension claims of households. Starting with a ratio in the neighborhood of 1 percent of national product in 1860–80, h (the ratio of the increase in thrift deposits and insurance claims to gross national product) rose steadily to fully 4 percent during 1923–29. After a temporary setback to 2 percent during the 1930's, h held close to a level of about 6 percent from 1940 to 1952. The share of h in ϕ rose from about two-fifths from 1860 to 1900 to about one-half in the first thirty years of the twentieth century. Reflecting the extraordinarily high share of m during World War II, the share of h in ϕ during that period was low—about one-third. Possibly the most significant development, however, is the sharp increase in the h/ϕ ratio to three-fourths in 1946–52, in part probably in reaction to the abnormally low ratio during the preceding five years, significant because it foreshadows the continued high level of the ratio that prevailed for the following fifteen years.

The statistics now available are not sufficient to allocate the observed values to the h ratio exactly among the four components distinguished in Chapter 1, section 3b. Enough is known, however, for an appraisal of the order of magnitudes involved.

Since two of these components—the ratio of personal disposable income to gross national product (p) and the personal saving ratio (s)—did not show a pronounced trend over the last 100 to 120 years, or at least not since the turn of the century (p has declined slowly from 0.85 to 0.70 and s has remained close to one-eighth except during the two world wars and the 1930's), the crucial factor in the contribution which h made to ϕ were the movements of the share of the accumulation of financial assets in personal saving (c) and the share of thrift deposits and insurance claims in personal financial saving (t).

Of these two factors, changes in t have been the more important and regular element: The ratio has risen from about one-fourth of personal financial saving in the first two decades of this century to two-fifths in 1923–29, and to fully two-thirds since the 1930's, with the exception of World War II. It may therefore be said that most of the increase of ϕ from a level of about 1 percent in the last forty years of the nineteenth century to about 5 percent in the 1946–52 period is due to the increase in saving through household thrift claims, a relation that will be found also to apply to the following fifteen years.

c. Other Sources

The movements of the ratio (x) of the issue of nonmonetary liabilities other than household thrift deposits and insurance claims by financial institutions to GNP (calculated as the difference between columns 4 and 5 in Table 2-6), as well as its contribution to ϕ, were erratic, partly because of the heterogeneous nature of this item. This component of ϕ was relatively most important in the periods 1923–29 and 1940–45. It amounted to 2.5 percent of GNP in both periods, but to less than one-third and one-eighth respectively of ϕ. The relatively high level of x during the 1920's reflected in part the rapid growth of the then new investment and finance companies. Their shares might well be combined with household thrift claims, since most of the former were bought by individual investors.

The issuance of equity securities by financial institutions, which is included in x except for the shares of insurance companies, has been a minor component of ϕ since 1900. (Comprehensive figures are not available for the earlier periods.) On the average, issues of equity securities by financial institutions have amounted to only three-quarters of 1 percent of GNP, reaching the maximum of $1\frac{1}{4}$ percent in 1923–29 when fairly large amounts of investment company stock were sold to the public. The share of equity securities in ϕ has been declining. During the second half of the nineteenth century it probably was about one-fourth. In 1901–12 and 1922–39 it amounted to about one-sixth, falling to about one-tenth in 1946–52.

From the fragmentary knowledge which we have about the extent of layering within financial institutions it does not appear that the layering ratio has shown substantial or continuous trends during the past century. In any case, the level of the ratio, approximately one-tenth, is too small for modest changes in it to influence the level of ϕ.

4. THE STOCK PORTFOLIO OF FINANCIAL INSTITUTIONS

a. Commercial Banks

Although commercial banks are the largest single group of financial institutions if measured by size of assets, they have hardly ever been important holders of corporate stock.[14] This fact is mostly due to regulation. National banks are virtually precluded from owning corporate stock

---

[14] Excluding, of course, their trust departments, for which see section 4h.

except that of the Federal Reserve banks. While the regulations are not as strict in many states, they still severely limit the freedom of state-chartered banks to invest in corporate stock even if they desire to. The holdings of the stock of Federal Reserve banks are, of course, in a category of their own, since they are compulsory for member banks, and in character are closer to a perpetual bond than to a corporate equity because of their guaranteed but limited dividend and the restricted right of member banks in the equity of the Federal Reserve banks.

In the century before 1939, holdings of common stock excluding those of Federal Reserve banks constituted between 1 and 1½ percent of the total assets of commercial banks, reaching the highest absolute and relative level in 1929 (Table 2-7). Unfortunately the make-up of these stock port-folios is not known before the Great Depression, an indication of their

TABLE 2-7

Holdings of Corporate Stock by Commercial Banks, 1860–1952

| | Stockholdings ($million) | | | Stock Other Than FRB Stock | |
	All Stock (1)	Federal Reserve Banks[a] (2)	Other (3)	Percent of Total Bank Assets (4)	Percent of All Stock Out-standing (5)
1860	10	—	10	(1.20)	1.30
1880	30	—	30	(1.10)	0.60
1900	103	—	103	1.03	0.74
1912	284	—	284	1.30	0.75
1922	508	107	401	0.84	0.53
1929	1,180	171	1,009	1.52	0.54
1939	609	136	473	0.71	0.47
1945	397	177	220	0.14	0.15
1952	403	253	150	0.08	0.07

SOURCES:
Col. 2. *Federal Reserve Bulletin.*
Col. 3. 1860, 1880: Rough estimates.
    1900–1939: *Financial Intermediaries*, pp. 339, 353.
    1945–52: *Studies in the National Balance Sheet*, Vol. II, p. 162.

[a] Par value. Book value in balance sheets of Federal Reserve banks (millions of dollars): 1922: 326; 1924: 448; 1939: 349; 1945: 587; 1952: 972.

insignificance. A substantial proportion probably consisted of stock of real estate, safe deposit, and similar operating affiliates, although some holdings of stocks of other banks were undoubtedly acquired for possible control. In 1934, when the book value of the holdings of stock other than that of Federal Reserve banks had been reduced to one-half of its 1929 level, approximately one-fifth of the total consisted of stocks of banks and bank affiliates, and one-seventh, of stock in real estate corporations. The remaining two-thirds were not further broken down. In 1941, the only other date for which this information is available, the proportion of stocks of banks and bank affiliates had increased to over two-fifths because of a sharp reduction in other holdings of corporate stock by commercial banks, but their absolute value was only about one-third higher than in 1934.[15] The stockholdings of commercial banks were even less important in comparison with the total volume of stock outstanding, accounting for only one-half of 1 percent of the total in 1929 and for only slightly higher fractions before World War I.

During World War II the book value of the holdings of corporate stock other than that of Federal Reserve banks was cut in half, and no details are known about this development. Since the total value of commercial bank assets increased sharply, the share of corporate stock (excluding Federal Reserve bank stock) in total assets fell precipitously from slightly more than 1 percent in 1939 to only one-seventh of 1 percent in 1945, and to less than one-tenth of 1 percent during the 1950's. Similarly, the importance of stockholdings of commercial banks, other than those of Federal Reserve banks, in total corporate stock outstanding has now been reduced to insignificance, falling to about 0.15 percent in 1945—compared with over 0.50 percent in 1929—and further declining to not much over 0.05 percent beginning with the late 1950's.

b. Mutual Savings Banks

During the late nineteenth century mutual savings banks held between 3 and 5 percent of their assets in corporate stocks, consisting mainly of a diversified portfolio of bank stocks (Table 2-8). At that time the bank stocks they held represented between 3 and 4 percent of all outstanding bank stocks in the United States, but a considerably higher proportion of the stock of banks in the states in which mutual savings banks operated, mainly the New England states, New York, and Pennsylvania. The motive for these holdings probably was the relatively high yield combined with fair security.

[15] Federal Deposit Insurance Corporation information.

TABLE 2-8

Stockholdings of Mutual Savings Banks, 1880–1952

	All Stock ($million) (1)	Bank Stock (2)	All Stock (percent of bank assets) (3)	Bank Stock (4)	All Stock (percent of stock outstanding) (5)	Bank Stock (6)	All Stock: Net Purchases[a] ($million) (7)
1880	40	37	4.52	4.22	.98		
1900A	83	40	3.57	1.69	.60	1.67	
1900B	43		1.77		.31	1.79[b]	
1912	41		1.02		.11	0.82[b]	−2
1922	48		0.73		.06	0.52[b]	7
1929	77		0.78		.04	0.49[b]	29
1939	136		1.15		.14	2.23[b]	59
1945	166	116	0.98	0.68	.11	1.25	30
1952	334	280	1.33	1.11	.15	2.15	100

SOURCES:
Cols. 1, 2. 1880–1900A: Estimated on basis of figures for six main states (New York, Massachusetts, Connecticut, Maine, New Jersey, and Rhode Island) taken from reports of their bank supervisory authorities.
 1900B–39: *Financial Intermediaries*, pp. 356–57.
 1945, 1952: National Association of Mutual Savings Banks, *National Fact Book of Mutual Savings Banking*, May 1969, p. 23 (book value less valuation reserve).
Col. 7. 1901–45: *A Study of Saving*, Vol. I, pp. 545–46.
 1945, 1952: *Flow of Funds Accounts 1945–1967*.

[a] Period ending at date indicated.
[b] Assuming virtually all stock to be bank stock.

From the turn of the century to 1922, however, the value of stocks held by mutual savings banks hardly changed, although their assets almost tripled. There is no obvious explanation for this change in their investment policy, except possibly the upward trend in interest rates which made the yield of bank stocks relatively less attractive. As a result, the share of bank stocks in the total assets of mutual savings banks fell to about three-fourths of 1 percent, while their holdings were reduced to about one-half of 1 percent of all bank stock outstanding in the United States.

Policy apparently was again reversed after 1929, and the portfolio of bank stocks was increased considerably during the 1930's, but only slowly during World War II. As a result, the share of bank stocks in total assets of mutual savings banks in 1945 stood at approximately 1 percent, compared with 0.8 percent in 1929, although their share in all bank stocks outstanding had risen substantially, from one-half of 1 percent to about $1\frac{1}{4}$ percent.

After 1945 mutual savings banks began to increase their stock portfolio, now for the first time acquiring considerable amounts of stocks of corporations other than banks. In 1952 this process was still in its initial stages, but the total value of all stocks was already twice as high as in 1945; the share of stocks in total assets was up from 1.0 to 1.3 percent; and the share of bank stocks held by mutual savings banks in all bank stock outstanding had increased from 1.3 to 2.2 percent.

c. Life Insurance Companies

The influence of statutory requirements on stockholdings is particularly evident in the case of life insurance companies, especially during the current century. Originally the limitations of investment in stocks by life insurance companies were not very strict, but because of the fixed value of the liabilities the companies held only moderate amounts, accounting for only approximately 2 percent of assets in the period 1860–80 (Table 2-9). Of these holdings fully one-fourth consisted of railroad stocks; among the others bank stocks appear to have played an important role, although exact figures are not available.

From about 1880 to 1905 stockholdings of life insurance companies increased substantially. Railroad and, later, public utility stocks presumably were acquired primarily for yield, but bank stocks were purchased by the large eastern life insurance companies also because of the influence and other advantages which they could give. The abuses in this direction, which were disclosed by the Armstrong-Hughes investigation of 1905, led to legislation that sharply limited the stockholdings permitted to companies operating in New York State and were a decisive factor in the investment policies of all American companies. For almost two decades after, the absolute volume of stocks held stagnated, and their share declined sharply in the face of a rapid advance in the total assets of life insurance companies. Whereas life insurance companies at the peak of 1906 had held more than 6 per cent of their total assets in stocks, the proportion had declined to only 1 percent by 1922. The proportion of all corporate stock outstanding held by life insurance companies always was

TABLE 2-9

Stockholdings and Transactions of Life Insurance Companies, 1860–1952

	Holdings									Net Purchases[a]		
	Total	Pre-ferred	Com-mon	Total	Pre-ferred	Com-mon	Total	Pre-ferred	Com-mon	Total	Pre-ferred	Com-mon
	($ million)			(percent of total assets)			(percent of stock outstanding)			($ million)		
	(1)	(2)	(3)	(4)	(5)	(6)	(7)	(8)	(9)	(10)	(11)	(12)
1860	1	—	—	2.30	—	—	(0.05)	—	—	—	—	—
1880	6	—	—	1.50	—	—	(0.10)	—	—	—	—	—
1900	62	8	54	3.56	0.46	3.10	0.45	0.28	.49	—	—	—
1912	84	12	72	1.91	0.27	1.63	0.22	0.16	.24	22	4	18
1922	75	16	59	0.87	0.18	0.68	0.10	0.12	.09	−9	4	−13
1929	352	255	97	2.01	1.46	0.55	0.19	1.33	.06	240	206	34
1939	568	435	133	1.94	1.49	0.46	0.57	3.18	.15	226	183	43
1945	1,000	820	180	2.23	1.83	0.40	0.68	6.10	.14	165	131	34
1952	2,450	1,490	960	3.30	2.01	1.29	1.12	9.28	.47	1,300	—	—

Sources:

Cols. 1–6.　1860–80:　L. Zartman, *The Investments of Life Insurance Companies*, 1906, p. 14.

　　　　　1900–1939:　*A Study of Saving*, Vol. I, p. 456.

　　　　　1945–52:　*Studies in the National Balance Sheet*, Vol. I, pp. 174–75.

Cols. 10–12.　1901–45:　*A Study of Saving*, Vol. I.

　　　　　1946–52:　*Flow of Funds Accounts 1945–1967*.

[a] Period ending with year indicated.

small. Even at the peak, life insurance companies' holdings amounted to less than one-half of 1 percent of all stocks outstanding and were important only in a few New York City banks. By 1922 the overall ratio was down to a mere one-tenth of 1 percent.

From the 1920's on, life insurance companies again began to build up their stock portfolios, but for several decades apparently primarily for yield and hence preferring high-grade stocks paying regular dividends. The absolute volume of stockholdings by life insurance companies increased, with few setbacks, from less than $100 million in 1922 to about $2,500 million in 1952. Their share in total assets also rose substantially, although with a marked setback during the 1930's, from 1 percent in 1922 to fully 3 percent in 1952. Similarly, the share of stockholdings of life insurance companies in all corporate stock outstanding advanced substantially, though even in the early 1950's it was only slightly above 1 percent, i.e., twice the previous maximum of the early 1900's but more than ten times the low of 1922.

The structure of the stock portfolio of life insurance companies reflects the change in emphasis from yield to appreciation (Table 2-10). The share of preferred stocks in the portfolio advanced from about one-eighth at the beginning of World War I to approximately three-fourths between the late 1920's and the mid-1940's. It then began to decline; by 1952, it had returned to the 1939 level of two-thirds. The industrial structure of the portfolio showed change in line with changes in the total supply of stock. While railroads accounted for nearly one-half of the total stock portfolio at the turn of the century, their share was down to one-fifth by 1929 and continued to decline to only 6 percent in 1952. Their share was in part taken by public utility stocks, which since 1929 have accounted for more than one-fourth of the total portfolio. Later, the share of industrials and a few other categories of stock gained considerably in the total portfolio, rising from about one-third before World War I to three-fifths at the end of World War II. These shifts were more pronounced in the composition of the portfolio of common than of preferred stocks, but changes occurred during the 1950's and 1960's rather than before 1952.

d. *Property Insurance Companies*

Until well into this century, property insurance companies (predominantly fire and marine companies until the turn of the century and later also casualty companies) were the only group of financial institutions that held a substantial proportion of their total assets in corporate stock; corporate stock constituted one of their most important assets, indeed in

TABLE 2-10

Distribution of Corporate Stock Held by Life Insurance Companies, Selected Dates, 1860–1945

(percent)

Type of Stock	1860 (1)	1870 (2)	1880 (3)	1890 (4)	1900 (5)	1906 (6)	1911 (7)	1922 (8)	1929 (9)	1939 (10)	1945 (11)
Preferred Stock											
Railroads						10	10	18	12	10	9
Public utilities						1	1	2	26	28	23
Other						2	2	3	34	39	47
Common Stock											
Railroads						23	35	26	8	4	3
Public utilities						11	19	12	3	5	4
Other[a]						53	33	40	17	14	14
All Stock											
Railroads	22	27	27	58	45	33	45	44	20	14	12
Public utilities	} 78	73	73	42	55	13	20	14	28	32	27
Other[a]						54	35	43	52	54	61

Sources:
Cols. 1–5. Zartman, *Investments of Life Insurance Companies*, p. 14.
Cols. 6–11. *Proceedings of 44th Meeting of Life Insurance Association of America*, p. 42.

[a] Through 1906 mostly bank stock.

most years the most important asset, next to corporate bonds. The relative prominence of corporate stock in the portfolios of property insurance companies may be explained on the one hand by the freedom from investment limitations that determined the structure of assets of other insurance companies and many other institutional investors; and on the other hand by the fact that their liabilities were mostly of an intermediate length, so that liquidity considerations were not dominant; not only current yields but long-term chances of appreciation could be given considerable weight in investment policies.

As far back as 1860, fire and marine insurance companies held nearly one-fourth of their total assets in corporate stock, primarily in a diversified portfolio of bank stocks which accounted for seven-eighths of their entire stock portfolio (Table 2-11). This concentration probably was due, as in the case of mutual savings banks, to the high quality of bank stocks and to the absence of large corporate issuers in other industries except the railroads. At that time, fire and marine insurance companies held approximately 1 percent of all corporate stock outstanding in the United States. However, because of their concentration on bank stocks the share of property insurance companies in total bank stocks outstanding was of the order of 3 or 4 percent and was considerably higher in the case of banks in the eastern states. The share of bank stocks declined rapidly from about one-fifth of total assets in 1860 to 6 percent in 1880 and 5 percent in 1900, but that of railroad stocks advanced from only 2 percent in 1860 to 4 percent in 1880 and shot up to nearly 20 percent in 1900. As a result, the proportion of corporate stock in the portfolio of fire and marine companies had increased to fully one-fourth by the turn of the century, after a drop to not much over one-tenth in 1880, but their share in total corporate stock outstanding had fallen to about three-fourths of 1 percent, reflecting the rapid rise in stock issues during the last fourth of the nineteenth century.

The share of corporate stock in the total assets of property insurance companies did not show a definite trend throughout the current century, although it was, of course, influenced by stock price fluctuations. At most benchmark dates between 1900 and 1952—with the exception of 1922— the share was in the neighborhood of 25 to 30 percent. The most pronounced increase occurred during the 1920's as a result both of heavy net purchases and the then pronounced rise in stock prices. It is remarkable, however, that property insurance companies also added substantially to their stock portfolios during the 1930's when some other institutional investors reduced theirs. As a result, the share of property insurance

TABLE 2-11

Stockholdings of Property Insurance Companies, 1860–1952

	All	Preferred	Common	All	Preferred	Common	All	Preferred	Common	All Stock: Net Purchases[a]
	($ million)			(percent of assets)			(percent of stock outstanding)			($million)
	(1)	(2)	(3)	(4)	(5)	(6)	(7)	(8)	(9)	(10)
Fire and Marine Companies										
1860	18			22.8			1.50			—
1880	25			11.5			0.50			
1900	106	25	81	25.7	6.1	19.6	0.76	0.86	0.74	
Fire, Marine, and Casualty Companies										
1900	122	29	93	25.7	6.1	19.6	0.88	1.00	0.85	—
1912	231	45	186	23.5	4.6	18.9	0.61	0.58	0.61	109
1922	370	95	275	16.0	4.1	11.9	0.49	0.73	0.44	139
1929	1,511	276	1,235	32.7	6.0	26.7	0.81	1.44	0.74	625
1939	1,457	330	1,127	30.5	6.9	23.6	1.46	2.41	1.30	270
1945	2,415	483	1,932	31.8	6.4	25.5	1.65	3.60	1.45	450
1952	4,320	800	3,520	26.9	5.0	21.9	1.97	4.98	1.73	600

SOURCES:
1860, 1880: Based on reports of 14 large companies in 1860 and 31 companies in 1880.
1900–45:   *A Study of Saving,* Vol. I, pp. 553, 555, 545–46.
1952:   *Studies in the National Balance Sheet,* Vol. II, p. 102 ff.

[a] Period ending at date indicated.

companies in total corporate stock outstanding in the United States increased from a low point of one-half of 1 percent in 1922 to about 1½ percent in the late 1930's and 2 percent in 1952.

During most of the period, preferred stock constituted between one-fourth and one-fifth of the total stock portfolio of property insurance companies. Within the common stock portfolio the predominance of bank stocks gave way, beginning around the turn of the century, to the accumulation of a fairly diversified portfolio, although the holdings of bank and insurance company stocks continued to represent a higher proportion of the total portfolio than corresponded to their share in the total volume of corporate stock outstanding in the United States. Since preferred stocks constituted a considerably larger proportion of the stock portfolio of property insurance companies than of total corporate stock outstanding, their share in all preferred stock outstanding was fairly substantial, reaching 5 percent in 1952.

e. Investment Companies

Investment companies in their varied forms (management-closed-end companies; open-end companies, now often called mutual funds; fixed and semifixed investment trusts; and face amount instalment contract investment companies) were of negligible importance until the early 1920's. After hectic growth during a few years and stagnation between the early 1930's and the end of World War II, investment companies started on a second and this time sustained period of growth in the late 1940's, the emphasis now shifting from closed-end management investment companies, which had predominated in the 1920's, and from fixed trusts, which had been of some importance during the 1930's, to open-end management companies (see Table 2-12).

All important types of investment companies—with the exception of face value contract companies—have always invested the bulk of their assets in corporate stock (see Table 2-13), and during the last two decades have become an important factor in the market, as they were temporarily during the late 1920's. In 1929 the corporate stocks held by investment companies accounted for slightly more than 1 percent of all stock outstanding in the United States, and this ratio was maintained through the 1930's. Beginning with World War II the share of the stockholdings of investment companies in total outstandings increased continuously, although with different speed, and it reached 3 percent by 1952.

Common stocks have always dominated the portfolio of investment companies. The share of preferred stocks was approximately 7 percent

TABLE 2-12

Stockholdings of Investment Companies,[a] 1922–52

	Value of Holdings ($million) (1)	Share in:		Net[b] Purchases ($million) (4)
		Assets (2)	Stocks Outstanding (3)	
		(percent)		
All Stocks				
1922	69[c]	69.0	0.09	
1929	2,189[d]	74.6	1.17	1,994
1939	1,204[d]	85.5	1.20	396
1945A	1,977[d]	82.4	1.35	−28
1945B	2,906	79.9	1.98	—
1952	6,583	84.8	3.00	1,360
Preferred Stock				
1922	12[c]	0.1	0.09	12
1929	191[d]	6.5	0.99	166
1939	72[d]	5.1	0.53	−103
1945A	201[d]	8.4	1.49	158
1945B	250	6.9	1.86	—
1952	290	3.7	1.81	40
Common Stock				
1922	57[c]	57.0	0.09	
1929	1,998[d]	68.1	1.19	1,828
1939	1,132[d]	80.4	1.31	499
1945A	1,776[d]	74.1	1.33	−186
1945B	2,656	73.0	1.99	—
1952	6,293	81.1	3.09	1,320

SOURCES:
Cols. 1–3. 1922–45A: *A Study of Saving*, Vol. I, p. 559 ff.
 1945B–52: *Studies in the National Balance Sheet*, Vol. II, pp. 168–69 (coverage is wider than for 1922–39).
Col. 4. 1923–45A: *A Study of Saving*, Vol. I, pp. 545–46.
 1945B–52: *Studies in the National Balance Sheet*, Vol. II, pp. 422–23.

[a] Excluding investment holding company and unclassified companies; Christiana Corporation classified until 1939 as investment holding company but as regular investment company beginning 1945.
[b] Period ending with year indicated.
[c] Closed-end investment companies only.
[d] Excluding face amount instalment companies; where no breakdown available, assumed allocation 90 percent common, 10 percent preferred.

TABLE 2-13

Stockholdings by Different Types of Investment Companies, 1922–52

	Closed-End Companies (1)	Open-End Companies (2)	Fixed and Semifixed Trusts (3)	Face Amount Investment Companies (4)	Total (5)
		Value ($million)			
1922	69	—	—	0	69
1929	1,927	109	153	2	2,191
1939	648	470	86	12	1,216
1945A	876	1,022	79	40	2,017
1945B	1,810	1,050		46	2,906
1952	3,110	3,400		73	6,583
		Percent of Total Assets			
1922	69.0	—	—	2.0	62.7
1929	73.0	81.3	93.3	3.8	73.3
1939	82.7	88.3	93.5	6.8	76.8
1945A	83.4	80.7	96.3	17.9	76.9
1945B	86.2	82.7		17.7	80.1
1952	94.8	85.2		15.0	84.9

Sources:
Cols. 1–4. 1922–45A: *A Study of Saving*, Vol. I, p. 559 ff.
        1945B–52: *Studies in the National Balance Sheet*, Vol. II, p. 168.

until the late thirties, but then declined to less than 4 percent in 1952. Among common stocks the proportion of railraods declined, in line with the development of the relative supply and price of this category, from approximately one-seventh of the total stock portfolio in the 1920's to 5 percent since World War II. Public utility shares constituted, except during the late 1930's, between one-tenth and one-sixth of the total stock portfolio and represented a somewhat higher proportion of the investment companies' holdings of preferred stock alone. Stocks of financial institutions accounted in 1952 for about one-tenth of the total stock portfolio— a ratio probably not much different from that prevailing earlier—leaving approximately three-fifths to industrial stock. Up to the mid-1950's foreign stocks, then almost all Canadian companies, were unimportant, except for a short period in the late 1920's. Partly as a result of federal regulation beginning in 1939 and partly as a reflection of the policies of most management investment companies—although, of course, not of management holding companies, which are not regarded as financial institutions in this report—the stock portfolio has been fairly widely diversified among individual issues.[16]

f. Private (Uninsured) Pension Funds

Private pension funds, whether administered by a commercial bank's trust department, as most of them are, or by independent trustees, were of very small importance among financial institutions or as owners of corporate stock until after World War II (Table 2-14). Thus, in 1945, the total shareholdings of private pension funds, amounting to less than $300 million, constituted only one-tenth of their total assets and accounted for only one-fifth of 1 percent of all corporate stock outstanding. In the following two decades, however, the growth of the assets of private pension funds was spectacular, as was the increase in the absolute and relative importance of their stockholdings.

As early as 1952 the stockholdings of private pension funds of nearly $2 billion, the result primarily of heavy net purchases during the preceding decade, accounted for about one-fifth of the funds' total assets and represented nearly 1 percent of all corporate stock outstanding.

The importance of private pension funds is even slightly more marked if attention is limited to common stock, since the proportion of preferred stock in their total stock portfolio declined from about one-third at the end of World War II to about one-fifth in 1952. Even though the share of preferred stocks in the total portfolio of private pension funds fell, the proportion of all preferred stock outstanding in the United States held by private pension funds increased from about 0.7 percent in 1945 to more than 2.5 percent in 1952.

g. Other Financial Institutions

The stockholdings of other financial institutions have been too small throughout the period to warrant separate discussion, either because of the small size of the institutions (e.g., savings bank life insurance departments) or because of the very small percentage of corporate stock held (e.g., savings and loan associations; government pension funds), or

---

[16] For the situation up to 1936 see U.S. Securities and Exchange Commission, *Investment Trusts and Investment Companies*, 1939, Part II, Chapter 8; for the 1950's and the then dominating mutual funds see *A Study of Mutual Funds*, prepared by the Wharton School of Finance and Commerce for the Securities and Exchange Commission, 1962, Chapter IV.

TABLE 2-14

Stockholdings of Private Pension Funds, 1922–52

	Value ($million) (1)	Share of Total Assets (percent) (2)	Share of Outstanding Stock (percent) (3)	Net Purchases[a] ($million) (4)	Share of Preferred Stock in (1) (percent) (5)
1922	18	20.0	0.02	13	
1929	100	20.0	0.05	58	
1939	210	20.0	0.21	51	
1945	289	10.8	0.20	246	32.5
1952	1,964	20.6	0.89	1,700	21.1

SOURCES:
Cols. 1, 2. 1922–39: *Financial Intermediaries*, p. 371.
　　　　　 1945, 1952: *Studies in the National Balance Sheet*, Vol. II, p. 178.
Col. 4.　 1922–45: *A Study of Saving*, Vol. I, p. 545.
　　　　　 1946–52: *Flow of Funds Accounts 1945–1967*, p. 71.
Col. 5.　 1945, 1952: *Studies in the National Balance Sheet*, Vol. II, pp. 178, 179.
[a] Period ending with date indicated (first period covers 1920 to 1922).

because of the special character of the holdings (e.g., the holding of stock in Federal Home Loan banks by member savings and loan associations), or because of the special and temporary character of the stock held (e.g., the holdings of certain government lending organizations during the 1930's), or because of a combination of these factors resulting in a very small volume of corporate stock held, notwithstanding the fact that the size of either the institution or of the share of corporate stock in its assets (e.g., fraternal order life insurance and health insurance organizations) is not negligible. The available figures on the stockholdings of these miscellaneous financial institutions are shown in Table 2-15 which also indicates the share of corporate stockholdings in the institutions' total assets.[17]

h. Personal Trust Departments of Commercial Banks

The personal trust departments of commercial banks and trust companies have always administered larger stockholdings than all other

[17] Information on holdings between 1945 and 1958 for some of these minor institutions is provided in Goldsmith, Lipsey, and Mendelson, *Studies in the National Balance Sheet*, Vol. II: state and local government pension funds, pp. 160–61; fraternal order life and health insurance organizations, pp. 188–91; savings bank life insurance, pp. 192–93.

TABLE 2-15

Stockholdings of Miscellaneous Financial Institutions, 1939–52ᵃ

	Agencies of Foreign Banks (1)	Security Brokers and Dealers (2)	Savings Bank Life Insurance (3)	Group Health Insurance (4)	Fraternal Orders Life Insurance (5)	State and Local Pension Funds (6)	Savings and Loan Associationsᵇ (7)	Government Lending Institutions (8)	Total (9)	Percent of Total Outstanding (10)
					All Stocks ($million)					
1939			1		11		41	816		
1945	17	294	1	2	44	40	72	325	795	0.54
1952	34	378	1	7	84	120	309	44	977	0.45
					Percent of Assets					
1939			3.13		0.92		0.76	8.36		
1945	2.00	5.93	1.64	2.22	2.61	1.32	0.82	1.00	1.53	
1952	3.00	9.54	0.76	1.78	3.73	1.61	1.37	0.15	1.44	

SOURCES:
1939: *Financial Intermediaries*, p. 368 ff.
1945, 1952: *Studies in the National Balance Sheet*, Vol. II, p. 160 ff.

ᵃ Holdings before 1939 were negligible.
ᵇ Stock of Federal Home Loan banks.

financial institutions taken together. Thus, at the turn of the century, the stockholdings administered by personal trust departments seem to have been nearly twice as large as those of all other financial institutions, and this ratio was apparently maintained without very marked changes until World War II.[18] It was only in the late 1950's that the aggregate stockholdings of all other financial institutions began to approach the size of the stocks in the personal trust funds administered by commercial banks, and only in the mid-1960's did the former decisively pass the latter. In making this comparison it must, of course, be kept in mind that while the other financial institutions are in full control of their stock portfolios, this is not the case for the stocks administered by the personal trust departments of commercial banks, since the trust instrument often limits the power of management, although these limitations seem to have been substantially relaxed in recent decades. Even then the personal trust departments of commercial banks are, of course, bound by the principles which govern the activities of trustees and hence have not had, at least until the more liberal interpretation of these obligations in recent years, as much freedom in the portfolio management of their trusts and estates as some other financial institutions, particularly property insurance companies, investment companies, and uninsured pension funds.

Corporate stock apparently always has constituted an important proportion of the total value of personal trust funds administered by commercial banks, partly because corporate stocks bulked heavily in many of the large estates that were entrusted to personal trust departments. Rough estimates indicate that the proportion of corporate stock in the total value of personal trust funds administered by commercial banks rose from about one-fifth at the turn of the century to two-fifths by the 1950's (Table 2-16). Very little is known about the structure of these portfolios, but it may be assumed that apart from a relatively small number of very large estates the administering commercial banks have tended to establish diversified portfolios of usually high-grade common stock. Preferred stocks accounted for only approximately 4 percent of the stock portfolio in 1958[19] but the share was undoubtedly considerably higher before World War II.

[18] Because of the scarcity and limited reliability of data and the absence of comprehensive statistics on the assets of personal trust departments before the late 1950's, all findings for earlier periods must be tentative.

[19] This is the first year for which a comprehensive survey of personal trust funds was undertaken by the American Bankers Association (cf. J. H. Wolfe, "Report of National Survey of Personal Trust Accounts," mimeographed). The figure for 1952 should have been on the order of 6 to 8 percent.

Since the custom of entrusting the administration of estates and trusts to specialized departments of commercial banks and trust companies originated only late in the nineteenth century, there is little doubt that the proportion of total common stock outstanding in the United States administered by these departments increased substantially over the first thirty years of this century. The rise may have been from a level of about 5 percent of all stock outstanding at the turn of the century to one of about one-tenth in the 1930's and 1940's. In recent years the growth of the stock portfolio administered by the trust departments of commercial banks does not seem to have kept full pace with the increase in the value of all corporate stock outstanding, since the proportion in the mid-1960's, when the figures were much more reliable, was somewhat below one-tenth.

More is known about the small part of the personal trust funds that is administered by commercial banks as common trust funds, i.e., the

TABLE 2-16

Stockholdings Administered by Personal Trust Departments of Commercial Banks and Trust Companies, 1900–52

	Value ($million) (1)	Share in Assets of Personal Trust Departments (percent) (2)	Share in Stock Outstanding (percent) (3)	Share of Preferred Stock in (1) (percent) (4)
1900	600	20.0	4.3	
1912	2,450	35.0	6.5	
1922	6,300	35.0	8.3	18.3
1929	12,600	42.0	6.8	14.7
1939	12,950	37.0	12.9	
1945	18,000	40.0	12.3	
1952	25,000	41.7	11.4	

SOURCES:
Cols. 1, 2. 1900–52:   *Financial Intermediaries*, p. 384.
Col. 4.   1922, 1929: N. G. Riddle, *The Investment Policy of Trust Institutions*, Chicago, Business Publications Co., 1934, p. 14; figures based on a small sample of accounts.

commingled funds of many trustors which are too small individually to justify separate management. These funds are more similar to other financial institutions, since they constitute separate legal entities—they most nearly resemble open-end investment companies—though participations in them are not marketable.

Common trust funds, started in the 1920's, have always been small compared to the personal trust funds administered by commercial banks on an individual basis. Even in 1952 after substantial growth in the postwar period, their assets equaled less than 2 percent of individually bank-administered personal trust funds. Common trust funds, in the portfolio selection of which the administering banks enjoy considerable freedom, have, since their introduction, kept about one-half of their assets

TABLE 2-17

Stockholdings of Common Trust Funds, 1929–52

	Value of Holdings ($million) (1)	Share in Total Assets (percent) (2)	Share in Stock Outstanding (3)
	All Stock		
1929	12	57.1	.006
1939	25	50.0	.025
1945	70	46.7	.047
1952	579	52.6	.264
	Preferred Stock		
1929	6	28.6	.031
1939	9	18.0	.066
1945	28	18.7	.208
1952	138	12.6	.859
	Common Stock		
1929	6	28.6	.004
1939	16	32.0	.019
1945	42	28.0	.032
1952	441	40.1	.217

SOURCE: *Financial Intermediaries*, p. 386.

in a diversified portfolio of corporate stock, the share rising to over three-fifths in the late 1950's, a ratio then corresponding to the average for individually bank-administered personal trusts (Table 2-17). As with other financial institutions, the proportion of preferred stocks in the total stock portfolio has declined sharply, from over one-half in 1929 to less than one-fourth in 1952.

i. Investment Advisers

The stockholdings subject to the investment management or advice of investment advisers—firms that may engage in this activity alone or combine it with investment banking, security brokerage, or publication of financial services—are similar to the stockholdings administered by personal trust departments of commercial banks in that for practical purposes the holdings are managed not by the beneficiary individual, nonprofit, or corporate owners but by the adviser. They are different in that legally no trustee relationship exists, the adviser may have a profit-sharing contract, and the securities generally are not kept physically with the manager but by a bank or other financial institution.

There is practically nothing known in quantitative terms about stocks under investment advisory management, and they are therefore excluded from all statistics used here. It may be estimated that in the mid-1930's total funds administered by investment advisory organizations were of the order of $5 billion, of which stocks probably constituted the majority. However, fully one-half of the total was funds of other financial institutions, which must be eliminated to avoid duplications. Individuals' funds administered by investment counsel firms seem to have been of the order of $1.5 billion.[20] At that time, therefore, the stockholdings managed by investment advisers were very small compared with stocks in personal trust departments or held directly by financial institutions. The rapid growth of stock under the management of investment advisers undoubtedly occurred only after World War II, in particular during the 1960's.

5. THE STOCKHOLDINGS OF ALL FINANCIAL INSTITUTIONS

Taking here as given the total assets of financial institutions, the determinants of which were discussed in sections 2 and 3, we need to survey the trend of three ratios: (1) the ratio of financial institutions'

---

[20] These estimates are based on data from 51 investment counsel organizations replying to a questionnaire and reporting funds administered of nearly $4 billion, assuming that they accounted for the bulk of the 394 firms then operating. (See Securities and Exchange Commission, *Investment Counsel . . . Services*, 1939, pp. 8–9.)

stockholdings to their total assets; (2) the ratio of stockholdings of all
financial institutions to the value of all corporate stock outstanding; and
(3) the ratio of net purchases of stock by all financial institutions to total
new issues of corporate stock during the same period. The first ratio
reflects portfolio policies of financial institutions within the constraints
provided by regulation and differential price movements among financial
assets, particularly the difference between movements of stock prices and
of claims of different types. The second and third ratios provide an indication of the role of financial institutions in the market for corporate
stocks.

a. The Share of Corporate Stock in the Assets of Financial Institutions

Table 2-18 shows that the share of stock in the assets of the various types
of financial institutions has fluctuated considerably over the past century
and without close synchronization among the different groups. This
diversity reflects developments specific to individual groups of financial
institutions. An example of this diversity is provided by the decline in the
share of stockholdings in the assets of life insurance companies early in
this century, and in the reduction of the proportion of stocks in the assets
of commercial banks and personal trust funds during World War I. One
important trend, however, is common to virtually all groups of financial
institutions, namely, the considerable rise in the share of corporate stock
in total assets during the 1920's and after World War II. Both movements
reflect net purchases of common stock as well as increases in their price.
Thus, the share of corporate stock in total assets rose between 1945 and
1952 from 2.3 to 3.3 percent for life insurance companies; from 11 to 21
percent for private pension funds; from 40 to 42 percent for common trust
funds; and from 0.8 to 1.3 percent for mutual savings banks (see Table
2-19). These are the harbingers of much sharper increases in the following
fifteen years, which will be discussed in Chapter 3. In 1952, however, the
share of corporate stock in total assets was still below the level which
prevailed at the turn of the century for commercial banks, mutual savings
banks, and life insurance companies and hardly above that level for
property insurance companies. In these important branches of financial
institutions, the previous peak ratio was not passed until the mid- or the
late 1950's; in the case of commercial banks this had not happened even
by the late 1960's.

If the balance sheets of all financial institutions are combined (but
personal trust departments are excluded), the share of corporate stock in
total assets declined from $2\frac{1}{4}$ percent in 1900 to $1\frac{1}{2}$ percent in 1922, but

by 1952 had reached 5 percent, equal to the previous peak of $4\frac{1}{2}$ percent in 1929. It is only during the last fifteen years that levels never before observed have been reached.

The distribution of the ratios of stock to total assets among the different types of financial institutions is bimodal. At one extreme are a few types of financial institutions for which stocks, and particularly common stocks, constitute the most important single type of asset and account for the majority, and often for two-thirds or more, of total assets. This category has always included investment companies and common trust funds and now also embraces private pension funds. In the case of property insurance companies, stocks accounted for less than half of total assets—the average for the period 1880 to 1930 was about one-third—but were the largest single asset. The situation of personal trust funds has been similar.

At the other extreme some financial institutions, and just the largest ones in terms of total assets, show only a very small proportion of total assets in corporate stock—say, less than 5 percent—so that the performance of the stock portfolio cannot decisively affect the financial position of the institutions. Commercial banks, mutual savings banks, savings and loan associations, credit unions, finance companies, life insurance companies, and (until the 1950's) state and local pension funds belong in this category. In some of them the share of corporate stock in total assets has fluctuated considerably over the last fifty years and has tended to increase during the postwar period. There is no group of financial institutions in which stocks ordinarily constitute a secondary but important asset.

b. The Share of Stockholdings of Financial Institutions in Total Corporate Stock Outstanding

The movements in this ratio in Table 2-20 are similar to those in the ratio of corporate stock to the total assets of financial institutions. Excluding personal trust funds, the share declined from about $3\frac{1}{2}$ percent in 1860 to $2\frac{1}{2}$ percent at the turn of century, mostly because of the relatively slow increase in the holdings of commercial banks and property insurance companies. The ratio fell further, to slightly more than $1\frac{1}{2}$ percent, in 1912, partly reflecting the reduction of stockholdings by life insurance companies and the only modest increases by the other groups in the face of a sharp rise in the volume of corporate stock issues. It was only the sharp increase in the net purchases of corporate stock during the 1920's, induced by the stock market boom then prevailing, which brought the share of financial institutions in total corporate stock outstanding back to 3 percent in 1929. Continuous purchases during the 1930's and World War II, in

TABLE 2-18

Financial Institutions' Holdings of Corporate Stock, 1860–1952

(*$million*)

	Commercial Banks[a] (1)	Mutual Savings Banks (2)	Life Insurance Companies (3)	Property Insurance Companies (4)	Private Pension Funds (5)	Investment Companies (6)	Common Trust Departments (7)	Total (1)–(7) (8)	Personal Trust Funds (9)	Total (10)
All Stock										
1860	10			18				28		
1880	30	40		25				95		
1900	103	43[b]	62	122				330	600	1,930
1912	284	41	84	231				640	2,450	3,090
1922	401	48	75	370	18	69		981	6,300	7,281
1929	1,009	77	352	1,511	100	2,189	12	5,250	12,600	17,850
1939	473	136	568	1,457	210	1,204	25	4,073	12,950	17,023
1945	220	166	1,000	2,415	289	1,977[c]	70	6,137	18,000	24,137
1952	150	336	2,450	4,320	1,964	6,580	579	16,379	25,000	41,379
Common Stock										
1860	10									
1880	30	40								
1900	103	43	54	93				293		
1912	284	41	72	186				583		

Year								
1922	401	48	59	275	11ᵈ	57		851
1929	1,009	77	97	1,235	60ᵈ	1,998	6	4,482
1939	473	136	133	1,127	126ᵈ	1,132	16	3,143
1945	220	166	180	1,932	195	1,776ᶜ	42	4,511
1952	150	336	960	3,520	1,550	6,290	441	13,247

Preferred Stock

Year								
1860								
1880								
1900			8	29				37
1912			12	45				57
1922			16	95	7ᵈ	12		130
1929			255	276	40ᵈ	191	6	768
1935			435	330	84ᵈ	72	9	930
1945			820	483	94	201ᶜ	28	1,626
1952			1,490	800	414	290	138	3,132

SOURCES: Tables 2-7 to 2-17.

ª Excluding stock of Federal Reserve banks.

ᵇ An alternative figure (83) has been estimated based on figures for six main states (New York, Massachusetts, Connecticut, Maine, New Hampshire, and Rhode Island) taken from reports of their bank supervisory authorities.

ᶜ Alternative figures (250 for preferred stock and 2,650 for common stock) can be found in *Studies in the National Balance Sheet*, pp. 168–69.

ᵈ Breakdown of preferred and common stock: 40 percent of total, preferred; 60 percent of total, common.

TABLE 2-19

Share of Stock in Assets of Financial Institutions, 1860–1952

(percent)

	Commercial Banks[a] (1)	Mutual Savings Banks (2)	Life Insurance Companies (3)	Property Insurance Companies (4)	Private Pension Funds (5)	Investment Companies (6)	Common Trust Departments (7)	Total (1)–(7) (8)	Personal Trust Funds (9)	Total (10)
					All Stock					
1860	1.20		2.30	22.80						
1880	1.10	4.52	1.50	11.50						
1900	1.03	1.77	3.56	25.68				2.25	20.00	5.27
1912	1.30	1.02	1.91	23.50				2.05	35.00	8.08
1922	0.84	0.73	0.87	16.02	20.00	57.12		1.50	35.00	8.88
1929	1.52	0.78	2.01	32.65	20.00	74.56	57.14	5.16	42.00	13.69
1939	0.71	1.15	1.94	30.45	20.00	85.51	50.00	3.55	37.00	11.46
1945	0.14	0.98	2.23	31.83	10.77	82.44	46.67	2.61	40.00	8.68
1952	0.08	1.33	3.30	26.87	20.62	84.79	52.64	5.06	41.67	10.83

Common Stock

Year							
1900	1.03	1.77	3.10	19.58				1.66
1912	1.30	1.02	1.63	18.92				1.53
1922	0.84	0.73	0.68	11.91	12.22	57.00		1.02
1929	1.52	0.78	0.55	26.69	12.00	68.05	28.57	3.40
1939	0.71	1.15	0.45	23.55	12.00	80.40	32.00	2.10
1945	0.14	0.98	0.40	25.46	7.27	74.06	28.00	1.61
1952	0.08	1.33	1.29	21.89	16.28	81.06	40.09	3.45

Preferred Stock

Year							
1900	0.46	6.11	7.78	0.12			0.21
1912	0.27	4.58					0.15
1922	0.18	4.11	8.00	6.51	28.57		0.16
1929	1.46	5.96	8.00	5.11	18.00		0.58
1939	1.49	6.90	3.51	5.11	18.00		0.62
1945	1.83	6.37	8.38	18.67			0.53
1952	2.01	4.98	4.35	3.74	12.55		0.82

SOURCES: Tables 2-7 to 2-17.
a Excluding stock of Federal Reserve banks.

TABLE 2-20

The Share of Financial Institutions in Total Stock Outstanding, 1860–1952

(*percent*)

	Commercial Banks[a] (1)	Mutual Savings Banks (2)	Life Insurance Companies (3)	Property Insurance Companies[b] (4)	Private Pension Funds (5)	Investment Companies (6)	Common Trust Departments (7)	Total (1)–(7) (8)	Personal Trust Funds (9)	Total (10)
					All Stock					
1860	1.30		0.10	1.50				3.00		
1880	0.60	.98	0.20	0.50				2.28		
1900	0.74	.31	0.45	0.88				2.38	4.32	6.70
1912	0.75	.11	0.22	0.61				1.69	6.45	8.14
1922	0.53	.06	0.10	0.49	0.02	0.09		1.29	8.28	9.57
1929	0.54	.04	0.19	0.81	0.05	1.17	.01	2.81	6.75	9.56
1939	0.47	.14	0.57	1.46	0.21	1.20	.03	4.08	12.93	17.01
1945	0.15	.11	0.68	1.65	0.20	1.35	.05	4.19	12.27	16.46
1952	0.07	.15	1.12	1.97	0.90	3.00	.26	7.47	11.39	18.86

Common Stock

Year								
1900	0.94	.39	0.49	0.85	0.02			2.67
1912	0.94	.14	0.24	0.61	0.04			1.93
1922	0.64	.08	0.09	0.44	0.15	0.09		1.36
1929	0.60	.05	0.06	0.74	0.15	1.19	.01	2.69
1939	0.55	.16	0.15	1.30	0.76	1.31	.02	3.64
1945	0.17	.12	0.14	1.45		1.33	.03	3.39
1952	0.07	.17	0.47	1.73		3.09	.22	6.51

Preferred Stock

Year								
1900	—		0.28	1.00	0.05			1.28
1912	—		0.16	0.58	0.21			0.74
1922	—		0.12	0.73	0.61	0.09		0.99
1929	—		1.33	1.44	0.70	0.99	.03	4.00
1939	—		3.18	2.41	2.58	0.53	.07	6.80
1945	—		6.10	3.60		1.49	.21	12.10
1952	—		9.28	4.98		1.81	.86	19.51

SOURCES: Tables 2-7 to 2-17.
a Excluding stock of Federal Reserve banks.
b Until 1880, only fire and marine companies.

the face of low stock prices and a very modest volume of new stock issues, raised the share to nearly 5 percent in 1945.

The real take-off in the ratio, however, started in the late 1940's, lifting it to more than 7 percent in 1952, a movement which was to double the ratio in the following fifteen years. This sharp increase reflected first the rapid growth in the total assets of financial institutions that concentrate their portfolios in corporate stocks, chiefly private pension funds and investment companies, and secondly the increase in the share of stock in the assets of other large financial institutions, particularly life and property insurance companies.[21]

If the rough estimates now available can be trusted, the ratio of stocks held in personal trust funds to total stock outstanding followed a movement which was in a direction opposite to that for the other institutions most of the time, rising from the late nineteenth century to 1922 but falling after World War II. As a result, the share of all financial institutions, including personal trust funds, in total corporate stock outstanding fluctuates less than either of the two components. The share appears to have increased from 3 percent in 1860 to about 10 percent in 1922; to have remained at that level during the 1920's; and to have increased sharply again to 17 percent at the end of the 1930's; rising also at the end of World War II. Even with the necessary reservations about the estimates for the stockholdings of personal trust funds, it is evident that the sharpest increase in the share of all financial institutions' holdings in total stock outstanding occurred from about 1880 to 1920 and during the Great Depression and World War II.

However, the character of the stockholdings of financial institutions and their ratio to total stock outstanding, changed during this century. Up to World War I the stockholdings of financial institutions were concentrated in bank and railroad stocks and represented a substantial

---

[21] All estimates of the share of financial institutions in the market value of corporate stock outstanding should be regarded as minima since some of the original figures, particularly those for some of the institutions with relatively small stockholdings, reflect book rather than market values. The resulting understatement, however, is not sufficient to affect substantially either the level, or the movement, of the estimates of the share for the aggregate of all financial institutions.

It should also be noted that the shares would be higher—during most of the period by about one-fourth—if the stockholdings of financial institutions were compared to total corporate stock outstanding excluding intercorporate holdings, a procedure that could be justified by the fact that most intercorporate holdings are not available for acquisition by financial institutions. The ratios would, of course, be further raised—and substantially so—if, following the same argument, the stock of closely held corporations were excluded from the denominator.

proportion of the total amount of such stock outstanding in the United States. In the postwar period the stockholdings of financial institutions have been more diversified. Another difference, and one of very significant economic importance, is that up to the Great Depression these stockholdings were largely attributable to upper wealth and income groups and were primarily holdings through personal trust funds. In contrast, in the postwar period the stockholdings of financial institutions may be regarded to an increasing extent—but probably to not more than one-half if stock administered by personal trust departments and investment advisers are included—as indirect holdings of individuals in the lower, and particularly the middle, income and wealth groups through insurance companies, pension funds, and investment companies.

Preferred stocks have always represented only a relatively small part of the total stockholdings of financial institutions and their movements in relation to the total volume of preferred stock outstanding in the United States have been generally similar to those observed for all stocks. Thus, the share declined from 1900 to 1922, but sharply increased during the remainder of the 1920's and during the 1930's. Differing from the case of common stock, however, the share of financial institutions' holdings in total preferred stock outstanding continued to increase during World War II. The share, now again paralleling the case of common stock, although in a less spectacular fashion, further increased in the 1950's and 1960's. As a result, the share of financial institutions in total preferred stock outstanding increased very sharply from only 1 percent in 1922 to 19 percent in 1952. The level of the share of financial institutions in the total value of stock outstanding has been considerably higher for preferred than for common stock since 1912. One of the reasons is the relatively moderate volume of new issues of preferred stock and the absence of a sharp price rise such as occurred in common stock, both factors which have resulted in a much slower increase in the value of preferred stock outstanding than in the total assets of financial institutions.

These conclusions, based on data excluding personal trust funds, have to be modified if an attempt is made to take account of the preferred stockholdings of these funds. If we assume, on the basis of scattered indications, that at the turn of the century about one-third of all stocks held in personal trust funds were preferred issues and that the ratio declined to about one-fifth in 1929 and dropped sharply to about one-twentieth in 1958—the last figure being fairly well documented—the share of preferred stock held by all financial institutions including personal trust funds would have risen from a negligible fraction in 1860 to about

TABLE 2-21

Institutional Holdings of All Stocks and of Stocks Listed on the New York
Stock Exchange, As of End of 1949

	Amounts		Share in Stock Outstanding	
	All Stocks	Stocks Listed on NYSE	All Stocks	Stock Listed on NYSE
	($billion)		(percent)	
	(1)	(2)	(3)	(4)
Commercial banks	0.15ᵃ		0.10ᵃ	
Mutual savings banks	0.16	0.2	0.11	0.3
Life insurance companies	1.72	1.1	1.17	1.4
Other insurance companies	2.15	1.7	1.46	2.2
Pension funds				
Corporate	0.75	0.5	0.51	0.7
Other private		0.0		0.0
State and local government		0.0		0.0
Investment companies				
Open-end	(1.60)	1.4 ⎱	2.44	1.8 ⎰
Closed-end	(2.00)	1.6 ⎰		2.1 ⎱
Common trust funds	0.25	0.0	0.16	0.0
Personal trust departments	20.00		13.60	
Total, including personal trust departments	28.78		19.55	
Total, excluding personal trust departments	8.78	6.5	5.95	8.5

NOTE: Figures in parentheses are rough estimates.
SOURCES:
Col. 1. *Financial Intermediaries*, Appendix A.
Col. 2. *New York Stock Exchange Research Report*, January 1970.
Col. 3. Col. 1 divided by $137.3 billion. From *Studies in the National Balance Sheet*, p. 51.

ᵃ Excluding stock in Federal Reserve banks.

8 percent in 1900, doubling to about 16 percent in 1929, and again doubling to about 32 percent in 1958. These figures, rough as they are, indicate
a sharp increase in the share of preferred stock held by financial institutions, an increase occurring almost continuously throughout the last century and proceeding at a level considerably above the share of their holdings of common stock. For example, the share of financial institutions in

the total volume of stock outstanding in 1958 was close to one-third for preferred stock, but in the neighborhood of only one-fifth for common stock. In 1929 the share for preferred stock, about one-sixth, was approximately twice as high as that for common stock; the difference in 1900 although smaller was still substantial.

Institutional holdings of corporate stock are concentrated in securities listed on the New York Stock Exchange. In 1949, for example, approximately seven-eighths of stockholdings of the main financial institutions, excluding personal trust departments of commercial banks, consisted of issues listed on the NYSE, while the share of stocks so listed in all corporate stock issues outstanding in the United States was only slightly in excess of one-half (Table 2-21). As a result, about $8\frac{1}{2}$ percent of the stock listed on the NYSE was held by financial institutions, compared to $6\frac{1}{2}$ percent for all corporate stock outstanding. If seven-eighths of the stock portfolios administered by personal trust departments consisted of issues listed on the NYSE, then at the end of 1949 all financial institutions would have held nearly one-third of all stock listed on the NYSE against a share in total stock outstanding of slightly less than one-fifth.

No similar figures are available for earlier dates, but it may be assumed that the concentration of the stockholdings of financial institutions in issues listed on the NYSE since World War I was not much different from the 1949 relationship. In the nineteenth century and the beginning of this century the ratio probably was lower because of the large share of bank stocks in institutional stock portfolios. (At that time, however, a considerable number of bank stocks were still listed on the NYSE.) Since the share of stocks listed on the NYSE increased from less than two-fifths in 1900 to about one-half in 1952 (if intercorporate holdings are excluded the rise was from about 45 to over 60 percent)[22] the difference between the share of institutional stockholdings in all corporate stock outstanding and in listed stock was more pronounced in those earlier periods than it is now.

c. The Share of Net Purchases of Stock by Financial Institutions in Total Net New Issues of Corporate Stock

The most spectacular movement in the share of financial institutions is observed if this share is measured by the ratio of institutions' net (cash) purchases to total net issues of corporate stock, i.e., the net addition to the supply of corporate stock resulting from cash offerings.

[22] See Goldsmith, *Financial Intermediaries*, Appendix F.

From the turn of the century, when the first estimates can be made, through World War II the share of net purchases by financial institutions in total new issues of corporate stock was never above 15 percent for any of the six periods distinguished. There were, however, considerable differences among these periods. The share of net purchases by financial institutions was relatively high, on the order of one-seventh of the total, for the periods 1897–1900, 1923–29, and 1940–45. The explanation is obvious for the 1920's: the appearance of investment companies as a new, important institutional buyer of corporate stocks and the sharp increase in the level of purchases, in this case mostly of preferred stock, by life insurance companies. During World War II total new issues of stock were so small that even very modest absolute net purchases by financial institutions, actually limited to preferred stock, produced a share of financial institutions in total net issues that was fairly high in historical perspective.

For the entire period from 1897 to 1945 net purchases by financial institutions were equal to a little less than one-tenth of total new issues of corporate stock.

A dramatic change occurred immediately after World War II. Already, in the 1946–52 period, net purchases of stock by financial institutions equaled nearly two-fifths of total net new issues, only a harbinger of the jump to 100 percent during the following fifteen years. This, of course, is the outstanding structural change in the role of financial institutions in the market for corporate stock in the postwar period, and as such it will be discussed in more detail in the following chapters.

The difference between the period before and after World War II would be somewhat less dramatic if it were possible to include the net purchases of corporate stock, or more correctly the addition to the holdings of corporate stock excluding valuation changes, by personal trust funds, although often—and possibly in most instances—this took place not through cash purchases but by transfer of previously personally held blocks of stock on the death of the owner or by the establishment of a trust fund while he was still alive. These purchases (or transfers) would considerably raise the ratio of institutional acquisitions to total net issues of corporate stock during the first four decades of this century, but would increase them relatively little during the 1950's and 1960's. As a result the increase in the ratio of acquisitions of corporate stock by financial institutions on this broader basis would be less pronounced than if the ratio is limited, as in Table 2-22, to the net cash purchases by financial institutions.

TABLE 2-22

Net Purchases of Corporate Stock by Financial Institutions, 1897–1952

(*$million, except column 9*)

	Total Net Issues (1)	Com-mer-cial Banks (2)	Mutual Savings Banks (3)	Life Insurance Com-panies (4)	Property Insurance Com-panies (5)	Pension Funds (6)	Invest-ment Com-panies (7)	All Financial Institutions	
								Value (8)	Percent of Net Issues (9)
All Stock									
1897–1900	981	55	−5	15	54	—	—	119	12.1
1901–1912	7,198	171	−2	22	109	—	—	300	4.2
1913–1922	10,727	115	7	−9	139	13	13	278	2.6
1923–1929	23,501	623	29	240	625	58	1,994	3,569	15.2
1930–1939	6,564	−535	59	228	270	51	396	469	7.1
1940–1945	4,349	−326	30	165	450	246	−28	537	12.3
1946–1952	12,700		100	1,300	600	1,700	1,360	5,060	39.8
Preferred Stock									
1897–1900	469	—	—	2	13	—	—	15	3.2
1901–1912	1,014	—	—	4	16	—	—	20	2.0
1913–1922	2,965	—	—	4	50	5	12	71	2.4

(*continued*)

TABLE 2-22 (*concluded*)

	Total Net Issues (1)	Commercial Banks (2)	Mutual Savings Banks (3)	Life Insurance Companies (4)	Property Insurance Companies (5)	Pension Funds (6)	Investment Companies (7)	All Financial Institutions Value (8)	All Financial Institutions Percent of Net Issues (9)
				Preferred Stock (continued)					
1923–1929	7,911	—	—	206	180	24	166	576	7.3
1930–1939	1,806	—	—	183	75	23	−103	178	10.0
1940–1945	2,013	—	—	131	150	120	158	559	27.8
				Common Stock					
1897–1900	512	55	−5	13	41	—	—	104	20.3
1901–1912	6,184	171	−2	18	93	—	—	280	4.5
1913–1922	7,762	115	7	−13	89	8	1	207	2.7
1923–1929	15,590	623	29	34	445	34	1,828	2,993	19.2
1930–1939	4,758	−535	59	45	195	28	499	291	6.1
1940–1945	2,336	−326	30	34	300	126	−186	−22	−0.9

Net Purchases by: (columns 2–9)

SOURCES:
1897–1949: *A Study of Saving*, Vol. I, pp. 493–98, 545–46.
1946–52: *Flow of Funds Accounts 1945–1967*, p. 60 ff.
Studies in the National Balance Sheet, Vol. II, pp. 422–23.

For the entire period from 1897 through 1949 (separate figures for the two types of stock are not available for later years) the share of net purchases by financial institutions was about the same for preferred as for common stock—about one-eighth. There are, however, substantial differences in some periods (particularly 1897–1900, 1923–29, and 1940–45) which can be followed in Table 2-22.

6. THE ECONOMIC SIGNIFICANCE OF INSTITUTIONAL STOCKHOLDINGS

The economic significance of the holdings of common stock by financial institutions has two main aspects. The first is the supply of equity funds to nonfinancial corporations embodied in the purchase of their stock by financial institutions. Supply may be direct, as when the financial institution acquires newly issued stock of nonfinancial corporations. It may be indirect and partial, as when financial institutions buy outstanding corporate stock and thus either set free part of the proceeds for reinvestment in new corporate stock, the proportion depending on the reactions of the sellers, or induce a rearrangement of the portfolios of the sellers in the direction of a reduction of corporate stock and an increase in other investments. The second economically relevant aspect of the holdings of nonfinancial corporate stock by financial institutions is their function as an outlet for the funds of these institutions, and the effects of this use of funds on the institutions' current earnings and capital gains and, at one degree removed, the effects on the rates which the institutions are able to pay to attract savings, and on their policy with regard to other uses of their funds.

a. As Suppliers of Equity Capital

Although direct evidence is almost entirely lacking, nevertheless the straightforward influence of financial institutions through acquisition of stock of nonfinancial corporations appears to have been small with few exceptions. One of these is the purchase of bank stocks by life insurance companies, property insurance companies, and mutual savings banks during the second half of the nineteenth century. That such an influence is possible, though it cannot have been decisive, is indicated by the fact that in 1880 fully 5 percent, and in 1900 about 8 percent, of all bank stock outstanding was held by financial institutions, excluding the personal trust departments of banks. Another, and more important, exception is the case of preferred stock, where beginning with the 1920's financial institutions probably absorbed a considerable part of new issues, the net purchases of institutions being equal to a considerable fraction of them. A less important exception is the purchase of industrial stocks by investment companies during the 1920's, which may have included a significant amount of recent issues.

To evaluate the role of financial institutions in the market for outstanding corporate stock we may use the proportion of shares outstanding and shares traded, as both figures are probably little affected by transactions in new issues. It is then rather unlikely that until the 1950's financial institutions can have had a major role, since their holdings never exceeded 5 percent of total corporate stock outstanding until the end of World War II, this mostly in the hands of life insurance companies, property insurance companies, and investment companies, all of which invested in a diversified portfolio of large, heavily capitalized companies. Because of concentration on the stocks of certain "blue chips," the proportion of financial institutions' holdings may, however, have been sufficiently large in a few cases to constitute an important factor in the market.

Detailed information of this type is limited to investment companies. In 1935 investment companies (excluding investment holding companies) owed slightly more than 5 percent of the common stocks of the 86 largest corporations traded on securities exchanges.[23] Their share, however, was as high as 15 percent for Missouri-Kansas-Texas Railroad, 13 percent for B–M–T and United Light and Power B, 11 percent for American Gas and Electric, and 9 percent for Pacific Gas and Electric and Pacific Lighting. But in most of the largest companies (such as American Telephone & Telegraph, Dupont, General Motors, Pennsylvania and New York Central Railroads, Standard Oil of New Jersey, and U.S. Steel), the proportion was considerably lower, averaging about 2 percent.

In 1952 open-end investment companies held $2\frac{1}{2}$ percent of all stocks listed on the New York Stock Exchange, but only $1\frac{1}{2}$ percent of a sample of 30 very large companies, although they accounted for over 4 percent of trading in these stocks on the exchange.[24] If the other institutional investors with diversified portfolios—closed-end investment companies, property insurance companies, private pension funds, and common trust funds—distributed their stock portfolio in the same way as open-end

---

[23] SEC, *Investment Trusts and Investment Companies*, Part II, p. 725 ff. At that time investment companies' holdings of common stock were equal to about 40 percent of all institutional holdings excluding, and 7 percent including, common stocks in portfolios administered by personal trust departments, excluding in both cases stock in Federal Reserve banks held by commercial banks.

[24] SEC, *A Study of Mutual Funds*, pp. 168–69.

investment companies, the aggregate holdings of all these financial institutions would have been equal to about 3 percent of the amount outstanding. The proportion, however, was considerably higher in a few open-end company favorites, e.g., 10 percent in Goodrich, 9 percent in Central and South West, and 6 percent in Goodyear. On the other hand, the proportion was below 1 percent for Standard Oil of New Jersey, General Motors, Dupont, and American Telephone & Telegraph.[25]

Another piece of evidence on the influence of transactions by financial institutions is the share of a group of large institutions (together accounting for about one-sixth of all institutional common stockholdings but nearly one-half of institutions other than personal trust departments) in the trading in 25 leading stocks on the New York Stock Exchange in 1953–55.[26] For the 25 stocks together the reporting institutions (other than the few reporting personal trust funds) accounted for a little over 5 percent of exchange trading in the 34 months ending October 1955. Their share, however, was as high as 23 percent for Sears Roebuck; 22 percent for Southern California Edison; 15 percent for General Public Utilities; 13 percent for Pacific Gas; 12 percent for American Can, CIT Financial, and United Gas; 11 percent for Goodyear; and 10 percent for Atchison. While it is obvious that for these and similar stocks the activities of financial institutions may have substantially influenced prices, it does not follow that they had a more marginal bearing on the equity financing of these companies, as most of them offered little if any new stock.

The situation is different for the stocks administered by the personal trust departments of commercial banks. From the fourth quarter of the nineteenth century to World War II, stocks held in these funds rose continually and substantially, finally accounting for over one-eighth of all corporate stock outstanding. These holdings, however, gave financial institutions much less direct and indirect influence on portfolio companies, on the market for corporate stock, and on the economy in general than direct holdings of similar size would have, because most of the blocks of stocks held in personal trust funds were the result of transfers at or before the death of the owner rather than of purchases in the open market, and because the turnover of the stock portfolios in personal trust funds after original transfer seems to have been moderate. Nevertheless, it is probably true that until World War II the influence of financial institutions on the market for corporate stock through ownership or management of such stocks

[25] *Ibid.*, p. 171.
[26] U.S. Joint Economic Committee, *Institutional Investors and the Stock Market*, 84th Cong., 2nd sess., 1956, p. 86 ff.

(and thus abstracting from the effect of loans on securities by commercial banks) probably lay more in the administration of large stockholdings by the trust departments of commercial banks than in the stock portfolios directly owned by other financial institutions.

Although the share of financial institutions (excluding personal trust departments) in corporate stock outstanding remained moderate until the postwar years, two significant long-term movements may be discerned within a period of nearly one century. The first is a decline in the share of financial institutions' holdings in total corporate stock outstanding from the late nineteenth century to the early 1920's; the second is the rapid increase in the two following decades. In fact, the increase from not much over 1 percent of total corporate stock outstanding in 1922 to nearly 5 percent in 1945 is relatively much larger, although considerably smaller in absolute terms and in percentage points, than the further increase in the twenty years after World War II.

b. As Outlets for Financial Institutions' Funds

Turning to the effects of the stockholdings of financial institutions as an outlet for their funds, a distinction must be made between two groups of institutions. For the first, corporate stock provides a substantial or even the major part of assets and hence of earnings and net worth (at market prices), indirectly strongly affecting the attraction of the institutions to investors. These institutions therefore are all strongly influenced by, or even dependent on, the performance of the stock portfolio. This is the case primarily for investment companies, the funds administered by personal trust departments of commercial banks, and private pension funds. It is true also, although less decisively, for property insurance companies. In all these cases, except for investment companies, the importance of the stock portfolio has been increasing since the 1930's and particularly since World War II. For the other types of financial institutions, stockholdings have been so small in proportion to total assets, at least until 1952, that the performance of the stock portfolio could exercise only a minor influence on the institutions' earnings, net worth, and attractiveness. This is the case particularly for commercial banks, mutual savings banks, savings and loan associations, credit unions, and finance companies, but it is also true of life insurance companies and state and local government pension funds.

3

The Position of Institutional Investors and of Corporate Stock in the National Balance Sheets and the Flow of Funds Accounts of the United States of America, 1952–68

RAYMOND W. GOLDSMITH

1. SCOPE AND LIMITATIONS OF DATA AND THEIR ANALYSIS

The purpose of this chapter is to provide an overview of the structure and development of the balance sheets and flow of funds accounts of the main financial and nonfinancial sectors of the American economy during the years 1952–68. This overview centers on corporate stock among assets and on financial institutions among sectors, and is intended to furnish a background for the more detailed studies of institutional investors' activities in the stock market during recent years which are being made by the Securities and Exchange Commission's Institutional Investors Study.

Because of the limited amount of time available for this study and because the basic framework of statistical data—the balance sheets and flow of funds statements for 1952–68—could be completed only shortly before the date on which the report was to be submitted to the SEC, it has not been possible to subject the data to substantial analysis. A few attempts in this direction are made in parts of Chapters 4 and 5, but these efforts are based essentially on data available before the material used in this chapter was assembled. The limitation to annual data precluded, of course, any detailed analysis of the effects of business cycles. The emphasis, therefore, was put on trends and structural changes.

Because of the limitations of time and resources noted above, and because of the unavailability of the extensive additional data which were collected by the Institutional Investors Study while this study was in progress, the latter was of necessity based essentially on existing statistical data insofar as financial assets were concerned, although a large part of the estimates of the level and changes in the stock of tangible assets—better known in their total for all sectors as national wealth—was developed specifically for this study.

The estimates of the market value of reproducible tangible assets and of their value in constant (1958) prices follow the perpetual inventory method, which has become accepted in this field in the postwar period, and are linked to existing estimates for 1952.[1] These estimates are explained in Appendix I. For most types of nonreproducible tangible assets (i.e., land) a new set of estimates was developed which is described in Appendix II. These figures are subject to substantial but indeterminate errors of estimation, as are all estimates in this field.

Financial assets outstanding and annual flows were essentially derived from the latest version of the Federal Reserve Board's flow of funds statistics.[2] However, new estimates were developed for two nonfinancial sectors that are not shown separately in past flow of funds statistics and for a few types of financial institutions which also are omitted from previous statistics.[3]

The elimination of the holdings and transactions of these groups makes the new "household" sector considerably more homogeneous than the old one. Unfortunately, due to lack of available data and of time and resources needed to develop new data, it was not possible to eliminate holdings of, and transactions in, financial assets of a few nonprofit institutions, particularly churches and hospitals. However, the holdings and transactions of these groups are relatively small, particularly in the case of corporate stock. More serious for the analysis of the market for corporate stock is the inability to separate funds administered by nonbank trustees and by investment advisers, funds which are supposed to be of substantial size, particularly in the latter case.

The new, more narrowly defined "household" sector still includes more than 60 million households and unattached individuals with a wide range of income and wealth and with very different structures of balance sheets and of stock portfolios. Therefore, an attempt (described in Appendix V) has been made to allocate the total assets and liabilities of the

---

[1] R. W. Goldsmith, *The National Wealth of the United States in the Postwar Period*, Princeton, Princeton University Press for National Bureau of Economic Research, 1962.

[2] This version is very similar to the figures published in *Flow of Funds Accounts 1945–1967* (February, 1968), *Federal Reserve Bulletin*, November, 1969, p. A 70 ff.; and *Flow of Funds . . . 4th Quarter 1969* (February, 1970), but embodies a number of minor revisions.

[3] For details see Chapter 1. The derivation of these estimates is described in Appendixes III and IV.

household sector among about half a dozen groups classified by total wealth, using estate tax returns and occasional sample surveys of financial assets and liabilities of households as the basis of the allocation. These estimates are necessarily very rough, but they are important for an under-standing of the capital market, and they deserve further development.

Of the groups for which balance sheets and flow of funds accounts were developed for this study, using partly existing and partly new data, five (personal trust departments, common trust funds, mortgage companies, closed-end and other investment companies, and fraternal insurance organizations) were added as new subsectors to the existing subsectors of the financial institutions sector. Together these five groups accounted in 1968 for about 15 percent of the assets and nearly one half of the stock-holdings of all financial institutions, represented mostly by the assets of personal trust departments. With the addition of these five groups all financial institutions with substantial stockholdings during the postwar period are included in the statistics, save investment advisers, who in 1969 administered for individual clients about 2 percent of all corporate stock outstanding, or about one-tenth of stock owned or administered by finan-cial institutions covered by the statistics.

The figures for the stocks and flows of financial assets are also subject to errors of estimation, the size of which cannot be precisely evaluated. These errors are particularly important in the case of the household sector because of its derivation as a residual. In order to improve the estimates of households' holdings of corporate stock, new estimates (described in Appendix VII) of the total market value of all corporate stock outstanding in the United States were prepared. A new estimate (described in Appen-dix I) was also made of corporate bonds outstanding, but it is still a very tentative one. The need for such a revised estimate is indicated by the fact that the residual between the previous estimate of the value of corporate and foreign bonds and the reported market value of the holdings of these securities by all sectors other than households—a residual measuring the holdings of corporate and foreign bonds by households (it is not as yet possible to separate the two components reliably)—was negative in some years, indicating either an underestimate of the amount outstanding or an overestimate of the holdings of other sectors.

Estimates of the flows (net purchases or sales) of long-term claims, particularly of marketable bonds, are subject—as already has been pointed out in Chapter 1—to the shortcoming that they are derived as the difference between the book value of holdings at the beginning and end of the year, which usually is equal to original cost or close to it. In this

TABLE 3-1

Distribution of Growth of Reproducible Tangible Civilian Wealth Among
Increases in Population, Price Level, and Real Wealth per Head,
1850–1968

(*percent*)

	Rate of Growth of Reproducible Tangible Wealth				Share in Growth of Total Reproducible Tangible Wealth			
	1952 to 1968 (1)	1930 to 1951 (2)	1901 to 1929 (3)	1851 to 1900 (4)	1952 to 1968 (5)	1930 to 1951 (6)	1901 to 1929 (7)	1851 to 1900 (8)
1. Nonmilitary wealth, current values	6.00	5.05	5.91	5.20	100.0	100.0	100.0	100.0
2. Population	1.55	1.10	1.62	2.40	25.9	21.8	27.4	46.2
3. Wealth per head	4.45	3.95	4.29	2.80	74.1	78.2	72.6	53.8
4. Price level	2.30	3.50	2.62	0.30	38.3	69.3	44.3	5.8
5. Real wealth per head	2.15	0.45	1.67	2.50	35.9	8.9	28.3	48.1
6. Real wealth	3.70	1.55	3.29	4.90	61.7	30.7	55.7	94.2

SOURCES:
Lines 1, 6. 1952–68: Appendix I.
   1929–52: R. W. Goldsmith, *The National Wealth of the United States in the Postwar Period.* Princeton, Princeton University Press, 1962, p. 114.
   1850–1929: *Ibid.,* p. 37.
Line 2. *Statistical Abstract of the United States.*
Line 3. Line 1 less line 2.
Line 4. 1850–1929: As for lines 1 and 6.
   1929–68: Difference between lines 3 and 5.
Line 5. Line 6 less line 2.
Line 6. Line 5 plus line 2.

method of calculation, realized capital gains and losses, as well as the less
common write-ups or write-downs, are included in net purchases or sales.
Fortunately the amounts of capital gains or losses realized when claims
were sold, or of write-ups and -downs—which have the same distorting
effect on calculated flows—probably were relatively small during the
postwar period, at least until 1965 when the sharp increase in interest
rates and the corresponding fall in the prices of long-term claims started.

TABLE 3-2

The Reproducible National Wealth of the United States and Its Main Components, 1900–68

(constant prices, $billion)

	1968	1960	1952B	1952A	1929	1900
	(1958 prices)			(1947–49 prices)		
	(1)	(2)	(3)	(4)	(5)	(6)
I. Structures	1,179	894	642	480	384	146
1. Private, residential	531	426	308	251	200	76
2. Private, nonresidential	290	213	156	135	139	60
3. Public, nonmilitary	358	255	178	94	45	10
II. Equipment	554	359	257	225	118	43
1. Private, producer durables	285	192	147	106	60	21
2. Private, consumer durables	227	140	95	116	57	22
3. Public, nonmilitary	42	27	15	3	1	0
III. Inventories[a]	204	143	125	98	64	32
IV. Reproducible wealth	1,937	1,396	1,024	803	566	221

SOURCES:
Cols. 1–3. Appendix I.
Cols. 4–6. Goldsmith, *National Wealth*, pp. 119–20.

[a] Including livestock.

2. MAIN CHARACTERISTICS OF NATIONAL AND SECTORAL BALANCE SHEETS AND FLOW OF FUNDS ACCOUNTS IN THE POSTWAR PERIOD[4]

a. Growth of National Wealth

In putting the essential features of the national balance sheet of the United States during the period 1952–68 into historical perspective, a few conclusions emerge, starting with the real infrastructure of tangible assets, which is summarized in Table 3-1.

(1) The average rate of growth of reproducible wealth per head in constant prices (excluding land, to which the concept of deflated values is difficult to apply) for the 17 years 1952–68 is 2.2 percent, substantially

[4] When Chapter 3 was written the final version of the figures shown in Appendix I was not available and preliminary estimates had to be used in some cases. Therefore, occasional discrepancies, mostly minor, exist between the figures of Chapter 3 and the corresponding figures of Appendix I.

TABLE 3-3

Distribution of the Reproducible National Wealth of the United States, 1900–68

(constant prices, percent)

	1968	1960	1952B	1952A	1929	1900
	(1958 prices)			(1947–49 prices)		
	(1)	(2)	(3)	(4)	(5)	(6)
I. Structures	60.9	64.0	62.7	59.8	67.9	66.0
1. Private, residential	27.4	30.5	30.2	31.3	35.3	34.3
2. Private, nonresidential	15.0	15.3	15.2	16.8	24.6	27.2
3. Public, nonmilitary	18.5	18.3	17.4	11.7	8.0	4.5
II. Equipment	28.6	25.7	25.1	28.0	20.8	19.5
1. Private, producer durables	14.7	13.8	14.4	13.2	10.6	9.5
2. Private, consumer durables	11.7	10.0	9.3	14.4	10.1	10.0
3. Public, nonmilitary	2.2	1.9	1.5	0.4	0.2	0.0
III. Inventories[a]	10.5	10.2	12.2	12.2	11.3	14.5
IV. Reproducible wealth	100.0	100.0	100.0	100.0	100.0	100.0

Sources:
Cols. 1–3. Appendix I.
Cols. 4–6. Goldsmith, *National Wealth*, pp. 127–28.

[a] Including livestock.

higher than the rate of 1.7 percent observed for the period 1901 through 1929 but slightly below the rate of 2.5 percent for the second half of the nineteenth century. By this test therefore, the rate of growth of the real infrastructure of the United States in the postwar period was in line with the trend over the preceding hundred years.

(2) Shifts within the real infrastructure during the postwar period were relatively small if measured in constant prices, as in Tables 3-2 and 3-3.[5] The main changes are the increase in the share of consumer durables from 9 to nearly 12 percent and a small decline in the share of

[5] The figures for the years 1968, 1960, and 1952B are not strictly comparable to those for 1952A, 1929, and 1900 because of the difference in the price bases and because of differences in the methods of estimation (particularly the assumed length of life) and in the exact coverage of the various components of reproducible wealth. Such differences are particularly marked in the estimates for consumer durables. Comparisons for the entire period should therefore be made by linking changes within the two subperiods.

residential structures and inventories. These tendencies are similar in direction to shifts occurring during the first half of the century. There was no continuation, however, of the sharp decline in the share of non-residential structures and the substantial increase in the share of producer durables observed in the earlier period. Similarly there was no major shift between the private and public sectors of the economy, although the share of the public sector increased slightly.

TABLE 3-4

The National Wealth of the United States and Its Main Components, 1900–68

(current values, $billion)

	1968 (1)	1960 (2)	1952 (3)	1929 (4)	1900 (5)
I. Land	716	413	200	113.5	31.0
1. Private, agricultural	153	93	67	38.0	16.1
2. Private, nonagricultural	419	241	98	60.2	10.9
3. Public	144	79	35	15.3	4.0
II. Structures	1,536	925	577	189.9	34.9
1. Private, residential	696	446	282	95.9	17.4
2. Private, nonresidential	362	217	142	70.6	15.5
3. Public, nonmilitary	479	261	153	23.4	2.0
III. Equipment	611	368	228	80.6	12.6
1. Private, producer durables	330	200	126	37.8	6.4
2. Private, consumer durables	234	141	90	42.2	6.1
3. Public, nonmilitary	47	27	12	0.6	0.1
IV. Inventories[a]	216	147	111	38.0	9.9
V. Monetary metals	11	18	23	4.8	1.6
VI. Net foreign assets	50	25	14	12.4	−2.3
VII. National wealth	3,141	1,895	1,153	439.2	87.7
VIII. Reproducible wealth	2,425	1,482	953	325.7	56.7

SOURCES:
Cols. 1–3. Line I. Appendix II.
　　　　　Lines II–VI. Appendix I.
Cols. 4, 5. Goldsmith, *National Wealth*, pp. 117–18.

[a] Including livestock.

TABLE 3-5

The National Wealth of the United States and Its Main Components,
1900–68

(*current values, percent*)

	1968 (1)	1960 (2)	1952 (3)	1929 (4)	1900 (5)
I. Land	22.8	21.8	17.3	25.8	35.3
1. Private, agricultural	4.9	4.9	5.8	8.7	18.4
2. Private, nonagricultural	13.3	12.7	8.5	13.7	12.4
3. Public	4.6	4.2	3.0	3.5	4.6
II. Structures	48.9	48.8	50.0	43.2	39.8
1. Private, residential	22.2	23.5	24.5	21.8	19.8
2. Private, nonresidential	11.5	11.5	12.3	16.1	17.7
3. Public, nonmilitary	15.3	13.8	13.3	5.3	2.3
III. Equipment	19.5	19.3	19.8	18.4	14.4
1. Private, producer durables	10.5	10.5	10.9	8.6	7.3
2. Private, consumer durables	7.5	7.4	7.8	9.6	7.0
3. Public, nonmilitary	1.5	1.4	1.0	0.1	0.1
IV. Inventories[a]	6.9	7.8	9.6	8.7	11.3
V. Monetary metals	0.4	0.9	2.0	1.1	1.8
VI. Net foreign assets	1.6	1.3	1.2	2.8	−2.6
VII. National wealth	100.0	100.0	100.0	100.0	100.0
VIII. Reproducible wealth	77.2	78.2	82.7	74.2	64.7

SOURCES:
Cols. 1–3. Table 3-2.
Cols. 4, 5. Goldsmith, *National Wealth*, pp. 125–26.

[a] Including livestock.

(3) In terms of current values and of aggregate rather than per head
values, terms which are probably more important for financial analysis
than the figures based on deflated values that have been used in the
preceding paragraphs, there was a significant shift in favor of land,
reflecting the more rapid rise in land prices than in the prices of other
durable assets (Tables 3-4 and 3-5). This is contrary to past experience
in which the share of land in total national wealth declined rapidly,
mainly because of the reduced importance of agriculture in the economy.

(4) The average price level of reproducible tangible assets rose by approximately 2.3 percent per year, or only slightly less than the 2.6 percent of the period 1900–29 and considerably less than the 3.5 percent of the period of the 1930's and 1940's. All these rates were far above the only very small increase experienced over the second half of the nineteenth century as a whole.

(5) As a result the increase in the current value of total reproducible tangible wealth of 6 percent per year was practically the same as that experienced in the period from 1900 to 1929, and it was only slightly higher than the rates prevailing from 1929 through 1952 and during the second half of the nineteenth century.

(6) Distribution of the total rate of increase of the current value of reproducible tangible assets from 1952 to 1968 was very similar to that observed in the 1900–29 period, population increase accounting for fully one-fourth, the price level for approximately two-fifths, and the remaining 30 to 35 percent representing an increase in real wealth per head. The distribution was, however, quite different in the second half of the nineteenth century when price rises contributed very little while population increase accounted for almost one-half of the growth in the current value of reproducible tangible wealth; or in the 1930's and 1940's when sharp price increases contributed over two-thirds, and less than one-tenth of the rise in total current value was contributed by an increase in real reproducible tangible wealth per head.

b. The Growth of Financial Assets

(1) The situation is rather different in the case of financial assets, the relevant figures for which are shown in Table 3-6. In this case there are considerable changes both in the average rate of growth between the four periods distinguished and in the relative share of the three components in the aggregate rate of growth of the current value of financial assets. As in the case of the real infrastructure, a substantial similarity exists between the two periods 1952–68 and 1901–29, and both these periods differ considerably from the periods 1930–51 and 1850–1900.

(2) In the postwar period 1952 through 1968, as in the first three decades of the current century, the market value of financial assets increased at an annual rate of nearly 8 percent (Table 3-7). The rate of growth of the value of corporate common stock was substantially above that of the rate of growth of claims in both periods, but the difference was

TABLE 3-6

Growth of Financial Assets in the United States, 1900–68

(*$billion*)

	All Financial Assets[a]	All	Claims						Corporate Stock		
			Against Nonfinancial Sectors			Against Financial Institutions					
			All	Federal Government	Other	All[b]	Banking System[c]	Other	All	Financial Institutions	Other
	(1)	(2)	(3)	(4)	(5)	(6)	(7)	(8)	(9)	(10)	(11)
1968	3,917.4	2,791.2	1,509.0	333.2	1,175.8	1,282.2	487.3	794.9	1,126.2	290.9	835.3
1960	2,001.4	1,555.5	889.4	263.4	626.0	666.1	260.1	406.0	445.9	92.9	353.0
1952B	1,161.5	971.8	567.0	243.7	323.3	404.8	208.1	196.7	189.7	34.6	155.1
1952A	1,293.7	1,074.2[a]	615.3	278.6	336.7	458.9	270.3	188.6	219.5	25.0	194.5
1929	504.0	317.3[a]	204.5	18.2	186.3	112.8	61.6	51.2	186.7	22.0	164.7
1900	58.7	44.8[a]	30.6	1.3	29.3	14.2	8.1	6.1	13.9	2.7	11.2

Notes to Table 3-6

SOURCES:
1900, 1929, 1952A. R. W. Goldsmith, R. W. Lipsey, and M. Mendelson, *Studies in the National Balance Sheet of the United States*, 2 vols., Princeton, Princeton University Press for NBER, 1963, pp. 56–57, 72–73, 78–79, 100–101.
1952B, 1960, 1968. Appendix I.

ᵃ Excluding proprietors' equities in unincorporated business enterprises.
ᵇ Including all investment companies, fraternal insurance organizations, and from 1952B on, personal trust funds administered by commercial banks. (Rough estimates of personal trust funds for 1900, $3 billion; for 1929, $30 billion; and for 1952A, $60 billion; according to R. W. Goldsmith, *Financial Intermediaries in the American Economy Since 1900*, Princeton, Princeton University Press for NBER, 1958, p. 384.)
ᶜ Monetary authorities and commercial banks.
ᵈ Taken as equal to liabilities of all domestic sectors.

more pronounced in the postwar period. The rate of expansion of claims, as a matter of fact, was about the same in both periods with approximately 7 percent per year. This rate also prevailed during the second half of the nineteenth century, but at 5 percent it was considerably lower in the 1930's and 1940's. On the other hand, the average rate of growth of the value of corporate common stock was slightly smaller in the second half of the nineteenth century (not too much importance should be attached to this difference as the amount of corporate stock outstanding was very small during the first few decades of this period), but of course, it was radically lower in the period 1930–51.

(3) It is only when account is taken of differences in the rate of population growth and, in particular, in the rate of change in the general price level that differences appear between the 1952–68 and 1901–29 periods, while those in the other two periods become even more accentuated (Table 3-8). In particular the rate of increase in the value of common stocks was considerably higher, with an annual average of 8 percent in the period 1952–68, than in either of the other periods. However, with slightly over 4 per cent, the rate of growth of all financial assets (deflated per head) was fractionally below that observed during the second half of the nineteenth century though it was considerably higher than that of the first three decades of this century and, of course, was far ahead of the rate prevailing between 1929 and 1951.

(4) The process of a considerable secular and practically uninterrupted increase in financial assets has been accompanied by substantial changes

TABLE 3-7

Average Annual Rate of Growth of Financial Assets, 1901–68

(*percent*)

	All Financial Assets[a] (1)	Claims[b]							Corporate Stock[c]		
		All (2)	Against Nonfinancial Sectors			Against Financial Institutions			All (9)	Financial Institutions (10)	Other (11)
			All (3)	Federal Government (4)	Other (5)	All (6)	Banking System (7)	Other (8)			
1961–1968	8.8	7.6	6.8	3.0	8.2	8.5	8.2	8.8	12.4	15.4	11.4
1952B–1960	7.0	6.1	5.8	1.0	8.6	6.4	2.8	9.5	11.2	13.2	10.8
1952B–1968	7.9	6.8	6.3	2.0	8.4	7.5	5.5	9.1	11.8	14.2	11.1
1930–1952A	4.2	5.4	4.9	12.6	2.6	6.3	6.6	5.9	0.7	0.6	0.7
1901–1929	7.7	7.0	6.8	9.5	6.6	7.4	7.2	7.6	9.4	7.5	9.7
1901–1952A	6.7	6.3	6.0	10.8	4.8	6.9	7.0	6.8	5.5	4.4	5.6

SOURCE: Table 3-6.
[a] Does not include proprietors' equities in unincorporated businesses.
[b] Face value.
[c] Market value.

TABLE 3-8

Distribution of Growth of Financial Assets Among Increase in Population, Price Level, and Deflated Assets per Head, 1850–1967

	Rate of Growth of Assets (percent per year)				Share in Growth of Total Assets (percent)			
	1952 to 1968	1930 to 1951	1901 to 1929	1850 to 1900	1952 to 1968	1930 to 1951	1901 to 1929	1850 to 1900
	(1)	(2)	(3)	(4)	(5)	(6)	(7)	(8)
	All Financial Assets							
1. Market value	7.90	4.40	7.70	6.70	100	100	100	100
2. Population	1.55	1.10	1.62	2.40	20	25	21	36
3. Assets per head[a]	6.35	3.30	6.08	4.30	80	75	79	64
4. Price level[b]	2.20	2.50	2.50	0	28	57	32	0
5. Deflated assets per head[c]	4.15	0.80	3.58	4.30	53	18	47	64
6. Deflated assets[d]	5.70	1.90	5.20	6.70	72	43	68	100
	Claims							
1. Market value	6.80	5.70	7.00	6.60	100	100	100	100
2. Population	1.55	1.10	1.62	2.40	23	19	23	36
3. Assets per head[a]	5.25	4.60	5.38	4.20	77	81	77	64
4. Price level[b]	2.20	2.50	2.50	0	32	44	36	0
5. Deflated assets per head[c]	3.05	2.10	2.88	4.20	45	37	41	64
6. Deflated assets[d]	4.60	3.20	4.50	6.60	68	56	64	100
	Corporate Common Stock							
1. Market value	11.70	0.70	9.30	7.00	100	100	100	100
2. Population	1.55	1.10	1.62	2.40	13	157	17	34
3. Assets per head[a]	10.15	−0.40	7.68	4.60	87	−57	83	66
4. Price level[b]	2.20	2.50	2.50	0	19	357	27	0
5. Deflated assets per head[c]	7.95	−2.90	5.16	4.60	68	−415	56	66
6. Deflated assets[d]	9.50	−1.80	6.80	7.00	81	257	73	100

SOURCES:
Cols. 1, 5.   Appendix I.
Cols. 2, 3, 6, 7. Table 3-6.
[a] For columns 1 to 4, line 1 less line 2.
[b] Gross national product deflator.
[c] Line 3 less line 4.
[d] Line 1 less line 4.

TABLE 3-9

Structure of Financial Assets, 1900–68

(percent)

	All Financial Assets[a]	Claims[b]								Corporate Stock[c]		
			Against Nonfinancial Sectors			Against Financial Institutions					
		All	All	Federal Government	Other	All	Banking System	Other	All	Financial Institutions	Other
	(1)	(2)	(3)	(4)	(5)	(6)	(7)	(8)	(9)	(10)	(11)
1968	100.0	71.3	38.5	8.5	30.0	32.7	12.4	20.3	28.7	7.4	21.3
1960	100.0	77.7	44.4	13.2	31.3	33.3	13.0	20.3	22.3	4.6	17.6
1952B	100.0	83.7	48.8	21.0	27.8	34.9	17.9	16.9	16.3	3.0	13.4
1952A	100.0	83.0	47.6	21.5	26.0	35.5	20.9	14.6	17.0	1.9	15.0
1929	100.0	63.0	40.6	3.6	37.0	22.4	12.2	10.2	37.0	4.4	32.6
1900	100.0	76.3	52.1	2.2	49.9	24.2	13.8	10.4	23.7	4.6	19.1

SOURCE: Table 3-6.
[a] Does not include proprietors' equities in unincorporated businesses.
[b] Face value.
[c] Market value.

in the structure of financial assets (Table 3-9). The chief characteristic is the increasing share of corporate stock from one-sixth at the end of 1952 to nearly three-tenths in 1968 (and probably still one-fourth at the end of 1969). Among claims, the share of the liabilities of financial institutions has remained practically unchanged at approximately one-third of all financial assets. The decline in the share of all claims is therefore concentrated on the liabilities of the nonfinancial sectors, whose share in total financial assets fell from slightly less than one-half in 1952 to somewhat below two-fifths in 1968. Here the decline occurred mostly in the debt of the federal government, whose share in total financial assets declined sharply from over one-fifth to only one-twelfth during this period. It should be remembered, however, that at the end of 1952 relationships were still affected by the extraordinary expansion of the federal debt during World War II. Compared to 1929 or 1900, the decline in the share of claims in total financial assets is concentrated in the liabilities of non-financial sectors other than the federal government. This share stood at 30 percent at the end of 1968 compared to 37 percent in 1929 and to as much as 50 percent in 1900.

c. Total National Assets

National assets, defined as the sum of tangible and financial assets, increased, as Table 3-10 shows, between the end of 1952 and 1968 from $2,400 billion to fully $7,000 billion (market value or reproduction cost), or at an average annual rate of $7\frac{1}{4}$ percent. This was substantially above the average of $5\frac{1}{2}$ percent for the first half of the century and that of 4 percent for the period 1930–52. It was higher, though only slightly, even when compared to the $6\frac{1}{2}$ percent for the first three decades of the century.

If the increase in the current value of national assets is adjusted for the increase in population and the decline in the purchasing power of the dollar as measured by the national product deflator (Table 3-11), it appears that the rate of increase in the postwar period was considerably higher than that in the first half of the century as a whole, and that it was slightly above even the rate prevailing from 1901 through 1929. The more appropriate but much more difficult and problematical deflation by price index specific to the different components of national assets—a deflation intended to transform the current value figures into measurements of quantities—also seems to indicate that the rate of expansion of national assets in the postwar period was more rapid than it had been in either the first three or the first five decades of this century.

TABLE 3-10

The Growth of National Assets of the United States, 1900–68

	Aggregate ($billion)			Per Head ($000)		
	National Wealth (1)	Financial Assets (2)	National Assets (3)	National Wealth (4)	Financial Assets (5)	National Assets (6)
1900	88	59	147	1.1	0.8	1.9
1929	439	504	943	3.6	4.1	7.7
1952A	1,186	1,294	2,480	7.6	8.3	15.9
1952B	1,153	1,162	2,315	7.4	7.5	14.9
1960	1,895	2,001	3,896	10.5	11.0	21.5
1968	3,141	3,917	7,058	15.6	19.4	34.9

NOTE: All figures at end of year or period indicated.
SOURCES: Tables 3-4 and 3-6.

d. The Financial Interrelations Ratio

More directly relevant to the connection of the financial superstructure to the real infrastructure is the "financial interrelations ratio," the ratio of the total market value of financial assets to national wealth. The figures shown in Table 3-12 for six benchmark dates since the turn of the century (1900, 1929, 1945, 1952, 1960, and 1968) for all financial assets as well as for their main components.

The postwar period 1952–68 witnessed a substantial increase in the overall financial interrelations ratio from 1.01 to about 1.25.[6] Most of the increase occurred during the second half of the period. Between the end of 1951 and 1960 the ratio went up by 5 percentage points while between 1960 and 1968 it increased by 20 points, or nearly one-fifth. The 1968 value of the financial interrelations ratio was still considerably below

---

[6] The level of these figures is somewhat below some other estimates (e.g., R. W. Goldsmith and R. E. Lipsey, *Studies in the National Balance Sheet of the United States*, Vol. I, Princeton, Princeton University Press for NBER, 1963, p. 80) partly because the latter define some items in the national balance sheet on a grosser basis and include proprietors' equity in unincorporated business enterprises as a separate asset. Note also that the sharp decline in stock prices since late 1968 has somewhat reduced the current value of the ratio. As of mid-1970 it may be estimated to have fallen to below 1.20.

TABLE 3-11

Rates of Growth of National Assets and Components, 1952–68 vs. 1901–51

(*percent per year*[a])

	1901–51 (1)	1952–68 (2)	Difference (3)
I. National assets in current prices	5.60	7.20	1.60
1. Tangible assets[b]	5.20	6.50	1.30
a. Reproducible tangible assets	5.70	6.10	0.40
b. Land	3.80	8.30	4.50
2. Financial assets	6.10	7.90	1.80
a. Claims	6.20	6.80	0.60
b. Equities	5.30	11.80	6.50
3. Debt	6.30	6.80	0.50
4. Net worth	5.10	7.10	2.00
II. General price level	2.50	2.10	−0.40
III. Population	1.40	1.65	0.25
IV. National assets in constant (1929) prices on basis of general price level	3.10	5.10	2.00
V. National assets per head at constant prices	1.70	3.45	1.75

SOURCES:
1900–1951: *Studies in the National Balance Sheet*, Vol. I, p. 54 ff.; Vol. II, p. 117 ff.
1952–68:   Tables 3-4 and 3-7.
[a] Calculated on the basis of value at beginning and end of period.
[b] Includes gold and net foreign assets.

the value reached at the end of World War II when price and wage controls and the sharp expansion of government debt and bank credit combined in lifting the ratio to an unprecedented level. The ratio was considerably higher, however, than the peaks reached before World War II in 1929 and again in 1939.[7]

Considerable differences are observed in the movements of the components of the financial interrelations ratio, differences which are closely

[7] If gross national product is used as the denominator of the ratio instead of national wealth, the direction of the movement is the same, but the changes are more pronounced. Thus, the ratio of the value of financial assets to national product rose from 3.7 in 1951 to 5.0 in 1968. The differences between the movements of the two ratios are, of course, due to changes in the wealth-income ratio.

TABLE 3-12

The Financial Interrelations Ratio, 1900–68

(*percent of national wealth*)

		Claims[b]							Corporate Stock[c]		
		Against Nonfinancial Sectors			Against Financial Institutions						
			Federal Government			Banking System				Financial Institutions	
All Financial Assets[a]	All	All	ment	Other	All	System	Other	All	tions	Other
(1)	(2)	(3)	(4)	(5)	(6)	(7)	(8)	(9)	(10)	(11)
1968	124.7	88.9	48.0	10.6	37.4	40.8	15.5	25.3	35.9	9.3	26.6
1960	105.6	82.1	46.9	13.9	33.0	35.1	13.7	21.4	23.5	4.9	18.6
1952B	100.8	84.3	49.2	21.1	28.0	35.1	18.0	17.1	16.5	3.0	13.5
1952A	109.1	90.6	51.9	23.5	28.4	38.7	22.8	15.9	18.5	2.1	16.4
1929	114.8	72.3	46.6	4.1	42.4	25.7	14.0	11.7	42.5	5.0	37.5
1900	66.7	50.9	34.8	1.5	33.3	16.1	9.2	6.9	15.8	3.1	12.7

SOURCES:

1900–51A: *Studies in the National Balance Sheet*, pp. 54–55, 72–73, 78–79, 100–101.
Financial Intermediaries, p. 340 for col. 7; *ibid.*, Appendix F for col. 10.

1951B–68: *Flow of Funds Accounts 1945–1968*, pp. 52–61; Appendix I for cols. 9–11.

[a] Does not include proprietors' equities in unincorporated businesses.
[b] Face value.
[c] Market value.

connected with basic developments in the postwar financial economy. The ratios for both main components of financial assets increased between the end of 1952 and 1968. While the ratio of claims to national wealth rose only from 0.84 to 0.89, the parallel ratio for corporate stock more than doubled, from 0.17 to 0.36, mainly due to an increase in stock prices by about 350 percent or an average rate of fully 9 percent per year (reduced by mid-1970 to about 220 percent or 6½ percent per year). As a result the ratio of the market value of corporate stock to national wealth in 1968 was close to its all-time peak of the late 1920's.

Here again considerable differences exist between the first and the second half of the postwar period. The ratio of the value of stocks to national wealth increased by 7 points in the period 1952–60 but by over 12 points in 1961–68, i.e., by fully two-fifths and one-half, respectively, of its starting value. On the other hand, the ratio of claims to national wealth, after declining slightly in the first period, advanced by 7 points, or nearly one-tenth, during the 1960's.

For a better understanding of the situation it is necessary to distinguish claims owed by nonfinancial sectors from those incurred by financial institutions. The first of these ratios decreased fractionally over the whole period. On the other hand, the ratio of claims against financial institutions to national wealth advanced over the period by five points or by one-seventh. As a result, the ratio of claims against financial institutions to those against the nonfinancial sectors had risen to 0.80 in 1968 compared to 0.72 at the beginning of the period.

Significant changes also occurred within the two main categories of claims. In the case of claims against nonfinancial sectors the share of the federal government declined sharply, from nearly 45 percent at the end of 1952 (already down substantially from the nearly two-thirds in 1945) to not much over one-fifth at the end of 1968, as the absolute amount of Treasury securities outstanding increased by only 40 percent in the face of an almost fourfold increase in the debt of business, households, and state and local governments. Similarly among claims against financial institutions the liabilities of the banking system declined from one-half in 1952 (and fully two-thirds in 1945) to only approximately two-fifths in 1968. Thus, the structure of claims changed in the direction of an expansion of the share of corporate, household, and state and local government debt and of the liabilities of nonbank financial institutions at the expense of the liabilities of the federal government and the banking system.

Developments during 1969 and the first half of 1970 (which are not covered in the statistical framework underlying this study) particularly the decline in common stock prices by about one-fourth, have undone a substantial part of the changes that occurred during the postwar period and particularly during the 1960's. Thus, the share of the market value of stock to national wealth may be estimated to have fallen back in mid-1970 to well below 0.30 against the ratio of 0.36 which it had reached at the end of 1968, but to have remained well above the value it had at the end of 1960. Similarly, the stocks-claims ratio in the national balance sheet was down to approximately 30 percent by mid-1970 against 40 percent at the end of 1968, returning to the levels prevailing at the beginning of the century but still remaining considerably above the minimum of about one-fifth reached between the end of World War II and 1952.

The movements of the financial interrelations ratio during this century are easier to follow in Table 3-13, which shows the average annual rate of change between five benchmark dates. Compared to an average annual rise of 1.1 percent for the entire period 1900–68—a trend which would double the ratio every 65 years—the average rate of increase of the ratio in the postwar period 1952–68 was 1.3 percent. This was mainly the result of a very rapid rise at the rate of 2.1 percent per year in the second half of the period, in which a sharp increase in the value of financial assets, both stocks and claims, was combined with a relatively slow (6½ percent) rate of growth of national wealth at current prices. Even this rate remained considerably below the extraordinarily rapid increase in the rate in the 1920's, which was close to 4 percent per year for the period 1923–29, the result primarily of a very rapid rise in the value of stock outstanding at an annual rate of 13½ percent—well above that of the postwar period or its two halves—in the face of a much slower rate of increase in the volume of claims (5½ percent) and a relatively modest expansion in national wealth at current prices (4 percent).

Table 3-14, which uses gross national product as denominator instead of national wealth, shows generally the same movements and relations. This is to be expected, as these ratios are linked to the financial interrelations ratio by the capital-output ratio (national wealth divided by national product), which has not moved sharply between the five benchmark years. The ratios of financial assets to national product are given, although they are conceptually inferior to the financial interrelations ratio (the denominator being the flow rather than the stock dimension) because figures on national product are available for many more dates and countries than are those for national wealth. Some differences in the movements of the two sets of ratios are, however, noticeable if the two halves of the

TABLE 3-13

Average Annual Rate of Growth in Financial Interrelations Ratio, 1901–68

(*percent*)

	All Financial Assets[a] (1)	Claims[b]							Corporate Stock[c]		
		All (2)	Against Nonfinancial Sectors			Against Financial Institutions			All (9)	Financial Institutions (10)	Other (11)
			All (3)	Federal Government (4)	Other (5)	All (6)	Banking System (7)	Other (8)			
1961–68	2.1	1.0	0.9	−3.4	3.6	1.9	1.6	2.1	5.5	8.3	4.6
1952–60	0.6	−0.3	−0.6	−5.3	2.1	0.0	−3.5	2.8	4.5	6.3	4.1
1952–68	1.3	0.3	−0.1	−4.4	1.8	0.9	−0.9	2.5	5.0	7.3	4.3
1930–51	−0.2	1.0	0.6	8.2	−1.8	1.9	2.2	1.4	−3.9	−4.0	−5.3
1901–29	1.9	1.2	1.0	3.6	0.8	1.6	1.5	1.8	3.5	1.7	3.8
1901–51	1.0	1.1	0.8	5.5	−0.3	1.7	1.8	1.6	0.3	−0.8	0.5

SOURCE: Table 3-12.
a Does not include proprietors' equities in unincorporated businesses.
b Face value.
c Market value.

TABLE 3-14

Relation of Financial Assets to GNP

(*percent*)

| | | Claims[b] | | | | | | Corporate Stock[c] | | |
| | | Against Nonfinancial Sectors | | | Against Financial Institutions | | | | | |
	All Financial Assets[a] (1)	All (2)	All (3)	Federal Government (4)	Other (5)	All (6)	Banking System (7)	Other (8)	All (9)	Financial Institutions (10)	Other (11)
1968	452.4	322.3	174.2	38.5	135.7	148.1	56.3	91.8	130.1	33.6	96.5
1960	397.2	308.6	176.4	52.3	124.1	132.2	51.6	80.6	88.5	18.4	70.1
1952B	336.0	281.1	163.9	70.5	93.4	117.2	60.2	56.9	54.9	10.0	44.9
1952A	374.4	310.9	178.1	80.6	97.5	132.8	78.2	54.6	63.5	7.2	56.3
1929	488.8	307.8	198.4	17.7	180.7	109.4	59.7	49.7	181.1	21.3	159.7
1900	404.8	309.0	211.0	9.0	202.1	97.9	55.9	42.1	95.9	18.6	77.2

SOURCE: Table 3-6.
[a] Does not include proprietors' equities in unincorporated businesses.
[b] Face value.
[c] Market value.

postwar period are compared. Because the capital-output ratio increased considerably between 1952 and 1960 and declined slightly from 1960 to 1968, the increase in the ratio of financial assets to national product is about the same in the two halves of the period while the ratio of financial assets to national wealth (the financial interrelations ratio) increases much more rapidly in the second than in the first half of the postwar period.

e. Distribution of National Assets and Their Main Components Among Sectors

In view of the rapid expansion of the economy and of the sharp changes that have occurred during the postwar period in the prices of land, structures, and corporate stock, it is remarkable that the distribution of national assets and its two main components, tangible and financial assets, as shown in Table 3-15, changed little during the postwar period.

In terms of their total assets, the shares of the three largest sectors changed only fractionally. Households increased their share very slightly; the share of business declined moderately from 26 to 22 percent, mainly because of a substantial relative decline in the share of farm business from nearly 6 to $3\frac{1}{2}$ percent; and the share of finance rose fractionally from 18 to 20 percent. The two government sectors together accounted for 11 percent of national assets in 1952, 1960, and 1968. However, the share of the federal government declined considerably over the period while that of state and local governments increased.

The distribution of tangible assets also showed only moderate changes, the most important of which were the increase in the share of state and local governments from 12 to 17 percent and a small decline in the share of business from 44 to 40 percent, again attributable mainly to agriculture. The shifts are more pronounced if attention is focused on the two main components, land and reproducible tangible assets. Changes in the distribution of the value of land are dominated by the sharp decline in the share of agriculture from 34 to 21 percent, reflecting the less rapid—though in absolute terms still very substantial—increase in the price of farm land. This was offset by substantial increases in the shares of households, corporate business, and state and local governments, all reflecting the rapid appreciation of urban land. More interesting are changes in the distribution of reproducible assets, because they result largely from differences in the rate of increase of capital formation rather than predominantly from price changes as is the case for land. Such changes, however, were moderate—a substantial increase in the share of state and local governments from 12 to 17 percent, small declines in the shares of

TABLE 3-15

Distribution of National Assets and Chief Components Among Sectors, 1952, 1960, and 1968

(all domestic sectors = 100)

| | House-holds | Nonprofit Institutions | Nonfinancial Business | | | | | Government | | Financial |
| | | | Total | Corpora-tions | Unincorporated | | | Federal | State and Local | |
					Agricul-ture	Other				
I. Total assets										
1952	44.0	1.3	25.7	16.3	5.8	3.6		4.9	6.2	17.8
1960	45.2	1.6	23.5	15.8	4.5	3.2		4.2	7.2	18.3
1968	45.4	1.7	21.9	15.1	3.7	3.1		3.5	7.8	19.7
II. Tangible										
1952	34.6	2.1	44.2	25.2	12.4	6.6		6.5	12.1	0.5
1960	36.2	2.4	39.9	24.1	9.7	6.1		6.4	14.4	0.7
1968	34.2	2.8	39.8	24.6	8.6	6.6		5.1	16.8	0.9
1. Land										
1952	28.9	3.1	48.8	10.4	33.1	5.3		5.3	11.6	2.3
1960	36.1	3.6	40.6	13.6	22.6	4.4		4.5	14.7	0.6
1968	35.1	4.0	39.8	14.4	21.3	4.1		4.7	15.5	1.0

2. Reproducible									
1952	35.8	1.8	43.0	28.4	7.7	6.9	6.7	12.2	0.5
1960	36.2	2.1	39.6	27.1	6.0	6.5	7.0	14.3	0.8
1968	33.9	2.5	39.9	27.7	4.8	7.4	5.6	17.2	0.9
III. Financial									
1952	24.4	1.1	16.9	14.2	0.9	1.8	5.6	2.3	49.6
1960	52.5	0.9	10.3	9.1	0.3	0.9	2.5	1.4	32.5
1968	53.4	0.9	9.1	8.3	0.2	0.6	2.1	1.4	33.1
1. Short-term									
1952	29.1	0.0	24.5	20.2	1.4	2.0	9.3	2.3	34.7
1960	32.6	0.0	25.4	22.2	0.8	2.4	6.3	2.6	33.1
1968	35.8	0.0	22.6	20.5	0.5	1.6	5.8	3.1	32.8
2. Long-term									
1952	45.5	0.7	2.1	2.1	—	—	0.6	2.0	49.0
1960	46.5	0.7	0.9	0.9	—	—	0.7	1.6	49.6
1968	44.2	0.5	0.6	0.6	—	—	0.7	1.5	52.3
3. Corporate stock									
1952	76.8	3.3	—	—	—	—	—	—	19.9
1960	73.5	3.0	—	—	—	—	—	—	23.5
1968	74.8	2.3	—	—	—	—	—	—	22.9
IV. Liabilities									
1952	9.8	0.3	19.7	17.0	1.4	1.3	25.1	3.4	41.7
1960	13.9	0.6	20.9	17.7	1.5	1.7	16.9	4.8	42.8
1968	14.7	0.7	21.9	17.9	1.8	2.2	11.9	4.8	45.9

(*continued*)

TABLE 3-15 (*concluded*)

	House-holds	Nonprofit Institutions	Nonfinancial Business		Unincorporated		Government		Financial
			Total	Corpora-tions	Agricul-ture	Other	Federal	State and Local	
IV. Liabilities (cont.)									
1. Short-term debt									
1952	7.7	—	22.8	20.7	1.3	0.8	14.1	0.5	54.8
1960	10.1	0.1	24.3	21.2	1.4	1.7	12.1	0.5	53.0
1968	11.4	0.2	23.7	20.4	1.6	1.7	8.9	0.6	55.2
2. Long-term debt									
1952	12.1	0.7	16.3	13.0	1.6	1.7	37.1	6.5	27.2
1960	17.8	1.2	17.6	14.1	1.7	1.8	21.8	9.2	32.4
1968	18.2	1.3	20.1	15.3	2.1	2.7	15.2	9.2	35.9
3. Net worth									
1952	65.7	1.9	29.5	15.8	8.6	5.1	−7.9	8.0	2.7
1960	64.1	2.1	25.1	14.7	6.3	4.1	−3.4	8.6	3.4
1968	64.0	2.3	21.8	13.3	4.9	3.6	−1.6	9.7	3.9

household and corporate business, and a substantial reduction in the share of agriculture.

Financial assets in the aggregate showed only small changes in distribution, a modest increase in the share of households and a decline in that of business. The share of financial institutions remained practically stable at slightly below one-third of the total.

There were more movements in the distribution of the main types of financial assets, particularly short-term claims. Here the share of households increased considerably, from 29 to 35 percent, while that of business declined from 24 to 22 percent, probably reflecting both a carry-over of excess liquidity from the war at the beginning of the period and the more effective management of liquid assets in the following two decades. The share of financial institutions showed a small net decline between 1952 and 1968. The distribution of long-term claims changed little, as a small decline in the share of households and a relatively substantial reduction in that of business were offset by an increase in the share of financial institutions from 49 to 52 percent, which testifies to the continuing high degree of institutionalization of long-term debt financing. The distribution of corporate stock, particularly interesting for this investigation, changed little. The share of financial institutions rose from 20 to 23 percent.

Much more pronounced changes appear in the distribution of debt among the sectors and reflect primarily the small expansion of the federal debt in absolute terms and its sharp reduction in proportion to all debt from 25 to 12 percent. As a consequence the share of all other sectors increased, although in varying proportions. The increase was sharpest for households, whose share rose from 10 to 15 percent of the total, and was substantial in relative terms for state and local governments, with a rise from $3\frac{1}{2}$ to 4 percent. The increase in the share of business was moderate. On the other hand, the share of financial institutions increased from 42 to 46 percent, another indication of the continuing institutionalization of the financial process. Changes were similar in direction and extent for short- and for long-term debt, the declining share of the federal government being somewhat more pronounced in the case of long-term debt, where its share was cut by three-fifths, than for short-term obligations.

In view of the relative stability of the distribution of tangible and financial assets and liabilities among sectors, it is not astonishing that changes in the share of net worth were also moderate. The most important of these was the reduction, and indeed the near disappearance, of the

TABLE 3-16

Growth of Total Assets of Main Sectors, 1952–68

	Growth (1952 = 100)		Annual Growth Rate (percent)		
	1960 (1)	1968 (2)	1953 to 1960 (3)	1961 to 1968 (4)	1953 to 1968 (5)
I. Households	169	305	6.8	7.6	7.2
II. Nonprofit institutions	197	376	8.8	8.4	8.6
III. Unincorporated business	135	213	3.8	5.9	4.8
1. Agricultural	127	188	3.0	5.0	4.0
2. Other	148	254	5.0	7.0	6.0
IV. Nonfinancial corporations	160	274	6.0	6.9	6.5
V. Federal government	144	212	4.7	4.9	4.8
VI. State and local government	191	372	8.4	8.7	8.6
VII. Finance	169	327	6.8	8.6	7.7
1. Banking system*	127	235	3.0	8.0	5.5
2. Other	210	416	9.7	8.9	9.3
VIII. All sectors	165	296	6.5	7.6	7.0
IX. General price level (GNP deflator)	118	142	2.1	2.3	2.2

SOURCE: Appendix I.
* Federal Reserve System and commercial banks.

negative net worth (excess of debt over assets) of the federal government.[8] Next in importance was the decline in the share of unincorporated business, both farm and nonfarm, which is responsible for most of the reduction of the share of total business from 29 to 22 percent of national net worth.

The changes in the distribution of national assets and their components just discussed are, of course, the result of differences in the growth rate of the aggregates and the main components of the assets of the different sectors. These are shown in Table 3-16.

[8] If military assets, excluded from Table 3-15 and throughout this discussion, were included, the federal government's net worth would be positive throughout, but probably declining.

For the period as a whole, for which total assets increased at an average rate of 7.0 percent per year, the most rapidly expanding sector was nonbank financial institutions, with an average annual growth rate of 9.3 percent, while the slowest-growing sector was unincorporated agricultural businesses, with a rate of only 4.0 percent a year. Ranking of the sectors was similar in the two subperiods, although the lead of the nonbank finance sector was much smaller in the second than in the first half of the period, and the most slowly growing sector in the second subperiod was the federal government rather than agriculture, which held that position in the first subperiod.

These rates of growth are the combined result of the sector's saving, its net external financing, and the increase in prices which affected its assets. For all sectors together, external financing and the residual primarily reflecting valuation changes (price increases) each accounted for approximately two-fifths of the increase in the value of assets between 1952 and 1958 as well as in both subperiods, leaving one-fifth to net saving. The share of valuation changes, however, was considerably higher than this for households and very much lower for financial institutions because the share of corporate stock in their total assets was low. External financing entirely dominated the increase in assets of the finance sector and, next to it, of the federal government, and was least important for households. Equity financing, however, was almost negligible in the two sectors in which it existed—nonfinancial corporations and finance. In both cases it accounted for only about 3 percent of the expansion of assets including, and 5 percent excluding, valuation changes.

An understanding of the changes in the distribution of national assets and its components among sectors, and of the rate of growth of total assets of the different sectors, requires an analysis of the balance sheets and flow of funds accounts of these sectors. While both statements have been constructed on an annual basis for the period from 1952 to 1968, after their completion there was not sufficient time for an adequate analysis. For the purposes of this report we shall have to be satisfied with a summary of the structure of the sectoral balance sheets for the three benchmark dates of 1952, 1960, and 1968, presented in Tables 3-17 and 3-18, and with a listing of a number of changes regarded as significant. This limitation is to some extent justified because some aspects of the structure of, and changes in, financial assets of households are discussed in Chapter 5, section 2; because a breakdown of the assets of the household sector by size of wealth for at least one recent date is presented in Appendix V; and because the position of corporate stock in the balance sheets and flow of

TABLE 3-17

Structure of Sectoral Balance Sheets, 1952, 1960, and 1968

(percent of total assets, except line VI)

	Households			Nonprofit Institutions[a]			Unincorporated Business[b]			Nonfinancial Corporations		
	1952 (1)	1960 (2)	1968 (3)	1952 (4)	1960 (5)	1968 (6)	1952 (7)	1960 (8)	1968 (9)	1952 (10)	1960 (11)	1968 (12)
I. Tangible assets	35.0	35.9	31.3	69.5	68.7	70.3	89.6	91.1	92.9	69.0	68.3	68.0
1. Land	5.3	8.0	7.5	19.0	22.9	23.0	33.0	34.8	36.0	5.2	8.6	9.2
2. Reproducible assets	29.7	28.0	23.8	50.5	45.8	47.3	56.6	56.4	56.9	63.8	59.8	58.7
a. Structures	21.5	20.4	16.9	45.3	41.8	44.7	22.1	24.0	29.8	28.5	26.4	24.4
b. Producer durables	—	—	—	5.1	4.0	2.6	18.7	19.6	16.7	19.1	19.9	20.9
c. Consumer durables	8.2	7.5	6.9	—	—	—	—	—	—	—	—	—
d. Inventories	—	—	—	—	—	—	15.8	12.7	10.5	16.2	13.4	13.4
II. Financial assets	65.0	64.1	68.7	30.5	31.3	29.7	10.4[i]	8.9[i]	7.1[i]	31.0	31.7	32.0
1. Short-term claims	13.0	12.7	14.3	0.3[h]	0.3[h]	0.4[h]	—	—	—	24.4	24.7	24.7
2. Long-term claims	19.1	19.2	17.7	9.7	8.4	5.7	9.1	7.4	5.4	2.4[i]	1.0[i]	0.8[i]
3. Corporate stock	12.9	17.2	24.6	18.7	20.1	20.6	—	—	—	—[k]	—[k]	—[k]
4. Miscellaneous assets	19.9[g]	15.0[g]	12.1[g]	1.8	2.5	3.0	1.2	1.5	1.7	4.2	5.9	6.5
III. Total assets	100.0	100.0	100.0	100.0	100.0	100.0	100.0	100.0	100.0	100.0	100.0	100.0
IV. Liabilities	8.6	11.6	12.2	10.3	15.1	16.6	11.1	15.8	22.3	40.6	42.1	44.8
1. Short-term	3.6	4.3	4.9	0.0	0.9	2.3	4.6	7.5	9.6	25.8	25.5	26.5
2. Long-term[f]	5.1	7.3	7.3	10.3	14.1	14.3	6.4	8.3	12.7	14.8	16.6	18.3
V. Net worth	91.4	88.4	87.8	89.7	84.9	83.4	88.9	84.2	77.7	59.4	57.9	55.2
VI. Total assets ($billion)	1,103.2	1,867.3	3,363.8	33.1	65.1	124.6	236.6	319.6	505.0	407.7	652.9	1,115.2

	Federal Government[c]			State and Local Governments[d]			Finance		
	1952 (13)	1960 (14)	1968 (15)	1952 (16)	1960 (17)	1968 (18)	1952 (19)	1960 (20)	1968 (21)
I. Tangible assets	59.0	68.1	64.6	86.6	89.6	89.3	1.1	1.7	2.0
1. Land	8.8	10.5	13.0	15.2	20.4	19.1	0.1	0.3	0.5
2. Reproducible assets	50.2	57.6	51.6	71.4	69.3	70.2	1.0	1.4	1.5
a. Structures	39.4	40.3	40.0	67.1	64.1	64.8	0.6	0.7	0.8
b. Producer durables	4.6	6.7	6.1	4.3	5.2	5.4	0.4	0.7	0.6
c. Consumer durables	—	—	—	—	—	—	—	—	—

I. Inventories	6.1	10.6	5.4	—	—	—	—	—	—
II. Financial assets	41.0	31.9	35.4	13.4	10.4	10.7	98.9	98.3	98.0
1. Short-term claims	37.7	26.3	30.0	7.3	6.3	7.1	38.3[i]	31.9[i]	30.2[i]
2. Long-term claims	2.4	3.3	3.8	6.1	4.1	3.6	50.9	50.7	48.1
3. Corporate stock	—	—	—	—	—	—	8.3	13.6	17.3
4. Miscellaneous assets	1.0	2.3	1.6	—	—	—	1.3	1.9	2.4
III. Total assets	100.0	100.0	100.0	100.0	100.0	100.0	100.0	100.0	100.0
IV. Liabilities	199.7	150.3	129.0	21.0	25.1	22.9	90.6	88.3	87.8
1. Short-term[e]	59.0	54.3	50.2	1.6	1.2	1.6	62.5	55.2	54.9
2. Long-term[f]	140.7	95.9	78.8	19.4	23.8	21.3	28.1	33.1	32.8
V. Net worth	-99.8	-50.3	-29.0	79.0	74.9	77.1	9.4	11.7	12.2
VI. Total assets ($billion)	122.0	175.2	258.2	155.9	297.3	580.3	446.8	754.5	1,460.8

SOURCE: Appendix I.

a Covers only foundations and educational institutions.

b Agricultural and nonagricultural businesses.

c Excludes military assets.

d Excludes state and local government pension funds, which are included in cols. 19–21.

e Includes miscellaneous liabilities.

f Mortgages only in cols. 1–9.

g Mostly equity in unincorporated business enterprises at value of their net worth (line V, cols. 7–9).

h Only currency and demand deposits.

i Only financial assets primarily associated with business activities; hence excludes securities and insurance claims of proprietors.

j Bonds only.

k Intercorporate stockholdings excluded.

l Includes currency and demand deposits (1952: 30.8 percent; 1960: 20.2 percent; 1968: 14.5 percent).

TABLE 3-18

Structure of Balance Sheet of Unincorporated Farm and Nonfarm Business
Enterprises, 1952, 1960, and 1968

(*percent, except line VI*)

	Farm Enterprises			Nonfarm Enterprises		
	1952	1960	1968	1952	1960	1968
	(1)	(2)	(3)	(4)	(5)	(6)
I. Tangible assets	94.3	95.7	96.6	82.0	84.4	88.4
1. Land	46.0	49.7	55.3	12.0	13.7	12.6
2. Reproducible assets	48.3	46.0	41.3	70.0	70.7	75.8
a. Structures	20.0	20.8	18.2	25.7[a]	28.5[a]	43.7[a]
b. Producer durables	12.6	12.9	12.4	28.7	29.1	21.8
c. Inventories[b]	15.9	12.3	10.7	15.6	13.2	10.2
II. Financial assets	5.7	4.1	3.4	17.8	15.5	11.6
1. Short-term claims	4.9	3.1	2.2	15.9	13.2	9.3
2. Miscellaneous assets	0.8	1.0	1.2	1.9	2.3	2.3
III. Total assets	100.0	100.0	100.0	100.0	100.0	100.0
IV. Liabilities	9.5	12.6	18.6	13.6	20.1	26.8
1. Short-term	4.6	5.8	8.6	4.7	9.9	10.8
2. Long-term[c]	4.9	6.8	10.0	8.9	10.2	16.0
V. Net worth	90.5	87.4	81.4	86.4	79.9	73.2
VI. Total assets ($billion)	146	187	276	90	133	229

SOURCE: Appendix I.
[a] Of which residential structures: 16.4; 16.3; 26.6.
[b] Including livestock.
[c] Mortgages.

funds of financial institutions forms the subject of section 5 of this
chapter.

1. The main change in the structure of the balance sheet of the household sector is the increase in the share of corporate stock from 13 percent
at the end of 1952 to 25 percent in 1968, a change completely due to the
rise in stock prices during the period, as households showed a net sales
balance of stock for the period as a whole.

2. Apart from the effects of the increase in stock prices on the distribution of assets of households some interest attaches to the increase in the
share of short-term claims, mainly claims against financial institutions;
the decline in the share of residential structures in contrast to the increase

in the share of land, which again reflects a price movement; the possibly unexpected decline in the share of consumer durables, which is attributable to the relatively slower rise in their prices; and to the modest increase in the debt-asset ratio, both for consumer credit and for home mortgages.

3. In agriculture the main changes on the asset side are the sharp increase in the share of land from 46 to 55 percent, reflecting a rapid increase in prices, and the proportionally even sharper decline in the share of livestock and other inventories. At the same time the debt-asset ratio, which had fallen to historically very low levels during World War II, doubled between 1952 and 1968, both for short- and for long-term liabilities.

4. Changes in the structure of assets of unincorporated nonfarm business enterprises were dominated by the sharp increase in the share of structures in the 1960's, mainly reflecting the rapid acceleration of multifamily residential construction. This development is also responsible for most of the rapid increase in mortgage debt in the 1961–68 period. The proportionally very pronounced decline in the share of producer durables, inventories, and liquid assets reflects the relatively low rate of growth of unincorporated nonfarm enterprises outside the real estate field.

5. Changes in the structure of the balance sheets of nonfinancial corporations were relatively small. The sharp increase in the share of land, of course, again reflects price movements. The declining share of structures continues a long-term trend.

6. The outstanding feature in the changes in the structure of the federal government is the reduction of the debt-asset ratio by one-third and the even sharper reduction in the long-term debt ratio, the result of a relatively small expansion of the absolute volume of debt in the face of a substantial increase in both the volume and price of assets.

7. Changes are again relatively small in the structure of the balance sheets of state and local government over the period as a whole, a substantial increase in the debt-asset ratio during the first period being partly undone in the second subperiod.

8. In the financial sector the main changes, at the high level of aggregation of Table 3-17, are a sharp increase, from 8 to 17 percent, in the share of corporate stock in assets; the reduction in the share of short-term claims in total assets from nearly 40 to 30 percent, mainly during the first subperiod; and the halving of the share of monetary liabilities in total liabilities and net worth, also primarily occurring during the first subperiod. These two changes reflect the much lower rate of growth of the

assets of the banking system compared to nonbank financial institutions during the first subperiod, a development which did not continue during the second subperiod.

3. THE DETERMINANTS OF NEW ISSUES AND TOTAL ASSETS OF FINANCIAL INSTITUTIONS

It remains to inquire briefly into the relation of some basic economic factors to the volume of new issues by financial institutions and the size of their total assets in the postwar period. These factors have been selected because statistics are available for them and the algebraic relations are simple, but they are only the immediate statistical determinants of the two magnitudes studied—new issues and assets of financial institutions. Each of them is, in turn, dependent on many other factors. An exploration of these ultimate factors would be necessary for an understanding of the level and movements of issues and assets of financial institutions, but such an inquiry would go far beyond the boundaries of this summary survey.

In Table 3-19 the decomposition of the change in assets of financial institutions discussed in Chapter 1 is applied to flow of funds data for the period 1952 through 1969. This means that the ratio of the change in the issues of financial institutions (monetary authorities, commercial banks, nonbank financial institutions, and federally sponsored lending agencies as defined in the flow of funds statistics) to gross national product is regarded as the sum of two ratios: (1) the ratio of the change in money outstanding to gross national product and (2) the ratio to national product of the change in household thrift deposits and claims against insurance organizations plus household purchases of open-end investment company stock. These two numerators leave (3) a rather heterogeneous remainder that includes, among other things, the issues of financial institutions other than the banking system, insurance organizations and investment companies, the issues of financial institutions to nonhouseholds (including, e.g., the recently important large certificates of deposit and Eurodollars), and changes in the net worth of all corporate financial institutions. The second ratio, in turn, is the product of four ratios: the ratio of personal disposable income to gross national product (p); the ratio of gross saving (as defined in the national accounts) to personal disposable income (s); the ratio of the acquisition of financial assets by households to their personal saving (c); and the ratio of the change in thrift deposits, claims against insurance organizations, and acquisitions of open-end investment companies stock to the net acquisition of financial assets (t).

TABLE 3-19

Determinants of New-Issue Ratio of
Financial Institutions, 1952–69

	Aggre-gate-Issue Ratio[a] (1)	Money-Issue Ratio[b] (2)	Household Claims Against Financial Institutions					Residual (1) − (2 + 3) (8)
			Total[c] (3)	p (4)	s (5)	c (6)	t (7)	
				Annual Data				
1952	7.93	1.90	4.72	.69	22.0	.42	0.74	1.31
1953	6.42	0.00	4.52	.69	22.4	.39	0.75	1.90
1954	7.62	1.23	4.85	.71	21.2	.37	0.87	1.54
1955	7.59	0.58	4.50	.69	22.4	.41	0.71	2.51
1956	6.30	0.43	4.78	.70	22.8	.41	0.73	1.09
1957	6.17	0.16	5.08	.70	22.3	.37	0.88	0.93
1958	8.41	1.30	5.55	.71	21.4	.43	0.85	1.56
1959	6.76	0.30	5.05	.70	21.5	.43	0.78	1.41
1960	7.25	0.02	4.98	.69	20.6	.34	1.03	2.25
1961	9.65	1.08	5.97	.70	20.8	.41	1.00	2.60
1962	10.42	0.80	6.88	.69	21.3	.45	1.04	2.74
1963	10.50	0.98	6.55	.69	21.1	.50	0.90	2.97
1964	10.64	1.17	6.45	.69	22.4	.48	0.87	3.02
1965	11.05	1.11	6.84	.69	23.0	.49	0.88	3.10
1966	8.58	0.35	5.62	.68	23.7	.42	0.83	2.61
1967	11.20	1.80	7.02	.69	23.8	.47	0.91	2.38
1968	11.35	1.24	5.89	.68	24.0	.41	0.88	4.22
1969	8.50	0.71	3.99	.68	23.3	.34	0.74	3.80
				Cycle Averages[d]				
1953–57	6.95	0.58	4.73	.70	22.2	.39	0.78	1.64
1957–60	7.29	0.56	5.21	.70	21.5	.41	0.86	1.52
1960–69	10.14	0.99	6.19	.69	22.5	.44	0.91	2.96
1960–65	10.07	0.92	6.35	.69	21.7	.45	0.95	2.80
1965–69	10.23	1.08	5.99	.69	23.7	.43	0.86	3.17
				Period Average				
1952–69	8.69	0.84	5.51	.69	22.2	.42	0.86	2.33

Notes to Table 3-19

p = ratio of personal disposable income to gross national product.
s = gross personal saving divided by personal disposable income (percent).
c = ratio of acquisition of financial assets by households to personal saving.
t = ratio of change in household claims against financial institutions to acquisition of
    claims by households.
SOURCE: Basic data from *Flow of Funds Accounts*.
  [a] Increase in liabilities of financial institutions plus sales of investment-company stock
divided by gross national product (percent).
  [b] Change in demand deposits and currency divided by GNP (percent).
  [c] Change in household claims against financial institutions plus sales of investment-
company stock divided by GNP (percent).
  [d] First and last years of cycle given half weight of other years in cycle.

For the seventeen-year period 1952–69 the aggregate-issue ratio averaged about 9 percent, ranging from 6.2 to 11.3 percent (see Table 3-19).
The money-issue ratio fluctuated without a definite trend from − 0.2 to
+ 1.9 percent with an average of about 0.85 percent for the entire period.
The ratio of changes in thrift deposits, claims against insurance organizations, and acquisition of stock of open-end investment companies to gross
national product averaged about $5\frac{1}{2}$ percent with a low of 4.6 and a high
of 6.9 percent and a slow upward trend over the period. As a result, the
remainder term averaged about $2\frac{1}{2}$ percent, ranging between 1.1 and
4.0 percent and also showing an upward trend. The sharp rise in the
second half of the 1960's is partly due to the greatly increased importance
of large certificates of deposit, commercial paper by banks, holding
companies, and Eurodollar deposits. The irregular movements of the
residual are, in part, a reflection of its heterogeneous character and the
fact that it absorbs all errors in the other three terms.

Of the four components of ratio (2), above, the first, p, averaged slightly
under 70 percent with only small fluctuations from year to year and without a trend. Fluctuations were also fairly small in the gross personal saving
ratio (s), which ranged from 20.6 to 23.8 percent with an average of
about 22 percent and only a very mild and not very definite upward
trend. Annual fluctuations were considerably larger in the two other
components: c averaged about 42 percent, fluctuating between 34 and 49
percent. Similarly, t, which had an average for the period as a whole of
90 percent, fluctuated between a low of 74 and a high of 103 percent. As
a result, ratio (2) showed an upward trend from about $4\frac{1}{2}$ percent in the
early 1950's to about $6\frac{1}{2}$ percent in the 1960's.

The crucial feature of the increasing trend in the new-issue ratio of
financial institutions in the postwar period, then, are the movements in the

share of saving through financial institutions (disregarding check deposits with commercial banks). These were sharply upward from the early 1950's to the peak of 1960–62, when saving through nonmonetary financial institutions came to account for the totality of personal financial saving; then slowly downward with troughs in 1966 and 1969, two years of marked "disintermediation" accompanying extraordinarily high levels of interest rates on marketable fixed-interest-bearing securities.

There is some indication that part, if not most, of the changes in the ratios are associated with business cycle movements. The relationship, however, is not very definite, which is not astonishing, since only annual data are used and the postwar recessions were relatively short and did not coincide with calendar years. All that can possibly be said is that the total aggregate-issue ratio as well as most of its components are positively associated with the business cycles, showing in general the highest values during the upswing. However, these values are reached in some cases in the earlier, and in others in the later, phases of the upswing. One component, however, saving through thrift deposits, claims against insurance organizations, and open-end investment company shares, is inversely related to the business cycle, reaching its highest values usually in or close to recession years. Using econometric methods, an attempt is made, in Chapter 5, section 2, to relate some of these series to each other and to broad economic factors such as interest rates.

Since most of the assets of financial institutions consist of claims that do not vary in market value or are subject only to relatively small fluctuations (fluctuations, moreover, that are not reflected in the customary statistics), the value of reported assets is essentially equal to the sum of past net acquisitions of assets, a magnitude which in turn is equal to the cumulation of net issues broadly defined to include retained earnings. An explanation of the level and movements of net issues acquired by financial institutions thus provides at the same time most of the explanation of the trend in assets of financial institutions.

This assertion must be qualified because in the postwar period financial institutions have held an increasing proportion of their assets in the form of corporate stock, which is subject to considerable price fluctuations. The share of corporate stocks in total assets rose from 7 percent at the end of 1951 to 17 percent in 1966 if personal trust funds are included, while the advance was from 3 to 11 percent if they are excluded, as in the flow of funds statistics used here. As a result, part of the change in the reported value of the assets of financial institutions reflects changes in stock prices rather than net purchases. This part may be estimated at one-eighth of the total reported increase in assets for the whole period 1952–68 if personal trust funds are included and at one-twelfth if they are excluded. Since stock prices have fluctuated considerably over this period as has the intensity of net purchases of stocks by financial institutions, and since the ratio of stocks to total assets varies for the different types of financial institution, the relative importance of the change in stock prices has fluctuated sharply over time and as between institutions.

4. THE SUPPLY OF CORPORATE STOCK

The outstanding characteristic of the supply of stock of nonfinancial corporations during the postwar period is its very low absolute and relative level. For the entire seventeen-year period from 1952 through 1968, gross issues of corporate stock averaged approximately $3.5 billion. Because retirements amounted to nearly $2 billion per year, the annual increase in the net supply of stock was only about $1½ billion. Gross cash issues alone averaged about $2½ billion per year, while annual net cash issues were below $1 billion. The proportion of stock issued by financial corporations (other than investment companies, which are excluded from all these statistics) is so small that the figures can be regarded as applicable as well to nonfinancial corporations alone. More details and annual data for these issues will be found in Chapter 4, section 1.

How small these figures are becomes evident when they are compared on the one hand with the total value of outstanding stock and on the other with the relevant figures from the balance sheets and flow of funds statements of nonfinancial corporations, or when they are compared with the historical record for the period before World War II (see Table 3-20).

The net additions to the supply of corporate stock during the postwar period averaged approximately one-half of 1 percent of the value of outstanding corporate stock,[9] compared to rates of between 8 and 11 percent for other important financial instruments except U.S. government securities (Table 3-16). These ratios are very low compared to either the period between the turn of the century and World War I or that of the 1920's, during both of which the average volume of net stock issues was on the order of 2 percent of the average market value of all corporate stock outstanding.[10]

[9] The figure of 1.6 percent of Table 3-20, line I-3, is considerably higher because it does not allow for the sharp rise in stock prices over this period.

[10] Based on net issues and estimates of value of corporate stock outstanding in Goldsmith, Lipsey, and Mendelson, *Studies in the National Balance Sheet*, Vol. II, p. 72 ff.

TABLE 3-20

Growth of Supply of Main Types of Financial Instruments, 1952–68

(*percent per year*[a])

	1952–60 (1)	1961–68 (2)	1952–68 (3)
I. Corporate stock			
1. Value of stock outstanding including investment companies	9.70	12.04	10.80
2. Value of stock outstanding excluding investment companies	9.54	11.74	10.65
3. Value of cumulated issues[b] including investment companies	1.71	1.37	1.55
4. Value of cumulated issues[b] excluding investment companies	1.34	0.42	0.90
II. Claims			
1. Seven main types	6.15	7.34	6.71
2. U.S. government securities	1.14	3.12	2.06
3. State and local government securities	10.84	8.03	9.51
4. Corporate bonds	7.61	7.66	7.64
5. Home mortgages	11.82	7.46	9.74
6. Other mortgages	9.22	12.71	10.85
7. Consumer credit	10.55	9.15	9.89
8. Bank loans n.e.c.	8.41	10.45	9.37

Sources: *Flow of Funds Accounts 1945–1968; Federal Reserve Bulletin*, November 1969.
[a] Geometric rate of increase between beginning and end of period.
[b] Value of stock outstanding at beginning of period plus net issues during period.

In Table 3-21 annual net new issues of stock in the postwar period are compared with bond issues and other external financing by nonfinancial corporations, on the basis both of absolute figures and of ratios to gross national product, in order to eliminate the influence of the strong upward trend in national product. The table also shows the value (market value for stocks; face value for other issues) of issues outstanding throughout this period.

It is immediately evident that for most individual years as well as for the period as a whole, the sharp increase in the value of corporate stock outstanding is due predominantly to the rise in stock prices rather than to

TABLE 3-21

The Supply of Stock of Nonfinancial Corporations, 1952–68

	Issues Outstanding[a] ($billion)				Net New Issues ($billion)				Issues Outstanding[a] (percent of GNP)		Net New Issues (percent of GNP)	
	Total (1)	Stocks[b] (2)	Bonds (3)	Other Debt (4)	Total (5)	Stocks (6)	Bonds (7)	Other Debt (8)	Total (9)	Stocks (10)	Total (11)	Stocks (12)
1952	318.3	152.8	44.1	121.4	11.2	2.3	4.9	4.0	92.1	44.2	3.24	.67
1953	325.1	151.2	48.1	125.8	9.7	1.8	3.9	4.0	89.2	41.5	2.66	.49
1954	392.1	213.7	51.3	127.1	5.8	1.6	3.3	0.9	107.5	58.6	1.59	.44
1955	459.4	257.9	54.1	147.4	25.0	1.9	2.8	20.3	115.4	64.8	6.28	.48
1956	477.2	259.2	57.8	160.2	18.6	2.3	3.7	12.6	113.8	61.8	4.44	.55
1957	450.7	222.0	64.3	164.4	13.0	2.4	6.5	4.1	102.2	50.3	2.95	.54
1958	560.2	318.5	70.1	171.6	14.8	2.1	5.8	6.9	125.2	71.2	3.30	.47
1959	613.9	351.3	73.0	189.6	22.8	2.2	2.8	17.8	127.9	72.6	4.71	.45
1960	623.4	348.4	76.3	198.7	13.8	1.6	3.3	8.9	123.8	69.2	2.74	.32
1961	722.7	444.5	80.9	197.3	20.8	2.5	4.6	13.7	139.0	85.5	4.00	.48
1962	691.1	390.4	85.3	215.4	22.9	0.6	4.4	17.9	123.3	69.7	4.01	.11
1963	822.2	496.9	89.6	235.7	23.7	-0.3	4.4	19.6	139.2	84.1	4.01	-.05
1964	914.3	567.9	94.7	251.7	22.4	1.4	5.1	15.9	144.6	89.8	3.54	.22
1965	999.3	616.6	99.5	283.2	35.9	0.0	4.8	31.1	145.9	90.0	5.24	.00
1966	988.4	566.8	110.2	311.4	39.9	1.2	10.7	28.0	131.8	75.6	5.32	.16
1967	1,191.2	738.2	125.0	328.0	33.2	2.3	14.9	16.0	150.1	93.0	4.18	.29
1968	1,328.8	828.9	136.8	363.1	46.2	-0.8	11.8	35.2	153.5	95.7	5.34	-.09

SOURCES: *Flow of Funds Accounts 1945–1968*. Cols. 6–8: *Flow of Funds Accounts, 4th Quarter 1969*.
[a] Market value at end of year (Appendix I).
[b] Excluding intercorporate holdings.

net new issues. At $25 billion, the latter are dwarfed by the increase of about $700 billion in the value of stock outstanding.

Similarly, the amounts raised by nonfinancial corporations through the sale of stock are very small compared to their aggregate or total external financing. Thus, for the entire period 1952–68, gross issues of stock accounted for only 6 percent of total sources of funds of nonfinancial corporations and for about 16 percent of total external financing. Since retirements were equal to about three-fifths of gross issues, the share of net issues of corporate stock in total sources of funds of nonfinancial corporations was below 3 percent and even their contribution to external financing was as low as about 7 percent. Moreover, there was a sharp decline in both ratios between the 1950's (1952–59) and the 1960's (1960–68). During the 1950's gross issues of corporate stock accounted for about $7\frac{1}{2}$ percent of total financing and 17 percent of external financing of nonfinancial corporations, while the contribution of net issues to total financing was about 5 percent and that to external financing 13 percent, retirements accounting for somewhat less than one-third of gross new issues. In the 1960's, on the other hand, gross issues contributed less than 5 percent to total financing and less than 15 percent to external financing, and the net contribution of corporate stock to financing amounted to not much over 1 percent of total sources of funds and to only about 3 percent of external financing, since retirements were equal to about four-fifths of gross new issues. These data are presented in greater detail in Chapter 4.

There is no satisfactory explanation for the extraordinarily low level of the issuance and the net increase in the supply of corporate stock in the period 1952–68, although numerous partial explanations have been advanced. Prominent among these are the tax advantages of debt financing, interest being deductible from corporate income but dividends not; the relatively high level of internal financing, particularly through rapidly increasing depreciation allowances following the liberalization in tax legislation in the early 1960's; the aversion of many managers to the dilution of stockholders' equity by issuing new stock at prices that are regarded as being below their intrinsic value (e.g., the reproduction cost of assets less liabilities), a situation particularly common during the earlier part of the period when stock prices were low; a disinclination to share control with new or outside stockholders, a factor applicable primarily to closely held and smaller corporations; and the high cost of issuing stock, particularly in small amounts.[11] An attempt to explore a new approach

[11] Securities and Exchange Commission, *Cost of Flotation of Registered Equity Issues, 1963–1965*, May 1970.

to the explanation of this remarkable phenomenon is made in sections 2, 3, and 5 of Chapter 4. One of the results of this attempt is negative; the other two are positive.

On the negative side it proved impossible to establish econometrically definite and reliable relationships between, on the one hand, gross issues, retirements, and net issues of stock by nonfinancial corporations, and on the other, economic factors such as changes in national product, in corporate capital expenditures or profits, in prices, and in yields on bonds or stocks. Given the limited resources available for this aspect of the investigation, the failure may be due to an insufficient amount of experimentation with alternative sets of data or alternative methods of econometric analysis; or to insufficient disaggregation, i.e., the limitation to totals for very large groups of corporations and the impossibility of separating straight preferred stock, convertible preferred stock, and common stock issues; or it may be due to the use of only annual data; or to peculiarities of the period 1952–68. It is entirely possible, however, that econometric explanations of corporate stock issues in this period will remain unsatisfactory until, and even after, we are in a position to compare individual corporations that have issued stock with those, otherwise similar, that have not found it necessary or advisable to resort to equity or to any external financing. An attempt in this direction, necessarily on a small scale, has been made in Chapter 4, section 5.

Of positive value is, first, the hypothesis suggested by the econometric analysis—a hypothesis which will need further and more extensive testing—that the sale of corporate stock for cash (in contradistinction to exchange issues) has in the postwar period been regarded by corporate management in most industries as the least desirable form of financing, to be resorted to only when debt financing, short or long, public or private, is impossible. This hypothesis, of course, is entirely compatible with the sudden sharp increase in cash offerings of stock by nonfinancial corporations in 1969 and 1970 when corporate profits declined and debt financing became extraordinarily difficult and expensive.

The second positive result of the econometric analysis concerns the cash retirements of stock. These were found to be positively correlated with both the total volume of internal financing and with stock prices if all three variables are measured in terms of the deviation of the annual values from their trend values for the period 1952–67. Stocks retired through exchange for debt securities of other corporations were found to be positively though weakly correlated to an index of merger activity in the American economy.

It is worth noting that the volume of issues of corporate stock has turned up sharply since the end of the period studied. Thus, the cash offerings of corporate stock in 1969 shot up to over $9 billion, 50 percent above the volume of 1968, more than $2\frac{1}{2}$ times that of the 1963–67 average, and almost three times as high as the issues of any year during the postwar period before 1968. The new higher level of issues of corporate stock continued in 1970, the volume of issues reaching that of 1969.[12] Even more dramatic is the increase in net new issues (all issues less retirements) from less than $1 billion a year in 1963–67—and a negative figure of about $1 billion in 1968—to $4.3 billion in 1969 and an expected fully $5 billion in 1970.[13] These figures nevertheless are equal to only about three-quarters of 1 percent a year of the market value of all corporate stock outstanding, a ratio which is still well below the 2 percent level prevailing in the first decade of the century and during the 1920's.

It remains to be seen whether this sudden upward surge in the issuance of corporate stock in 1969 and 1970 is a temporary phenomenon, associated with the credit stringency and the extremely high cost of debt financing, or whether it presages a sharp change in the methods of financing nonfinancial corporations and in the share of corporate stock in the total issuance of financial instruments.

While it is thus not yet possible to provide a satisfactory explanation of the basic factors responsible for the low volume of new issues of corporate stock during the postwar period and to allocate the responsibility among them, it may be worthwhile to put the new issues of corporate stock of nonfinancial corporations into a broader framework, following the suggestion made in Chapter 1. This approach treats the ratio of net issues of stock of nonfinancial corporations to gross national product—a ratio which may be regarded as possibly the least objectionable simple measure of the importance of these issues in the economy—as being the result of four relationships: the share of the issues of corporate stock in total external financing of nonfinancial corporations; the relationship of total external financing to the capital expenditures of nonfinancial corporations—a relationship which assumes that capital expenditures are one of the important factors determining the volume of external financing; the share of nonfinancial corporations in national gross capital formation; and finally the well-known national capital formation ratio, i.e., the proportion of total gross capital formation to gross national product. Of course,

---

[12] Bankers Trust Company, *The Investment Outlook for 1970*, New York, 1969, Table 11.
[13] Actual issues during the first half of 1970 were running at an annual rate of $5\frac{1}{2}$ billion. (*Flow of Funds . . . 2nd Quarter 1970.*)

such a breakdown is useful only if some of the ratios are relatively stable or if they follow a reasonably simple pattern so that movements of the ratio in which we are interested—here the proportion of stock issues of nonfinancial corporations to national product—depend chiefly on the movements of one or two other factors. Annual data on these ratios are given in the upper part of Table 3-22; the lower part shows the average values for business cycles that can be distinguished in the 1952–68 period.[14]

We find that during the period from 1952 through 1968 the national gross capital formation ratio averaged 28.1 percent, while the share of nonfinancial corporations in national capital formation averaged 28.0 percent, so that the average ratio of gross capital formation of nonfinancial corporations to gross national product was 7.9 percent. Since the share of external financing in gross capital formation of nonfinancial corporations averaged 50.7 percent, and the share of net issues of corporate stock in total external financing of nonfinancial corporations amounted, on the average, to 10.2 percent, the ratio of net issues of stock of nonfinancial corporations to gross national product averaged 0.4 percent.

Two of the four ratios that determine the proportion of stock issues by nonfinancial corporations to gross national product, namely, the national capital formation ratio and the relationship between external financing of nonfinancial corporations and their capital expenditures (columns 1 and 4 in Table 3-22), show no trend over the period, as can be seen from the stability of the cycle averages. On the other hand, a slight upward trend appears in the share of nonfinancial corporations in national capital formation, the proportion rising from 26 percent for the first cycle, to 33 percent in 1965–68, though it is doubtful whether this trend will continue. If the other three ratios are stable, such a trend implies an increase in the proportion of stock issues of nonfinancial corporations to national product. The sharp decline observed in the ratio of nonfinancial corporations' stock issues to national product (Table 3-22, column 7)—from 0.50 percent in the first cycle to 0.09 percent in 1965–68 or 0.15 percent in 1960–68—is due entirely to the fall in the share of corporate stock in the external financing of nonfinancial corporations (Table 3-22, column 6) from 17 percent in the first cycle to only 2 percent in 1965–68. Thus, the decline in the ratio of nonfinancial corporations' stock issues to

[14] The dating of business cycles follows the annual chronology of the National Bureau of Economic Research. The long cycle starting in 1960 and probably ending in 1969 has been split in two at the end of 1964 because of the very different character of the capital market, in general, and the market for corporate stock, in particular, in the two periods.

TABLE 3-22

The Determinants of the Ratio of Corporate Share Issues to Gross
National Product, 1952–68

	$\dfrac{k_n}{y}$ (1)	$\dfrac{k_c}{k_n}$ (2)	$\dfrac{k_c}{y}$ (3)	$\dfrac{e}{k_c}$ (4)	$\dfrac{e}{y}$ (5)	$\dfrac{a}{e}$ (6)	$\dfrac{a}{y}$ (7)
				Annual Data			
1952	.272	.260	.071	.425	.030	.221	.0067
1953	.267	.253	.067	.337	.023	.217	.0049
1954	.268	.221	.059	.268	.016	.276	.0044
1955	.303	.262	.079	.794	.063	.076	.0048
1956	.300	.286	.086	.515	.044	.124	.0055
1957	.291	.270	.079	.368	.023	.188	.0054
1958	.261	.234	.061	.538	.033	.143	.0047
1959	.281	.272	.076	.623	.047	.096	.0046
1960	.278	.279	.078	.351	.027	.117	.0032
1961	.267	.264	.070	.572	.040	.119	.0048
1962	.278	.283	.079	.525	.041	.026	.0011
1963	.282	.274	.077	.507	.039	−.013	−.0005
1964	.286	.287	.082	.408	.033	.066	.0022
1965	.297	.309	.092	.580	.053	.000	.0000
1966	.295	.348	.103	.510	.053	.030	.0016
1967	.277	.330	.091	.455	.041	.070	.0029
1968	.277	.321	.089	.615	.055	−.017	−.0009
				Cycle Averages[a]			
1953–57	.288	.258	.075	.483	.037	.170	.0050
1957–60	.276	.260	.072	.507	.036	.131	.0045
1960–68	.283	.299	.085	.505	.043	.044	.0017
1960–65	.280	.280	.079	.496	.039	.051	.0018
1965–68	.286	.331	.095	.521	.049	.030	.0013
				Period Average			
1952–68	.281	.280	.079	.494	.039	.102	.0033

y = gross national product;
k_n = national gross capital formation;
k_c = corporate gross national formation;
e = total issues of nonfinancial corporations;
a = stock issues of nonfinancial corporations.
SOURCE: Basic data from *Flow of Funds Accounts 1945–1968*.
[a] First and last years of cycle given half weight of other years in cycle.

national product is due to the change, permanent or otherwise, in the method of external financing of corporations, not to changes in the national capital formation ratio, the share of nonfinancial corporations in national capital formation, or the relationship between external financing and capital expenditures of nonfinancial corporations.

On an annual basis the national capital formation ratio, the share of nonfinancial corporations in national capital formation, and the relationship between nonfinancial corporations' capital expenditures and their external financing were all high late in the upswing (1955–56, 1959, 1965–66). As a result the ratio of total external financing by nonfinancial corporations to national product (Table 3-22, column 5) was then at a high level: 5.4 percent in 1955–56, 5.3 percent in 1965–66, and 4.7 percent in 1959 in the weak upswing of 1957–60. The share of corporate stock in the total external financing of nonfinancial corporations was highest in 1954, 1957, 1961 and 1967, i.e., in the recession or early in the upswing. As a result, the movements of the ratio of nonfinancial corporations' stock issues to national product showed little relationship to the cycle either during the 1950's or the 1960's, although during the second period they were at a much lower average (4.9 percent for the period 1952–61 against 0.9 percent for 1962–68).

5. THE POSITION OF FINANCIAL INSTITUTIONS IN HOLDINGS OF
AND TRANSACTIONS IN CORPORATE STOCK

Since the stock portfolios of the main types of financial institutions will be discussed in Chapter 5, section 3, and statistics of the aggregate holdings and net purchases and sales of corporate stock by about twenty groups of financial institutions will be presented in Appendix I, it may suffice here to summarize the most important figures, both in the stock and the flow dimensions.

The basic figures for flows—the annual net purchases of all corporate stock by the main types of financial institutions for which primary data are available—are shown in Table 3-23. The distribution of the annual totals among main types of institutions is shown in Table 3-24. Table 3-25, which presents the ratio of annual net purchases or sales by each type of institution to the value of its stockholdings at the beginning of the year, indicates how rapidly the portfolios have been expanded. The annual net purchases of corporate stock are then related to all purchases of financial assets by these institutions to yield a ratio which indicates the proportion of the year's acquisition of financial assets that was allocated to corporate stock (Table 3-26); to all new net issues of corporate stock (Table 3-27);

TABLE 3-23

Net Purchases or Sales of Corporate Stock by Financial Institutions, 1952–69

(*$billion*)

	Total (1)	Mutual Savings Banks (2)	Life Insur- ance Com- panies (3)	Pension Funds		Other Insur- ance Com- panies (6)	Open- End Invest- ment Com- panies (7)
				Private (4)	State and Local Govern- ments (5)		
Annual Data							
1952	1.42	.11	0.16	0.48	0.02	0.18	0.47
1953	1.51	.10	0.09	0.55	0.02	0.19	0.56
1954	1.60	.14	0.27	0.71	0.02	0.16	0.30
1955	1.59	.08	0.07	0.74	0.03	0.16	0.51
1956	1.72	.05	−0.00	0.94	0.03	0.14	0.56
1957	2.24	.06	0.04	1.14	0.05	0.13	0.82
1958	2.74	.10	0.08	1.38	0.06	0.13	0.99
1959	3.53	−.05	0.19	1.74	0.08	0.27	1.30
1960	3.69	.02	0.35	1.95	0.09	0.26	1.02
1961	4.34	.07	0.47	2.26	0.15	0.26	1.13
1962	4.14	.15	0.43	2.20	0.20	0.25	0.91
1963	3.67	.12	0.25	2.17	0.21	0.16	0.76
1964	4.36	.10	0.55	2.21	0.27	0.10	1.13
1965	5.68	.17	0.71	3.12	0.35	0.09	1.24
1966	6.21	.04	0.27	3.68	0.49	0.39	1.34
1967	9.59	.22	1.06	4.99	0.67	0.59	2.06
1968	10.39	.25	1.43	4.71	1.28	1.07	1.65
1969	12.60	.30	1.60	4.90	1.80	1.50	2.50
Cycle Averages[a]							
1953–57	1.70	.09	0.10	0.81	0.03	0.16	0.52
1957–60	3.08	.03	0.16	1.56	0.07	0.20	1.07
1960–69	6.28	.14	0.68	3.20	0.51	0.42	1.33
1960–65	4.24	.11	0.45	2.28	0.21	0.19	1.01
1965–69	8.83	.19	0.98	4.35	0.88	0.71	1.73
Period Average							
1952–69	4.50	.11	0.45	2.22	0.32	0.34	1.07

NOTE: Sales are indicated by a minus sign.
SOURCE: Basic data from Appendix I.
[a] First and last years of cycle given half weight of other years in cycle.

TABLE 3-24

Distribution of Net Purchases or Sales of Corporate Stock by Financial
Institutions, 1952–69

(*percent*)

	Total (1)	Mutual Savings Banks (2)	Life Insur- ance Com- panies (3)	Pension Funds Private (4)	Pension Funds State and Local Govern- ments (5)	Other Insur- ance Com- panies (6)	Open- End Invest- ment Com- panies (7)
				Annual Data			
1952	100.0	7.7	11.3	33.8	1.4	12.7	33.1
1953	100.0	6.6	6.0	36.4	1.3	12.6	37.1
1954	100.0	8.8	16.9	44.4	1.3	10.0	18.8
1955	100.0	5.0	4.4	46.5	1.9	10.1	32.1
1956	100.0	2.9	0.0	54.6	1.7	8.1	32.6
1957	100.0	2.7	1.8	50.9	2.2	5.8	36.6
1958	100.0	3.6	2.9	50.4	2.2	4.7	36.1
1959	100.0	−1.4	5.4	49.3	2.2	7.6	36.8
1960	100.0	0.5	9.5	52.8	2.4	7.0	27.6
1961	100.0	1.6	10.8	52.1	3.5	6.0	26.0
1962	100.0	3.6	10.4	53.1	4.8	6.0	22.0
1963	100.0	3.3	6.8	59.1	5.7	4.4	20.7
1964	100.0	2.3	12.6	50.7	6.2	2.3	25.9
1965	100.0	3.0	12.5	54.9	6.2	1.6	21.8
1966	100.0	0.6	4.3	59.3	7.9	6.3	21.6
1967	100.0	2.3	11.1	52.0	7.0	6.2	21.5
1968	100.0	2.4	13.8	45.3	12.3	10.3	15.9
1969	100.0	2.4	12.7	38.9	14.3	11.9	19.8
				Cycle Averages[a]			
1953–57	100.0	5.4	6.3	47.3	1.7	9.4	30.1
1957–60	100.0	1.3	4.7	50.5	2.2	6.2	35.0
1960–69	100.0	2.3	10.4	52.5	6.9	5.8	22.1
1960–65	100.0	2.5	10.3	53.8	4.9	4.6	23.9
1965–69	100.0	2.0	10.5	50.9	9.4	7.4	20.0
				Period Average			
1952–69	100.0	3.2	8.5	49.1	4.7	7.4	27.0

NOTE: Sales are indicated by a minus sign.
SOURCE: Basic data from Appendix I.
[a] First and last years of cycle given half weight of other years in cycle.

TABLE 3-25

Growth of Stock Portfolio of Financial Institutions, 1952–69

(*percent*)

	Total (1)	Mutual Savings Banks (2)	Life Insurance Companies (3)	Pension Funds Private (4)	Pension Funds State and Local Governments (5)	Other Insurance Companies (6)	Open-End Investment Companies (7)
				Annual Data			
1952	13.4	55.0	7.3	34.3	—	4.6	16.2
1953	12.4	33.3	3.8	30.6	20.0	4.4	17.0
1954	11.9	35.0	10.4	29.6	20.0	3.6	8.6
1955	8.6	13.3	2.1	23.1	30.0	2.7	9.4
1956	7.1	7.1	—	15.4	30.0	2.0	8.1
1957	8.4	8.6	1.1	16.0	25.0	1.8	10.4
1958	10.5	12.5	2.4	18.4	30.0	1.9	13.4
1959	9.5	−5.6	4.6	15.0	26.7	3.2	11.1
1960	8.5	2.5	7.6	13.4	30.0	2.9	7.3
1961	9.3	8.8	9.4	13.7	37.5	2.8	7.6
1962	6.6	16.7	6.8	9.6	33.3	2.2	4.5
1963	6.2	12.0	4.0	9.9	26.3	1.4	4.2
1964	6.0	8.3	7.7	8.0	27.0	0.8	5.1
1965	6.9	13.1	9.0	9.3	26.9	0.6	5.2
1966	6.3	2.9	3.0	9.3	30.6	2.5	4.3
1967	10.3	14.7	12.0	13.0	31.9	4.3	7.1
1968	8.5	14.7	12.1	9.5	45.7	6.0	4.2
1969	8.8	15.8	12.1	8.2	43.9	8.3	5.4
				Cycle Averages[a]			
1953–57	9.5	19.1	3.8	22.9	25.6	2.9	10.0
1957–60	9.5	4.2	3.8	16.0	28.1	2.5	11.1
1960–69	7.6	11.2	8.2	10.3	32.9	2.9	5.4
1960–65	7.2	10.7	7.2	10.5	30.5	1.8	5.5
1965–69	8.3	11.7	9.4	10.1	35.9	4.3	5.2
				Period Average			
1952–69	8.8	14.9	6.4	15.9	28.6	3.1	8.3

SOURCE: Basic data from Appendix I.

[a] First and last years of cycle given half weight of other years in cycle.

TABLE 3-26

Ratio of Net Acquisition of Corporate Stock by Financial Institutions
to Their Total Acquisition of Financial Assets, 1952–68

(*percent*)

| | | Insurance Organizations | | | |
| | | Pension Funds | | | Open-End Investment Companies (6) |
	Mutual Savings Banks (1)	Life Insurance Companies (2)	Private (3)	State and Local Governments (4)	Other Insurance Companies (5)	
			Annual Data			
1952	5.6	4.3	27.8	0.0	15.4	80.0
1953	5.3	2.0	25.0	0.0	14.3	100.0
1954	4.5	5.9	33.3	0.0	18.2	75.0
1955	5.0	1.8	30.4	0.0	20.0	71.4
1956	5.0	0.0	33.3	0.0	16.7	75.0
1957	5.6	0.0	35.5	6.3	10.0	88.9
1958	3.8	1.9	43.8	6.7	8.3	83.3
1959	0.0	3.6	45.9	5.0	17.6	71.4
1960	0.0	7.0	47.5	4.3	25.0	72.7
1961	4.3	8.2	57.5	8.0	23.1	71.4
1962	3.0	5.9	52.4	8.0	10.5	78.6
1963	2.8	2.9	48.9	8.3	18.2	75.0
1964	2.2	6.4	44.9	10.7	10.0	63.6
1965	5.0	8.0	55.4	12.1	8.3	60.0
1966	0.0	3.6	60.7	12.5	19.0	40.0
1967	3.7	11.7	74.6	15.2	26.1	136.4
1968	6.5	15.1	73.4	30.2	32.4	60.0
			Cycle Averages[a]			
1953–57	5.0	2.2	31.8	0.8	16.8	79.0
1957–60	2.2	3.0	43.7	5.7	14.5	78.5
1960–68	3.0	7.2	56.9	11.5	18.0	73.9
1960–65	3.0	6.2	51.0	8.6	15.7	71.0
1965–68	3.2	9.0	66.6	16.3	21.8	78.8
			Period Average			
1952–68	3.7	5.2	46.5	7.5	17.2	76.6

SOURCE: Basic data from Appendix I.
[a] First and last years of cycle given half weight of other years in cycle.

TABLE 3-27

Ratio of Net Acquisitions of Corporate Stock by Financial Institutions
to All Net Issues of Corporate Stock, 1952–68

(*percent*)

			Pension Funds			Open-
		Life		State	Other	End
		Insur-		and	Insur-	Invest-
	Mutual	ance		Local	ance	ment
	Savings	Com-		Govern-	Com-	Com-
	Total	Banks	panies	Private	ments	panies	panies
	(1)	(2)	(3)	(4)	(5)	(6)	(7)
				Annual Data			
1952	45.1	3.5	5.1	15.2	0.6	5.7	14.9
1953	62.9	4.2	3.8	22.9	0.8	7.9	23.3
1954	60.4	5.3	10.2	26.8	0.8	6.0	11.3
1955	53.0	2.7	2.3	24.7	1.0	5.3	17.0
1956	44.2	1.3	0.0	24.2	0.8	3.6	14.4
1957	56.1	1.5	1.0	28.6	1.3	3.3	20.6
1958	63.9	2.3	1.9	32.2	1.4	3.0	23.1
1959	83.4	−1.2	4.4	40.6	1.9	6.3	30.3
1960	101.6	0.6	9.6	53.7	2.5	7.2	28.1
1961	70.1	1.1	7.6	36.5	2.4	4.2	18.3
1962	130.6	4.7	13.6	69.4	6.3	7.9	28.7
1963	269.9	8.8	18.4	159.6	15.4	11.8	55.9
1964	116.6	2.7	14.7	59.1	7.2	2.7	30.2
1965	171.6	5.1	21.5	94.3	10.6	2.7	37.5
1966	111.5	0.7	4.8	66.1	8.8	7.0	24.1
1967	137.4	3.2	15.2	71.5	9.6	8.5	29.5
1968	197.2	4.7	27.1	89.4	24.3	20.3	31.3
				Cycle Averages[a]			
1953–57	54.3	3.1	3.7	25.4	0.9	5.1	16.2
1957–60	75.4	0.7	3.9	38.0	1.7	4.9	25.9
1960–68	114.7	3.6	14.3	78.5	9.2	7.3	31.7
1960–65	144.8	4.0	14.0	79.7	7.6	6.3	33.2
1965–68	144.5	2.9	14.8	76.5	12.0	9.0	29.3
				Period Average			
1952–68	104.5	3.0	9.5	53.8	5.6	6.7	25.8

SOURCE: Basic data from Appendix I.
[a] First and last years of cycle given half weight of other years in cycle.

TABLE 3-28

Ratio of Net Acquisitions of Corporate Stock by Financial Institutions to Net Issues Excluding Intercorporate and Investment Company Issues, 1952–68

(*percent*)

				Pension Funds			Open-End Invest-ment Com-panies (7)
	Total (1)	Mutual Savings Banks (2)	Life Insur-ance Com-panies (3)	Private (4)	State and Local Govern-ments (5)	Other Insur-ance Com-panies (6)	
1952	54	4	6	19	1	7	17
1953	80	5	5	29	1	10	30
1954	78	7	13	35	1	8	15
1955	77	4	3	36	2	8	25
1956	65	2	0	35	1	5	21
1957	82	2	2	42	2	5	30
1958	111	4	3	56	2	5	40
1959	137	−2	7	68	3	11	51
1960	207	1	20	110	5	15	57
1961	146	2	16	76	5	9	38
1962	524	19	54	279	25	32	115
1963	−1,184	−39	−81	−700	−68	−52	−245
1964	357	8	45	181	22	8	93
1965	−1,721	−52	−215	−946	−106	−27	−376
1966	437	3	19	259	35	28	94
1967	415	10	46	216	29	26	89
1968	−1,423	−34	−196	−645	−175	−147	−226

SOURCE: Basic data from Appendix I.

and finally to the total value of all corporate stock outstanding, excluding intercorporate holdings and open-end investment company stock (Table 3-28). These ratios give an idea of the influence of net purchases and sales by financial institutions in the market for corporate stock.[15]

Similar information is provided on the stock dimensions of the holdings, at market value, of corporate stock of financial institutions. Thus, Table 3-29 shows the absolute values of the holdings at each year-end from 1951 through 1968; Table 3-30 expresses these figures as percentages of the holdings of all financial institutions, thus showing changes in the distribution of these holdings within the financial institutions sector; and Table 3-31 relates the holdings of corporate stock by the main types of financial institutions to total outstandings, again excluding intercorporate holdings and open-end investment company stock from the outstandings.

Since net purchase and sales balances of the different groups of financial institutions are substantially smaller than their gross purchases and sales, it is also necessary to appraise the intensity of stock trading of the different groups, i.e., the turnover ratio of their stock portfolios (Table 3-32), and to look at their share in the trading on the single most important market for stocks in the United States, the New York Stock Exchange (Table 3-33).

From this material the following main conclusions emerge regarding the role of financial institutions in the aggregate, and that of their main types, in the market for corporate stock.

1. The value of the corporate stock held by all financial institutions increased from about $35 billion at the end of 1951 to $250 billion in 1968 or at an average rate of slightly more than 12 percent a year.[16] The average rate of growth was more rapid in the 1950's (about 15 percent a year) than in the 1960's (about 11 percent a year).

2. Most of the increase in the value of stockholdings—about two-thirds to judge by the figures of the groups of institutions for which information on net purchases is available—reflected the rising level of stock prices

---

[15] All tables omit the groups of financial institutions without or with only small (in absolute amounts) holdings of corporate stock: commercial banks, savings and loan associations, credit unions, federal lending institutions, closed-end investment companies, brokers and dealers, mortgage companies, finance companies, and fraternal insurance organizations. Their omission does not affect the discussion, as their total stockholdings amount to only a small fraction of the group included in the tables (about 5 percent in 1968 although over 10 percent in 1954). The tables omit personal trust funds because no reliable information is available on them. However, rough estimates of the net purchases by personal trust funds, closed-end investment companies, and brokers and dealers are occasionally used in the text. The tables on holdings of stocks (Tables 3-29 to 3-31) include the first two of these three groups.

[16] By mid-1970 the figures were approximately $200 billion and 10 percent a year.

TABLE 3-29

Holdings of Corporate Stock by Financial Institutions, 1951–68

(*$billion*)

| | | Insurance Organizations | | | | | | | |
| | Total (1) | Life Insurance Companies (2) | Pension Funds | | Other Insurance Companies (5) | Open-End Investment Companies (6) | Other Investment Companies (7) | Mutual Savings Banks (8) | Personal Trust Funds (9) |
			Private (3)	State and Local Governments (4)					
1951	33.2	2.2	1.4	0.0	3.9	3.5	3.0	0.2	19.0
1952	36.3	2.4	1.8	0.1	4.3	3.4	3.2	0.3	20.8
1953	37.2	2.6	2.4	0.1	4.5	3.6	3.3	0.4	20.3
1954	51.1	3.3	3.2	0.1	5.9	5.5	4.7	0.6	27.8
1955	63.4	3.6	6.1	0.1	6.9	7.1	5.7	0.7	33.2
1956	67.8	3.5	7.1	0.2	7.2	8.0	5.2	0.7	35.9
1957	63.3	3.4	7.5	0.2	6.7	7.5	4.8	0.8	32.4
1958	85.7	4.1	11.6	0.3	8.4	11.8	5.6	0.9	43.0
1959	97.1	4.6	14.5	0.3	9.1	14.4	5.9	0.8	47.5

1960	102.0	5.0	16.5	0.4	9.4	15.5	5.9	0.8	48.5
1961	131.8	6.3	22.9	0.6	11.8	21.3	6.6	0.9	61.4
1962	124.8	6.3	21.9	0.8	11.1	19.6	6.5	1.0	57.6
1963	150.2	7.1	27.7	1.0	13.0	23.7	7.6	1.2	68.9
1964	164.8	7.9	33.5	1.3	14.7	25.8	7.8	1.3	72.5
1965	186.8	9.1	39.7	1.6	15.3	33.3	6.9	1.4	79.5
1966	178.3	8.8	38.5	2.1	13.8	31.1	6.5	1.5	76.0
1967	221.9	11.8	49.5	2.8	17.7	43.1	8.7	1.7	86.6
1968	252.7	13.2	59.6	4.1	18.1	50.5	9.4	1.9	95.9

SOURCES: *Flow of Funds Accounts* and Appendix I (for columns 7 and 9).

TABLE 3-30

Distribution of Holdings of Corporate Stock by Financial Institutions, 1951–68

(*percent*)

	Total (1)	Life Insurance Companies (2)	Insurance Organizations				Open-End Investment Companies (6)	Other Investment Companies (7)	Mutual Savings Banks (8)	Personal Trust Funds (9)
			Pension Funds		Other Insurance Companies (5)				
			Private (3)	State and Local Governments (4)					
1951	100.0	6.6	4.2	0.0	11.7	10.5	9.0	0.6	57.2
1952	100.0	6.6	5.0	0.3	11.8	9.4	8.8	0.8	57.3
1953	100.0	7.0	6.5	0.3	12.1	9.7	8.9	1.1	54.6
1954	100.0	6.5	6.3	0.2	11.5	10.8	9.2	1.2	54.4
1955	100.0	5.7	9.6	0.2	10.9	11.2	9.0	1.1	52.4
1956	100.0	5.2	10.5	0.3	10.6	11.8	7.7	1.0	52.9
1957	100.0	5.4	11.8	0.3	10.6	11.8	7.6	1.3	51.2
1958	100.0	4.8	13.5	0.4	9.8	13.8	6.5	1.1	50.2
1959	100.0	4.7	14.9	0.3	9.4	14.9	6.1	0.8	48.9

1960	100.0	4.9	16.2	0.4	9.2	15.2	5.8	0.8	47.5
1961	100.0	4.8	17.4	0.5	9.0	16.2	5.0	0.7	46.6
1962	100.0	5.0	17.5	0.6	8.9	15.7	5.2	0.8	46.2
1963	100.0	4.7	18.4	0.7	8.7	15.8	5.1	0.8	45.9
1964	100.0	4.8	20.3	0.8	8.9	15.7	4.7	0.8	44.0
1965	100.0	4.9	21.3	0.9	8.2	17.8	3.7	0.7	42.6
1966	100.0	4.9	21.6	1.2	7.7	17.4	3.6	0.8	42.6
1967	100.0	5.3	22.3	1.3	8.0	19.4	3.9	0.8	39.0
1968	100.0	5.2	23.6	1.6	7.2	20.0	3.7	0.8	38.0

SOURCE: Table 3-29.

TABLE 3-31

Ratio of Holdings of Corporate Stock[a] by Financial Institutions to Total Corporate Stock Outstanding, 1951–68

(*percent*)

		Insurance Organizations							
			Pension Funds						
	Total	Life Insurance Companies	Private	State and Local Governments	Other Insurance Companies	Open-End Investment Companies	Other Investment Companies	Mutual Savings Banks	Personal Trust Funds
	(1)	(2)	(3)	(4)	(5)	(6)	(7)	(8)	(9)
Annual Data									
1951	18.9	1.3	0.8	.0	2.3	1.7	1.3	.1	11.4
1952	19.9	1.3	1.0	.0	2.4	1.9	1.7	.2	11.4
1953	20.6	1.4	1.3	.0	2.5	2.0	1.8	.2	11.4
1954	20.6	1.3	1.3	.0	2.4	2.2	1.9	.2	11.3
1955	21.6	1.2	2.1	.0	2.4	2.4	1.9	.2	11.4
1956	23.0	1.2	2.4	.0	2.5	2.7	1.8	.2	12.2
1957	23.8	1.3	2.8	.1	2.5	2.8	1.8	.3	12.2
1958	22.7	1.1	3.1	.1	2.2	3.1	1.5	.2	11.4
1959	23.1	1.1	3.4	.1	2.2	3.4	1.4	.2	11.3

1960	24.2	1.2	3.9	.1	2.2	3.7	1.4	.2	11.5
1961	23.6	1.1	4.1	.1	2.1	3.8	1.2	.2	11.0
1962	26.2	1.3	4.6	.2	2.3	4.1	1.4	.2	12.1
1963	24.9	1.2	4.6	.2	2.1	3.9	1.3	.2	11.4
1964	24.2	1.2	4.9	.2	2.2	3.8	1.1	.2	10.6
1965	24.4	1.2	5.2	.2	2.0	4.3	0.9	.2	10.4
1966	25.6	1.3	5.5	.3	2.0	4.5	0.9	.2	10.9
1967	25.0	1.3	5.6	.3	2.0	4.8	1.0	.2	9.7
1968	24.0	1.3	5.6	.4	1.7	4.8	0.9	.2	9.1

Cycle Averages [b]

1953–57	21.9	1.3	2.0	.0	2.5	2.4	1.9	.2	11.7
1957–60	23.3	1.2	3.3	.1	2.3	3.3	1.5	.2	11.5
1960–68	24.8	1.2	4.9	.2	2.1	4.2	1.1	.2	10.8
1960–65	24.6	1.2	4.6	.2	2.2	3.9	1.2	.2	11.2
1965–68	24.9	1.3	5.5	.3	2.2	4.6	0.9	.2	10.1

Period Average

1952–68	23.1	1.2	3.5	.1	2.2	3.3	1.4	.2	11.2

Sources: Tables 3-23 and 3-29.
[a] Excluding investment-company shares.
[b] First and last years of cycle given half weight of other years in cycle.

Institutional Investors

TABLE 3-32

Common Stock Activity Rates, 1955–69

(*percent*)

	Noninsured Private Pension Funds	Open-End Investment Companies	Life Insurance Companies	Other Insurance Companies	New York Stock Exchange
1955	11.8	15.9	11.8	n.a.	17.0
1956	11.8	18.6	11.5	n.a.	14.0
1957	11.9	18.8	12.0	n.a.	13.0
1958	12.0	21.7	13.0	n.a.	14.0
1959	11.7	19.8	10.9	n.a.	15.0
1960	11.1	17.6	10.1	n.a.	12.4
1961	12.1	20.0	13.5	n.a.	15.2
1962	9.7	17.3	9.8	7.1	12.0
1963	11.0	18.6	11.2	7.8	13.1
1964	10.8	18.7	11.9	8.0	13.2
1965	11.3	21.2	13.6	8.2	14.5
1966	12.7	33.5	15.8	8.3	19.7
1967	18.2	42.3	18.5	9.9	25.8
1968	18.9	46.6	26.2	15.7	29.0
1969	22.3	49.8	28.1	26.1	32.7

n.a. = not available.
SOURCE: U.S. Securities and Exchange Commission, *Statistical Bulletin*, April 1970, p. 25.

over the period. Variations of stock prices have hardly any noticeable effect on the changes in assets of banks and thrift institutions but account in some years for a considerable proportion of the total variation in assets of institutions such as pension funds, non-life-insurance companies, investment companies, and personal trust funds.

3. The decisive increases occurred in two sectors, private pension funds, whose holdings rose dramatically from $1½ billion to $60 billion; and open-end investment companies, whose holdings shot up from $3 billion to $46 billion. In absolute amount the increase in the value of the holdings administered by personal trust funds was also very large—they are

TABLE 3-33

Distribution of Stock Trading on New York Stock Exchange

(total number of shares = 100)

| Date | Public Individuals (1) | NYSE Members (2) | Total (3) | Institutions and Intermediaries | | | |
				Commercial Banks[a] (4)	Brokers and Dealers[b] (5)	Investment Companies[c] (6)	Other (7)
Sept. 1952	57.0	18.4	24.6	7.1	4.6	3.9	9.0
March 1953	61.4	19.3	22.3	6.2	4.7	2.4	9.0
March 1954	56.4	20.1	23.5	7.5	4.3	2.7	9.0
Dec. 1954	62.3	20.2	17.5	5.3	3.9	1.4	6.9
June 1955	59.2	21.3	19.5	6.5	3.9	1.7	7.4
March 1956	58.9	21.0	20.1	6.8	3.7	2.2	7.4
Oct. 1957	54.3	22.4	23.3	8.8	3.4	2.0	9.2
Sept. 1958	55.8	21.3	22.9	5.7	3.4	13.8	
June 1959	53.5	23.7	22.8	9.2	3.2	10.4	
Sept. 1960	52.6	23.1	23.3	9.4	2.6	4.0	7.3
Sept. 1961	51.4	22.4	26.2				
May 1962	56.9	24.4	18.7				
Oct. 1963	53.4	22.7	23.9	9.0	2.6	4.8	7.5
March 1965	48.5	20.1	31.4				
Oct. 1966	43.2	24.3	32.5	12.6	2.0	8.4	9.6
Dec. 1969	33.4	24.2	42.2	15.9	3.1	12.3[d]	10.9[e]

SOURCES:
Cols. 1–3. 1952–62: NYSE, *Public Participation in the Stock Market*, May 1962.
1966, 1969: NYSE, *Public Transactions Study*, 1969.
Cols. 4–7. 1952–60: NYSE, *The Institutional Investor and the Stock Market*, 1960.
1963: NYSE, *Institutional Activity, Week of October 24, 1966*, 1966.
1966–69: NYSE, *Public Transactions Study*, 1969.

[a] Including trust departments.
[b] Excluding members of NYSE.
[c] Open-end companies only until 1960.
[d] Includes hedge funds (1.7).
[e] Includes insurance companies (2.1), nonbank trusts or estates (1.5), noninsured pension funds (2.1), and other (5.2).

estimated to have risen from slightly less than $20 billion to nearly $100 billion—but proportionately the rise was much smaller than for the other two leading groups and most of it, possibly more than four-fifths, was due to an increase in stock prices.

4. As a result radical changes occurred in the distribution of stock-holdings of financial institutions among their main groupings. The share of private pension funds rose from 5 to 25 percent while that of open-end investment companies advanced from 10 to nearly 20 percent. The sharpest decline occurred in the holdings administered by personal trust funds, whose share fell from almost two-thirds of the total in 1951 to only two-fifths in 1968. The share of non-life-insurance companies also declined substantially, from 13 to 8 percent, and a smaller reduction occurred in the share of life insurance companies. (This would disappear if the comparison were limited to common stock.)

5. From the point of view of the capital market the share of financial institutions in the total value of corporate stock outstanding (excluding intercorporate holdings and open-end investment companies and disregarding the small holdings of foreign stocks by financial institutions) is more important than the dollar value of holdings. This share rose from 18 to 24 percent, the advance being about equally divided among the 1950's and the 1960's. While this is a substantial rise it does not imply a radical change in the distribution of ownership of American corporations. However, since the share of corporate stock administered by personal trust funds declined slightly, sharp increases occurred in the share of the holdings of the other types of financial institutions. For all of these together, the share increased from 6 percent in 1951 to 14 percent in 1968. Here again, the increase was about equally large in percentage points in the 1950's and in the 1960's, but proportionately it was more pronounced during the first half of the period. Particularly impressive increases in the share in total corporate stock outstanding were registered by private pension funds with an advance from less than 1 percent to 6 percent and by open-end investment companies, whose share advanced from less than 2 to almost 5 percent.

6. The influence of financial institutions in the market for corporate stock, is however, more adequately reflected in the flow dimension. The net acquisition of common stock by the six groups of financial institutions for which information on net purchases or sales is available amounted to over $80 billion in the period 1952–69 (Table 3-23). Furthermore, over two-thirds of them were made during the second half of the period (1961–69) with peaks of more than $10 billion each in 1968 and 1969. Net

purchases by these financial institutions did not fall below $3 billion in any year after 1958.

7. By far the largest purchases were made by private pension funds ($40 billion) and by open-end investment companies ($16 billion). By comparison the net purchases of non-life-insurance companies, life insurance companies, and personal trust funds administered by banks and trust companies were considerably smaller. What may be equally import-ant, they were much more irregular although by no means negligible in absolute amounts.

8. Since no direct information is available on the net purchases and sales of these other important groups of institutional holders of corporate stock —bank trust departments, closed-end investment companies, and brokers and dealers—the results of their transactions must be inferred from the movements of the known or estimated values of their stock portfolios and from the movements of a stock price index assumed to reflect the structure of their portfolios. This somewhat hazardous procedure suggests that for the entire period 1953–68 personal trust departments bought on balance approximately $15 billion of corporate stock, such net purchases being concentrated in the last three years of the period. This would add only about one-fifth to the known net purchases of the six groups for the period as a whole, but would increase net purchases in 1966–68 by more than one-third.

The inferred net purchases of the other two groups—closed-end investment companies and brokers and dealers—were too small to affect significantly the figures of Table 3-23, either for the period as a whole or for subperiods of substantial length.

9. Because of the low volume of new issues of corporate stock during this period, the net purchases of financial institutions have been in excess of the total increase in the supply of corporate stock in every year since 1958. For the entire period, the known net purchases by financial institu-tions of $90 billion were three times as large as total new issues. The dis-crepancy, moreover, showed a clearly increasing trend over the period. While from 1952 through 1960 the known net purchases of corporate stock by financial institutions were only about equal to total net issues of all corporate stock (excluding investment company stock), from 1961 through 1969 net issues of about $10 billion were dwarfed by the known net purchases of financial institutions, which amounted to more than $65 billion (see Table 3-34). As a result (since foreign investors also had a small net purchase balance) large amounts of corporate stock were transferred from domestic individual ownership to that of financial

TABLE 3-34

Share of Valuation Changes in Growth of Assets of Financial Institutions,[a]
1952–68

(*$billion*)

	Increase in:		Net Stock Purchases (3)	Valuation Change:	
	Assets of Financial Institutions (1)	Stockholdings of Financial Institutions (2)		Absolute Value (4)	Share in (1) (5)
1952–55	$115	$14	$6	$8	7%
1956–60	168	22	12	10	6
1961–64	339	51	16	35	10
1965–68	263	45	31	14	5
1952–68	885	132	65	67	8

Sources: *Flow of Funds Accounts 1945–1968*, except for personal trust fund figures, which are taken from Appendix I.
[a] Not including closed-end investment companies, brokers and dealers, and personal trust funds.

institutions. These transfers may be estimated during the 1960's at about one-tenth of the entire portfolio of corporate stock (excluding investment companies) held by households at the beginning of the period. They amounted to an only slightly smaller fraction during the first half of the period (1952–59).

10. On the average, the net purchases by financial institutions amounted to 1 percent per year of corporate stock outstanding (excluding inter-corporate holdings and investment company stock). It is remarkable that the ratio was fairly stable, remaining between 0.8 and 1.2 percent of total stock outstanding in ten of the seventeen years of the period and being only slightly higher (averaging 1.5 percent) in another four years (1961 and 1966–68). They were substantially lower in only two years in the period (1955 and 1964).

11. The importance of financial institutions as traders in corporate stock is evident in two statistics—the velocity of turnover of their portfolios and their share of stock trading on the New York Stock Exchange. From both bodies of data it is evident that the participation of financial

institutions in stock trading during the postwar period increased at least as much as their share in total corporate stock outstanding.

12. While financial institutions, as determined by the periodic surveys of the NYSE, accounted for about one-fifth of all trading on the exchange in the mid-1950's and for one-fourth of public trading (i.e., excluding trading by member brokers and dealers), their share rose considerably and almost continuously during the 1960's to reach about two-fifths of total trading and over one-half of public trading during the first half of 1969.

13. The turnover ratios of the stock portfolios of financial institutions, indicative of the intensity of their trading activities, rose for all types of institutions from 1955 (when the statistics begin) through 1969. The increase was most pronounced for open-end investment companies. For them the velocity rose from one-sixth of the portfolio in 1955 and one-fifth in 1965 to one-half in 1968 and 1969. This acceleration was due to the spread of the performance orientation, involving numerous but relatively short-term engagements and increasing emphasis on in-and-out trading. The same sharp acceleration in turnover ratios in the late 1960's can be observed in the other main groups of financial institutions. Although it occurred here later than in the case of open-end investment companies—in 1967 or 1968 rather than in 1966—it was no less pronounced. Thus, the turnover ratio of life insurance companies nearly doubled between 1966 and 1969 as did that of private pension funds, while the turnover ratio of fire and casualty companies more than tripled. However, the ratios for all of these groups still remained well below those for open-end investment companies. The acceleration of trading by financial institutions was about in line with the movements of the overall turnover ratio on the New York Stock Exchange, which increased from 15 percent in 1965 and 20 percent in 1966 to 33 percent in 1969.

14. The sharp increase in the net purchases of corporate stock by financial institutions in the 1950's and 1960's was the result of two factors: the increase in the total funds available for investment and the change in investment policy that allocated a larger share of available funds to the acquisition of corporate stock. While the first factor was the result of basic forces in the economy which were only in part under the influence of the institutions themselves, the changes in portfolio policy were largely autonomous although they were in some cases influenced by changes in the statutes governing the investments of the respective institutions.

For all types of financial institutions, excluding investment companies (which always had invested the bulk of their funds in corporate stock), the share of corporate stock in the net acquisition of financial assets sharply increased over this period. Comparing three-year averages to avoid erratic movements, the share of corporate stock in total net acquisitions of financial assets increased from 1952–54 to 1967–69 from less than 30 to over 80 percent for uninsured private pension funds; from $1\frac{1}{2}$ percent to 25 percent for state and local pension funds; from 15 to nearly 40 percent for non-life-insurance companies; and from 4 to over 6 percent for mutual savings banks. It is this dramatic change in investment policy, discussed in somewhat more detail in Chapter 5, section 2, that must be regarded as the most important aspect of the postwar activities of financial institutions in the market for common stock.

6. PARTICIPATION OF FOREIGN INVESTORS IN THE AMERICAN STOCK MARKET

The transactions of foreign investors in American corporate stock are of particular interest for three reasons: (1) They are sometimes an important factor in the demand for or the supply of stock. In this respect foreigners are in the same position as institutional and noninstitutional groups of domestic investors as buyers or sellers of stock, or as financial corporations as issuers. (2) To the extent of net foreign purchases or sales of American corporate stock there may be a net sales or purchase balance by all domestic investors. (3) These transactions are important to the balance of payments and thus, indirectly, to monetary policy. Continuous substantial net purchases of American corporate stock by foreign investors obviously permit larger net imports of commodities and services, larger net exportation of capital, or larger accumulation of monetary metals than would otherwise be possible. Protracted net sales have the opposite effect.

From 1952 through 1968 the net purchases of American corporate stock by foreign investors totalled $3.7 billion as shown in Table 3-35.[17] This amount is small compared to the net purchases by some domestic investor groups—particularly investment companies ($16 billion) and uninsured pension funds ($35 billion)—during the same period and equals only 5 percent of net purchases by all domestic financial institutions. Still, it is substantial in relation to the total increase in the supply of stock. Net foreign stock purchases were about one-seventh of total net stock issues in the period 1953–68 and accounted for about one-fourth of total net cash issues. From 1952 through 1968, American open-end investment companies sold $1.5 billion, or about 4 percent, of their shares

[17] For the methods of calculating the figures and their limitations, see Appendix VII.

TABLE 3-35

Transactions by Foreign Investors in United States Corporate Stock, 1958–68

	Trading[a] ($billion) (1)	Average Holdings[b] ($billion) (2)	Turnover Ratio (3)	Trading on Securities Exchanges[c] ($billion) (4)	Share of Foreigners[d] (percent) (5)	Net Purchases ($billion) (6)	Ratio of Trading to Net Purchases (7)	Stock Price Changes[e] (percent) (8)
1958	2.85	7.20	0.40	77	3.7	-0.05	-57.0	34.0
1959	4.08	8.85	0.46	104	3.9	0.36	11.3	7.3
1960	3.75	9.35	0.40	90	4.2	0.21	17.8	-0.5
1961	5.81	10.55	0.55	128	4.5	0.33	17.6	20.5
1962	4.41	11.05	0.40	110	4.0	0.11	40.1	5.1
1963	5.25	11.40	0.46	129	4.1	0.19	27.6	2.0
1964	6.51	13.15	0.50	145	4.5	-0.35	-18.6	12.9
1965	7.77	14.20	0.55	189	4.1	-0.51	-15.2	8.8
1966	9.82	13.60	0.72	247	4.0	-0.34	-29.8	-10.4
1967	15.31	14.05	1.09	324	4.7	0.75	20.4	14.8
1968	23.97	17.50	1.43	394	6.1	2.27	10.6	9.5

SOURCE: Appendix VII.

[a] Purchases plus sales.

[b] Average of value of holdings at beginning and end of year.

[c] Twice volume of trading (*35th Annual Report of U.S. Securities and Exchange Commission*, p. 193).

[d] Slightly too high because trading by foreigners off exchanges is disregarded.

[e] Standard and Poor's 500 stock average; year end to year end.

to foreigners. If the redemption rates had been the same for foreign as for domestic stockholders (about 50 percent) open-end-company shares would have accounted for about one-fifth of the net purchases of American corporate stock by foreigners.[18]

Thus, the net purchases or sales by foreign investors are likely to have exercised a considerable effect on the supply-demand situation in corporate stock during the period, and certainly during those parts of it when either net sales or net purchases were substantial in relation to the increase in the total supply of corporate stock. In 1956, for example, net foreign purchases were equal to 7 percent of all net new stock issues and to 10 percent of issues excluding investment companies. The latter may be the more relevant comparison since probably only a small fraction of foreign purchases was directed toward investment company issues. The corresponding ratios were as high as 15 and 33 percent respectively in 1957, and in 1968 large net foreign purchases occurred in the face of a small net reduction in the supply of domestic corporate stock.

These purchases, however, resulted in the transfer of only approximately 0.5 percent of the total amount of American corporate stock into foreign hands. The percentage was considerably higher in individual issues popular with foreign investors.

There is little evidence of a trend over the entire postwar period in the net purchase or sales balance of American corporate stock by foreign investors (Table 3-36). Small purchase balances prevailed from 1952 through 1963, except for a very small sales balance in 1958, a year of recession, and a somewhat larger than average purchase balance in 1956, 1959, and 1961, all years in which stock prices rose substantially. Movements were more pronounced during the last half-dozen years. Foreigners' sales exceeded their purchases by $1.2 billion from 1964 through 1966, a period in which American stock prices advanced substantially. This was due mainly to sales of American stock held by the British government, a transaction presumably reflecting that country's contemporary balance of payments difficulties. On the other hand, heavy purchase balances developed during 1967 and particularly during 1968 when they exceeded $2.2 billion in the period in which American stock prices reached their peak. The volume of net purchases was much reduced in 1969, when stock prices began to decline.

It is apparent from an examination of the net purchases column of Table 3-35 that until recent years, foreign purchases of U.S. stocks were

---

[18] Based on figures in *Mutual Fund Fact Book 1970*, pp. 14, 68 ff.

TABLE 3-36

Ratio of Net Purchases of American Corporate Stock by Foreigners
to Total Issues and Outstandings, 1952–68

	Net Purchases ($billion) (1)	Ratio (percent) to:		
		Net Issues of Domestic Corporate Stock (2)	Domestic Corporate Stock Outstanding (3)	Net Purchases by Domestic Financial Institutions (4)
1952	0.00	0.0	.000	0.0
1953	0.06	2.5	.027	4.0
1954	0.14	6.1	.054	8.8
1955	0.13	4.8	.040	8.2
1956	0.26	7.0	.074	15.1
1957	0.14	3.6	.042	6.2
1958	−0.05	−1.4	−.013	−1.8
1959	0.36	8.8	.076	10.2
1960	0.21	6.6	.042	5.7
1961	0.33	6.3	.057	7.6
1962	0.11	4.2	.018	2.7
1963	0.19	19.0	.030	5.2
1964	−0.35	−10.6	−.047	−8.0
1965	−0.51	−17.0	−.061	−9.0
1966	−0.34	−6.9	−.040	−5.5
1967	0.75	15.6	.081	7.8
1968	2.27	59.7	.201	21.8
1952–68 average	0.22	5.9	.032	5.1

Source: Appendix VII.

insignificant. The single most influential cause of the recent apparent shift
in investor attitudes in favor of U.S. equities has been expansion of investor
interest and mutual fund sales activities abroad. Both newly formed and
older, more established open-end investment companies have aggressively
sought out new markets outside the United States for their own shares on
the strength of their performance during the mid-sixties. Overseas expansion and concomitant changes in attitudes were conditioned to some extent

by a U.S. government program of encouraging investment in U.S. securities by foreigners and removing barriers to it.

The 1965 and 1968 direct investment restraint programs, aimed at alleviating pressure on the U.S. balance of payments, forced American firms to increase their reliance on the Eurobond market to maintain foreign direct investment levels. The unprecedented increase in new issues of U.S. securities on this market provided new opportunities for the European investor to purchase American equities, often in the form of convertible bonds.

European investment behavior during the period under discussion was further influenced by exogenous economic and political factors that probably induced capital migrations to the United States. Among them were currency instability, the 1967 Middle East crisis, the 1968 events in France, and the Soviet invasion of Czechoslovakia.

Since foreign holders of American shares participated in the generally upward trend in stock prices during the period, the aggregate value of their holdings of American corporate securities increased sharply from about $3 billion at the end of 1951 to nearly $20 billion seventeen years later. Of the increase in value, about five-sixths were due to the rise in stock prices and less than one-sixth to net purchases. The share of foreign investors in the total market value of corporate stock outstanding (excluding intercorporate holdings) stayed at around 2 percent throughout the period. Since it may be assumed that foreign holdings of American corporate stock are heavily concentrated in issues listed on the New York Stock Exchange, their share there may be about 3 percent.

As in the case of domestic investor groups, the purchase and sales balances of foreign investors are the result of much larger transactions. From 1958 through 1968, the only period for which these figures are available, purchases and sales combined came to $90 billion, a sum about thirty times as large as the net purchase balance of $3.0 billion. Assuming that most of the trading took place on exchanges, foreign investors would have accounted for about 4 percent of total stock trading against a share of only 2 percent in holdings of American corporate stock. This indicates that the velocity of turnover of foreign investors' portfolios of American corporate stock was higher than the average for all domestic investors. An average ratio of slightly over 60 percent for the period 1958–68 compares with one of a little over 20 percent for all stocks listed on exchanges (excluding intercorporate holdings). The ratio is higher than that for American individual holders of corporate stock and is closer to that of the more actively trading institutional holders of corporate stock—open-end investment companies.[19] This is not unexpected as a probably considerable part of foreign holdings of American corporate stock are in the hands of, or are administered by, financial institutions. As is the case for American investors, particularly institutional holders of corporate stock, the turnover ratio, which had been fairly stable at around 50 percent from 1958 through 1965, rose rapidly in the last three years of the period, exceeding 135 percent in 1968. Thus, foreign investors in American corporate stock conformed in this respect also to the behavior of American investors, apparently being no more immune to this trend than they were to the speculative fever of the late 1960's.

European investors (or more correctly, investors handling their transactions in American securities through European banks, brokers, or dealers) accounted for about two-thirds of the total trading in American corporate stock by foreigners. About one-half of this amount was accounted for by transactions from Switzerland, but it is certain that residents of that country were responsible for only part of the volume originating there. British investors or organizations originated about one-fifth of all European transactions and about one-seventh of all transactions by foreign investors. Canadian investors accounted for almost one-fifth of all foreign trading in American corporate stock, Latin American investors for about one-tenth; while the rest of the world contributed not much more than 5 percent. Net purchases of American securities, however, were distributed in a quite different way among the different regions. Thus, Canadian investors, although originating less than one-fifth of all foreign purchases and sales, were on balance purchasers and accounted for more than two-fifths of the net purchase balance of all foreign investors. In contrast, British investors had net sales balances in most years, and for the period as a whole they showed a sales balance of more than $1.1 billion, probably in part a result of British foreign exchange control. Details about the geographic distribution of transactions, sales balances, and holdings by foreign investors may be observed in Tables 3-37 to 3-39, below.

---

[19] For the velocity of their stock portfolios, see Table 3-32.

TABLE 3-37

Net Purchases or Sales of U.S. Corporate Stock by Foreign
Investors in Main Regions, 1952–68

(*$billion*)

	All Countries (1)	Canada (2)	United Kingdom (3)	Switzer- land (4)	Other European Countries (5)	Latin America (6)	Other Countries (7)
1952	0.00						
1953	0.06						
1954	0.14						
1955	0.13						
1956	0.26						
1957	0.14						
1958	−0.05	− .05	.00	.01	− .04	.01	.02
1959	0.36	− .02	.02	.21	.09	.03	.03
1960	0.21	− .01	− .04	.12	.10	.01	.03
1961	0.33	− .03	− .01	.16	.10	.04	.07
1962	0.11	.04	− .04	.13	.02	− .02	− .02
1963	0.19	.00	.20	− .03	.00	.01	.01
1964	−0.35	.04	− .18	− .22	− .02	.03	.00
1965	−0.51	.05	− .40	− .12	− .04	− .01	− .01
1966	−0.34	.23	− .52	− .06	− .06	.04	− .07
1967	0.75	.27	− .12	.25	.21	.08	.06
1968	2.27	.38	− .03	.82	.78	.15	.17

NOTE: Sales are indicated by a minus sign.
SOURCE: *Treasury Bulletin*, various issues.

TABLE 3-38

Activities of Foreign Investors in U.S. Corporate Stocks, by
Main Regions, 1958–68

(*$billion*)

	Trading (1)	Net Purchase (2)	Increase in Value of Holdings (3)	Average Holdings (4)	Ratio: Col. (1) to Col. (4) (5)	Ratio: Col. (2) to Col. (3) (6)	Turnover Ratio: Col. (1) to Col. (4) (7)
Canada	16.44	0.90	2.39	1.68	18.2	.38	9.8
Europe	59.05	1.31	8.57	8.57	45.0	.15	6.9
Switzerland	30.67	1.27			24.2		
United Kingdom	12.54	−1.12			11.2		
Other Europe	15.84	1.16			13.7		
Latin America	8.90	0.40	0.92	0.94	22.3	.43	9.5
Other countries	5.14	−0.41	1.56	0.63	12.5		8.2
All foreign countries	89.53	2.27	13.44	11.82	40.0	.17	7.6

SOURCE: Derived from *Treasury Bulletin*.

TABLE 3-39

Foreign Holdings of U.S. Corporate Stock, 1953–68

(*$billion*)

	Total (1)	Canada (2)	Western Europe (3)	Latin America (4)	Other Countries (5)
1953	3.65	0.68	2.53	0.29	0.15
1954	5.25	0.94	3.66	0.42	0.23
1955	6.58	1.09	4.64	0.52	0.33
1956	6.96	1.09	4.97	0.56	0.34
1957	6.09	0.88	4.42	0.49	0.30
1958	8.31	1.17	6.03	0.66	0.45
1959	9.36	1.25	6.86	0.74	0.51
1960	9.30	1.21	6.84	0.73	0.52
1961	11.81	1.46	8.71	0.93	0.71
1962	10.34	1.24	7.70	0.79	0.61
1963	12.49	1.49	9.31	0.94	0.75
1964	13.84	1.73	10.16	1.08	0.87
1965	14.60	1.93	10.53	1.17	0.97
1966	12.64	1.93	8.74	1.08	0.89
1967	15.51	2.54	10.51	1.27	1.19
1968	19.53	3.27	12.99	1.41	1.86

NOTE: All figures for end of year indicated.
SOURCES: *Survey of Current Business*, various issues.

4

The Supply of Equity Securities, 1952–68

JOHN J. McGOWAN

YALE UNIVERSITY

THIS chapter describes trends in the supply of equity financing during the years 1952 to 1968 and trends in corporate financing over this period. An attempt is also made to identify the determinants of the volume of equity financing for nonfinancial corporations and for several subsectors within that group, namely, manufacturing, utilities, and communications. In addition, an effort is made to explain equity financing behavior by studying a sample of large manufacturing corporations, each of which made at least one issue of common stocks during the period. Finally, an attempt is made to identify the determinants of the volume of equity securities retired.

1. TRENDS IN THE SUPPLY OF EQUITY SECURITIES, 1952–68

During the period under study, domestic corporations issued $58.3 billion of new equity securities and at the same time retired $31.8 billion of outstanding equity securities. As a result net new issues over the period added $26.5 billion to the stock of outstanding equity securities. Yearly data on new issues and retirements are presented in Table 4-1.

While the total market value of outstanding stocks of domestic corporations increased by $983.4 billion between 1952 and 1968, net new issues accounted for only 2.7 percent of this increase, with the balance arising from appreciation of outstanding issues. Moreover, there has been a significant decline over the period in the contribution of net new issues to the growth in market value of equity securities. Between 1953 and 1959, 6.6 percent of the increase in market value was attributable to new issues

TABLE 4-1

Domestic Corporate Securities Issued and Retired,[a] 1952–68

(*$million*)

	1952	1953	1954	1955	1956	1957
Issues						
1. Cash issues	1,933	1,815	2,029	2,820	2,937	2,927
2. Conversions of debt into stocks						
a. Cash	194	125	213	203	169	55
b. Stock issued	541	366	752	802	694	277
3. Exchanges[b]	0	0	0	2	11	39
4. Other additions[c]	75	113	188	151	317	203
5. Deductions[d]	157	203	182	359	207	193
6. Total issues	2,586	2,216	2,999	3,619	3,920	3,309
Retirements						
7. Called for payment	98	115	397	590	187	42
8. Repurchases and other retirements[e]	46	170	712	1,008	1,112	507
9. Exchanges[b]	0	0	88	176	103	69
10. Deductions[f]	0	0	0	48	30	23
11. Total retirements	145	284	1,196	1,725	1,373	596
12. New issues less retirements	2,441	1,932	1,802	1,893	2,548	2,713

NOTE: Data prior to 1955 are not strictly comparable with the current period because of differences in coverage. Transactions reflecting mergers and liquidations, as well as adjustments for intercorporate transactions, were not covered.

SOURCE: Securities and Exchange Commission, Branch of Capital Markets.

* Less than half a million dollars.

[a] Excluding investment company shares.

[b] Exchange transactions are covered only when they involve the issuance and retirement of different types of securities, e.g., debt issues for equity issues.

whereas they accounted for only 1.2 percent of the increase between 1960 and 1968.

The data in Table 4-2 show that over the period as a whole, manufacturing corporations accounted for almost 32 percent of gross new issues, while public utility corporations, communications corporations, and others (including mining, transportation, fire insurance, real estate, and commercial corporations) each accounted for between 23 and 24 percent

1958	1959	1960	1961	1962	1963	1964	1965	1966	1967	1968
1,906	2,554	2,071	3,748	1,738	1,361	3,093	2,272	2,513	2,873	4,549
253	41	7	5	1	*	4	0	0	0	0
851	451	308	236	122	163	156	392	530	1,071	992
17	6	4	20	11	5	15	0	1	23	98
324	572	569	783	652	657	762	815	1,388	944	910
280	247	234	337	268	240	282	275	263	187	492
3,070	3,378	2,725	4,454	2,255	1,948	3,748	3,205	4,169	4,724	6,057
123	85	95	157	298	425	408	602	121	118	86
608	861	869	1,546	1,232	1,688	1,804	2,519	2,344	2,390	5,402
233	77	123	106	88	206	212	199	753	244	2,362
21	22	58	5	52	122	107	79	218	355	891
943	1,002	1,029	1,804	1,567	2,197	2,317	3,242	3,000	2,397	6,959
2,127	2,376	1,696	2,650	688	−249	1,431	−37	1,169	2,327	−900

c Includes issues such as sales by affiliated companies, private sales to foreigners, and sales to employees.

d Deductions are made for certain transactions, such as foreign issues sold in the United States, sales to other corporations, and estimated amounts of issues offered but not sold.

e Repurchases by public tender, open-market repurchases, and cash payments in connection with liquidations, reorganizations, and mergers.

f Retirements of issues held by other corporations and in items 8 and 9.

of gross new issues. However, there were some shifts in the roles of the individual sectors as sources of new equity securities between the 1950's and 1960's. Corporations both in manufacturing and in the miscellaneous group increased their share in gross new issues between these two periods, while the shares of both public utility and communications corporations declined. Additional detail on new issues and retirements by sector is given in Table 4-3.

TABLE 4-2

Distribution of Gross New Issues of Equity Securities by Industry, 1952–68

(*percent*)

	Manufacturing (1)	Utilities (2)	Communications (3)	Other (4)
1968	40.9	15.2	2.3	41.6
1967	50.7	15.7	10.6	23.0
1966	43.1	13.3	14.4	29.2
1965	37.6	18.7	17.4	26.3
1964	15.8	17.2	48.4	18.2
1963	27.4	22.2	25.8	24.6
1962	26.1	26.4	16.6	30.9
1961	25.8	16.9	33.3	24.0
1960	35.9	25.3	13.3	25.5
1959	29.7	31.6	13.5	25.2
1958	16.2	34.4	35.2	14.2
1957	51.1	25.3	6.5	17.1
1956	29.1	20.5	31.6	18.2
1955	30.3	24.5	24.5	20.7
1954	15.4	31.3	33.0	20.3
1953	8.7	50.7	28.6	12.0
1952	24.3	32.9	31.6	11.2
Annual Averages				
1952–68	31.5	23.1	21.7	23.7
1960–68	33.7	19.0	20.2	27.1
1952–59	25.6	31.4	25.6	17.4

SOURCE: Calculated from the data in Table 4-3.

Throughout the period, the bulk of new issues apparently was rather small. Table 4-4 shows that individual issues of $15 million or more accounted, on average, for only 30 percent of gross new issues, although the individual sectors exhibited considerable variation in this respect. Large issues accounted for slightly more than 50 percent of total issues by public utility corporations and comprised by far the largest share. Large issues by communications corporations accounted for an average of

30 percent of total issues by corporations in that sector, while the large issues have accounted for approximately 24 percent of the total in manufacturing and approximately 18 percent in the miscellaneous sector.

Perhaps the most striking trend in the supply of equity securities over the period has been the dramatic increase in the volume of retirements. The data in Table 4-5 indicate that with the exception of the earliest years of the period, a relatively small proportion of the retirements represents preferred stock called for payment. In particular, such retirements accounted for less than 5 percent of the total in the years 1966–68 when approximately 35 percent of the total amount of retirements during the period occurred. Most retirements fall into the category of repurchases by the issuing corporations and retirements associated with mergers and liquidations. Within this category there is some evidence that the bulk is accounted for by repurchases on the part of the initial issuer.

Table 4-6 shows estimates, derived by Leo Guthart, of the market value of shares repurchased by corporations listed on the New York Stock Exchange from 1954 to 1963. In six of the ten years these estimated repurchases accounted for over 50 percent of the retirements falling into the category of repurchases and retirements associated with mergers and liquidations. The balances listed as exchanges (i.e., exchanges of debt for equity securities) are probably closely associated with merger activity.

As can be seen by referring back to Table 4-3, it is manufacturing corporations which are responsible for most of the retirement of stocks. In most years such corporations account for somewhat more than half of all retirements and in only one year (1961) were they responsible for less than 45 percent of total retirements. Most of the balance of retirements are accounted for by firms in the extractive industries, in fire insurance and real estate, and in the commercial and other group. Retirements by firms in the utility, transportation, and communications groups generally account for a very small proportion of total retirements.

2. TRENDS IN CORPORATE FINANCING

The net supply of equity securities reflects, of course, corporate decisions as to uses and sources of funds. By far the largest corporate use of funds is capital expenditures. Table 4-7 shows that throughout the period under consideration over 60 percent of total funds used were allocated to capital expenditures. As is to be expected, the proportion spent varies closely with the level of business activity. Variations in the proportion of funds used for capital expenditures are offset primarily by compensating variations in the acquisition of financial assets. In most years capital expenditures

TABLE 4-3

Net New Issues of Corporate Stock by Industry, 1952–68

(*$million*)

	1952	1953	1954	1955	1956	1957
All industries						
New issues	2,586	2,216	2,999	3,619	3,920	3,309
Retirements	145	284	1,196	1,725	1,373	596
Net change	2,441	1,932	1,802	1,893	2,548	2,713
Manufacturing						
New issues	629	193	463	1,096	1,140	1,690
Retirements	104	133	607	814	685	283
Net change	525	61	−145	282	455	1,407
Extractive						
New issues	n.a.	54	125	125	140	72
Retirements	n.a.	11	101	104	272	29
Net change	n.a.	42	23	22	−133	43
Electricity, gas, and water						
New issues	850	1,124	940	888	803	837
Retirements	4	54	146	40	7	22
Net change	845	1,069	794	849	796	815
Railroad						
New issues	1	—	5	7	1	*
Retirements	16	12	41	242	52	32
Net change	−15	−12	−35	−236	−51	−32
Other transportation						
New issues	42	6	5	46	62	48
Retirements	*	13	19	70	42	16
Net change	42	−8	−15	−24	20	32
Communication						
New issues	817	634	989	888	1,238	215
Retirements	*	12	7	8	42	26
Net change	817	622	982	879	1,196	189
Fire insurance and real estate						
New issues	129	177	366	483	473	374
Retirements	7	12	145	308	177	102
Net change	122	165	220	175	297	272
Commercial and other						
New issues	119	30	107	86	64	72
Retirements	14	37	130	139	95	86
Net change	165	−8	−23	−53	−31	−14

1958	1959	1960	1961	1962	1963	1964	1965	1966	1967	1968
3,070	3,378	2,725	4,454	2,255	1,948	3,748	3,205	4,169	4,664	6,057
943	1,002	1,029	1,804	1,567	2,197	2,317	3,242	3,000	2,397	6,959
2,127	2,376	1,696	2,650	688	−249	1,431	−37	1,169	2,267	−900
496	1,004	977	1,147	589	534	593	1,204	1,798	2,365	2,477
542	562	515	733	831	1,198	1,109	1,774	1,767	1,532	4,319
−46	442	462	415	−242	−664	−516	−570	32	833	−1,842
81	44	47	57	48	43	89	75	78	139	318
10	9	76	619	282	276	468	100	532	27	52
72	35	−29	−562	−234	−233	−379	−25	−454	112	266
1,057	1,067	689	753	596	433	643	600	556	734	922
30	39	54	49	116	188	167	504	22	83	30
1,027	1,028	635	704	479	245	476	96	534	652	892
—	—	—	1	1	*	1	33	9	64	53
109	18	26	43	9	9	4	38	22	9	81
−109	−18	−26	−42	−8	−9	−3	−5	−10	55	−28
33	68	18	42	21	74	57	109	766	204	170
17	49	34	7	37	84	84	105	38	98	292
16	20	−16	35	−17	−10	−27	4	728	108	−122
1,080	457	363	1,483	374	502	1,814	559	600	494	167
10	12	8	26	17	55	115	41	27	28	46
1,070	445	356	1,457	157	447	1,699	518	573	466	−120
250	427	439	664	419	276	429	439	166	189	611
92	129	107	136	100	182	144	449	256	318	1,355
158	298	331	528	319	94	285	−10	−90	−121	−744
73	309	193	307	207	86	132	185	193	472	1,337
134	182	210	192	175	205	225	229	336	303	782
−61	127	−17	115	33	−119	−104	−45	−143	169	755

n.a. = not available.
SOURCE: Securities and Exchange Commission.
* Less than half a million dollars.

TABLE 4-4

Large Equity Issues as a Percent of Total, by Sector, 1953–67

	Manufacturing and Extractive (1)	Utilities (2)	Communications (3)	Other (4)	Total (5)
1953	14.7	45.2	3.7	34.6	28.9
1954	20.6	27.0	—	43.0	19.4
1955	39.5	46.1	6.1	20.8	28.6
1956	18.2	34.9	48.7	39.9	35.5
1957	57.2	51.8	24.5	23.9	48.7
1958	14.0	3.7	4.2	12.9	22.7
1959	11.6	2.2	28.3	16.1	27.5
1960	8.4	42.9	6.2	3.4	15.4
1961	5.0	61.6	69.2	14.6	38.1
1962	4.9	62.5	—	3.0	18.8
1963	13.3	49.2	9.5	5.5	18.6
1964	—	50.6	79.3	17.0	49.9
1965	27.2	32.8	12.8	14.2	22.6
1966	44.3	73.5	16.9	7.0	34.0
1967	15.1	80.0	11.6	28.2	27.2
Annual average	23.5	50.6	30.4	17.5	30.3

SOURCES: Reports prepared by the Business Finance and Capital Markets Section Division of Research and Statistics, Board of Governors of the Federal Reserve System.

and the acquisition of financial assets together account for slightly more than 90 percent of total uses, and there is no apparent trend in this figure. Capital expenditures and acquisition of financial assets averaged 90.7 percent of yearly total uses during 1952–59 and 90.1 percent during 1960–68.

The remaining 10 percent of funds has been used for the retirement of outstanding debt and equity securities. Within this component of total uses there has been a noteworthy, if not dramatic, increase in the importance of retirements of equity issues. While, on average, such retirements accounted for 2.0 percent of uses during the years 1952–59, retirement of stock consumed 3.2 percent of funds annually during the period 1960–68.

TABLE 4-5

Distribution of Total Retirements by Type, 1952–68

(*percent*)

	Called for Payment	Repurchases and Other Retirements	Exchanges
1968	1.1	68.8	30.1
1967	4.3	86.8	8.9
1966	3.8	72.8	23.4
1965	18.1	75.9	6.0
1964	16.8	74.4	8.7
1963	18.3	72.9	8.9
1962	18.4	76.1	5.4
1961	8.7	85.5	5.9
1960	8.7	79.9	11.3
1959	8.3	84.1	7.5
1958	12.8	63.1	24.2
1957	6.8	81.9	11.1
1956	13.3	79.3	7.3
1955	33.3	56.9	9.9
1954	33.2	59.5	7.4
1953	40.5	59.5	—
1952	68.1	39.9	—

SOURCE: Calculated from the data in Table 4-1.

At the same time the annual average proportion of funds used for the retirement of debt securities declined from 7.3 percent in the fifties to 5.8 percent during the sixties.

The major proportion of funds used by corporations is internally generated, primarily from depreciation reserves and retained earnings. While internally generated funds exhibited short-run variation, they showed no apparent trend at this level. In most years such funds accounted for more than 60 percent of total sources. Over the years 1952–59 internally generated funds accounted for 64.8 percent of the funds used each year; they

TABLE 4-6

Market Value of Shares Repurchased by New York Stock Exchange
Companies, 1954–63

	Estimated Repurchases by NYSE Companies ($million)	Percent of Total Repurchases and Other Retirements
1963	1,302.9	77.2
1962	1,056.7	85.8
1961	793.6	47.8
1960	598.4	68.9
1959	647.5	75.2
1958	465.7	76.6
1957	382.3	75.4
1956	414.3	37.3
1955	387.8	38.5
1954	273.9	38.5

SOURCE: Leo A. Guthart, "More Companies are Buying Back Their Stock," *Harvard Business Review*, March-April 1965, Exhibit 1, p. 44.

accounted for 63.5 percent during the years 1960–68. As a consequence, the role of external financing, except for short-run variations, has remained relatively unchanged throughout the period.

The sources of external finance, however, show significant shifts over the period. In particular the roles of both debt and equity securities as sources have been markedly smaller in the 1960's than in the 1950's. While issues of debt securities provided, on average, 19.4 percent of total funds annually from 1952–59, this proportion fell to 16.1 percent during 1960–68. More dramatic is the reduced importance of new equity issues as a source. On average, such issues accounted for 7.5 percent of total funds from 1952–59 but for only 4.8 percent of total funds from 1960–68. These reductions in the role of securities have been offset by a marked increase in the proportion of funds supplied by other sources, primarily commercial banks. Bank debt and other sources, which provided, on average, 8.3 percent of total funds during the 1950's, supplied almost twice that, or 15.6 percent, in the 1960's.

Thus there are two trends in corporate financial behavior which have acted to limit the supply of equity securities during the period under study. On the one hand, corporations as a group have increased the extent to which funds are used to retire their outstanding equity issues. On the other hand, there has been a notable shift away from the issuance of new equity securities as a source of funds. Explanations for these two trends would, to a large extent, provide explanations for the behavior of the supply of equity securities during the 1950's and 1960's.

Before proceeding to examine some explanations for these trends, it would be desirable to examine corporate financial behavior on a less aggregative basis. This can be done for three broad sectors—manufacturing, electric and gas utilities, and communications. Information on uses and sources of funds, other than that relating to retirements and issues of debt and equity securities, is available from reports of various regulatory agencies. Thus data for manufacturing were calculated from the FTC–SEC Quarterly Surveys of Manufacturing; data for electric and gas utilities, from reports on class A and class B privately owned electric utilities and natural gas pipelines, and utilities filed with the Federal Power Commission; and data for class A telephone companies, from reports filed with the Federal Communications Commission. Such data do not cover all firms in these categories; and, particularly in the case of the FTC–SEC Survey of Manufacturing, changes in number and identity of reporting firms introduce additional errors. Nevertheless, included firms account for very high percentages of total activity in each sector. Furthermore, these data should provide reasonably reliable indicators of trends in the relative importance of various sources and uses of funds within each sector. Information on the financing behavior of a miscellaneous group of firms including those in transportation, mining, commercial and fire insurance, and real estate was obtained by subtracting the data for manufacturing, utilities, and communications from the flow of funds data for all nonfinancial corporations.

In Table 4-8, annual average percentage data on the uses and sources of funds are presented for each sector for the periods 1952–59 and 1960–68; yearly data for each sector are in Tables 4-9 through 4-12. The relative constancy of the proportion of funds used for reductions in liabilities which was observed at the aggregate level extends only to the manufacturing sector. Utilities and the miscellaneous group both exhibit a tendency toward increasing use of funds for the retirement of securities though the tendency is much more pronounced for the latter. In communications, however, there is a contrary trend toward a reduction in the use of funds

TABLE 4-7

Sources and Uses of Funds, All Nonfinancial Corporations, 1952–68

(*percent of total uses*)

	1952	1953	1954	1955	1956	1957
Total ($billion)	33.2	29.3	32.6	55.2	46.8	43.9
Uses of funds (percent)						
Capital expenditures	73.5	84.0	66.3	57.1	76.7	79.0
Net average of financial assets	19.0	8.5	17.8	33.7	13.5	13.7
Retirements	7.5	7.5	16.0	9.2	9.8	7.3
Stocks	0.3	1.0	3.7	3.1	3.0	1.4
Bonds	7.2	6.5	12.3	6.1	6.8	5.9
Sources of funds (percent)						
Gross internal	63.9	72.0	71.5	52.9	61.8	69.7
External	36.1	28.0	28.5	47.1	38.2	30.3
Stocks	7.8	7.5	9.2	6.5	8.3	7.5
Bonds	22.0	22.9	23.9	13.8	16.7	21.9
Other	6.3	−2.4	−4.6	26.8	13.2	0.9

for retirements. Likewise, the trend toward a decrease in the proportion of funds used for the retirement of debt securities at the aggregate level does not extend uniformly to the individual sectors. While retirement of debt securities absorbed a decreasing proportion of funds in manufacturing and communications, utilities showed a slight increase, and the miscellaneous group exhibited no change. The one aggregate tendency which extends to each sector without exception is an increase in the proportion of funds used to retire outstanding equity securities. While the proportion of funds so used is still relatively minor in each sector, it has approximately doubled in the 1960's as compared to the 1950's in both the communications and the miscellaneous sectors, and has quadrupled in the utility sector. Thus, one of the important trends influencing the supply of equity securities has apparently been a general phenomenon throughout the corporate sector.

The absence of any substantial trend in the role of external financing at the aggregate level obscures more varied behavior at the level of the

1958	1959	1960	1961	1962	1963	1964	1965	1966	1967	1968
45.1	57.1	47.8	58.0	65.3	70.5	71.3	93.7	100.1	93.7	115.8
60.5	64.6	81.6	63.3	67.4	64.7	73.1	67.0	77.0	77.4	66.3
29.0	28.4	9.8	26.7	24.5	25.1	18.0	24.7	15.5	14.4	23.0
10.4	7.0	8.6	10.0	8.1	10.2	8.9	8.3	7.5	8.2	10.7
2.0	1.8	2.1	3.1	2.5	3.1	3.2	3.4	3.0	2.3	6.0
8.4	5.2	6.5	6.9	5.6	7.1	5.7	4.9	4.5	5.9	4.7
65.4	61.3	72.0	61.4	64.0	62.3	70.8	60.4	61.2	65.3	54.4
34.6	38.7	28.0	38.6	36.0	37.7	29.2	39.6	38.9	34.7	45.6
6.9	6.0	5.6	7.8	3.5	2.7	5.2	3.4	4.2	5.0	5.3
21.5	12.4	16.9	15.9	13.2	15.0	15.0	13.6	15.6	22.7	16.8
6.2	20.3	5.4	15.0	19.3	20.0	9.0	22.6	19.1	7.0	23.5

Sources: Calculated from *Flow of Funds Accounts 1945–1968*; *Federal Reserve Bulletin,* November 1969.

individual sectors. There has, in fact, been a dramatic increase in the role of external financing for manufacturing corporations, with 42.1 percent of funds coming from external sources on average over the years 1960–68 as compared with only 29.1 percent during 1952–59. At the same time there have been substantial reductions in the role of external funds in the utility and communications sectors, and a more minor reduction in their role in the miscellaneous group.

The trend toward decreasing reliance on equity issues as a source of funds was, nevertheless, common to all sectors other than the miscellaneous group, where there was an insignificant increase in the share of funds derived from new equity issues. Of the other three sectors, the decline in the role of equity financing was pronounced in communications, where the average annual share of new equity in total financing fell from 35.6 percent in the fifties to 23.7 percent in the sixties, and in the utility sector, where the fall was from 17.5 percent to 8.7 percent between the two periods.

TABLE 4-8

Comparative Sources and Uses of Funds, Annual Averages, 1952–59 and 1960–68

(percent of total uses)

	All Nonfinancial Corporations		Manufacturing		Utilities		Communications		Miscellaneous	
	1952– 59 (1)	1960– 68 (2)	1952– 59 (3)	1960– 68 (4)	1952– 59 (5)	1960– 68 (6)	1952– 59 (7)	1960– 68 (8)	1952– 58 (9)	1960– 68 (10)
Increase in assets	90.7	91.0	92.1	92.9	89.2	85.8	79.6	92.5	86.6	77.5
Retirement of debt securities	7.3	5.8	5.4	4.0	9.9	11.0	19.8	6.2	6.6	6.6
Retirement of equity securities	2.0	3.2	2.5	3.1	0.8	3.2	0.7	1.3	1.6	3.2
Net reduction in other liabilities	—	—	—	—	—	—	—	—	5.2	12.7
Total	100.0	100.0	100.0	100.0	100.0	100.0	100.0	100.0	100.0	100.0
Internal funds	64.8	63.5	70.9	57.9	27.7	38.4	22.5	34.9	75.8	79.3
External funds	35.2	36.5	29.1	42.1	72.3	61.6	77.5	65.1	24.2	22.7
Equity	7.5	4.8	4.3	2.8	17.5	8.7	35.6	23.7	2.9	3.0
Debt securities	19.4	16.1	14.9	9.7	41.0	34.5	40.3	32.8	14.5	16.2
Net increases in other liabilities	8.3	15.6	9.1	30.3	13.8	18.5	1.9	8.5	6.8	3.5

Sources: Calculated from the data in Tables 4-9 through 4-12.

TABLE 4-9

Sources and Uses of Funds, Manufacturing Corporations, 1952–68

(percent of total uses)

	Increase in Assets	Debt Retire-ment	Stock Retire-ment	Total Uses	Internal Funds	External Funds	Equity	Debt Securities	Other
1968	91.4	3.0	5.6	100.0	45.9	54.1	3.2	8.8	42.1
1967	93.4	3.9	2.6	100.0	54.7	45.3	4.1	16.5	24.7
1966	94.3	3.0	2.7	100.0	52.0	48.0	2.8	9.6	39.6
1965	93.4	3.4	3.2	100.0	53.2	46.8	2.2	8.1	36.6
1964	93.1	4.0	2.9	100.0	63.0	37.0	1.6	7.4	30.6
1963	91.4	4.8	3.8	100.0	65.3	34.7	1.7	10.5	22.5
1962	93.0	4.3	2.7	100.0	63.9	36.1	1.9	8.7	25.5
1961	93.1	4.4	2.5	100.0	57.0	43.0	3.9	11.3	27.8
1960	92.9	4.9	2.2	100.0	65.8	34.2	4.1	6.6	23.5
1959	94.2	4.0	1.8	100.0	55.4	44.6	3.3	5.1	36.2
1958	89.9	6.7	3.4	100.0	84.8	15.2	3.2	20.6	−8.6
1957	94.2	4.5	1.3	100.0	72.1	27.9	8.0	12.9	7.0
1956	87.8	7.8	4.4	100.0	72.5	27.5	7.3	18.1	2.1
1955	93.2	4.2	2.6	100.0	53.8	46.2	3.5	6.6	36.2
1954	88.1	6.9	5.0	100.0	84.8	15.2	3.8	18.6	−12.9
1953	94.6	4.4	1.0	100.0	78.9	21.1	1.6	13.9	5.6
1952	95.0	4.3	0.7	100.0	65.0	35.0	4.5	23.1	7.4

SOURCES: Calculated from data in *FTC-SEC Quarterly Surveys of Manufacturing*.

TABLE 4-10

Sources and Uses of Funds, Public Utility Corporations, 1952–67

(percent of total uses)

	Increase in Assets	Debt Retire- ment	Stock Retire- ment	Total Uses	Internal Funds	External Funds	Equity	Debt Securities	Other
1967	85.6	6.6	7.8	100.0	25.4	74.6	6.9	39.0	28.7
1966	91.0	6.5	2.5	100.0	44.4	55.6	6.2	36.1	13.3
1965	83.1	10.2	6.7	100.0	38.9	61.1	8.0	28.2	24.9
1964	86.4	11.0	2.6	100.0	47.8	52.2	9.9	32.7	9.6
1963	76.8	20.3	2.9	100.0	41.6	58.4	6.9	34.2	17.3
1962	83.8	14.4	1.8	100.0	38.9	61.1	9.0	33.7	18.4
1961	89.9	9.3	0.8	100.0	34.7	65.3	11.8	35.3	18.3
1960	89.7	9.5	0.8	100.0	35.3	64.7	11.1	36.5	17.1
1959	91.5	7.9	0.6	100.0	34.5	65.5	16.0	34.0	15.4
1958	87.5	11.3	0.5	100.0	31.0	69.0	17.3	46.1	5.6
1957	93.8	5.9	0.3	100.0	24.8	75.2	11.6	41.7	21.9
1956	91.8	8.0	0.2	100.0	30.6	69.4	15.3	33.7	20.5
1955	88.6	10.5	0.9	100.0	27.4	72.6	18.8	34.6	19.2
1954	76.2	21.0	2.8	100.0	22.9	77.1	17.9	54.7	4.5
1953	92.3	6.6	1.1	100.0	26.4	73.6	24.6	42.6	6.4
1952	92.1	7.9	—	100.0	24.1	75.9	18.6	40.4	16.9

Sources: Calculated from data in reports to the Federal Power Commission of Class A and Class B privately owned electric utilities and natural gas pipelines.

TABLE 4-11

Sources and Uses of Funds, Communications Corporations, 1952–67

(percent of total uses)

	Increase in Assets	Debt Retirement	Stock Retirement	Total Uses	Internal Funds	External Funds	Equity	Debt Securities	Other
1967	97.8	1.5	0.7	100.0	37.8	62.2	10.9	39.8	11.6
1966	97.6	1.7	0.7	100.0	35.7	64.3	14.3	41.2	8.8
1965	96.6	2.3	1.1	100.0	39.8	60.2	15.9	20.7	23.6
1964	92.2	4.5	3.3	100.0	33.5	66.5	50.6	16.8	-1.4
1963	81.8	16.0	2.2	100.0	40.9	59.1	18.6	32.0	8.6
1962	97.0	2.2	0.8	100.0	29.7	70.3	13.8	45.9	10.4
1961	80.5	18.5	1.0	100.0	26.8	73.2	49.7	23.5	—
1960	96.5	3.1	0.4	100.0	35.1	64.9	15.8	42.5	6.6
1959	91.9	7.6	0.5	100.0	37.8	62.2	24.9	33.0	5.9
1958	74.9	24.8	0.3	100.0	22.8	77.2	35.2	41.0	1.0
1957	94.7	3.7	1.6	100.0	26.3	73.7	11.1	68.4	-5.8
1956	83.7	14.6	1.7	100.0	16.7	83.3	51.9	30.5	0.8
1955	78.7	21.0	0.3	100.0	18.7	81.3	33.3	37.0	10.9
1954	63.7	35.8	0.5	100.0	24.5	75.5	48.5	29.9	-2.9
1953	78.7	20.8	0.5	100.0	17.2	82.8	35.4	44.4	3.4
1952	70.3	29.7	—	100.0	16.2	83.8	44.3	37.8	1.6

Sources: Calculated from data in reports of Class A telephone companies to the Federal Communications Commission as summarized in FCC *Common Carrier Statistics*, annual editions.

TABLE 4-12

Sources and Uses of Funds, Miscellaneous Corporations, 1952–67

(percent of total uses)

	Increase in Assets	Retirement of Debt Securities	Retirement of Equity	Net Retirement of Other Debt	Total Uses	Internal Funds	External Funds	Equity Securities	Debt Securities	Net Increase of Other Debt
1967	57.8	7.5	2.5	32.2	100.0	78.7	21.3	2.8	18.4	—
1966	65.7	6.6	4.2	23.5	100.0	81.3	18.7	3.8	14.9	—
1965	84.6	6.8	3.1	5.5	100.0	78.5	21.5	2.7	18.8	—
1964	73.9	6.1	3.2	16.8	100.0	79.6	20.4	2.1	18.2	—
1963	91.6	5.7	2.7	—	100.0	65.3	34.7	1.3	18.5	14.8
1962	92.5	5.1	2.4	—	100.0	74.7	25.3	2.4	9.5	13.4
1961	84.4	8.0	5.0	2.5	100.0	79.9	20.0	5.0	15.0	—
1960	69.7	6.7	2.6	21.0	100.0	80.0	20.0	3.6	16.4	—
1959	89.2	6.5	2.2	2.2	100.0	81.2	18.8	4.3	14.5	—
1958	91.1	6.9	2.0	—	100.0	66.5	33.5	2.0	11.8	19.7
1957	76.1	6.9	1.9	15.0	100.0	81.8	18.9	3.1	15.7	—
1956	92.7	4.7	2.6	—	100.0	66.5	33.5	2.6	10.3	20.6
1955	88.4	6.1	5.5	—	100.0	64.0	36.0	3.7	17.7	14.6
1954	82.6	9.4	2.9	5.1	100.0	81.9	18.1	3.6	14.5	—
1953	80.0	5.6	0.8	13.6	100.0	80.0	20.0	1.6	18.4	—
1952	93.0	7.0	—	—	100.0	83.6	16.4	2.3	12.5	1.6

SOURCES: Based on the data of Table 4-7 and Tables 4-9 through 4-11, as explained in section 2, above.

As is the case at the aggregate level, the three sectors in which the share of equity financing was declining—manufacturing, utilities, and communications—also exhibited reductions in the role of debt securities as a source of funds. In all three sectors reliance on other forms of debt financing increased. The expanded role of other forms of debt financing was most dramatic in manufacturing, where the share of such debt rose from an annual average of 9.1 percent to 30.3 percent between the 1950's and the 1960's, and in communications, where it rose from 1.9 percent to 8.5 percent. In contrast to these sectors, the miscellaneous sector exhibited a slight increase in the role of debt securities and a substantial reduction in the role of other debt financing as sources of funds.

There were, then, significant intersectoral variations in financing behavior during the period. But both trends, when observed at the aggregate level—the most important for explaining the supply of equity securities—seem broadly to have characterized the pattern of behavior within sectors. In all sectors retirement of equity absorbed an increasing share of funds, while in all but the miscellaneous group the role of equity and debt security issues as sources of funds has been declining, with an accompanying shift toward greater reliance on other forms of debt financing.

3. DETERMINANTS OF THE COMPOSITION OF EXTERNAL FINANCING

Broadly speaking the sources of funds for firms may be divided into four categories, as we have done in the preceding tables: (1) internal funds, (2) debt securities, (3) equity securities, and (4) other sources including bank loans, trade debt, profit tax accruals, and mortgages. Whatever level of funds firms wish to raise, they can be expected to distribute these requirements over the various sources in such a way as to minimize the total cost of funds for a given level of financing. As a consequence the composition of financing should shift in response to changes in the relative cost of obtaining funds from the several sources.

Let us assume that in any period a firm has some desired level of total financing, TF^*, which is equal to its desired increase in physical capital plus replacement investment, plus its desired increase in financial assets.[1] The financing problem of the firm is then that of determining the level of funds to be raised from each source in such a way as to minimize cost, subject to the constraint that the sum of the funds raised be equal to the desired level of financing.

---

[1] This might be formalized through the use of an accelerator-adjustment model of desired total financing but it would serve no useful purpose at this juncture.

Among the four sources of funds recognized here, internal funds have the special attraction that the firm incurs no transactions costs in their use. Thus, while it may be difficult in practice to determine the opportunity cost of the marginal dollar of internal funds reinvested in the business, it would seem safe to assume that the cost of any given amount of funds will be minimized if it can be obtained from internal funds. Consequently, funds will be raised from the other three sources only if desired financing exceeds the amount of internally generated funds available. The excess of desired financing over internal funds gives the firm's required level of external financing, *REF*. If we accept this simplification, the financing problem becomes one of obtaining the required level of external financing at minimum cost.

The cost of funds from any source is made up of the interest charges the firm must pay plus certain transactions costs such as arranging for bank loans, or flotation costs in the case of bond or equity financing. While these transactions costs tend to be relatively insensitive to the amount of funds raised, the interest rates which must be paid are likely to increase with the amount raised from any source. This means that the marginal cost of funds from each source increases with the amount raised.

In addition, the levels of the cost curves probably differ among the sources of funds. Thus, because of the special tax advantages of debt financing, the cost curves for both bond and "other" financing lie below that for equity financing over some range. Furthermore, if as seems likely, the transactions costs of obtaining "other" funds are lower than the flotation costs of securities, the cost curve will be below both those for bond and equity financing over some range.

These properties of the cost curves mean that an optimal, i.e., cost minimizing, financial policy need not involve the use of all sources of external funds. Rather, there will be some level of required external financing below which it would be optimal to rely solely on "other financing." Let us denote this level as *REF'*. There will be another level of required external financing *REF''* below which cost minimization requires that no funds be obtained from equity issues. Thus firms whose required external funds fall below *REF'* and *REF''* will use both "other" and bond financing, while only those firms with requirements in excess of *REF''* would use all three sources. This dependence of optimal financing policy for individual firms upon their level of required external financing relative to two critical levels, *REF'* and *REF''*, makes it difficult to analyze the determinants of financing behavior.

Since we must rely on aggregate data on the amounts of different types of financing and on total external financing, we can only attempt to explain financing behavior by equations such as:

$$\overline{F} = \alpha_0 + \alpha_1\overline{EF} + \alpha_2 r_f + \alpha_3 r_b + \alpha_4 r_e$$
$$\overline{B} = \beta_0 + \beta_1\overline{EF} + \beta_2 r_f + \beta_3 r_b + \beta_4 r_e$$
$$\overline{E} = \eta_0 = \eta_1\overline{EF} + \eta_2 r_f + \eta_3 r_b + \eta_4 r_e$$

where $\overline{F}$ = aggregate "other" financing
$\overline{B}$ = aggregate bond financing
$\overline{E}$ = aggregate equity financing
$\overline{EF}$ = aggregate external financing
r_f = interest rate on "other" funds
r_b = interest rate on bonds
r_e = required rate of return on equity

But because the optimal financing policy for individual firms depends upon required external funds relative to the critical levels *REF'* and *REF"*, the "other" financing equation should have as separate variables: (1) external financing by firms which have requirements less than *REF'*, (2) external financing by firms which have requirements between *REF'* and *REF"*, and (3) external financing by firms with requirements greater than *REF"*. Similarly, the bond equation should have as separate variables: (1) external financing by firms with requirements less than *REF'*, and (2) external financing by firms with requirements between *REF'* and *REF"*. Finally, the equity financing equation should have as a variable only the external financing by firms with requirements in excess of *REF"*. The use of aggregate external financing as a single variable in each of the equations thus introduces errors which limit the usefulness of analysis of aggregate data for making inferences about financing behavior at the firm level.

One consequence of such errors will be a reduction of the estimated explanatory power of the model as measured by the coefficient of multiple determination, R^2. This in itself might not be too serious provided the problem is recognized. Nevertheless, since the errors lead to a magnification of unexplained variance, the standard errors of the estimated coefficients will be magnified. Thus, even if the properties of the errors are such as still to lead to unbiased estimates of these coefficients, casual application of standard significance tests is to be avoided.

But even more serious problems may beset the analysis if the magnitudes of the errors are correlated with other explanatory variables in the model. And there is some reason to expect this to be the case, since the critical levels of required external financing, REF' and REF'', are not independent of the interest rates on funds from the various sources. It is therefore quite likely that the errors arising from the use of aggregate external financing as an explanatory variable are correlated with other variables in the model. As a consequence estimates of the coefficients in the model are likely to be biased in unknown directions and magnitudes.

All of this suggests that extreme caution is necessary in making inferences on the basis of aggregate financial data. Yet something may be gained from it. The nearer together are the total cost curves of the various sources of funds, the more firms there are whose external financing requirements are greater than REF'', and hence the smaller is the error introduced by estimating the financing equations through use of aggregate external financing as an explanatory variable. Thus, if the assumption of nearly identical cost functions were true, the estimated equations would have closely similar R^2's. If, on the other hand, firms view the cost of "other" financing as significantly lower than the cost of bond financing over a large range, and the cost of bond financing as lower than that of equity financing over a substantial range, then the errors introduced by using aggregate external financing as an explanatory variable should be least for the "other" financing equation and greatest for the equity financing equation. Consequently, if the assumptions on the cost curves were true we should expect R^2 to be highest for the "other" financing equation, lowest for the equity-financing equation, and intermediate for the bond-financing equation. Since it is commonly believed that such a hierarchy of sources of funds exists, it would be interesting to see to what extent actual financing behavior supports the belief.

Regressions of F, B, and E on EF and measures of r_f, r_b, and r_e are presented in Table 4-13. The rate on short-term commercial bank loans was taken as a measure of r_f, while the rate on AAA corporate bonds was taken as a measure of r_b. Two measures of r_e were used. The first was the inverse of the current price-earnings ratio for the Standard and Poor's composite group. The second was constructed by taking the earnings-price ratio for the Standard and Poor's composite group and adding to it the trend rate of growth of earnings per share of stocks in the same group. The trend used was calculated for each observation year by computing a

TABLE 4-13

Estimated Financing Equations, All Nonfinancial Corporations, 1952–67

Dependent Variable	Constant	$\overline{EF}$	r_b	r_e	r'_e	R^2	d
$\overline{F}$	15.910	.859* (.102)	−4.770* (1.659)	−1.017 (.633)	—	.892*	1.933
$\overline{B}$	−18.099	.116 (.085)	4.586* (1.388)	1.045* (.529)	—	.742*	2.100
$\overline{E}$	2.189	.025 (.031)	.184 (.510)	−.028 (.194)	—	.226	1.891
$\overline{F}$	7.821	1.000* (.126)	−4.400* (1.434)	—	−.296* (.161)	.890*	1.561
$\overline{B}$	−8.524	−.002 (.110)	3.893* (1.215)	—	.254* (.136)	.733*	1.516
$\overline{E}$	1.041	.004 (.039)	.412 (.427)	—	.041 (.048)	.269	2.115

NOTE: Figures in parentheses are standard errors.
* Significant at the 5 percent level or better on a one-tailed test.

semilogarithmic regression of earnings per share for the observation year and the preceding four years. The measures are denoted r_e and r'_e, respectively. Initial results showed the measures of r_f and r_b to be almost perfectly correlated, so r_f was eliminated; the regressions reported here used only r_b and r_e.

The resulting pattern of R^2 conforms with the expectations based on the proposition that "other" financing is viewed as much less costly than the other forms of financing, while equity financing is viewed as the most costly. The magnitudes of all coefficient estimates are sensitive to the specification of r_e, but neither the explanatory power of the equations nor the signs of the coefficients are. While the interest rate coefficients are mostly insignificant or barely significant, what is more disturbing is their sign pattern. The coefficient of r_b has the right sign in the "other" financing and in the equity financing equations, while r_e has the right sign in both the bond and equity financial equations. Of the incorrect signs the most disturbing is the positive sign on r_b in the bond equation, since the estimated coefficient is highly significant. One explanation for this result would be that in periods of tight money, when both r_f and r_b rise, the availability of funds from "other" sources contracts, and firms are forced into the debt securities market even at market rates they would prefer not to adopt. In terms of the underlying specification of the financing model, the perverse sign on r_b in the bond equation is an indication that the parameters of the "other" funds cost function, a_0 and a_1, are not constant over time but increase as interest rates rise.

Similar equations were estimated for the manufacturing, utilities, and communications sectors. The results are presented in Tables 4-14 to 4-16. For manufacturing, the rate on AAA industrial bonds was used as a measure of r_b while r_e and r'_e were calculated using the procedures outlined above and employing earnings-price ratios and earnings per share data for Standard and Poor's industrial stocks. For both utilities and communications, r_b was based on data for AAA utility bonds while r_e was based on Standard and Poor's utility stocks.

The results show little variation from those for all nonfinancial corporations when r_e is measured by the current earnings-price ratio. The explanatory power is highest for the "other" financing equation for both manufacturing and utilities, but this equation ranks lower than those for

TABLE 4-14

Estimated Financing Equations, Manufacturing Corporations, 1952–67

Dependent Variable	Constant	$\overline{EF}$	r_b	r_e	r'_e	R^2	d
$\overline{F}$	10.788	.937* (.082)	−2.666* (1.374)	−.579 (.415)	—	.966*	1.813
$\overline{B}$	−9.751	.042 (.670)	2.285* (1.175)	.534 (.355)	—	.619*	2.120
$\overline{E}$	−1.172	.020 (.023)	0.392 (0.381)	.057 (.115)	—	.508	1.099
$\overline{F}$	5.567	.976* (.097)	−2.023* (1.066)	—	−.146 (.105)	.966*	1.374
$\overline{B}$	−4.176	.025 (.086)	1.529 (0.944)	—	.106 (.094)	.590*	1.496
$\overline{E}$	−1.230	.003 (.025)	0.451 (0.279)	—	.037 (.028)	.560*	1.189

NOTE: Figures in parentheses are standard errors.
* Significant at the 5 percent level or better on a one-tailed test.

TABLE 4-15

Estimated Financing Equations, Utility Corporations, 1952–67

Dependent Variable	Constant	$\overline{EF}$	r_b	r_e	r_e'	R^2	d
$\overline{F}$	.320	.477* (.126)	−.025 (.259)	−.195 (.164)	—	.771*	2.226
$\overline{B}$	−.787	.478* (.111)	.127 (.227)	.106 (.144)	—	.619*	2.704
$\overline{E}$	.483	.045 (.057)	−.102 (.118)	.088 (.075)	—	.440	1.641
$\overline{F}$	−1.843	.398* (.117)	.183 (.173)	—	.042 (.047)	.761*	2.398
$\overline{B}$	.280	.517* (.102)	.005 (.151)	—	−.009 (.041)	.798*	2.778
$\overline{E}$	1.564	.085 (.049)	−.186 (.073)	—	−.034 (.020)	.498*	1.716

NOTE: Figures in parentheses are standard errors.
* Significant at the 5 percent level or better on a one-tailed test.

bond and equity financing for communications. In all three sectors the sign on r_e in the "other" financing equation is negative rather than positive; however, in no instance is the estimated coefficient significantly different from zero. Both in manufacturing and in utilities the sign on r_b is negative rather than positive although the coefficient is significant only for the manufacturing equation. Once again this suggests that while the market rates for "other" funds and bonds move closely together, a rise in rates is accompanied by a contraction in the availability of "other" funds, forcing firms to seek alternative sources.

This is further borne out by the positive sign on r_b in the bond equation for each sector and by its significance in both manufacturing and communications. The coefficient on r_e in the bond financing equations is also positive in all cases, as it should be, although it is significant only in communications.

The equity financing equation performs rather poorly in all cases. While the equation explains slightly more than 50 percent of the variance in equity financing for both manufacturing and communications, it does less

TABLE 4-16

Estimated Financing Equations, Communications Corporations, 1952–67

Dependent Variable	Constant	$\overline{EF}$	r_b	r_e	r'_e	R^2	d
$\overline{F}$	−.374	.116 (.141)	.107 (.119)	−.020 (.093)	—	.298	2.606
$\overline{B}$	−.328	.319* (.145)	.447* (.122)	.303* (.096)	—	.691*	2.106
$\overline{E}$	3.654	.565* (.207)	−.554* (.174)	−.283* (.136)	—	.533*	2.889
$\overline{F}$	−.645	.085 (.160)	.121 (.089)	—	.014 (.033)	.305	2.574
$\overline{B}$	−.533	.229 (.221)	.183 (.122)	—	.028 (.045)	.452*	1.809
$\overline{E}$	1.178	.686* (.268)	−.304* (.149)	—	−.042 (.055)	.395	2.261

NOTE: Figures in parentheses are standard errors.
* Significant at the 5 percent level or better on a one-tailed test.

well for utilities. While all coefficients are significant in the equity financing equation for communications, none is individually significant in the equations for manufacturing and utilities. Furthermore, the sign on r_b is negative rather than positive in both manufacturing and communications, while the sign on r_e is positive rather than negative in both manufacturing and utilities.

As was the case for nonfinancial corporations as a group, using the more sophisticated measure of the cost of equity capital has little qualitative impact on the results, although there are often substantial changes in the magnitudes of the coefficient estimates. In general, the equations employing r_e have slightly different R^2's, and the standard errors of the coefficients on r_b and r'_e are smaller, while the standard errors of the coefficients of $\overline{EF}$ are slightly larger. These changes are probably due to the fact that r'_e is less strongly correlated with r_b and more highly correlated with $\overline{EF}$ than is the simpler measure of the cost of equity capital, r_e. In any event the changes have no material effects on the observations made above.

Nevertheless, taken together, these somewhat disappointing results seem to indicate that for nonfinancial corporations as a whole, and for the subsectors we have examined, equity financing is a source of last resort except for communications firms. Put another way, for almost all corporations equity capital is viewed as a markedly inferior substitute for funds from other sources. As a result changes in relative costs of equity, as measured by the approximate required rate of return to holders of equity, have very little impact on most firms' financing decisions. In addition most firms seem to prefer to raise funds by means other than the issuance of securities. They resort to securities not in response to changes in the relative costs of funds as measured by market interest rates but in response to contractions in the availability of other types of funds, a condition which is imperfectly reflected by changes in interest rates.

4. EQUITY FINANCING BY LARGE MANUFACTURING CORPORATIONS

As a further test of the financing decision model presented in the previous section, a study was undertaken of the determinants of the volume of equity financing by large manufacturing corporations which had issued common stock during some year of the period under study. Fifty industrial corporations had at least one equity issue in excess of $15 million in the period 1953–67. A sample of 50 corporations was randomly drawn from *Fortune*'s 500 for 1968, making a total sample of 100 corporations. An attempt was then made to determine all equity issues of these 100 corporations and their predecessors during the years 1953–67.

Only 53 of the 100 corporations were found to have made equity issues during the period. These corporations had 63 issues of common stocks totaling $2,848.2 million and 29 issues of preferred stocks totaling $524.7 million. Since concentration on issues of common stock was decided upon, and since data on certain characteristics of the issuing firms were lacking in some cases, a number of issues had to be deleted from the sample. In the end, our sample was composed of 35 firms that had made a total of 43 issues of common stocks during the period.

In line with the model presented in the previous section, it was postulated that the volume of equity financing by the ith firm in year t could be expressed by

$$E_{it} = \gamma_0 + \gamma_1 EF_{it} + \gamma_2 r_{b_{it}} + \gamma_3 d_{it} + \gamma_4 r_{e_{it}} + u_{it}$$

where E_{it} = dollar value of common stock issued
$\quad EF_{it}$ = total external financing
$\quad r_{b_{it}}$ = the yield on corporate bonds

d_{it} = the firm's debt-equity ratio
$r_{e_{it}}$ = the required rate of return on equity
u_{it} = a random error term

The debt-equity ratio was added to the equation, since a firm's capital structure is widely believed to influence cost of funds. More specifically, traditional views of corporate financing would indicate that the cost of additional debt financing is higher, the higher the existing debt-equity ratio. On the other hand, those views suggest that at least up to some point, firms with higher debt-equity ratios should be able to raise additional equity on more favorable terms. For both these reasons one would expect the debt-equity ratio to be an important determinant of equity financing and the coefficient on the ratio to be positive.

Unfortunately, estimation of such an equation from the available sample raises several problems. Since no firm in the sample had more than two issues during the period, time-series estimation of the equity financing equation for individual firms was not possible. Likewise, in no single year were there enough firms issuing common stocks to constitute a sample of acceptable size for cross-sectional estimation. As a result it was necessary to pool observations, treating each issue and the characteristics of the issuing corporation as an observation.

Pooling of the observations in this way raises several problems. First, the parameters of the financing equation may not have remained constant over the period. To allow for this possibility the equation was estimated in three ways: (1) pooling all 43 observations; (2) using only the observations on issues between 1953 and 1959; and (3) using only the observations on issues between 1960 and 1967.

Second, if there is little variability among firms in the sample with respect to debt-equity ratios, and if at the same time the sample firms tend on average to have quite different debt-equity ratios from firms which did not issue equities, then we might find this variable to have no influence on equity financing behavior even though it was an important determinant of equity financing. This, however, does not seem to be a problem. The average debt-equity ratio for firms in the sample is 0.45 with a standard deviation of 0.44. Data from the FTC–SEC Quarterly Survey of Manufacturing Corporations indicates that over the period studied the average debt-equity ratio for firms with assets in excess of $25 million has varied between 0.4 and 0.6.

Third, the importance of the required rate of return on equity might be similarly disguised if there were little variability in required rates of return among firms in the sample and if these firms at the same time had required rates of return quite different from firms which did not issue equity securities. Again this does not seem to be the case. The average earnings-price ratio for firms in the sample was 5.64 percent with a standard deviation of 2.89. Over the period studied, the average earnings-price ratio for Standard and Poor's industrials was 6.8. Thus, sample firms did apparently tend to have below average earnings-price ratios but there was considerable variation among them in this respect.

Fourth, the data could mask the importance of interest rates as a determinant of equity financing if most issues occurred in years with high interest rates. Such bunching of observations would tend to reduce the amount of a variation in the interest rate variable, particularly since that variable has the same value for all firms in any one year. This does appear to be a real problem since over half of the issues in the sample occurred in the four years 1956 (5 issues), 1957 (10 issues), 1966 (5 issues), and 1967 (6 issues).

These considerations indicate that the results to be presented should be viewed as highly tentative and, at best, suggestive. Much larger samples need to be analyzed with more sophisticated models and techniques in order to gain a solid understanding of the determinants of equity financing.

Data on the value of common issues were obtained from records maintained by the Federal Reserve Board. Total external financing and debt-equity ratios were computed from balance sheet and income statements of issuing corporations, published in *Moody's Industrials Manual.* The corporate bond yield variable was taken as the yield on AAA corporate industrial bonds. The same two measures of the required return on equity capital used in the previous section were also employed here. These measures were calculated from data in *Moody's Industrials* and *Moody's Handbook of Common Stocks.* Common issues and external financing were measured in millions of dollars. Bond yields and required return on equity were expressed as percentages, but the debt-equity ratio was expressed simply as a ratio.

The initial regressions run had uniformly very low R^2's and seemed to indicate the presence of heteroscedasticity. To counteract this problem all variables were deflated by the total assets of the issuing corporation in the year prior to the issue (A_{t-1}), and $1/A_{t-1}$ was entered as an independent variable. The results of this estimation when the required rate of return on equity is measured by the current earnings-price ratio are shown in Table 4-17. Table 4-18 shows the results when the required return on

TABLE 4-17

Deflated Equity-Financing Equations Based on Current Earnings-Price Ratio

	Number of Issues	Dependent Variable	Constant	$\dfrac{EF_t}{A_{t-1}}$	$\dfrac{r_b}{A_{t-1}}$	$\dfrac{d}{A_{t-1}}$	$\dfrac{r_e}{A_{t-1}}$	$\dfrac{1}{A_{t-1}}$	R^2
1953–67	43	$\dfrac{E}{A_{t-1}}$	.089	.068* (.039)	−0.732 (3.088)	−7.196 (5.865)	−1.409* (0.530)	16.461 (13.430)	.750*
1953–59	23	$\dfrac{E}{A_{t-1}}$	.069	.382* (.108)	−2.519 (6.624)	−12.845* (7.164)	−1.767 (1.090)	27.019 (28.837)	.632*
1960–67	20	$\dfrac{E}{A_{t-1}}$	.073	.038 (.042)	3.118 (6.179)	4.997 (10.058)	−2.142* (1.090)	0.147 (25.250)	.860*

NOTE: Figures in parentheses are standard errors.
* Significant at the 5 percent level or better on a one-tailed test.

TABLE 4-18

Deflated Equity-Financing Equations Based on Current Earnings-Price Ratio plus Trend Rate of Growth of Earnings per Share

	Number of Issues	Dependent Variable	Constant	$\dfrac{EF}{A_{t-1}}$	$\dfrac{r_b}{A_{t-1}}$	$\dfrac{d}{A_{t-1}}$	$\dfrac{r'_e}{A_{t-1}}$	$\dfrac{1}{A_{t-1}}$	R^2
1953–67	43	$\dfrac{E}{A_{t-1}}$	.086	.041 (.038)	4.257 (2.619)	−17.868* (5.809)	.039 (.058)	−6.849 (11.055)	.704*
1953–59	23	$\dfrac{E}{A_{t-1}}$	.064	.360* (.118)	4.743 (5.264)	−13.900* (7.788)	−.068 (.124)	−7.747 (19.576)	.582*
1960–67	20	$\dfrac{E}{A_{t-1}}$	.066	.044 (.047)	−2.058 (6.338)	−0.166 (12.738)	.001 (.074)	19.235 (26.546)	.818*

NOTE: Figures in parentheses are standard errors.
* Significant at the 5 percent level or better on a one-tailed test.

equity is measured by the current earnings-price ratio plus the trend rate of growth of earnings per share over the previous five years.

These regressions were estimated with a constant term; however, in strict accordance with the model specified above, the constant term in the regressions should be zero. For that reason, the regressions were rerun with the constant term forced to zero. The resulting equations had very substantially lower and statistically less significant R^2's than the equations reported in Tables 4-17 and 4-18, indicating that the size of the firms as measured by total assets exerted a significant independent effect on the amount of equity financing.[2] Consequently, additional regressions using undeflated values of the variables and including A_{t-1} as an independent variable were run. These results are reported for each of the measures of the required return on equity in Tables 4-19 and 4-20. On the whole the undeflated form of the equation which included A_{t-1} as an independent variable seems to provide the more reliable estimates, not only because the R^2's are higher for that formulation but also because deflation of the variables by A_{t-1} introduced rather high (.8 or higher) levels of inter-correlation among the independent variables.

But regardless of the formulation of the equation there is little evidence to suggest that equity financing decisions are sensitive to the bond yield, the measures of the required return on equity capital, or the debt-equity ratio. The coefficient on r_b is not significant in any equation and has the wrong sign in seven of the twelve regressions. While the coefficient of the debt-equity ratio is significant in three equations, it has the wrong sign in each of these cases and in six additional ones. The current earnings-price ratio has the right sign in all six regressions in which it is entered but is significant in only half of them and is never significant for the 1953–59 subsample. When the required return on equity is measured by the current earnings-price plus the trend rate of growth of earnings per share, its co-efficient is never significant and is negative only in the regressions for the 1953–59 subsample. These observations suggest that the current earnings-price ratio is a more satisfactory approximation to the required rate of return on equity in explaining equity financing behavior.

Nevertheless, total external financing and the size of the issuing corporation appear to be the overriding determinants of equity financing. The total external financing as an important determinant of the magnitude of equity financing is, of course, not surprising. The positive and significant

[2] It should be noted that external financing and size, as measured by the previous period's total assets, are not highly correlated. The simple correlations are .140 for the sample as a whole, .025 for the 1953–59 subsample; and .497 for the 1960–67 subsample.

TABLE 4-19

Undeflated Equity-Financing Equations Based on Current Earnings-Price Ratio

	Number of Issues	Dependent Variable	Constant	EF	r_b	d	r'_e	A_{t-1}	R^2
1953–67	43	E	74.149	.269*	−10.639	−17.157	−2.955	.047*	.833*
				(.060)	(9.918)	(13.899)	(2.372)	(.004)	
1963–69	23	E	117.224	.788*	−25.245	−22.045	−2.312	.042*	.897*
				(.166)	(23.898)	(22.621)	(3.272)	(.004)	
1960–67	20	E	−17.778	.120*	8.878	−11.500	−5.204*	.078*	.959*
				(.037)	(0.162)	(8.864)	(2.119)	(.006)	

NOTE: Figures in parentheses are standard errors.
* Significant at the 5 percent level or better on a one-tailed test.

TABLE 4-20

Undeflated Equity-Financing Equations Based on Current Earnings-Price Ratio plus Trend Rate of Growth of Earnings per Share

	Number of Issues	Dependent Variable	Constant	EF	r_b	d	r'_e	A_{t-1}	R^2
1953–67	43	E	386.398	.267*	−5.258	−17.458	−.147	.046*	.826*
				(.061)	(9.160)	(14.157)	(.266)	(.004)	
1953–59	23	E	77.133	.799*	−18.190	−20.717	−.124	.041*	.890*
				(.169)	(21.594)	(22.861)	(.452)	(.004)	
1960–67	20	E	−16.923	.107*	4.613	−13.959	.026	.078*	.939*
				(.045)	(10.762)	(10.500)	(.200)	(.007)	

NOTE: Figures in parentheses are standard errors.
* Significant at the 5 percent level or better on a one-tailed test.

coefficient on the size of the corporation seems to indicate that larger firms can raise equity capital on more favorable terms, other things being equal.

The two formulations which employ the current earnings-price ratio indicate a fall in the coefficients of both total external financing and the required return on equity in the 1960's. On the other hand, both formulations indicate an increase in the coefficients of the bond yield, the debt-equity ratio, and the size of firm. It is interesting to note that all of these shifts are in accord with what one would expect if funds from sources other than the securities market were more easily available during the 1960's than they were in the 1950's. In terms of the model presented in the previous section, such an increase in availability would be reflected in decreases in the values of the parameters of the total cost curve for other financing. These decreases would in themselves give rise to the observed pattern of changes in the coefficients of the equity financing equations. This suggests that an explanation for the reduced reliance on both equity and bond financing in the sixties as opposed to the fifties may lie in an increase in the availability of funds from sources other than the securities markets.

These findings require further qualification, however, because the dependent variable, equity financing, is included in total external financing. The two are thus quite highly correlated and it is this correlation which accounts for a substantial portion of the explanatory power of the equations presented above.

To avoid this problem the ratio of equity financing to total external financing was regressed on bond rates, current earnings-price ratios, and debt-equity ratios. To allow for shifts in this equity financing function over time, dummy variables were introduced to permit a different intercept for each year. In this formulation none of the coefficients, including those for the dummy variables, was significant. In addition the signs on both the earnings-price ratio and the debt-equity ratio were contrary to expectations.

These results reinforce the finding that the volume of equity financing is not sensitive to the cost of equity capital relative to the cost of funds from other sources—at least in the ranges encountered over the period studied here. Additional tests indicate that the decision to engage in equity financing, irrespective of the amounts so raised, is also insensitive to indicators of the relative cost of capital.

It might be expected that even though the volume of equity financing was not closely related to earnings-price ratios, firms which engaged in some equity financing would tend to have below average earnings-price ratios. However, only 54 percent of the issues in our sample took place at times when the issuing corporations had earnings-price ratios below the average for all manufacturing corporations. Statistically, this percentage is not significantly different from what one would expect if issuing corporations were equally likely to have above, or below, average earnings-price ratios.

Similarly, only 49 percent of the issues were made by corporations which had debt-equity ratios in excess of the average for all manufacturing corporations at the time of issue. Comparison of the debt-equity ratios of issuers with the average debt-equity ratio for corporations in the same industry group (SIC 2-digit) showed that issuers had above average debt-equity ratios in the case of 59 percent of the issues. Once again this percentage is not statistically different from what one would expect if issuers were equally likely to have debt-equity ratios above or below the average for firms in the same industry.

5. DETERMINANTS OF RETIREMENTS

To the extent that retirements of equity securities are not associated with merger activity or liquidations or the retirement of preferred stocks, they reflect a decision by management that cash distributions to stockholders are a more attractive use of funds than the internal investment opportunities available to the firm. Various other reasons have been offered for retirements, such as the desire to increase the debt-equity ratio. However, if a firm has sufficient profitable investment opportunities, the preferred method of increasing its debt-equity ratio would be to engage in debt financing. Consequently, retirement of equity should only occur when internal fund flows exceed the amount that can profitably be absorbed by the investment opportunities available to the firm. Of course, dividend payments offer an alternative means of distributing excess cash to the stockholders. But if the excess cash were distributed in the form of dividends, stockholders would become liable for tax on the full amount of the distribution and at ordinary income tax rates. On the other hand, when cash distributions are accomplished through stock repurchases, shareholders need only pay tax, at capital gains rates, on the excess of the repurchase price over the initial purchase price of the shares retired.

For corporations as a group, internal fund flows have not in any year exceeded the amounts by which the firms have been willing to add to their physical and financial assets, and they have absorbed funds from other sectors in every year. Nor, as we have seen, is there any observable tendency for the ratio of internal funds to other capital expenditures or total asset expansion to increase over the period for corporations as a group.

These observations do not, however, rule out the possibility that individual corporations have at times during the period experienced internal cash flows in excess of the amounts they could profitably re-invest in the business. Furthermore, one might expect to observe a high positive correlation between internal fund flows and stock repurchases. One might also expect firms to be more prone to distribute excess cash through repurchases of their stocks when stock prices are low. Consequently, a negative correlation between stock prices and repurchases is to be expected.

A regression of cash retirements (T) on Standard and Poor's index of stock prices (SP) and on the level of internal funds over the period gave the following result:

$$T_t = -.771 + .018\,SP_t + .025\,IF_t$$
$$\ (.012)\ (.020)$$
$$R^2 = .910$$

However, these results are unreliable because all the variables exhibit strong time trends over the period. Thus the correlation coefficient of stock prices on time is .986; that between internal funds and time is .965; and that between repurchases and time is .917. As a result stock prices and internal funds are highly correlated ($r = .970$), and the above equation provides only a slightly better prediction of repurchases than a simple time trend.

As an alternative, the deviations of T_t from its trend value were regressed on the deviations of stock prices and internal funds from their trend values with the following results:

$$\overline{T_t} = 0.0 + .043\,\overline{SP_t} + .032\,IF_t$$
$$\phantom{\overline{T_t} = 0.0 +}\ (.017)\phantom{\overline{SP_t} +}\ (.018)$$
$$R^2 = .542$$

While both stock prices and internal funds are significant in this equation, repurchases are apparently more closely related to stock prices than to internal funds, and the relationship is positive rather than negative. This strange result is probably a statistical quirk arising from the use of highly aggregated data. Consequently, while it seems reasonable to attribute the rising trend in repurchases to rising liquidity in some corporations, no satisfactory test of that explanation can be performed with the data on hand.

The other quantitatively important category of retirements includes cases where stock has been retired with debt securities issued in exchange. These types of retirements have also shown an upward trend over the period, and as noted earlier, the most obvious explanation for this lies in the rising trend of merger activity over the period. A regression of the value of exchanges (EX) on the estimated market value of acquired firms (M) gave the following results:[3]

$$EX_t = -43.728 + .053 \, M_t$$
$$(.020)$$
$$R^2 = .395$$

Thus, while the expected relationship exists, merger activity alone provides a relatively weak explanation of the value of exchanges. This is not surprising, since it is unlikely that the percentage of the total value of mergers consummated through exchanges has been constant from year to year throughout the period.

6. SUMMARY

While the value of outstanding equity securities has grown substantially over the period studied, a minor proportion of this growth is accounted for by net new issues and the proportion has been declining. This is a reflection of two phenomena which have characterized corporate financing in all nonfinancial sectors; namely, a trend away from equity securities relative to other types of financing and an increasing trend in the retirement of equity securities as a proportion of total uses of funds.

The first of these trends is particularly surprising in the face of a general trend toward lower earnings-price ratios on common stocks relative to bond yields. Indeed, statistical studies of equity financing behavior based on time-series data for the aggregate of all nonfinancial corporations, and for the manufacturing, utilities, and communications subsectors, indicate that equity financing decisions are quite insensitive to changes in the costs of equity capital, as measured by the required rate of return on equity and the cost of debt capital as measured by market interest rates. This same insensitivity of equity financing behavior to market measures of the costs of funds from various sources is also found in studying the determinants of the volume of equity financing by individual manufacturing corporations.

[3] The market value of mergers was estimated by applying the average of market to book value for Standard and Poor's stocks to estimates of the assets value of large mining and manufacturing firms acquired, as reported by the Federal Trade Commission.

Both of these findings suggest that equity financing is a "source of last resort." Nonfinancial corporations seem to turn to equity financing only when all other sources of capital have been exhausted. This further suggests that the decline in the share of funds raised through issues of equity securities in the 1960's relative to the 1950's may be due to an increase in the availability of external funds from other sources, particularly bank credit.

The rising trend in the share of funds used to retire equity seems most reasonably explained by the growth of internally generated funds relative to internal investment opportunities for some corporations. Tests of this hypothesis are, however, hampered by lack of appropriate data. At the aggregate level, cash retirements are not highly correlated with internal funds flow once the strong time trends are removed from both variables. Nor is there any evidence that retirements behavior is strongly influenced by the behavior of stock prices. The rising trend of noncash retirements, that is, exchanges of debt for equity, might plausibly be explained by trends in merger activity. However, since the share of mergers consummated through exchanges of debt for equity is likely to vary widely from year to year, there is not a strong correlation between the volume of exchanges and the estimated market value of mergers.

5

The Demand for Corporate Stock in the Postwar Period

MAHLON R. STRASZHEIM

UNIVERSITY OF MARYLAND

1. INTRODUCTION

The demand for corporate equity is influenced by the preferences of households for investing their wealth, by the financial market structure through which intermediation occurs, and by the investment behavior of financial institutions. Financial institutions have assumed an ever increasing role in the market for corporate stock. The causes are twofold—a gradual shift in household preferences away from direct holdings of stocks in favor of indirect holdings through mutual fund shares and pension savings, and a change in the investment strategy of institutions in favor of stocks.

Household preferences for financial savings are discussed in section 2 below. Households may choose among a wide range of alternative means of holding financial assets, each with different attributes (expected return, variance of return, marketability, negotiability). Financial intermediation has grown increasingly specialized in the postwar period as particular types of institutions adapted to meet specific needs of different borrowers and lenders. While fund flows to financial intermediaries are dominated by rather strong trends, in the short run there are notable fluctuations in the flows of household savings to different types of financial intermediaries in response to changes in income, prices, interest rates, and stock prices. Both the trend and cyclic variations in savings flows to financial institutions influence these institutions' investment decisions.

The investment strategies of financial institutions differ widely. Historically, institutional considerations have been the most important determinant of investment portfolios. For example, there are statutory restrictions on the types of investments that some institutions may make.

Fiduciary trustees operate in a context established by statute, the courts, and traditions. This institutional environment has evolved very slowly, and hence investment portfolios of financial institutions in the postwar period are characterized by rather stable trends. Changing stock market prices or rates of return on other financial assets appear to exert a relatively minor influence on institutions' portfolio decisions. The most dramatic shift in the demand for corporate equities occurred only near the end of the period—since 1967—when life, fire, and casualty insurance companies, state and local retirement funds, and corporate pension funds all very sharply increased their share of new funds invested in corporate stock. The investment decisions by financial institutions, particularly their decisions regarding common stock, are discussed in sections 3 and 4, with special attention devoted to the period since 1967.

2. FINANCIAL SAVINGS BY THE HOUSEHOLD SECTOR

a. Issues in Model Specification and Estimation

Household financial saving shifted over several decades from real assets (residential housing, farms, unincorporated businesses, and so on) to financial assets. This trend has continued in the postwar period. Continued industrialization, a longer life span, and greater reliance on group over self-insurance have all been contributing causes.[1] In addition, the value of corporate stock increased much more than income as a result of the increase in price-earnings multiples during the 1950's. Thus, while saving as a percentage of income has been constant, household holdings of financial assets have grown more rapidly than income in the postwar period. As shown in Table 5-1, the ratio of household financial assets to income has risen from slightly less than 2 in 1950 to $2\frac{3}{4}$ in 1968.

The long-run trends in household choices among financial assets are evident in Table 5-1. Most notable is the huge rise in the value of corporate stock holdings, from $155 billion in 1951 to $873 billion in 1968. This accounts for most of the increase in household holdings of marketable securities. Households have only moderately increased their net purchases of bonds and other fixed-income securities. While the value of their corporate stock holdings has risen continuously, households have shifted from being net purchasers of corporate stock to being large net sellers over this time period. That household stockholdings have increased in recent years in spite of households' net sales is attributable to increases in equity prices.

[1] Raymond W. Goldsmith, *The Flow of Capital Funds in the Postwar Economy*, New York, National Bureau of Economic Research, 1965.

TABLE 5-1

Asset Holdings and Net Fund Flows of Households,[a] 1951–68

	Billions of Dollars				Percentage Distribution			
	1951 (1)	1960 (2)	1964 (3)	1968 (4)	1951 (5)	1960 (6)	1964 (7)	1968 (8)
	Financial Asset Holdings							
1. Currency and demand deposits	58.3	65.0	80.6	109.7	12.1	6.8	6.1	5.9
2. Savings accounts	71.6	165.3	252.9	357.4	14.9	17.3	19.0	19.0
3. Life insurance reserves	57.8	85.2	101.1	120.0	12.0	8.9	7.6	6.4
4. Pension fund reserves	27.5	90.7	137.3	202.9	5.7	9.5	10.3	10.8
5. Bonds	82.1	110.5	120.2	149.8	17.1	11.6	9.0	8.0
6. Corporate stock	155.4	394.2	587.4	873.2	32.3	41.2	44.1	46.5
7. Other financial assets[b]	28.4	46.2	52.0	63.5	5.9	4.8	3.9	3.4
8. Total financial assets	481.0	957.1	1,331.4	1,876.4	100.0	100.0	100.0	100.0
	Net Fund Flows[c]							
1. Currency and demand deposits		10.4	16.0	28.6		4.2	10.1	12.9
2. Savings accounts		97.9	87.7	105.7		39.6	55.7	47.6
3. Life insurance reserves		29.0	15.5	18.7		11.7	9.8	8.4
4. Pension fund reserves		61.1	38.5	55.9		24.7	24.4	25.2
5. Bonds		28.0	8.7	30.6		11.3	5.5	13.8
6. Corporate stock		11.1	4.5	15.5		4.5	2.9	7.0
7. Other financial assets[b]		19.3	5.7	11.5		7.8	3.6	5.2
8. Total financial assets		247.4	157.5	221.9		100.0	100.0	100.0

Notes to Table 5-1

SOURCE: Board of Governors of the Federal Reserve System, *Flow of Funds Accounts 1945–1968*, 1970.
ª Including personal trust funds and nonprofit institutions.
ᵇ Excluding net investment in corporate business.
ᶜ Period ending with year indicated at top of column.

Conventional portfolio theory of asset management provides the conceptual framework for empirically analyzing the interrelationships between alternative forms of financial asset holdings and their changes. In conventional portfolio theory, desired financial asset holdings are assumed to be positively related to income and expected asset prices or rates of return.[2] Uncertainty is represented by including higher moments of the joint probability distribution for rates of return for the different types of assets. Most analysis has focused on the variance, with investors assumed to accept greater risk in exchange for a higher expected return. If there are positive covariances between rates of return of different types of assets, the investor trying to achieve the least risk associated with any target expected return will diversify his portfolio.

The simplest representation of the income effect is a positive relationship between desired asset holdings and current income (independent of other variables such as asset prices). Assuming changes in asset prices or other variables are independent of changes in income, observed savings flows would therefore also be positively related to changes in income. The common upward trends in income and in the accumulation of financial assets are such that this type of equation statistically accounts for a significant share of the total variance in financial flows. However, while taking full advantage of the common trends, this specification poorly represents the short-run variations in flows of funds. The above formulation implies that net additions to financial asset holdings would have the same sign as changes in income. Aggregate data for the accumulation of most financial assets do not substantiate this formulation. Typically, net accumulation of most types of assets continues even when income falls. More sophisticated versions would introduce lag structures in the formation of households' expectations regarding changes in income and asset prices, and in households' reactions to changes in these variables. Thus, for example, the relevant measure of income to which households

[2] Harry Markowitz, *Portfolio Selection*, New York, Wiley, 1959; Donald Farrar, *The Investment Decision Under Uncertainty*, Englewood Cliffs, N.J., Prentice-Hall, 1962; Donald H. Hester and James Tobin, eds., *Studies of Portfolio Behavior*, Cowles Foundation Monograph 20, New York, Wiley, 1967.

respond might be a weighted sum of current and previous years' incomes. This would explain the continued accumulation of virtually all types of financial assets in years when income declines—"permanent" income based on a lag structure over several years has continually risen though current income has occasionally declined for one year.

Unfortunately aggregate annual data for the postwar period are insufficient to provide empirical estimates of these more complex models of the formation of expectations and the associated lag structures. Variables describing income and the accumulation of financial assets are trend dominated. These trends make it virtually impossible to test alternative hypotheses about medium- or longer-term lag structures with a short annual time series.

However, after certain simplifying assumptions are made, the data do permit examination of the short-run responses to changes in income and asset prices. The model below assumes that actual asset holdings in any time period coincide with desired levels of such holdings. Dynamic stock-adjustment models in which there are lags in adjustment are popular in econometric estimation, especially for durable goods. There are several reasons why no attempt was made to specify lagged adjustment processes in the model below. The costs of entry into the capital markets are generally quite low, and "indivisibilities" would not appear to have large effects on transactions costs for most assets. Low transactions costs greatly reduce the likelihood that desired and actual asset holdings diverge. Also, for annual data aggregated for the entire household sector, there is likely to be little variation over time in the nature of adjustments of actual holdings to desired levels and certainly little or no prospect of specifying such differences econometrically with annual time-series data.

Because of data limitations the model does not attempt to choose among alternative lag structures between income and asset changes. Financial flows by asset type are linearly related to income, rather than to changes in income. The dependent variable was expressed in ratio form, the ratio of net purchases (or sales) of each asset type to income

$$(1) \qquad \frac{dA_{it}}{Y_t} = \alpha_i + \sum_j \beta_{ij} X_{jt}$$

where A_{it} equals assets of type i at time t, Y_t is income, and X_{jt} are independent variables. An equation was estimated independently for each asset type i. Since the marginal propensity to save varies from year to year, it is inappropriate to constrain the estimates of the individual equations to a constant savings rate. However, decisions about several forms of saving are interrelated. Several equations are estimated below relating ratios of one asset type to another (or to the sum of several others) to changes in income and asset prices.

This model is based on income and individual asset prices, and excludes total wealth as an independent variable. Asset prices and wealth are, of course, related. Changes in interest rates or stock prices appear in most of the flow equations; these changes are highly correlated to the value of corporate stock or fixed-income security holdings. Thus, while market prices or yields are included in the flow equations rather than asset values, there is no statistical basis for determining whether the correlation of market prices with flows represents households' reaction to changes in rates of return or to changes in the market value of particular asset holdings.

This model formulation implies that the ratios of particular asset holdings or total wealth to income may assume different values, depending on initial conditions and the estimated flow equations. While this assumption is at variance with conventional portfolio theory, it is substantiated by the postwar experience. The biggest source of changes in total wealth arises from changing stock-market prices. Household reactions to rather large changes in stock prices or the value of their aggregate financial-wealth holdings, sometimes 20 percent in a year, have, in fact, been rather modest; no change in aggregate savings is evident, and flows of funds in and out of stocks in any year are usually less than one percent of total stockholdings. Thus, short-run changes in total wealth generally do not prove to be significant in explaining short-run changes in holdings. If the ratio of total wealth to income matters, the effects occur only over a long period of time, and are presumably one of the factors influencing the long trends underlying the data on financial-asset accumulation.

Finally, the equations assume that causation runs from income or capital market conditions, as represented by interest rates or stock prices, to household savings rather than vice versa. The implicit causal assumption in the analysis below is that monetary and fiscal policies interacting with private demands for goods and services determine income and interest rates. These in turn affect household saving flows. This is not to deny the important interdependencies between decisions regarding financial asset holdings and income or credit market conditions. However, the available evidence suggests that the lags are long. Changes in household saving decisions, in fiscal or monetary policies, or in private demand affect the level and composition of income and the credit markets only after a lag. Econometric models have made little progress to date in describing the interrelationships between the processes of financial intermediation and real economic activity.

The following types of household financial assets are included in the model below:

DD = demand deposits (millions of dollars)
SD = savings deposits
LI = life insurance contracts
PF = pension fund reserves
F = fixed income securities (public and private bonds, mortgages)
S = corporate stock
MF = mutual fund holdings.

Annual data from *Flow of Funds Accounts 1952–1968* (Board of Governors of the Federal Reserve System) are used. The distinctions between the several types of assets in the class "fixed-income securities" are relatively insignificant in the context of a general model representing aggregate financial savings decisions. The one significant component of household savings and financial asset holdings not included is that of "unincorporated business investment."

In the analysis below, income and expected returns on assets, as reflected in current and lagged market yields, were employed as explanatory variables. The sample size was too small to yield significant estimates of the effects of change in the variance of returns on portfolio choices. Independent variables used in the equations included income, interest rates, and stock yields. Definitions and data sources are as follows:

Y = personal money income (billions of dollars) (Board of Governors of the Federal Reserve System, *Flow of Funds Accounts*)
RB = rate of return on three- to five-year government securities (*Economic Report of the President*)
RS = rate of return on equity; price appreciation plus dividends for NYSE 500 index (NYSE, *Fact Book*, 1969)
t = time trend (assumed values 1, 2, . . . , 17 for this sample)

Since the short-run variations in the several popular stock market indices are highly correlated, there is little or no advantage statistically in using a different equity price index. Nor has more than one of the several available interest rates series been included. While the yield curve does fluctuate in the short run, most interest rate variables are highly correlated over time. Thus, in the equations below, the bond rate variable is a proxy for all interest rates; the variable denoting the annual change in interest rates on bonds serves as a proxy for changing credit market conditions generally.

b. Empirical Estimates of the Model

1. *Demand Deposits.* The concept of household preferences for money balances has been a cornerstone of macroeconomic theory and the subject of a considerable theoretical literature.[3] Several empirical formulations of such demand functions have been estimated.[4] The controversy revolves around the elasticity of interest rates.

Annual data for the period 1952–68 were used to test the competing hypotheses. The early postwar years were excluded for two reasons—households had acquired unusually large amounts of liquid assets during World War II, which affected their decisions concerning financial asset holdings, and the capital markets were substantially affected by the Federal Reserve System's policy of fixing the interest rate on long-term Treasury securities at a low level. This policy was abandoned with the Accord of 1952. The dependent variable in the equation is the share of income which households used to add to their demand deposits holdings.

$$(2) \qquad \frac{DD_t}{Y_t} = \underset{(1.33)}{-99.00} + \underset{(1.76)}{.4807t} - \underset{(1.91)}{43.63} \frac{RB_t}{RB_{t-1}} + \underset{(1.58)}{13.60} \frac{Y_t}{Y_{t-1}}$$

$$R^2 = .4970$$

$$D.W. = 2.15$$

where DD_t represents the change in demand deposits in year t (millions of dollars), Y_t is income (billions of dollars), and RB is the bond rate (three- to five-year government securities).

[3] Irving Fisher, *The Purchasing Power of Money*, New York, Macmillan, 1911; John M. Keynes, *The General Theory of Employment, Interest and Money*, London, Macmillan, 1936; W. J. Baumol, "The Transactions Demand for Cash: An Inventory Theoretic Approach," *Quarterly Journal of Economics*, November 1952, pp. 545–56; Milton Friedman, "The Quantity Theory of Money—A Restatement," in *The Optimum Quantity of Money and Other Essays*, Chicago, Aldric, 1969; James Tobin, "Liquidity Preferences as Behavior Toward Risk," *Review of Economic Studies*, February 1958, pp. 65–68; James Tobin, "The Interest Elasticity of the Transactions Demand for Cash," *Review of Economics and Statistics*, August 1956, pp. 241–47.

[4] Allan Meltzer, "Demand for Money: The Evidence from Time Series." *Journal of Political Economy*, June 1963, pp. 219–46; Milton Friedman, "The Demand for Money: Some Theoretical and Empirical Results," *Journal of Political Economy*, August 1959, pp. 327–51; Karl Bruner and Allan Meltzer, "Predicting Velocity," *Journal of Finance*, May 1963, pp. 319–34; Gregory Chow, "On the Long-Run and Short-Run Demand for Money," *Journal of Political Economy*, April 1966, pp. 111–31.

The explanatory variables include a time trend, the transactions demand for money, as evidenced by the significance of the change-in-income term, and short-run changes in interest rates. The negative coefficient of RB_t/RB_{t-1} indicates that households economize on their holdings of demand deposits as interest rates rise in the short run. The positive coefficient of Y_t/Y_{t-1} implies that one of the responses in the short run to changes in income is a more than proportionate increase in demand deposits. As will be seen below, the sum of all financial savings increases more than proportionally in the short run as income rises. This is consistent with the econometric literature on consumption functions, which employ distributed lag functions on income as the explanatory variable.[5]

2. *Savings Deposits.* A similar equation fitted for additions to savings deposits includes both the level of interest rates and their short-run changes. Short-run changes in income did not prove statistically significant.

$$(3) \qquad \frac{SD_t}{Y_t} = 81.22 + 7.398\,RB_t - 70.60\,\frac{RB_t}{RB_{t-1}}$$
$$\phantom{(3) \qquad \frac{SD_t}{Y_t} = } (3.38) \quad (3.86) \qquad\quad (2.89)$$

$$R^2 = .5574$$

$$D.W. = 1.67$$

The level of interest rates, RB_t, reflects a strong trend in the share of income devoted to savings. The negative coefficient on the interest rate change variable reflects the process of disintermediation, households switching from savings accounts to fixed-income securities when interest rates rise sharply. Interest rate regulation on commercial banks, mutual savings banks, and savings and loan associations, and other institutional

---

[5] M. Friedman, *A Theory of the Consumption Function*, Princeton, Princeton University Press for NBER, 1957; A. Ando and F. Modigliani, "The Life Cycle Hypothesis of Savings: Aggregate Implications and Tests," *American Economic Review*, March 1953, pp. 55–84; H. S. Houthakker and L. D. Taylor, *Consumer Demand in the United States*, Cambridge, Harvard University Press, 1966; N. Leviatan, "Estimates of Distributed Lag Consumption Functions from Cross Section Data," *Review of Economics and Statistics*, February 1965, pp. 44–53; F. Modigliani and A. Ando, "The Permanent Income and the Life Cycle Hypothesis of Savings Behavior: Comparisons and Tests," in *Proceedings of the Conference on Consumption and Saving*, Vol. 2, Philadelphia, 1960; J. Simon and D. Aigner, "Cross Section and Time-Series Tests of the Permanent-Income Hypothesis," *American Economic Review*, June 1970, pp. 341–51.

considerations are such that interest rates on savings deposits rise less rapidly than bond rates during periods of tight credit. As a result, disintermediation occurs and households switch to bonds. For example, during the period 1963 through 1965 households added an average of $24.4 billion to their savings deposits each year and acquired an average of $4.2 billion of public and private bonds and mortgages. During the tight money period of 1966, households acquired $12.9 billion of these fixed-income securities while increasing their savings deposits by only $19.0 billion. In 1967, when market rates on bonds had fallen rapidly relative to savings deposits rates, the pattern was reversed; savings deposits were increased by $32.5 billion, fixed-income securities by $3.5 billion. This pattern occurred throughout the postwar period and is the fundamental source of the countercyclical pattern in mortgage lending and, hence, in residential construction.

3. Pension Fund Holdings. Pension programs have grown rapidly in the postwar period. The reasons for this growth have been extensively described elsewhere.[6] Since the Supreme Court ruled in 1948 that fringe benefits were a proper part of labor contract negotiations, coverage of pension programs has grown enormously, and both contributions and benefit payments have risen sharply. Public pension plans for state and municipal employees also grew rapidly during the 1950's, as did union and other multiemployer plans.[7] Pension retirement plans for self-employed individuals received tax free status in 1962 with the Smathers-Keough Act, which permitted individuals to contribute sums (limited to $2,500 annually) to a common trust to be managed on a pooled basis. Liberalization in 1968 resulted in many more such plans being initiated; 100,000 plans registered in 1968 as compared to about half that number over the previous four years.[8]

Net fund flows to pension programs are the stablest of all forms of household financial savings. The equation for pension fund flows, including a logarithmic trend and the short-run change in income, is quite

[6] Daniel M. Holland, *Private Pension Funds: Projected Growth*, Occasional Paper 97, New York, NBER, 1966; Phillip Cagan, *The Effect of Pension Funds on Aggregate Savings: Evidence from a Sample Survey*, Occasional Paper 95, New York, NBER, 1965; and Roger F. Murray, *Economic Aspects of Pensions: A Summary Report*, New York, NBER, 1968.

[7] H. Robert Bartell, Jr., and Elizabeth T. Simpson, *Pension Funds of Multiemployer Industrial Groups, Unions, and Nonprofit Organizations*, Occasional Paper 105, New York, NBER, 1968.

[8] Wiesenberger Financial Services, Inc., *Investment Companies: Mutual Funds and Other Types*, 1969 edition, p. 90.

simple. Changes in interest rates or stock prices proved to be statistically insignificant.

$$(4) \qquad \ln\left(\frac{PF_t}{Y_t}\right) = \underset{(27.69)}{2.44} + \underset{(8.40)}{.0271t} + \underset{(1.76)}{.1610} \frac{Y_t}{Y_{t-1}}$$

$$R^2 = .8378$$

$$D.W. = 1.80$$

That short-run increases in income raise the share of income devoted to pension reserves may be attributed to several factors. Periods of prosperity extend the coverage of pension fund programs at a rate above the long-term trend by employing the marginal work force. More liberal pension agreements may be realized in times of prosperity and vice versa. Finally, there is a growing percentage of workers whose benefits are based on final compensation. This implies that short-run increases in income will lead to a higher share of income devoted to pension funds in the short run.

4. Life Insurance Reserves. Life insurance companies provide a guaranteed fixed-dollar payment to their customers, with premiums based on rather conservative investment assumptions. Life insurance was the first form of nonbank financial intermediation serving a wide market. Coverage has grown extensively throughout the twentieth century, so that, by 1965, 83 percent of all households had at least one member insured.[9] Currently about 15 percent of insurance company assets are held to cover the liabilities of insured pension funds. Historically, insured pension funds were the predominant form of pension savings, but insured pension plans have grown much less rapidly during the postwar period than uninsured plans.

A very small share of life insurance reserves is accounted for by variable annuity plans. Since 1963, some states have permitted life insurance companies to establish so-called "separate accounts" in which they invest pension reserves in equities. These are essentially equivalent to the common trust funds which commercial banks use to manage small pension accounts collectively. To date most variable-annuity offerings are oriented toward serving those who qualify under the Keough Act; there are few variable-annuity plans that are not sheltered.

The growth of life insurance reserves net of policy loans exhibits both a trend and short-run variations. While the trend in fund flows is positive,

[9] Institute of Life Insurance, *Life Insurance Fact Book*, 1966, p. 7.

the share of income that households devote to life insurance has steadily fallen.

(5) $\dfrac{LI_t}{Y_t} = 5.574 - 1.526\,RB_t - 9.794\,\dfrac{RB_t}{RB_{t-1}} + 19.16\,\dfrac{Y_t}{Y_{t-1}} - .0349\,RS_t$
$\phantom{(5)\ \dfrac{LI_t}{Y_t} = }$ (2.80)$\quad$ (5.99)$\qquad\quad$ (1.86)$\qquad\qquad$ (1.98)$\qquad$ (1.94)

$$R^2 = .7469$$

$$D.W. = 1.96$$

The cause for the downward trend in life insurance premiums as a share of income, as represented by the negative coefficient for RB_t, is the growth of alternative forms of savings yielding higher returns—corporate pension plans and mutual funds. Each yields higher returns by being more heavily invested in corporate equities. In addition, pension savings are tax free. It seems likely that life insurance contracts defined by current premiums and fixed payment obligations will continue to receive a lesser share of the consumer savings dollar. Insurance companies might enhance their product by offering variable-annuity plans as an inflation hedge or by reducing the premiums on straight life and term insurance, either policy requiring that insurance companies become more active in the equity market. Life insurance companies appear to have chosen another alternative, that of entering the mutual fund business. In 1968 and 1969, there was a large-scale merging and comingling of insurance companies and mutual fund management and equity. By the third quarter of 1969, 153 mutual funds were linked to 79 insurance companies or groups; $8 billion of mutual fund shares was involved—16 percent of the industry.[10] The economics of the mass marketing of both insurance and mutual fund shares are obvious. It would appear that life insurance premiums will continue to be based on fixed-income investments and that the trends in household choices for fixed obligation insurance described in equation (5) are likely to persist.

Short-term fluctuations in fund flows to life insurance have become significant since the middle 1950's. These variations are highly correlated with changes in money markets; in particular, life insurance flows are negatively correlated with short-run changes in interest rates. In each period of tight credit and rising interest rates since 1957, life insurance fund flows as a share of household income declined more than would be

[10] Wiesenberger Financial Services, Inc., *Mutual Affairs*, November 1969, p. 104.

indicated by the long-run downward trend in the share of household savings devoted to life insurance. There are several explanations. Life insurance companies are committed to lending to policy holders at fixed rates of interest; these lending terms inevitably become very attractive when market interest rates rise sharply and credit rationing occurs. While the 1966 credit crunch was the first in which this mechanism received much public attention, the negative coefficient on the term for changes in interest rates in equation (5) suggests that it has been operative and of empirical significance for some time. An additional explanation for the significance of the change-in-interest-rate variable is simply that rising market rates of interest are attracting household savings into fixed-income securities. This is discussed further below.

Stock prices also are significant in the equation, the negative coefficient implying that rising (stock) prices attract funds from life insurance. In the subsequent equations for household purchases of stock, stock prices appear to influence stock purchases with a one-year lag. Thus, the exact relationship between life insurance and net stock purchases, particularly the timing of such switches in asset holdings, remains unclear.

5. *"Fixed Interest" Long-Term Claims: Bonds and Mortgages.* No trend is evident in the share of income devoted to fixed-income securities, but there are very considerable cyclical variations. Additions to bond holdings are negatively correlated with short-run changes in income. The response of fixed-income security holdings to short-run changes in interest rates is very pronounced; households substitute bonds for savings deposits during periods of tight credit. This substitution is made largely by upper-income households. Holdings of marketable securities other than stock are more concentrated among wealthy households than any other form of investment assets. In 1963, the top tenth of the income distribution held 45 percent of total wealth, and 80 percent of total investment in marketable securities other than stock.[11] In recession years the actual share of income devoted to fixed-income securities falls. The equation below suggests that this negative income effect is more than offset by interest rate effects.

Stock prices are also significant in the equation for bond holdings, and are positively correlated when a one year lag is allowed. As will be seen below, households react to stock prices after a lag, switching out of stocks

[11] Dorothy S. Projector and Gertrude S. Weiss, *Survey of Financial Characteristics of Consumers*, Board of Governors of the Federal Reserve System, 1966, pp. 14–15.

after the stockmarket declines; the equation below suggests that some of these funds are finding their way into bonds and mortgages.

$$(6) \quad \frac{F_t}{Y_t} = 96.16 + 74.51 \frac{RB_t}{RB_{t-1}} - 160.9 \frac{Y_t}{Y_{t-1}} + .2129 \, RS_{t-1}$$
$$\quad\quad\quad (1.56) \quad (3.29) \quad\quad (2.38) \quad\quad (2.48)$$

$$R^2 = .6068$$
$$D.W. = 1.66$$

where F equals additions to holdings of fixed income securities, and RS_{t-1} equals return on stock with a one year lag.

Data for 1969 have only recently become available. Extrapolation with the above equation provides an estimate of the impact of tight credit during 1969. Based on the 22.5 percent increase in interest rates during 1969, equation (6) predicts that households will devote 1.7 percent of their income to fixed-income securities, compared with a mean level of about one-half of 1 percent during the postwar period. The actual percentage was 2.5 percent. The $23.1 billion invested in bonds was nearly double the rate during the 1966 credit crunch; 1969 was clearly a year of extraordinary participation in the bond markets by the household sector.

The tradeoffs between fixed-income securities, savings deposits, and life insurance reserves, all sensitive to short-run changes in interest rates, deserve brief summary.

$$(7) \quad \frac{F_t}{(F + SD)_t} = -.7255 + .9268 \frac{RB_t}{RB_{t-1}}$$
$$\quad\quad\quad\quad\quad\quad\quad\quad (2.082)$$

$$R^2 = .1857$$
$$D.W. = 1.32$$

$$(8) \quad \frac{F_t}{(F + SD + LI)_t} = -.9885 - .0360 \, RB_t + 1.276 \frac{RB_t}{RB_{t-1}}$$
$$\quad\quad\quad\quad\quad\quad\quad (3.18) \quad (1.46) \quad\quad (4.06)$$

$$R^2 = .5407$$
$$D.W. = 1.74$$

$$(9) \quad \frac{SD_t}{(F + SD + LI)_t} = 1.689 + .0667 \, RB_t - 1.257 \frac{RB_t}{RB_{t-1}}$$
$$\quad\quad\quad\quad\quad\quad\quad (5.71) \quad (2.83) \quad\quad (4.19)$$

$$R^2 = .5845$$
$$D.W. = 1.85$$

(10)
$$\frac{LI_t}{(LI + SD)_t} = \underset{(.96)}{.0891} - \underset{(6.47)}{.0476\, RB_t} + \underset{(3.05)}{.2859}\, \frac{RB_t}{RB_{t-1}}$$

$$R^2 = .7525$$

$$D.W. = 1.76$$

Equations (7) and (8) reveal the shift into fixed-income securities as interest rates rise in the short run. Equation (10) indicates that life insurance reserves fall less rapidly than do savings deposits when credit conditions are tightened and disintermediation occurs.

The sum of savings by fixed-income holdings, savings accounts, and life insurance as a percent of income is increasing over time, the increase in holdings of fixed-income securities and savings deposits having more than offset the decline in life insurance savings. This trend is reflected in a positive coefficient on interest rates in equations (11) and (12).

(11)
$$\frac{(F + SD)_t}{Y_t} = \underset{(1.39)}{-116.6} + \underset{(2.70)}{4.808\, RB_t} - \underset{(1.65)}{158.3}\, \frac{Y_t}{Y_{t-1}}$$

$$R^2 = .6060$$

$$D.W. = 1.38$$

(12)
$$\frac{(F + SD + LI)_t}{Y_t} = \underset{(1.29)}{-95.24} + \underset{(2.12)}{3.681\, RB_t} + \underset{(1.79)}{130.5}\, \frac{Y_t}{Y_{t-1}}$$

$$R^2 = .5385$$

$$D.W. = 1.12$$

While changes in income also appear in these equations, the significant autocorrelation reduces the statistical significance of the estimated co-efficients. Conspicuous by its absence in these equations is the short-run change in interest rates, which proves statistically insignificant.

This suggests that the reduced fund flows into life insurance and savings deposits associated with increasing market interest rates in the short run is essentially offset by higher flows into fixed-income holdings.

6. Corporate Stock and Mutual Fund Shares. Ownership of corporate stock is not nearly as widespread throughout the income distribution as pension funds, life insurance, or savings deposits. In 1963 one person in six held stocks,[12] and the wealthiest 10 percent of the population held 62 percent of the equity in publicly traded stock.[13] A trend toward a more even distribution of corporate stock ownership has prevailed throughout the twentieth century. From 1952 to 1956 the median money income of stockholders actually declined from $7,100 to $6,200, or 15 percent; while for the populace as a whole, median income rose by about that same percentage. However, since the early 1960's this trend has been altered due to the growth in mutual funds. Mutual funds provide a relatively inexpensive means for the small investor to diversify. As a result, direct investment in corporate stock is being displaced by investment in mutual funds. Both the 1962 and 1965 *Census of Stockholders* revealed the same proportion of the population holding corporate stock directly. During this three year period, median household income of shareowners increased 16 percent, the same increase as for median household income generally.[14] At the same time, mutual fund growth has been rapid and ownership increasingly widespread. Mutual funds had 9.1 million accounts by 1968 yearend versus 300,000 in 1940.

Two other characteristics of mutual fund purchasers deserve mention. In very recent years, the median family income of mutual fund holders has accelerated, rising from $8,100 in 1963 to $11,350 in 1966, an increase well in excess of the rise in income for the population generally. Also, the average age of those in accumulation plans rose sharply, from 42.8 to 46.4 years. This suggests that mutual funds are becoming an increasingly important means of providing retirement savings for middle- and upper-income households.[15]

Second, household acquisitions of mutual funds have shifted in favor of those with greater risk. In 1958, the share of the investment in mutual funds to be found in funds classified as "diversified common stock" was 60 percent; a decade later that figure had risen to 80 percent. "Balanced" funds, with 20 to 50 percent of their assets invested in fixed dollar holdings, saw their share of the mutual fund market decline from 26 to 14 percent.[16] As will be seen below, mutual fund market performance approximated the

---

[12] New York Stock Exchange, *Fact Book, 1968*, p. 40. The next survey was scheduled for 1970. There is no evidence on how the distribution of dollar amounts of stock held, by income class, is changing.

[13] Projector and Weiss, *op. cit.*, p. 15.

[14] NYSE, *Fact Book, 1968*, p. 40.

[15] Investment Company Institute, *Mutual Fund Fact Book*, 1969, p. 47.

[16] *Investment Companies: Mutual Funds and Other Types*, pp. 42–44.

return achieved by the market averages until 1965. Since 1965, the performance of the growth funds has improved substantially. By accepting higher risk, the growth funds were able to earn a significantly higher return, though it was accompanied by a higher variance. Whether households will continue to exhibit this preference for more risk remains to be seen.

Household annual acquisitions of corporate stock (both direct holdings and the sum of direct holdings and mutual fund shares) have turned from a marginal plus to a rather large negative amount during the postwar period. Households sold $12 billion in stocks (other than investment company shares) in 1968 and nearly $11 billion in 1969. One striking feature about this series is that its magnitude is very small, a tiny fraction of 1 percent of either total personal income or the total valuation on stock held. Moreover, it does not change much when stock prices change dramatically. A sizable portion of stockholdings is very inactive. A 1965 survey indicated that only one-half of all household stockholders acquired any stock that year, and that only one in eight made as many as five transactions. The average income of the small share who were more active in the market was very much higher than that for all shareholders generally.[17]

There are several explanations for the downward trend in net acquisitions. One is the long-run shift in relative prices in favor of fixed-income holdings. Bond rates have risen over these two decades, while returns on stock were lower in the 1960's than 1950's; for the period 1950–59 the compound rate of growth (price appreciation plus dividends) for the Standard and Poor's index of 500 stocks was 20.3 percent, versus 10.9 percent from 1958 to 1968.[18] Another explanation is the rise in pensions as an alternative means of savings. The declining share of income, or the share of financial savings, devoted to direct stock investment and mutual fund shares combined is represented by equation (13), revealing a negative correlation with the bond rate.

$$(13) \qquad \frac{(S + MF)_t}{Y_t} = 16.83 - 4.165\ RB_t$$
$$(7.69)$$

$$R^2 = .7476$$
$$D.W. = 1.41$$

[17] NYSE, *Public Transactions Survey*, 1965.
[18] NYSE, *Fact Book, 1969*.

The bond rate is essentially a trend proxy in this equation, reflecting the several sources of change discussed above. Neither short-run changes in interest rates or bond prices, nor a distributed lag or weighted average of current and past stock prices, proved statistically significant in this equation.

Disaggregation of direct and indirect stockholdings reveals more about household investment behavior. Both strong trends and short-run variations are apparent in household acquisitions of mutual funds. The rate of return in the stock market is correlated with net mutual fund sales (sales less redemptions) after allowing for a lag. The sharp stock market declines in 1962 and 1966 resulted in much lower mutual fund sales a year later. The following equation was fitted.

$$(14) \qquad \frac{MF_t}{Y_t} = .00053 + \underset{(8.76)}{.2537t} - \underset{(1.68)}{.0179}\ RS_{t-1}$$

$$R^2 = .8137$$
$$D.W. = 1.74$$

Short-run changes in income or interest rates did not prove statistically significant. The upward trend in mutual fund sales has been interrupted only by sharp variations in stock prices.

Direct corporate stock acquisitions and sales present a different picture. In addition to a downward trend, represented by a significant coefficient on the bond rate, short-run changes in income and interest rates are also statistically significant. Short-run increases in income coincide with a lower share of income devoted to stock purchases. The positive coefficient on changes in bond rates indicates that rate increases attract more money into stocks. This is not easily explained. As noted, fixed-income securities also attract funds during periods of rising interest rates. There have been several periods when stock prices fell as interest rates moved up. However, attempts to include stock prices in the equation, in either current or lagged terms, or by a weighted average, proved unsuccessful. The explanation for the positive correlation of net stock purchases with short-run changes in the interest rate remains unclear.

$$(15) \qquad \frac{S_t}{Y_t} = 20.52 - \underset{(13.95)}{6.301}\ RB_t - \underset{(1.57)}{26.17}\frac{Y_t}{Y_{t-1}} + \underset{(3.55)}{27.90}\frac{RB_t}{RB_{t-1}}$$

$$R^2 = .9210$$
$$D.W. = 2.14$$

Disaggregation of households' net stock purchases provides further insight. Odd-lot transactions are made largely by the small investor, primarily in the household sector. Net purchases of odd lots on the NYSE amount to about one-fifth of the total household sector's net flows. An equation for the ratio of odd-lot net purchases to income is

(16)

$$\frac{S_{1t}}{Y_t} = 7.555 - \underset{(4.98)}{.8987\ RB_t} - \underset{(1.66)}{10.79\ \frac{Y_t}{Y_{t-1}}} + \underset{(2.30)}{7.525\ \frac{RB_t}{RB_{t-1}}} + \underset{(2.03)}{.0220\ RS_{t-1}}$$

$$R^2 = .7035$$

$$D.W. = 1.21$$

where S_{1t} equals net odd-lot purchases on NYSE in year t. Stock prices enter with a one-year lag, while current stock prices are not statistically significant. Odd-lot purchases thus behave much like mutual fund net purchases. Households appear to react in belated fashion to stock prices, increasing their net selling of direct holdings *and* their redemption of mutual funds *after* stock prices decline. This is testimony to the familiar cliche that "the odd-lotters are always wrong." The most recent illustration is their actions during the 1966–67 market decline and recovery. Household mutual fund redemptions *and* net sales of direct stockholdings were much higher than usual in 1967, following the sharp market drop in 1966. The stock market was staging a huge recovery in 1967. While annual data is not suited to a determination of the precise timing of this phenomenon, the general outlines are clear.

The same equation for round lot net purchases (i.e., all household net purchases less those in odd lots) is similar, but stock prices in this case do not prove statistically significant.

(17) $$\frac{S_{2t}}{Y_t} = \underset{(2.10)}{54.65} - \underset{(8.85)}{4.8971\ RB_t} - \underset{(1.96)}{58.536\ \frac{Y_t}{Y_{t-1}}} + \underset{(2.68)}{21.967\ \frac{RB_t}{RB_{t-1}}}$$

$$R^2 = .9043$$

$$D.W. = 2.34$$

The "household" sector in the flow of funds accounts is an agglomeration of several types of accounts, including personal trusts and estates, colleges and universities, and nonprofit foundations. At year-end 1968 colleges and nonprofit foundations held $25 billion in corporate stock, while personal trusts held $95 billion. Together this was nearly one-eighth of the stock held by the "household" sector as defined in *Flow of Funds Accounts*. Trusts and foundations are likely to behave differently than households, but unfortunately no flow of funds data are available on their actions. By making explicit assumptions about the annual price appreciation of stockholdings by each group, the flow of money into or out of corporate stocks can be estimated. Together with reported asset holdings at the beginning and end of the year, estimates of flows of new funds into stocks (or withdrawals) can be derived. That estimate will be only as reliable as the assumptions about portfolio appreciation. It was assumed that portfolio appreciation for personal trusts, colleges, and foundations equaled the rate of price appreciation plus dividends for the Dow-Jones industrial average (DJIA). While this assumption is a reasonable approximation over the long run, the estimates for any given year are subject to some error. The error is probably largest when stock price changes are largest. Excluding estimated "fund flows" of personal trusts, colleges, and foundations from round lot net purchases, the relationship is

$$(18) \quad \frac{S_{3t}}{Y_t} = -27.68 - 8.048\ RB_t + 49.92\ \frac{RB_t}{RB_{t-1}} + .4050\ RS_t$$
$$\phantom{(18)\quad \frac{S_{3t}}{Y_t} = } (4.00) (1.78) \phantom{\frac{RB_t}{RB_{t-1}}} (3.50)$$

$$R^2 = .7864$$

$$D.W. = 2.59$$

where S_{3t} equals net purchases by "household" sector less odd-lots on the NYSE, and less estimated net purchases by personal trusts and estates, colleges and universities, and foundations. The significance of the stock price term is by no means unambiguous, since it may reflect misspecification in the net fund flows by personal trusts and estates.

Estimated net purchases by personal trusts and estates as a share of income reveal neither trend nor short-run responsiveness to income or interest rate changes. However, stock prices are negatively correlated with net flows.

$$(19) \quad \frac{PT_t}{Y_t} = 2.715 - .2048\ RS_t$$
$$\phantom{(19)\quad \frac{PT_t}{Y_t} = 2.715 - } (2.41)$$

$$R^2 = .3097$$

$$D.W. = 2.71$$

where *PT* equals net purchases of stocks by personal trusts and estates. The coefficient on stock prices is subject to two different interpretations: stock price declines may attract funds of personal trusts into stocks or their past holdings of stocks may fluctuate less in value than the DJIA, the assumption used to derive net flows.

7. Summary. Short-run increases in income raise the share of income devoted to financial savings in the aggregate, indicating that the short-run marginal propensity to consume is below its long-run level. Higher interest rates in the short run also induce households to devote a higher share of income to financial savings and to shift from life insurance and savings deposits into direct bond holdings.

Over the long run households are reducing their direct participation in the equities markets, while at the same time increasing their indirect holdings, by investing in mutual funds and uninsured pension funds. Currently, the increase in pension fund holdings and mutual fund shares more than offsets the decline in household sales of stock. The short-run variations in stock prices affect household investment decisions; stock market declines hasten the liquidation of households' direct stockholdings and reduce their willingness to buy mutual funds, in each case the reaction occurring after a time lapse.

3. THE STOCK INVESTMENT POLICIES OF THE MANY TYPES OF FINANCIAL INSTITUTIONS

An overview of the trends in the holdings and net purchases and sales of corporate stock by financial institutions in the postwar period was given in section 5 of Chapter 3. Also in that section was a summary of the relationship of these holdings and transactions to total acquisition of financial assets by financial institutions, to total net issues of corporate stock, to total volume of trading in corporate stock on exchanges in the U.S., and to the velocity of turnover of the stock portfolio of financial institutions. The present section reviews, still very summarily, the policies followed by the main types of financial institutions and their relation to other uses of their funds, employing a standard table (e.g., Table 5-2), and summarizes the scarce available information on the structure of the stock portfolios of these institutions.[19]

---

[19] It is expected that these matters will be analyzed in the Commission's own report in much greater detail for the last four years on the basis of new primary data specifically collected for this purpose.

TABLE 5-2

Structure of Assets and Transactions of Private Uninsured Pension Funds, 1951–69

(*percent*)

	1951 (1)	1955 (2)	1960 (3)	1965 (4)	1969 (5)
Distribution of financial assets					
1. Cash	3.8	2.2	1.3	1.2	1.7
2. U.S. govt. securities	26.9	15.8	7.1	4.6	3.2
3. State and local govt. securities	—	—	—	—	—
4. Mortgages	1.3	1.6	3.4	4.5	4.1
5. Loans	—	—	—	—	—
6. Corporate bonds	45.1	43.2	41.2	31.3	27.5
7. Corporate stocks	17.8	33.3	43.3	54.7	59.0
8. Miscellaneous assets	5.1	3.8	3.7	3.3	4.5
Total ($billion)	7.8	18.3	38.1	72.6	96.6
Distribution of net acquisition of financial assets[a]					
1. Cash		2.4	0.6	1.3	2.4
2. U.S. govt. securities		10.8	−1.9	3.5	−1.2
3. State and local govt. securities		—	—	—	—
4. Mortgages		1.2	5.6	8.7	2.7
5. Loans		—	—	—	—
6. Corporate bonds		53.0	48.4	30.3	15.7
7. Corporate stocks		28.9	43.5	51.9	73.7
8. Miscellaneous assets		3.6	3.8	4.3	6.7
Total ($billion)		8.3	16.1	23.1	25.5

SOURCES: *Flow of Funds Accounts 1945–1968* and *ibid., First Quarter, 1970.*
[a] Period ending with year indicated at top of column, derived from annual figures. Hence, occasional small differences may appear when compared with final differences between benchmark years.

a. Uninsured Pension Funds

Net fund flows into pension funds are growing rapidly, are unusually stable, and can be easily predicted on an actuarial basis, given assumptions about employee contributions, rates of retirement, and benefit payments. Pension funds do not face a liquidity problem arising from sudden changes in fund flows.

Originally, the investment objective of pension funds was that of achieving a return to meet a dollar target payment at some future date. Until about 1950, private pension funds were about equally divided between insured and uninsured plans. Insured pension funds were very conservatively invested, life insurance companies being severely limited in their opportunity to acquire corporate stock.

In the decade following World War II, corporate treasurers gradually adopted the investment strategy of maximizing returns subject to a risk limitation, rather than that of investing to minimize the risk associated with meeting a specified target based on particular conservative actuarial assumptions. In the years immediately following the war, the interest rates on long-term government bonds (pegged at $2\frac{1}{2}$ percent) kept interest rates on private bonds at similar low levels. The higher returns on common stock investments were strong inducement for bank trustees to invest an increasing share in stocks. Accordingly, uninsured pension funds quickly sold off the government securities which they had accumulated during World War II and invested primarily in corporate stocks and bonds, a process that can be followed in Table 5-2. This change was made possible by a revision in the New York State law allowing trustees to invest up to 35 percent of a fund in stocks.[20] The largest companies with established records were the obvious investment vehicle. A steadily rising trend is exhibited in the share of fund flows invested in corporate stock throughout the postwar period.

There is no statistical correlation between changes in the portfolio composition of pension funds shown in Table 5-2 and changes in rates of return on stocks or bonds. An important qualification must be made in interpreting this result. Aggregated data for all pension funds may conceal relationships that exist at the individual-firm level. If fund managers have different bases for forming price or interest rate expectations or if they respond at varying speeds to change in relative rates of return, aggregated data on portfolio composition will reflect the sum of these behavioral effects. For example, the gradual shift to stocks appearing in the aggregate

[20] Murray, *op. cit.*, pp. 72–80.

data may reflect a series of decisions, each made at a fairly discrete point in time by one of the various corporate treasurers (and their bank trust department advisers), that their funds should be more heavily invested in corporate stock. Many pension funds adopt a fixed percentage of fund flows as their target for corporate stock investment, which they do not change for many years. If the decisions by individual firms to change that target occur at different points through the sample period (for example, in response to changes in expected rates of return on stocks versus bonds, each fund employing very different lags in forming those expectations), aggregated data on portfolio composition may be trend dominated even though relative prices on stocks and bonds are important to the decision.

While aggregation in the data may conceal the role of relative prices in decisions regarding portfolio composition, it is likely that the real effects of changing interest rates or stock yields in portfolio decisions are not great. The predominant focus in most trust agreements is on long-term growth. As will be noted in section 4, bank trustees have tended to invest conservatively, essentially placing stock funds in medium and large companies with long-term growth potential. Turnover rates on pension funds are well below those of mutual funds (see Table 5-3). Short-run variations in business conditions and interest rates apparently have little effect on decisions regarding the share of portfolios devoted to stocks. In addition, trust departments manage a huge volume of assets, with large new fund flows. This makes it more difficult to pursue an aggressive investment policy which is responsive to short-run changes in bond and equity markets.

The future course of pension fund investment has been the subject of considerable speculation. The direction of future fund flows will reflect rates of return on alternative credit instruments. A recent suggestion that the flow of funds into corporate stock might stabilize or peak at about 60 percent, and similarly the suggestion that pension funds would increase their involvement in mortgages, are contradicted by the 1967–68 experience.[21] Corporate stock accounted for approximately 85 percent of fund flows in 1967 and 1968 and for 75 percent in 1969.

A limited number of pension accounts have adopted a riskier market strategy since 1967. Aggregate turnover rates for pension funds have increased significantly since that date. Some pension accounts have been switched from bank trust departments or self-management to private investment advisers or brokers managing special equity funds. These managers are generally offering a level of expected yield and associated

[21] *Ibid.*, pp. 92–97.

TABLE 5-3

Structure of Assets and Transactions of State and Local Government
Retirement Funds, 1951–69

(*percent*)

	1951 (1)	1955 (2)	1960 (3)	1965 (4)	1969 (5)
Distribution of financial assets					
1. Cash	1.8	1.9	1.0	0.9	0.9
2. U.S. govt. securities	51.8	43.9	30.3	23.6	15.5
3. State and local govt. securities	30.4	25.2	22.6	7.9	4.3
4. Mortgages	1.8	2.8	7.7	11.2	11.4
5. Loans	—	—	—	—	—
6. Corporate bonds	12.5	23.4	34.4	49.4	54.3
7. Corporate stocks	—	0.9	2.1	4.8	11.4
8. Miscellaneous assets	1.8	1.9	2.1	2.1	2.2
Total ($billion)	5.6	10.7	19.5	33.0	51.0
Distribution of net acquisition of financial assets[a]					
1. Cash					1.1
2. U.S. govt. securities		36.7	13.6	14.7	0.6
3. State and local govt. securities		20.4	19.3	−13.2	−2.2
4. Mortgages		4.1	13.6	16.9	11.7
5. Loans		—	—	—	—
6. Corporate bonds		36.7	48.9	69.9	62.8
7. Corporate stocks		—	4.5	9.6	23.9
8. Miscellaneous assets		2.0	—	2.2	2.2
Total ($billion)		4.9	8.8	13.6	18.0

SOURCES: Same as Table 5-2.

[a] Period ending with year indicated at top of column, derived from annual figures.
Hence, occasional small differences may appear when compared with final differences
between benchmark years.

risk that lies between the traditional conservative bank trust department philosophy and the high risk strategy represented by the smaller "performance"-oriented mutual funds. Bank trust departments have also responded in a limited way to their treasurers' interest in assuming more risk, by creating pooled equity funds within the bank that are oriented toward a higher turnover, high "performance" objective. A modest share of individual pension accounts are invested in such accounts, at the discretion of the corporate treasurer (often limited to 10 percent). In one instance, such a pooled equity fund constituted $800 million of the bank's total trust assets of $12 billion.[22] How much risk corporate treasurers will assume in managing their pension funds in the future is difficult to predict.

b. State and Local Retirement Funds

The characteristics of fund flows and investment objectives of state and local retirement funds are not unlike those of private pension funds. However, up until now political factors have resulted in a rather conservative investment strategy—a large share of funds invested in public securities and a very small share in corporate stock (Table 5-3). Public retirement funds have generally been managed by state or municipal treasurers. Funds have been gradually shifted from U.S. government and state and local securities into corporate bonds and, more recently, into mortgages. The share invested in stock has been quite small, less than 5 percent of new funds up until the middle 1960's. Throughout this period the performance on such portfolios has been disappointingly low.[23] A weak negative correlation exists between changes in interest rates and the share of funds devoted to corporate stock. For the period 1948–68, the share of funds devoted to stock by state and local retirement funds can be represented as follows:

$$(20) \qquad \left(\frac{S}{TA}\right)_t = \underset{(1.52)}{.1728} + \underset{(3.34)}{.0042(t)} - \underset{(1.48)}{.1651} \frac{RB_t}{RB_{t-1}}$$

$$R^2 = .3955$$

$$D.W. = 1.86$$

where S is net stock purchases, TA is the change in total assets, and RB is

[22] Robert L. Donerstein, "Bankers Trustman Furnum Has Most of the Answers," *Finance*, February 1970, pp. 10–15.

[23] Murray, *op. cit.*, pp. 102–10.

the interest rate on three- to five-year government bonds. Stock prices were not statistically significant in the equation.

The investment policies of public retirement programs appear to be changing rather dramatically in very recent years. Since 1967, the share of funds devoted to corporate stock has been rising rapidly; in 1967 and 1968, 15 to 20 percent of net fund flows were allocated to corporate stock versus less than 5 percent in earlier years. While the process of liberalizing legal restrictions and political constraints on the investment of such funds is likely to progress in an uncertain fashion, there appears to be a potential for a further dramatic shift to corporate equities. In 1969, Oregon pioneered a new approach, that of allowing outside professional managers to handle a portion of equity funds with full discretion. Other states appear headed in the same direction.[24] It seems likely that state and local government retirement funds will devote a much larger share of their funds to corporate stocks, as corporate pension funds have already done.

c. Life Insurance Companies

Historically, life insurance companies have been very conservative investors, on the presumption that their fundamental objective should be safety of principal. As a result over three-fourths of all life insurance assets have been invested in corporate bonds and mortgages (Tables 5-3 and 5-4). A variety of statutory and institutional considerations reduced the investment alternatives in corporate stock that were available to life insurance companies; state laws provide very strict limitations.[25] Most life insurance company assets are held by companies licensed in New York. Originally, New York State law prohibited investment in corporate stock. Relaxation of this restriction in 1951 allowed life insurance companies to invest up to 3 percent of total assets in common stock; an amendment in 1957 raised the limit to 5 percent. The law also prescribes limits on the type of company whose stock is eligible. A company must have paid a dividend in each of the previous ten years, and dividends must not have exceeded earnings in any year. Obviously, these restrictions severely limit the choice of stocks open to life insurance companies.

The extent to which statutory limitations have reduced the share of fund flows that life insurance companies have devoted to equities is the subject of some dispute. Brimmer noted that in 1951 when the first significant

[24]"Oregon Blazes the Pension Trail," *Institutional Investor*, February 1970, pp. 41–47.
[25] For a review of state laws and their effects, see Commission on Money and Credit, *Life Insurance Companies as Financial Institutions*, Englewood Cliffs, N.J., Prentice-Hall, 1962, pp. 75–159.

TABLE 5-4

Structure of Assets and Transactions of Life Insurance Companies, 1951–69

(*percent*)

	1951 (1)	1955 (2)	1960 (3)	1965 (4)	1969 (5)
Distribution of financial assets					
1. Cash	1.6	1.5	1.1	0.9	0.8
2. U.S. govt. securities	16.5	9.8	5.6	3.3	2.1
3. State and local govt. securities	1.8	2.3	3.1	2.3	1.7
4. Mortgages	28.9	33.6	41.6	39.7	37.9
5. Loans	3.9	3.9	4.3	5.9	7.8
6. Corporate bonds	41.2	42.1	36.1	39.0	38.5
7. Corporate stocks	3.3	4.1	4.7	5.2	6.9
8. Miscellaneous assets	2.7	2.8	3.4	3.7	4.2
Total ($billion)	66.7	87.9	115.8	154.0	190.0
Distribution of net acquisition of financial assets[a]					
1. Cash		1.0	—	0.5	—
2. U.S. govt. securities		−12.1	−8.1	−3.8	−3.6
3. State and local govt. securities		4.8	5.5	−0.3	−0.8
4. Mortgages		48.8	45.2	50.0	33.8
5. Loans		3.9	8.1	7.1	19.0
6. Corporate bonds		46.9	41.2	35.2	33.2
7. Corporate stocks		3.4	2.6	6.3	12.3
8. Miscellaneous assets		3.4	5.5	4.9	6.1
Total ($billion)		20.7	27.2	36.6	35.8

SOURCES: Same as Table 5-2.

[a] Period ending with year indicated at top of column, derived from annual figures. Hence, occasional small differences may appear when compared with final differences between benchmark years.

liberalization in the New York State law occurred, life insurance companies invested 40 percent less in stocks than in the year before.[26] A survey of the industry in 1959 revealed that an overwhelming majority opposed substitution of the prudent-man rule in place of statutory limitations. However, more than half the industry wanted the New York State law liberalized to allow 10 percent of a portfolio to be invested in stocks.[27] In general, the investment policy of life insurance companies through 1965 was quite conservative.[28] Annual acquisitions of common and preferred stock since 1958 are shown in Tables 5-5 and 5-6.

The rules for valuation of assets constitute the second major deterrent to stock investment by life insurance companies. Most life insurance companies are mutual companies and are required by law to return profits in excess of a stated level of net policy liabilities. Thus, determining asset values critically affects a company's cash flow and almost since its beginning has been the subject of dispute in the industry.[29] Valuation of stocks is required to be at market value, though in 1957 some modification was made for preferred stocks. This in turn is the basis for determining the reserves from which dividend payments are made. "Overvaluation" of assets due to temporary price increases leads to higher dividend payments, while "undervaluation," by using temporarily depressed security prices, produces huge paper losses. In actual practice, valuation rules are often changed and often suspended when large changes occur in securities prices. Fraine's study of the effect of valuation policy and practices suggests that the industry's valuation procedures may have reduced real solvency.[30] For present purposes, the most significant consequence is that the rules have discouraged investment in securities with above average risk, in both common and preferred stock.[31] The disincentives to investment in preferred stock have cost the industry a substantial amount, since their return in the long run has been well above corporate bonds.[32] The

[26] Andrew Brimmer, *Life Insurance Companies in the Capital Markets*, E. Lansing, Michigan State University Press, 1962, pp. 340–41.

[27] *Ibid.*, pp. 347–57.

[28] R. Hart, "Life Insurance Companies and the Equity Capital Market," *Journal of Finance*, 1965, pp. 362–67.

[29] For a good historical review, see *Life Insurance Companies as Financial Institutions* (note 25, above), pp. 166–73.

[30] Harold G. Fraine, *Valuation of Security Holdings of Life Insurance Companies*, Homewood, Ill., Richard D. Irwin, 1962, pp. 20–21.

[31] Lawrence D. Jones, *Investment Policies of Life Insurance Companies*, Boston, Graduate School of Business Administration, Harvard University, 1968, pp. 143–45.

[32] Alden C. Olson, *The Impact of Valuation Requirements on the Preferred Stock Investment Policies of Life Insurance Companies*, Occasional Paper No. 13, Graduate School of Business Administration, Michigan State University, 1964.

TABLE 5-5

Acquisition of Corporate Stock by Life Insurance Companies, 1958–68

(*$billion*)

	Total (1)	Preferred		Common	
		Total (2)	Public Utility[a] (3)	Total (4)	Public Utility[a] (5)
1958	0.37	.09	.07	0.28	.06
1959	0.51	.15	.10	0.36	.06
1960	0.66	.25	.21	0.41	.07
1961	0.92	.31	.21	0.61	.10
1962	0.77	.22	.12	0.55	.07
1963	0.79	.26	.16	0.53	.08
1964	1.07	.32	.23	0.75	.09
1965	1.46	.48	.31	0.98	.13
1966	1.32	.22	.12	1.10	.14
1967	2.07	.38	.21	1.69	.20
1968	3.32	.39	.18	1.93	.24

SOURCE: Institute of Life Insurance, *Life Insurance Fact Book*, 1969, p. 81.
[a] Includes very small amounts of railroad stock (for 1958–68, $35 million of preferred and $82 million of common).

opportunity cost of remaining largely out of the equity market in common stocks is even greater.

d. Non-Life-Insurance Companies

The growth of fire and casualty insurance companies has been much more sporadic than that of life insurance companies, and short-run changes in fund flows tend to be substantial. From 1946 through 1965, net fund flows fluctuated from $600 million to $1,800 million yearly, with little evidence of trend or business cycle effects. Since 1966, growth has been much more rapid. In both 1966 and 1967, fund inflows exceeded $2 billion, and in 1968 they were over $3 billion.

Instability in fund flows has induced non-life-insurance companies to invest significant amounts in government securities, which serve largely as a hedge against uncertainty. The observed short-run variation in

TABLE 5-6

Industrial Structure of Stockholdings of Life Insurance Companies, 1951–68

(percent of all stocks)

	Preferred Stock				Common Stock			
	Total (1)	Railroad (2)	Public Utility (3)	Other (4)	Total (5)	Railroad (6)	Public Utility (7)	Other (8)
1951	63.1	4.1	23.7	35.3	36.1	1.4	8.9	26.7
1952	60.6	4.3	24.3	32.0	39.4	1.6	10.1	27.8
1953	59.5	4.0	26.0	29.6	40.5	1.3	10.8	28.3
1954	53.0	3.0	26.4	23.6	47.0	2.0	11.8	33.2
1955	48.0	2.2	26.0	19.8	52.0	1.9	12.4	37.7
1956	44.3	1.8	24.8	17.7	55.7	1.6	12.8	41.4
1957	44.9	1.8	25.9	17.2	55.1	1.1	13.7	40.3
1958	38.0	1.5	22.7	13.8	62.0	1.4	15.0	45.6
1959	35.2	1.3	22.0	11.9	64.8	1.0	13.4	49.2
1960	36.1	1.2	23.6	11.4	63.9	0.8	16.4	46.8
1961	32.5	0.9	21.7	9.9	67.5	0.7	16.8	50.1
1962	34.6	1.0	23.0	10.7	65.4	0.7	16.6	48.1
1963	32.5	0.9	21.9	9.7	67.6	0.6	16.1	50.9
1964	31.7	0.9	21.7	9.1	68.3	0.6	16.4	51.2
1965	31.4	0.9	21.9	8.6	68.6	0.7	14.8	53.2
1966	32.0	0.7	23.0	8.3	68.0	0.6	13.8	53.6
1967	28.2	0.6	20.2	7.2	71.8	0.5	11.6	59.7
1968	24.5	0.4	17.6	5.6	75.6	0.5	10.4	64.7

SOURCE: Institute of Life Insurance, *Life Insurance Fact Book*, 1969.

TABLE 5-7

Structure of Assets and Transactions of Non-Life-Insurance Companies,
1951–69

(*percent*)

	1951 (1)	1955 (2)	1960 (3)	1965 (4)	1969 (5)
Distribution of financial assets					
1. Cash	8.7	6.2	4.6	3.3	2.8
2. U.S. govt. securities	39.9	28.9	19.9	15.2	8.4
3. State and local govt. securities	10.1	19.9	28.8	28.5	82.3
4. Mortgages	0.7	0.9	0.4	0.3	0.4
5. Corporate bonds	5.8	5.7	6.0	7.6	13.3
6. Corporate stocks	28.3	32.7	33.5	38.6	35.1
7. Miscellaneous assets	6.5	5.7	6.8	6.7	7.6
Total ($billion)	13.8	21.1	28.1	39.6	49.8
Distribution of net acquisition of financial assets[a]					
1. Cash		2.0	—	—	0.9
2. U.S. govt. securities		12.2	−7.0	4.6	−17.8
3. State and local govt. securities		55.1	68.4	50.8	43.9
4. Mortgages		—	—	—	—
5. Corporate bonds		6.1	8.8	18.5	33.6
6. Corporate stocks		16.3	15.8	13.8	29.0
7. Miscellaneous assets		8.6	14.3	12.3	10.3
Total ($billion)		4.9	5.7	6.5	10.7

SOURCES: Same as Table 5-2.

[a] Period ending with year indicated at top of column, derived from annual figures. Hence, occasional small differences may appear when compared with final differences between benchmark years.

government security holdings mainly reflects variation in claims (cf. Table 5-7). As with other financial institutions, government securities made up a large share of their assets after World War II. These were sold in the postwar period. Government securities have now been reduced to about one-tenth of the asset holdings of nonlife insurance companies.

Nonlife company investment portfolios exhibit several distinct trends and tradeoffs. First, a large share of funds is invested in state and local securities; unlike pension funds, nonlife companies are subject to corporate income tax and hence the tax-free status of municipal securities has proven attractive. However, their share in total funds has fallen over time while investments in corporate bonds and mortgages have risen, even though the after-tax yield on state and local government securities has been considerably higher. Relative rates of return are not statistically significant in explaining this tradeoff, nor are short-run changes in interest rates. However, during periods of declining fund flows the share of funds devoted to bonds falls, while conversely an increasing share is devoted to state and local securities. The following equations using annual data for the postwar period illustrate these tradeoffs. Net fund flows were defined exclusive of variation in government security holdings, which approximates the portion of assets that may be invested with a longer time horizon.

$$(21) \qquad \frac{SLG_t}{(TA - G)_t} = \underset{(1.99)}{.9701} - \underset{(1.87)}{.0714}\, RB_t - \underset{(2.19)}{.1838}\, \frac{(TA - G)_t}{(TA - G)_{t-1}}$$

$$R^2 = .4008$$

$$D.W. = 1.54$$

$$(22) \qquad \frac{B_t}{(TA - G)_t} = \underset{(2.29)}{.1120} + \underset{(2.08)}{.0797}\, RB_t + \underset{(2.22)}{.1874}\, \frac{(TA - G)_t}{(TA - G)_{t-1}}$$

$$R^2 = .4065$$

$$D.W. = 1.82$$

where B equals net purchases of bonds, SLG equals net purchases of state and local government securities, and $TA - G$ equals the change in total assets less government securities.

Finally, there is no statistical explanation for the share of funds devoted to stocks. Neither fund flows, relative rates of return, or short-run changes in the capital markets appear relevant. The most noticeable occurrence is the rise in the share of funds devoted to corporate stock since 1967. This may be the result of a change in investment strategy or it may simply reflect the more than doubling of net fund flows over this two-year period.

e. Mutual Funds[33]

Investment strategy varies among different types of mutual funds, though only those most interested in safety of principal or income hold any appreciable part of their funds outside of stocks. In the aggregate, the industry invests 85 percent of fund flows in corporate stock. The industry's "portfolio response" to changes in interest rates or stock prices in the aggregate is to alter marginally (by a few percent) its cash holdings.

The most significant change in investment strategy by mutual funds occurred very recently. Many funds have increased the risk they are willing to take, placing greater emphasis on short-run performance. A much larger share of assets has been invested in smaller companies and unlisted securities. Also, turnover rates have increased sharply, from their long-run norm of about 20 percent through 1965 to levels twice that high in 1968 (Table 5-8). A recent survey indicated that the funds expect their turnover rates to remain at these high levels in 1975.[34] These changes are discussed below.

An adequate analysis of the portfolio structure of investment companies and changes in portfolios for the entire postwar period would have gone far beyond the scope of this study. Moreover, such a study has been made for limited periods in the 1950's (the Wharton Study), and another, for recent years, is now being undertaken in the Securities and Exchange Commission's Institutional Investor Study. It may therefore suffice to indicate in Table 5-9 the industrial breakdown of stockholdings of open-end investment companies at a few benchmark dates between 1952 and 1968 and to compare it with a similar breakdown of all common stocks listed on the New York Stock Exchange. The comparison will indicate the industrial sectors favored or neglected by open-end investment companies. Thus, for instance, mutual funds have always held a considerably smaller proportion of their portfolio in stocks of public utilities, railroads, automobiles, and chemicals than would correspond to those industries' share in NYSE listings or total stock outstanding.[35] On the other hand, mutual

[33] Investment Company Institute, *Management Investment Companies*, Englewood Cliffs, N.J., Prentice-Hall, 1962; University of Pennsylvania, Wharton School of Finance and Commerce, *A Study of Mutual Funds*, House Report No. 2274, 87th Cong., 2nd sess., Philadelphia, 1962; Securities and Exchange Commission, *Public Policy Implications of Investment Company Growth*, House Report No. 2337, 89th Cong., 2nd sess., Washington, D.C., 1966.

[34] Daniel Nordby and George DeVoe, "Secret Sales Tools for Researching Tomorrow's Institutional Buyer," *Finance*, December 1969, p. 26.

[35] The apparently high share of stock of financial companies in mutual fund portfolios reflects of course the fact that only relatively few companies in this sector are listed on the NYSE.

TABLE 5-8

Structure of Assets and Transactions of Open-End Investment
Companies, 1951–69

(*percent*)

	1951 (1)	1955 (2)	1960 (3)	1965 (4)	1969 (5)
Distribution of financial assets					
1. Cash[a]	2.9	21.5	2.4	1.8	6.0
2. U.S. govt. securities	2.9	3.8	3.5	3.0	1.2
3. Corporate bonds	8.8	6.3	7.1	7.8	7.0
4. Corporate stocks	85.4	87.4	87.0	87.4	85.8
Total ($billion)	3.4	7.9	17.0	27.1	52.6
Distribution of net acquisition of financial assets[b]					
1. Cash[a]		4.8	3.7	10.2	31.2
2. U.S. govt. securities		9.5	5.6	2.0	−2.8
3. Corporate bonds		9.5	13.0	18.4	12.8
4. Corporate stocks		76.2	77.7	69.4	58.8
Total ($billion)		2.1	5.4	4.9	10.9

SOURCES: Same as Table 5-2.
[a] Includes open market paper.
[b] Period ending with year indicated at top of column.

funds have invested more heavily in electronic,[36] drug, and building
material companies than would correspond to the relative supply of
shares of this type.

f. Personal Trusts and Common Trusts

Systematic data on the investment portfolios of personal and common
trusts are unfortunately unavailable. Common trust funds were initiated

---

[36] The comparison should be made for the sum of lines 1 and 2 in Table 5-9 because of
apparent differences in industrial classification of identical companies (probably including
IBM) in the two sources used in the comparison.

TABLE 5-9

Industrial Structure of Common Stock Portfolios of Open-End Investment Companies and of Common Stock Listed on NYSE, 1952–68

(*percent*)

	Holdings of Open-End Investment Companies					Listings on New York Stock Exchange			
	Dec. 1952[a]	Sept. 1958[a]	Dec. 1958	Dec. 1965	Dec. 1968	Dec. 1952	Dec. 1958	Dec. 1965	Dec. 1968
	(1)	(2)	(3)	(4)	(5)	(6)	(7)	(8)	(9)
Selected Industries with Substantially Rising Shares[b]									
1. Office equipment	1.2	2.6	3.3	5.0	9.4	1.0	2.8	1.3	1.8
2. Electrical equipment	3.4	2.5	3.5[c]	6.1[c]	7.9[c]	3.2	4.0	9.4	12.1
3. Drugs	1.8	3.6	4.7[d]	4.1[d]	5.6[d]	n.a.	n.a.	n.a.	4.5
4. Building materials	2.0	2.2	3.7	1.3	4.0	1.2	1.6	1.0	1.4
5. Foods and beverages	2.6	1.8	1.6	2.5	3.5	3.8	3.1	4.0	4.5
Selected Industries Without Trend[b]									
1. Finance	9.0	9.2	10.5	10.5	8.4	2.6[e]	2.3[e]	2.4[e]	4.0[e]
2. Retail trade	4.1	2.4	2.2	2.5	4.0	4.7	4.1	4.6	4.7
3. Mining	3.0	3.2	4.5[f]	3.8[f]	3.1[f]	3.1	3.0	2.2	2.9

(*continued*)

TABLE 5-9 (*concluded*)

	Holdings of Open-End Investment Companies					Listings on New York Stock Exchange			
	Dec. 1952ᵃ	Sept. 1958ᵃ	Dec. 1958	Dec. 1965	Dec. 1968	Dec. 1952	Dec. 1958	Dec. 1965	Dec. 1968
	(1)	(2)	(3)	(4)	(5)	(6)	(7)	(8)	(9)
	Selected Industries with Substantially Declining Sharesᵇ								
1. Utilities	17.0	12.7	13.6	10.5	6.3	16.1	17.3	18.5	14.3
2. Oil	14.8	14.1	15.8	10.0	12.8	18.6	16.7	13.7	14.6
3. Chemicals	8.7	7.3	7.0	6.5	7.0	14.2	14.5	15.0	9.3
4. Automobiles	3.3	2.9	2.3	4.6	2.2	8.1	7.0	7.9	5.5
5. Railroads	6.3	4.2	3.9	3.6	3.2	4.8	3.0	2.1	3.4
6. Rubber and tires	2.4	2.4	3.1	1.2	1.3	1.0	1.4	0.9	1.0
7. Steel	2.7	6.0	6.8	2.3	1.2	3.3	5.0	2.3	1.7

n.a. = not available.

SOURCES: Cols. 1, 2. *A Study of Mutual Funds*, 1962, p. 71; columns 3–5. *Mutual Fund Fact Book*, p. 22; columns 6–9. NYSE, Department of Research and Statistics.

ᵃ As a percentage of domestic stocks only; foreign stocks accounted for 2.4 percent in 1952 and 6.3 percent in 1958.
ᵇ Based on holdings of open-end investment companies.
ᶜ Includes electronics.
ᵈ Includes cosmetics.
ᵉ Includes real estate.
ᶠ Includes metals.

in the 1930's as a means by which banks could exercise fiduciary responsibility for small trusts at low cost. After the passage of the Keough Act in 1962, common trust fund assets grew from $3.6 billion in 1962 to $9.5 billion in 1968.[37] Generally a conservative investment strategy has been followed. Turnover rates have historically been well below those for other institutional investors. During the 1960–64 period, one study showed that over half of the equity common trust funds surveyed had turnovers ranging from 3 to 9 percent.[38] During this period only half of the funds outperformed the DJIA and only one-fourth exceeded the S&P 500 index.[39] More recent studies for the period 1961–68 indicate that common trust investment performance has been comparable to that of the S&P 500.[40] During this period a gradual evolution toward investing a higher percentage of funds in corporate stock occurred, as is evident in Table 5-10. Compared to other institutional investors, common trust funds have kept a relatively large part of their stock portfolio in conservative preferred and utility stocks (see Table 5-11).

Much less is known about the investment decisions of personal trusts. The share of total assets held in stock has risen over th postwar period, from 48 percent in 1951 to 70 percent in 1968 (see Table 5-12). As noted earlier, fund flows can only be derived from reported changes in asset holdings at year end and, hence, investment decisions regarding new commitments cannot be accurately determined. It appears that trustees have pursued very conservative policies. One survey indicated that turnover rates on private trusts during the week of October 21–25, 1963, were 2.5 percent, a level well below that of pension accounts.[41]

g. Commercial Banks and Thrift Institutions

Commercial banks and savings and loan associations are prohibited by law from holding corporate stock. Mutual savings banks are permitted to hold stock, but up until now have chosen to make little commitment in this area. Even in 1968, stocks represented less than 3 percent of their

[37] Edwin W. Hanczaryk, *Bank Trusts: Investments and Performance*, Office of the Comptroller of the Currency, 1970, p. 34.

[38] Frank L. Voorheir, "Bank Administered Pooled Equity Funds for Employee Benefit Plans," Graduate School of Business Administration, Michigan State University, 1967, p. 53.

[39] *Ibid.*, pp. 60–72.

[40] Edward Gill, "Equity Common Trust Funds," *Trusts and Estates*, February 1969, pp. 109–200; Hanczaryk, *op. cit.*, pp. 52–56.

[41] NYSE, *Institutional Shareownership*, 1965, p. 41.

TABLE 5-10

Structure of Assets and Transactions of Common Trust Funds, 1952–68

(*percent*)

	1952 (1)	1955 (2)	1960 (3)	1965 (4)	1968 (5)
Distribution of financial assets					
1. Cash	—	0.6	0.8	1.0	1.3
2. U.S. govt. securities	30.2	17.2	7.9	9.2	5.2
3. State and local govt. securities		1.7	1.6	14.9	16.3
4. Mortgages	75.6	1.1	1.6	2.4	2.4
5. Corporate and foreign bonds		19.2	28.8	25.0	23.9
6. Corporate stock preferred	12.5	11.5	7.6	2.9	2.6
7. Corporate stock common	40.1	48.7	51.7	44.2	47.7
8. Other assets	1.6	—	—	0.2	0.6
Total ($billion)	1.1	1.8	2.8	7.5	9.5
Distribution of net acquisition of financial assets[a]					
1. Cash		−314.3	−8.1	2.8	3.3
2. U.S. govt. securities			−37.2	28.9	−3.0
3. State and local govt. securities		566.6	47.6	6.5	17.6
4. Mortgages			−1.5	2.5	5.8
5. Corporate and foreign bonds			10.7	15.2	22.1
6. Corporate stock preferred		39.9	−5.0	2.8	5.4
7. Corporate stock common		−188.8	80.3	11.2	39.2
8. Other assets		−3.5	13.3	30.1	9.6
Total (percent)		100.0	100.0	100.0	100.0

SOURCES: 1952: R. W. Goldsmith, *Financial Intermediaries in the American Economy Since 1900*, Princeton, Princeton University Press for National Bureau, 1958; 1955–68: *ibid.*, Appendix I.

[a] Period ending with year indicated at top of column.

assets although net stock purchases in 1967–68 accounted for 5 percent of total fund uses (Table 5-13). Stock portfolios are concentrated on preferred shares and common stocks of banks and an investment company jointly owned by a number of savings banks (Table 5-14). It seems unlikely that banks will become active participants in the equities market.

TABLE 5-11

Industrial Structure of Stockholdings of Common Trust Funds, 1952–68

(*percent*)

	Preferred Stock (1)	Common Stock			
		Total (2)	Bank and Finance (3)	Utilities (4)	Other (5)
1952	24.1	75.9	n.a.	n.a.	n.a.
1953	22.9	77.1	n.a.	n.a.	n.a.
1954	20.2	79.8	9.2	16.8	53.7
1955	19.1	80.9	8.3	16.8	55.8
1956	17.5	82.5	7.6	16.9	58.0
1957	17.9	82.1	7.8	18.2	56.1
1958	14.6	85.4	8.4	19.0	58.0
1959	12.8	87.2	8.4	18.5	60.4
1960	12.8	87.2	8.6	21.3	57.3
1961	10.4	89.6	10.6	21.9	57.1
1962	12.0	88.0	10.0	22.8	55.1
1963	9.0	91.0	9.2	21.4	60.4
1964	7.3	92.7	8.3	20.9	63.5
1965	6.2	93.8	7.6	18.9	67.3
1966	5.4	94.6	8.1	19.2	67.3
1967	4.7	95.3	7.1	15.0	73.1
1968	5.2	4.8	3.0	14.3	72.6

n.a. = not available.

SOURCES: 1951–53: R. W. Goldsmith, R. E. Lipsey, and M. Mendelson, *Studies in the National Balance Sheet of the United States*, Princeton, Princeton University Press for NBER, 1963, Vol. II, p. 123; 1954–62: *Federal Reserve Bulletin*, various issues; 1963–68: Edwin W. Hanczaryk, *National Banking Review*, 1965, p. 365, and *ibid.*, 1967, p. 442.

h. Summary

The shift of institutions into stocks over the postwar period does not lend itself to any complex econometric explanation. Rates of return on equity have been much above bond rates throughout the period. The shift to stocks appears a belated and long process of adaptation to these circumstances.

TABLE 5-12

Structure of Assets and Transactions of Personal Trust Funds
Administered by Banks and Trust Companies,[a] 1951–68

(*percent*)

	1951 (1)	1955 (2)	1960 (3)	1965 (4)	1968 (5)
Distribution of financial assets					
1. Cash	2.2	2.4	1.0	1.0	1.0
2. U.S. govt. securities	23.8	12.2	5.9	7.2	5.7
3. State and local govt. securities	12.2	12.9	14.2	9.7	9.7
4. Mortgages	2.7	2.1	1.4	1.2	1.5
5. Corporate bonds	4.4	5.5	5.2	5.7	6.3
6. Corporate stock preferred	4.2	3.5	2.2	1.7	1.9
7. Corporate stock common	44.5	56.8	65.3	67.5	67.5
8. Other assets	6.6	4.6	4.8	6.6	6.4
Total ($billion)	39.1	55.0	71.9	115.0	138.4
Distribution of net acquisition of financial assets[b]					
1. Cash		3.5	0.0	1.7	3.3
2. U.S. govt. securities		−3.4	−16.3	12.7	−13.4
3. State and local govt. securities		10.3	2.1	29.1	29.6
4. Mortgages		6.5	4.0	3.7	3.3
5. Corporate bonds		59.3	74.0	29.0	27.2
6. Corporate stock preferred		24.5	−0.2	0.1	2.0
7. Corporate stock common		4.9	36.4	22.8	46.0
8. Other assets		−5.6	−0.0	0.8	1.8
Total (percent)		100.0	100.0	100.0	100.0

Source: Appendix I.

[a] Includes common trust funds; separate figures for these are shown in Table 5-11.

[b] Period ending with year indicated at top of column.

TABLE 5-13

Structure of Assets and Transactions of Mutual Savings Banks, 1951–69

(*percent*)

	1951 (1)	1955 (2)	1960 (3)	1965 (4)	1969 (5)
Distribution of financial assets					
1. Cash	3.8	2.9	2.0	1.7	1.2
2. U.S. govt. securities	42.1	27.5	16.5	10.7	6.3
3. State and local govt. securities	0.4	1.9	1.7	0.5	0.3
4. Mortgages	42.1	55.9	66.7	76.9	75.3
5. Loans	0.9	0.6	1.0	1.4	2.6
6. Corporate bonds	9.4	8.3	9.4	5.0	9.3
7. Corporate stocks	0.9	2.2	2.0	2.4	3.1
8. Miscellaneous assets	0.4	0.6	0.7	1.4	2.0
Total ($billion)	23.5	31.3	40.5	58.1	74.4
Distribution of net acquisition of financial assets[a]					
1. Cash		1.2	−2.1	0.6	−0.6
2. U.S. govt. securities		−26.7	−19.8	−3.4	−10.1
3. State and local govt. securities		6.8	—	−2.3	−0.6
4. Mortgages		107.0	100.0	100.6	71.1
5. Loans		—	1.0	2.3	6.3
6. Corporate bonds		5.8	14.6	4.5	25.8
7. Corporate stocks		4.7	3.1	3.4	5.0
8. Miscellaneous assets		1.2	3.1	3.4	3.1
Total ($billion)		8.6	9.6	17.7	15.9

SOURCES: *Flow of Funds Accounts, 1945–1968. Ibid., First Quarter, 1970.*

[a] Period ending with year indicated at top of column, derived from annual figures. Hence, occasional small differences may appear when compared with final differences between benchmark years.

TABLE 5-14

Industrial Structure of Stockholdings of Mutual Savings Banks, 1953–68

(*percent*)

	Preferred Stock			Common Stock				
	Total (1)	Convertible (2)	Straight (3)	Total (4)	Banks (5)	Insurance (6)	Investment Companies (7)	Other (8)
1953	n.a.	n.a.	n.a.	n.a.	65.9[a]	n.a.	n.a.	34.1[b]
1954	n.a.	n.a.	n.a.	n.a.	56.2[a]	n.a.	n.a.	43.8[b]
1955	26.3	1.5	24.8	73.5	49.9	3.9	3.5	16.2
1956	28.7	1.6	27.0	71.4	47.5	4.1	3.8	16.0
1957	29.0	1.3	27.8	71.1	44.7	3.8	5.2	17.3
1958	30.8	1.4	29.4	69.1	41.3	3.8	5.5	18.5
1959	32.4	1.0	31.5	67.6	40.1	3.6	6.8	17.1

1960	32.7	0.7	32.1	67.2	39.4	3.7	8.1	16.0
1961	30.0	0.5	29.5	69.9	36.7	3.7	8.8	20.8
1962	30.6	0.8	29.8	69.4	33.3	3.9	9.8	22.5
1963	30.9	0.9	29.9	69.1	31.5	3.5	10.2	23.9
1964	29.8	0.8	29.0	70.3	32.0	3.5	9.8	24.9
1965	29.3	1.60	27.7	67.4	30.7	3.5	10.3	22.9
1966	31.2	n.a.	n.a.	68.8	29.9	3.2	10.3	25.3
1967	32.0	n.a.	n.a.	68.1	26.9	2.5	11.6	27.2
1968	30.1	2.00	28.1	69.9	25.0	1.2	13.1	30.5

n.a. = not available.

SOURCES: 1953–60: Unpublished data of the National Association of Mutual Savings Banks; 1961–68: *Savings Bank Journal*, various issues.

a Includes both common and preferred.
b Includes all stock, both common and preferred, not held by commercial banks.

4. THE RETURN ON EQUITY AND INSTITUTIONAL INVESTMENT SINCE 1967

The sharp shift to stock by all major institutional investors in 1967 and 1968 occurred at a time when returns on equity were less attractive relative to bonds than at any other time throughout the postwar period. Institutions appear to have changed their expectations regarding the future return on equity investment in response to the high return earned by a

TABLE 5-15

Price Appreciation Plus Dividend Yield: Selected Stock Market Indices, 1952–69

	DJIA	S&P 500	NYSE Composite	AMEX	Over the Counter[a]
1952	21.3	23.4			
1953	14.2	17.7			
1954	11.8	−1.2			
1955	50.2	51.2			
1956	7.0	6.4			
1957	−8.5	−10.5			
1958	38.6	42.4			
1959	20.0	11.8			
1960	−6.2	0.3			
1961	22.4	26.6			
1962	−7.6	−5.4			
1963	20.6	22.5			
1964	18.7	16.3			
1965	14.2	12.3	9.5	39.5	30.1
1966	−15.6	−10.0	−12.6	−6.6	−1.5
1967	18.9	23.7	23.1	76.5	54.0
1968	7.4	11.1	9.7	33.2	20.8
1969	−15.2	−11.4	−12.5	−19.7	

SOURCE: New York Stock Exchange, *Fact Book*.
[a] 35 industrials (National Quotation Bureau).

segment of the mutual fund industry. "Growth funds" have increased the proportion of their asset holdings in medium-sized and smaller companies and have assumed more risk, a strategy contrasting sharply with traditional practice, e.g., the policy of most bank trust departments. The publicity about growth funds' "performance" and their approach to investment since 1967 apparently induced some pension and other trusteed accounts to assume more risk, and inflated expectations regarding the return on equity for all types of institutional investors.

a. The Return on Equity

Several indices which measure the return (price appreciation plus dividends) on different groups of equity investments are shown in Table 5-15. Dividend yields have been falling relative to capital gains throughout the postwar period. Rising tax rates, the provision for lower capital gains taxation, and the advantages to corporations of internal financing seem to be the principal reasons for this change.

The explanations for the trends in stock prices and much of their short-run fluctuation lie in fundamental economic factors, which affect the expectations of all actual and potential corporate stockholders. The level of stock prices responds in turn to these changes in expectations. Price-earnings ratios are the best single measure of investors' expectations concerning the further return on equity investments. A doubling of price-earnings ratios occurred from the end of World War II to their peak in 1961 (see Table 5-16). The upward revision in these ratios during the 1950's suggests the increasing belief of investors that equity investments were undervalued relative to bonds in that decade. This increase in multiples accounted for over half of the growth in stock prices during this period (their annual rate of increase was about 20 percent). Since 1961, multiples have fluctuated in the 13–20 range. The 10 percent annual rate of increase in stock prices from 1960 through 1968 essentially mirrors the growth in after-tax corporate profits.

In addition to these changing trends, the composition of returns among companies has changed. While the indices of stock prices are highly correlated, the more broadly based averages, the Standard and Poor's 500 index or the New York Stock Exchange index of all stocks on the Exchange, have a higher long-term growth rate than the Dow-Jones industrial average, which is made up of thirty of the larger, more established companies. From 1950 through 1959 the compound rate of growth was 19.5 percent for the DJIA, versus 20.3 percent for the Standard and

TABLE 5-16

Stock-Bond Yield Differentials, 1952–68

| | Common Stock Return | | | Bond Return Rate[c] | Yield Gap | | Price-Earnings Multiple | Implicit Price Deflator for GNP | Corporate Profits After Taxes |
| | Dividend Yield[a] | Capital Gains[b] | Total Yield | | Current (1) − (4) | Total (3) − (4) | | | |
	(1)	(2)	(3)	(4)	(5)	(6)	(7)	(8)	(9)
1952	5.80%	9.4%	17.8%	2.96%	2.84%	14.8%	9.3%	87.5	$17.0
1953	5.80	−4.4	−1.2	3.20	2.60	−4.4	10.5	88.3	15.5
1954	4.95	4.0	57.2	2.90	2.05	48.3	9.7	89.6	16.0
1955	4.08	26.8	31.0	3.06	1.02	27.9	11.3	90.9	22.2
1956	4.09	2.6	6.4	3.36	0.73	3.0	14.1	94.0	22.1
1957	4.35	−11.3	−10.5	3.89	0.46	−14.4	12.9	97.5	20.9
1958	3.97	34.0	42.4	3.79	0.18	38.6	16.6	100.0	17.5
1959	3.23	7.3	11.8	4.38	−1.15	7.4	17.1	101.6	22.5

1960	3.47	−0.5	0.3	4.41	−0.94	−4.3	17.1	103.3	20.6
1961	2.98	20.9	26.6	4.35	−1.37	22.2	21.1	104.6	20.5
1962	3.37	−9.4	−5.4	4.33	−0.96	−9.7	16.7	105.8	23.8
1963	3.17	17.5	22.5	4.26	−1.09	18.2	17.6	107.2	26.3
1964	3.01	12.9	16.3	4.40	−1.39	11.9	18.1	108.8	31.5
1965	3.00	8.8	12.3	4.49	−1.49	7.8	17.1	110.9	38.2
1966	3.40	−10.4	−10.0	5.13	−1.73	−15.1	14.9	113.9	41.1
1967	3.20	14.8	23.7	5.51	−2.31	18.2	17.5	117.6	38.1
1968	3.07	9.6	11.1	6.18	−3.11	4.9	17.2	122.3	40.0
1969	3.24	−13.0	−9.8	7.03	−3.79	−16.8		128.1	40.3

SOURCE: *Economic Report of the President, 1970.*
[a] 500 stocks, Standard and Poor's stock index.
[b] Year-end to year-end percentage in Standard and Poor's stock index.
[c] Moody, AAA corporate bonds.

Poor's 500 index. From 1959 through 1968, the rates of increase were 9.2 percent and 10.9 percent respectively. From 1967 through 1969 the differences between these two indices became even more pronounced, about 4 percent annually. The indices of American Stock Exchange stocks and of industrial stocks traded over the counter (Table 5-15), which are based primarily on the shares of smaller, younger companies, also illustrate this growing differential between large and small companies. From 1965 through 1968 the American Stock Exchange index rose 120 percent, and over-the-counter stocks rose 83 percent, against 24 percent for the S&P index.

The basis for this ever increasing gap between the DJIA and the broader-based averages reflects a long-run shift in the pattern of economic growth. A systematic examination of growth by corporations in the United States economy would go well beyond the scope of this study. However, a brief review of the experience of the *Fortune* 500 indicates that the smaller companies are growing the fastest. (The *Fortune* 500 are the 500 largest manufacturing firms, comprising 63.7 percent of all manufacturing sales in 1969. Statistics for the "Second 500" largest firms, first compiled by *Fortune* for 1969, revealed that this group accounted for 6.5 percent of sales.) The 50 largest manufacturing firms in the *Fortune* 500 have sustained a slower growth rate since the beginning of the economic expansion in 1961,[42] through periods of both rapid and slower growth. In 1969, sales by the 50 largest firms rose 6.5 percent over the previous year, while the sales growth of the entire 500 was 9.7 percent. Sales growth for the "Second 500" firms was 11.7 percent. In earnings, the top 50 registered a decline of 4 percent in 1969 compared to a rise for the 500 of 2 percent and a rise of 8.6 percent for the "Second 500."[43]

Much the same pattern appears in earnings per share, a critical determinant of stock prices in the long run. For the entire decade 1960–69, the 50 largest firms achieved an average growth rate in earnings per share of 5.94 percent; for the entire 500 the growth rate was 7.01 percent; for the "Second 500" it was 7.50 percent; and for the 50 smallest firms of the "Second 500" it was 10.21 percent.[44] In short, the highest growth in sales, earnings, and opportunities for equity investment has generally been outside the largest companies.

---

[42] *Fortune 500 Directory*, 1967, p. 1.
[43] *Fortune*, May 1970, pp. 182–83; *Fortune*, June 1970, pp. 982–99.
[44] *Fortune 500 Directory*, May 1970, pp. 182–83; *Fortune*, June 1970, pp. 98–116.

b. Bank Trust Department Equity Management

As noted earlier, there are two major money-management groups in the financial community, bank trust departments and the mutual fund organizations. In recent years the differences in management strategy of these two groups have become pronounced, as have the results. Examination of these differences is important in analyzing the current flow of institutional funds to the equity market and in predicting likely trends in the future.

A trust agreement is an arrangement by which the trustee assumes fiduciary responsibility for managing assets for the benefit of another.[45] The agreement typically defines that responsibility, the degree of discretion of the trustee, and the rules for distributing benefits of the trust. The definition of fiduciary discretion has many dimensions. Often it limits the extent of corporate stock and other types of investments; it may impose limits on the share of funds that may be invested in a single company; and it may lay out guidelines, indicating which companies are eligible. Also, state laws and state courts interpret the nature and limits of trustee discretion differently. In some cases the trustee is limited to selecting from a "legal list" of eligible investments maintained by many states. Within the agreed upon limits of fiduciary responsibility trustees typically are limited by the "prudent man" rule.[46]

Trust agreements and investment policies vary for different kinds of accounts. For example, the uncertainty associated with the liquidation date of many personal trusts forces the trustee to be more attentive to liquidity and short-run changes in portfolio values. Tax considerations also matter; for example, corporate pension funds are tax free and hence have not invested in state and local government securities. However, despite these differences the percentage of assets invested in stocks by these three groups in 1968 was nearly identical: 64.1 percent by employee benefit accounts, 63.8 percent by personal trusts and estates, and 59.6 percent for employee pension accounts.[47]

Historically the investment strategy for investing in stock on behalf of pension funds has been conservative, with most funds invested in large companies and with turnover rates on such holdings well below those of mutual funds. The first comprehensive survey of pension fund holdings was

[45] Cf. Austin W. Scott, *The Law of Trusts*, 3rd ed., Boston, Little Brown & Co., 1967. For application to pension funds, see Commerce Clearing House, Inc., *Pension Plan Guide*. Chicago, 1964.

[46] Harvard College versus Amory (1835).

[47] Hanczaryk, *op. cit.*, p. 21.

conducted in 1955 by the New York State Banking Department. The survey revealed that the stock portion of pension funds trusteed by New York banks were mainly concentrated in the largest stocks. As of December 31, 1954, almost 61 percent of pension fund investments were in stocks of companies whose capitalization had a market value in excess of $500 million, with 14 percent in stocks of companies with valuations under $200 million; the comparable figures for all outstanding common stock were 52.6 percent and 25 percent respectively.[48] The 1956 Fulbright Committee investigation of thirty large pension funds revealed the same concentration of stock investments in a few large, well-established companies. From 1953 to 1955, almost 25 percent of the equity investment of corporate pension funds was in 25 leading companies. In contrast, such companies attracted only 15 percent of mutual fund investment during that period.[49]

Trust departments gradually diversified their equity investment during the 1950's. The survey of the portfolios of ten large bank trust departments for 1958–59 bore this out: only 16.5 percent of purchases were in the above-mentioned group of 25 companies.[50] This process of diversification has continued into the 1960's. However, turnover rates have remained relatively stable, about 12 percent, in the decade through 1965—less than half the level of mutual funds.

The aggregate return on trusteed pension funds can be inferred from various sources. A questionnaire survey of the largest 200 firms among the *Fortune* 500 revealed that the common stock portfolios of these pension funds appreciated at a compound rate of 7.2 percent from January 1, 1957, to December 31, 1962.[51] During that same period the average annual increase (price appreciation plus dividends) of the DJIA was 9.1 percent; for the S&P 500 index, 10.9 percent. Dietz found similar results in his examination of the return on six large pension funds for 1953–62. The average annual appreciation for the funds was 12.0 percent over the period versus 13.1 percent for the DJIA and 13.6 percent for Standard and Poor's index of 425 industrials. There were no subperiods during which the

[48] George A. Mooney, *Pension and Other Employee Welfare Plans: A Survey of Funds Held by State and National Banks in New York State*, New York State Banking Department, 1955; and Norman C. Miller, "Concentration in Institutional Common Stocks Portfolios," *Journal of Finance*, March 1961, pp. 40–41.

[49] U.S. Senate, Committee on Banking and Currency, *Institutional Investors and the Stock Market, 1953–1955*, Washington, 1956.

[50] Murray, *op. cit.*, pp. 81–82.

[51] F. William Graham II and Richard D. Bower, "Corporate Responsibility in Pension Fund Management," Graduate School of Business Administration, Harvard University, unpublished monograph, Exhibits 13 and 14.

performance of the funds differed appreciably from the averages. He also found no evidence that these pension funds attempted to shift the share of funds devoted to equities in response to market conditions.[52]

The results are little different for more recent years. A recent survey of some 894 profit-sharing pension trusts' records of asset appreciation during the period 1959–66 reveals much the same result.[53] The asset size of these funds ranged from under $50,000 to over $25 million; taken together they had assets valued at $4.1 billion at year-end 1961, equal to 12 percent of all uninsured pension fund accounts. About one-half of these funds made their own investment decisions, while the other half relied on a trustee. Most of the trust agreements did not restrict the trustee to the "legal list." Generally bank and trust companies were the trustees, hence this sample should reflect the experience of a wide group of bank trustees.

For the 46 largest of these profit-sharing trusts, i.e., all those with assets in excess of $10 million, the average overall return for the period 1959–63 was 8.4 percent.[54] At the end of 1961 these profit-sharing trusts held 64 percent of their funds in common stock. Assuming a return on the nonequity portion of their investments of 3 to 4 percent implies that these funds have earned 10.9 to 11.5 percent on the equity portion of the portfolio. This return is slightly above the return on the DJIA, which rose 7.3 percent in price over this period and yielded slightly over 3 percent in dividends. Within this group of 46 profit-sharing trusts, there is a distinct correlation between rate of return and the share of funds held in equities.[55] As one might suppose, in the 1966 market decline the portfolios of these funds declined more than the aggregate of all pension funds, 7.9 percent versus 5.7 percent.[56]

Finally, the return on all uninsured pension funds for the period 1959–66 has been estimated to be 5.8 percent.[57] With roughly 50 percent of the portfolio in nonequity investments yielding from 3 to 4 percent, the implied return on the equity portion of the investment is 7.5 to 8.5 percent.

[52] Peter O. Dietz, *Pension Funds: Measuring Investment Performance*, New York, Graduate School of Business Administration, Columbia University and Free Press of Glencoe, 1966, pp. 80–83.

[53] Bert L. Metzger, "Investment Practices, Performance, and Management of Profit Sharing Trust Funds," Profit Sharing Research Foundation, Evanston, Illinois, 1969.

[54] *Ibid.*, p. 360.

[55] *Ibid.*, pp. 372–75.

[56] *Ibid.*, pp. 427–28.

[57] *Ibid.*, p. 359.

During that period the rate of return on an unmanaged portfolio made up of the DJIA stocks was 8.6 percent.

In short, it appears that historically the average appreciation of equity investments of the bank trust departments is not significantly different from that realized by the more conservative stocks of companies with large capitalizations, as represented, e.g., in the DJIA. What appears to have occurred as a result of the diversification in trust department investments in the late 1950's and early 1960's is that average performance now is better approximated by the more comprehensive stock price indices. As noted above, concentrating stock investments in the stocks of the companies with the largest capitalization is likely to result in lower rates of return. This difference in growth rates has widened since 1966, as evidenced by the increasing gap between the DJIA and the more comprehensive stock market indices.

c. The Investment Record of Mutual Funds

The investment record of the mutual fund industry has been scrutinized several times.[58] In every case asset appreciation of the mutual funds was essentially the same as that of the relevant securities price averages.[59] In the Wharton School examination of the period 1953–58, it was concluded that the mutual funds had not outperformed the DJIA. The same conclusion could be reached in 1964. However, since 1965 the performance of the "growth funds" has been distinctly better than that of all the popular averages. In the most recent study, Friend examined forty-one growth stocks (those in existence at the beginning of 1964) from 1964 to mid-1968. The mean return exceeded the return on a weighted average of all NYSE issues—the weights proportionate to the dollar value of stock outstanding —and was comparable to an unweighted random selection of all NYSE stocks.[60] These weighted and unweighted averages exceeded the return on the DJIA. This is evident in Table 5-17. As a result, the cumulative appreciation of an investment in the growth funds over the ten-year period 1960–69 was well above that realized by the averages, about 145 percent versus 60 percent for the DJIA.

[58] U.S. Securities and Exchange Commission, *Investment Trusts and Investment Companies,* 1939: Wharton Report (see note 33, above); SEC, *Public Policy Implications of Investment Company Growth.*

[59] This was first noted in the SEC study of the period 1927–37 (*Investment Trusts and Investment Companies,* Part II, Chapter VI and Appendix J).

[60] Irwin Friend, Marshall Blume, and John Crockett, *Mutual Funds and Other Institutional Investors,* New York, Twentieth Century Fund, 1970, pp. 150–52.

The higher rates of asset appreciation by the growth funds is the result of adopting a higher-risk strategy, diversifying to smaller companies and small-capitalization stocks. This strategy, of course, leaves the growth funds more susceptible to downside risk as well. These funds sustained sizable losses during the 1969–70 stock market decline. During 1969 the growth funds depreciated 15.8 percent, comparable to the decline in the DJIA but slightly more than that in the broader averages, e.g., the NYSE index. In 1970 the performance of the growth funds relative to the market worsened; during the first six months of 1970, they had fallen 31.0 percent, while the NYSE index declined about 23 percent. However, for the two and one-half year period January 1, 1968, to June 30, 1970, the growth funds' decline was just comparable to that of the NYSE index. Given their much superior performance relative to the market from 1965 to 1967, their cumulative appreciation since 1965 still greatly exceeds that of the market. The mutual funds' gains relative to the market when stock prices were rising more than offset their disproportionate losses in the market decline.

These comparisons were made as of June 30, 1970, the last date for which data were available. Because of the higher-risk strategy adopted by the growth funds, the low point of a "market cycle" provides the worst possible basis for comparing their performance to the averages. It seems unlikely that further stock market declines will be of sufficient size to invalidate the conclusion that the growth funds can significantly "out-perform" the averages, though at the same time they raise the variance on returns.

Nor is this conclusion necessarily invalidated by the speculative market environment of 1967, which contributed to the very high rates of return of the smaller growth funds. The equities markets did provide unusually large rewards to speculative investment in small issues during 1967 and 1968. While the NYSE index increased by 23.1 percent in 1967 and 9.7 percent in 1968, the increases on the American Exchange were 76.5 percent and 33.2 percent, and those for the National Quotation Bureau's over-the-counter index were 54.0 percent and 20.8 percent. Also, the performance figures of many funds were inflated by the acquisition of "letter stock," unlisted stock (which the company would list at a subsequent registration or offering) purchased from a company at below the market price and valued by the fund each quarter at the current market price. Acquisition of letter stock was a source of large gains by the purchasing fund if the market price of the company's stock continued up and there was a market for its sale after public listing.

TABLE 5-17

Average Annual Return of Mutual Funds: Capital Gains Reinvested,
Dividends in Cash, 1960–69

(percent change)

		Growth Funds				
	Large (1969 year-end assets over $300 mill.) (1)	Small: Maximum Capital Gain (2)	Small: Long-Term Growth (3)	Growth and Current Income (4)	Growth and Current Income, with Relative Stability (5)	Balanced Funds (6)	Income Funds (7)
Annual change[a]							
1960	6.4	4.8	1.9	1.4	2.7	5.1	0.8
1961	27.2	28.8	26.1	24.7	23.6	19.5	19.0
1962	−18.1	−19.4	−15.3	−12.0	−8.1	−5.4	−3.6
1963	22.5	20.3	17.4	18.0	17.1	13.2	16.0
1964	15.0	11.6	12.5	15.1	14.3	12.2	14.4
1965	32.4	35.3	21.5	16.9	14.5	10.4	14.0

1966	-1.6	-2.4	-4.1	-6.7	-6.5	-5.5	-6.5
1967	39.1	58.3	31.7	25.3	24.2	19.7	23.9
1968	10.1	21.1	14.1	15.0	17.4	14.4	21.3
1969	-10.4	-16.3	-10.7	-11.4	-12.6	-11.3	-15.9
Cumulative percentage change							
1960–64[b]	48.0	37.0	48.0	49.0	54.0	47.0	50.0
1965–69[a]	78.3	91.4	53.4	37.0	35.7	25.7	33.0
1960–69[a]	148.0	144.3	112.4	97.0	99.4	80.0	90.9

NOTE: Cumulative percentage change, Dow-Jones industrial average: 1960–64, +46.6; 1965–69, +9.2; 1960–69, +60.1.
[a] Wiesenberger Financial Services, Inc., *Investment Companies: Mutual Funds and Other Types*, 1970 ed., New York, pp. 124–31.
[b] *Ibid*, 1966 ed., pp. 118–23.

On the other hand, it is always hazardous to make too much of "extenuating circumstances" in the stock market. The opportunity for speculative investment in 1967 was by no means unprecedented. The downside risk associated with speculative investment, e.g., in "letter stock," may well be fully reflected in the losses sustained by the growth funds in 1969–70. In essence, the higher gains by the growth funds over the entire period since 1965 reflect their realization that market opportunities were shifting away from the largest companies. It is their wider diversification and their greater flexibility, enabling them to adjust their portfolios more rapidly, that have produced the very sharp contrast in rates of appreciation on equity investments compared to the bank trust departments.

These and subsequent comparisons of mean returns do not include specific measures of the risk element. It is clear that the growth funds have raised the variability of returns together with their expected value. Both the expected return and its variability need to be included in measuring portfolio performance.[61] The proper measure of risk remains the subject of some controversy.[62] Abstracting from an explicit risk measure in this discussion is not critical since the differences between the rates of return for the trust departments and many of the growth funds is very large; penalties for the variance which would offset these differences in expected returns would need to be very large, especially if one had a time horizon of several years.

One other important dimension to mutual fund performance since 1967 is the interrelationship between fund performance and fund size.[63] Neither the Wharton School study of the period 1953–58, the SEC study for 1956–65, nor Friend's recent study of the 1964–68 period have revealed any correlation of mutual fund performance with size, after stratifying funds by their different objectives.[64] However, year to year comparisons of the growth funds since 1967 reveal that size has been significantly

[61] Jack Treynor, "How to Rate Management of Investment Funds," *Harvard Business Review*, January-February 1965, pp. 63–79; William F. Sharpe, "Market Fund Performance," *Journal of Business*, Supplement, June 1966, pp. 119–30; Ira Horowitz, "The Reward to Variability Rates and Mutual Fund Performance," *Journal of Business*, October 1966, pp. 485–88.

[62] Eugene Fama, "Risk and the Evaluation of Pension Fund Portfolio Performance," Bank Administration Institute, Park Ridge, Ill., 1969.

[63] For the period 1930–55 the correlation between size and performance was significant in only two of the years, and in those two the larger companies performed better than the smaller ones (*ibid.*, p. 474).

[64] Wharton Report, pp. 210–30; SEC Report, pp. 255–73; Friend, Blume, and Crockett, *op. cit.*, pp. 60, 156.

correlated with performance, the highest rates of appreciation being achieved by the smaller funds.

Table 5-18 presents yearly performance of all growth funds, classified by size of assets in each year, since 1964.[65] In 1965 the two funds with assets in excess of $1 billion had a significantly lower average gain than the rest, and in 1966 funds with less than $100 million in assets sustained below-average losses. Beginning in 1967, the size effects are rather pronounced. Average fund appreciation declined markedly with fund size, except for the Dreyfus Fund, the largest of all, with assets of over $2 billion. None of the ten funds with over $500 million in assets achieved an increase equal to the *mean* level of gains by all 37 funds with less than $300 million in assets at the year's end. In 1968, the same inverse correlation of average performance and fund size appears, again with the exception of the Dreyfus Fund *and* excluding one other entry—the Enterprise Fund—from the size class $500 million to $1 billion.[66] In the 1969–70 market decline, the smaller funds sustained the largest losses.[67]

Several reasons may explain why Friend's recent study did not reveal these size effects. First, his sample was confined to 44 firms, those in existence in 1964; this excludes many new smaller firms which tended to assume more risk. Second, data for the entire 1964–68 period may conceal the size effects which only appear since 1967. This tends to overstate the growth of larger funds; many funds classified as large in 1967 were much smaller when they achieved their highest growth. The typical experience in the mutual fund industry during this period was for smaller funds with the highest rates of asset appreciation to attract rather large fund inflows.

Several factors influence these relationships between assets appreciation and fund size. First, important economies can be realized by managing larger amounts. There are obvious administrative and management

[65] The same analysis was conducted on funds classified as having the objective of "long-term growth and income." These funds represent a step toward a more conservative investment policy. The role of size in this class of funds would not be expected on *a priori* grounds to be so important, since the objective of a more stable return lends itself to investment in high-capitalization stocks and implies a lower premium for high turnover rates. There were no size effects.

[66] The Enterprise Fund's performance of +44.3 percent in 1968 is four times the average of funds of its size (whose performances range from +0.4 to +14.3 percent). The mean value of this 10-fund group is raised from 7.1 to 11.5 percent when Enterprise is included. Enterprise's performance has been exceptional; it grew from under $10 million in 1964, and has each year consistently outperformed its competitors of similar size. (In 1969, it fell by 26.4 percent; by contrast, other funds in its asset class fell 10.9 percent.)

[67] In the first 6 months of 1970, growth funds with assets from $25 million to $100 million declined 30.57 percent, versus −26.7 percent for those with assets over $500 million (Arthur Lipper Service, "Mutual Fund Performance Analysis," June 30, 1970).

TABLE 5-18

Performance of Growth Funds by Asset Size: Average Percentage Gain, 1964–69

(number of firms in parentheses)

	Mean Level of Funds with Assets Over $300 Mill. on Dec. 31, 1968	Asset Size at Year End						
		$10 Mill. but Under $50 Mill.	$50 Mill. but Under $100 Mill.	$100 Mill. but Under $300 Mill.	$300 Mill. but Under $500 Mill.	$500 Mill. but Under $1 Bill.	$1 Bill. but Under $2 Bill.	$2 Bill. or More
1964	14.3	13.9 (1)	18.4 (10)	13.4 (3)	13.3 (4)	14.5	None	None
1965	34.6	38.2 (9)	39.8 (6)	34.1 (7)	31.2 (6)	34.9 (3)	22.2 (2)	None
1966	−1.1	−1.1 (12)	−0.1 (7)	−3.3 (6)	−2.9 (6)	−2.0 (4)	−2.2 (2)	None
1967	43.6	62.1 (9)	66.9 (13)	66.7 (7)	42.2 (8)	33.4 (6)	25.7 (3)	26.5 (1)
1968	8.3	19.1 (9)	18.1 (10)	20.5 (14)	7.3 (7)	7.1ᵃ (10)	4.7 (4)	11.6 (1)
1969	n.a.	−18.7 (9)	−24.0 (11)	−18.3 (14)	−22.1 (7)	−10.9 (10)	−11.0 (4)	−13.9 (1)
Cumulative return, 1967–69[b]		57.0 (9)	49.8 (11)	66.1 (14)	18.9 (7)	27.3 (10)	17.1 (4)	21.5 (1)

n.a. = not available.

SOURCE: Calculations by the author, based on data reported by Wiesenberger Financial Services, various years.

[a] Average excludes Enterprise Fund. See text note 66.

[b] By asset size as of December 31, 1967.

---

economies in employing specialized personnel to perform the diverse tasks of marketing, trading, research, and portfolio management. Also many cost items akin to overhead can be spread as fund size increases; e.g., visits to companies being considered as potential investments, an important part of the institutional investors' research which those managing small funds are generally unable to afford. These economies have been well documented. One study of mutual funds revealed that those funds with assets over $400 million achieved a per unit cost 50 percent lower than that of funds with assets below $5 million.[68]

There are other potential gains. For example, larger companies have greater leverage in buying research or other market information from brokerage houses because they generate large commissions. The absence of sufficient taper in commission rates for large transactions provides an obvious opportunity for those making large-block trades to receive this sort of nonprice transfer in exchange for their commission business. As in any regulated market where prices and costs diverge, the competitive response is that of service or product competition and various nonprice transfers.

On the other hand, large funds have little or no size advantage in dealing in low-capitalization stocks. The "size of the market" in any stock will limit the amount of money any given investor can place in a stock without reducing his own liquidity or the flexibility to sell his position. The capitalization of the company and how closely the stock is held help determine the size of the market in a stock. A large fund may have to diversify its portfolio very widely when investing in small companies. Large funds apparently enjoy no scale economies in investing small amounts in many issues.

The potential economies and market advantage for large funds have not been realized in practice, as has become evident from this review of their investment record. Invariably those with large amounts to manage (both mutual funds and bank trust departments) have conceded some degree of

[68] SEC Report, p. 253.

market flexibility by reason of their size. One common tendency is to deal in the larger companies, which reduces average expected returns. The largest accumulations of funds have also tended to be less active in the market. The much lower turnover of trust accounts relative to mutual funds was noted earlier. Among mutual funds, there is an inverse correlation of turnover rates with fund size.[69] This is not to suggest high turnover as an end in itself, but rather to indicate that the larger fund accumulations are pursuing a different market strategy.

d. Summary and Concluding Observations

The contrast between investment practices and results of the bank trust departments and those of the smaller, capital-appreciation oriented mutual funds is striking. The trust departments are essentially investing with limited risk and achieving results reflecting the rate of equity price appreciation of the more established companies. The investment return in the largest companies has steadily fallen below equity returns in the corporate sector generally, a difference which has increased markedly since 1966.

In sharp contrast, some of the mutual funds have assumed more risk and have achieved records of price appreciation—even discounting "special circumstances"—which are well above the broadly based averages. Moreover, these above-average rates of asset appreciation are *not* being achieved by the largest funds, e.g., those with assets in excess of $1 billion, which perform essentially as the broader-based market averages or at best very marginally above that level.[70] Large fund size need not *preclude* asset appreciation above the "averages," though this has been the result to date. Given this experience among the mutual funds, it is hardly surprising that the huge agglomerations of funds managed by the bank trust departments, in some cases as much as $10 billion in a single bank, perform essentially as "the market".

The long-term implications for institutional investment of these very different investment strategies, a contrast which has been clearly drawn only since 1967, remain to be seen. Risk preferences of institutional investors vary widely and appear to be changing fairly rapidly over time. In addition, prices in the capital markets have changed dramatically in recent years. Price inflation resulted in long-term bond rates of over 8

---

[69] Wharton Report, pp. 210–28; SEC Report, pp. 254–55.

[70] These observations are based on "expectations" in the statistical sense; individual large funds may perform better.

percent for a period, a rate which compares favorably with returns in the stock market in recent years, certainly during 1969–70. Moreover, the losses sustained by the performance funds during the recent stock market decline will surely be a reminder of the expected yield-risk tradeoff, and have undoubtedly temporarily undermined the appeal of a riskier market strategy.

However, reductions in the rate of inflation and the long-term bond rate, and resumption of economic growth are likely to reward equity holders once again, raising returns on equity above that of bonds. And unlike households, institutional investors' preferences for stocks and their portfolio choices have not been much influenced by previous stock market declines. This suggests that the long-run shift of financial institutions in favor of equity investments is likely to continue.

How much risk institutional investors will assume in their equity investments is more difficult to predict. A return on equity comparable to the broad market averages will surely continue to be quite acceptable to many corporate treasurers and other endowment and private trust accounts. Nevertheless, if professional money managers are able to show that they can again achieve rates of equity appreciation better than "the market," as they did in the 1965–70 period, this will very likely entice the owners of some pension fund and trust accounts. Private investment advisers and brokers managing special equity funds now offer a range of options to institutional accounts, allowing them to choose a level of expected yield and associated risk premium from a continuum ranging between the two extremes: a very conservative strategy or a high-risk one dealing in the stocks of the smallest companies. The most attractive policy for significant amounts of pension and private trust money may well lie somewhere between these two end points.

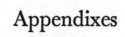
Appendixes

Appendix I

Basic Statistical Data

HELEN STONE TICE

BOARD OF GOVERNORS OF THE FEDERAL RESERVE SYSTEM

and

VIRGINIA A. DUFF

UNIVERSITY OF MARYLAND

A. INTRODUCTION

The data used in this portion of the report were taken from the flow of funds accounts wherever possible.[1] In three areas, however, we found it necessary to supplement the flow of funds estimates. First, the published accounts contain no data on the value of tangible assets; we incorporated such estimates as were available from the Office of Business Economics and developed our own series for housing and for public sector tangibles. The data are given in Tables IA-1 through IA-7.

Second, there are several financial institutions which are not shown explicitly in the flow of funds accounts; instead they are included in other sectors, particularly in the household sector. In the interest both of measuring more accurately the financial position of true households and of being able to study the behavior of these institutions which are important participants in the securities market, we created time series for them. These estimates are shown in Tables IA-8 through IA-18.

Third, the focus of the Institutional Investors Study on the market for corporate securities made us reexamine the flow of funds estimates of the amounts outstanding of, and transactions in, such securities. In the case of corporate shares, the market value outstanding series in the flow of

---

[1] Board of Governors of the Federal Reserve System, *Flow of Funds Accounts 1945–1968*, Washington, D.C., 1970.

funds was replaced by that developed in Appendix VI [2] although the flow of funds net issue series was retained. In the case of corporate bonds, both the stock and the flow series were replaced by series which, although still based on par values, at least have the virtue of allowing households to hold nonnegative amounts of such securities, a characteristic not shared by their predecessors. These data are given in Tables IA-19 through IA-22.

Finally, these new estimates are combined with the flow of funds estimates of financial assets and liabilities to produce the sector balance sheets shown in Tables IB-1 through IB-9 for selected years. [3]

B. ESTIMATES OF TANGIBLE ASSETS

1. Land

The land estimates used in this appendix are those given in Milgram's Appendix II with a few exceptions. The land of financial corporations was estimated by multiplying the Internal Revenue Service estimates of the book value of land of all financial institutions by the market-to-book ratio developed in Appendix II for "finance, insurance, and real estate." No adjustment was made for unincorporated financial institutions. These tend to be brokerage houses; and the land holdings of the finance, insurance, and real estate aggregate for partnerships and proprietorships are accounted for primarily by the holdings of real estate firms.

The estimated value of farm land used here differs from that reported in Appendix II. Although both estimates were made by subtracting the value of buildings from the U.S. Department of Agriculture's estimate of the value of farm real estate, Appendix II used the USDA's estimates of structures, while we used the estimates described below.

Transactions were measured by first differences in the holdings, since the net purchase data of Appendix II were rather spotty.

2. Reproducible Tangible Assets

All the estimates of depreciable assets reported here were made using the perpetual inventory method. This method involves the computation of a weighted moving sum of annual data on gross investment in the asset in question; the weights are determined by the particular life and depreciation assumptions employed in the calculation. The difference between the gross investment of a given year and the change in the stock

---

[2] The value of investment company shares outstanding differs from the estimates of Appendix VI. See sections C1 and D2 below.

[3] At the time of writing, publication of full balance sheets for major sectors on a flow of funds basis was planned.

during that year is by definition the depreciation which has occurred. To derive the replacement cost estimates used in this report, the calculation is first made in terms of constant dollars, and then the stock and depreciation estimates are reflated to current year prices.

The gross investment series used for the estimates of the private stock of depreciable assets are in all cases those used in the gross investment component of the income and product accounts produced by the Office of Business Economics at the Department of Commerce. In the case of public sector estimates, the construction data and equipment series were taken from the income and product accounts wherever possible; data are regularly published, although the two government sectors are not credited with capital formation in the OBE's accounts.

a. Private Nonresidential Structures and Equipment. Stocks of plant and equipment for the private sector were obtained from the OBE's Capital Stock Study; the variant used was straight-line depreciation at Bulletin F lives.[4] This concept was selected both for comparability with the earlier NBER estimates and because there is some presumption that in their own internal decision making, at least, firms use a much less rapid write-off of their plant and equipment than they demand for tax purposes. A theoretically preferable present-value measure of the stock of capital was not available. To calculate such a measure would have necessitated the specification of a discount rate parameter in addition to the life estimate; furthermore, the OBE estimates embodied much more refined adjustments for the retirement distribution and for asset categories than we could have readily duplicated in calculations using the present-value method.

The flow of funds estimates of corporate and noncorporate investment in plant and equipment are obtained from the OBE. Such estimates were also used by Allan Young in his study of depreciation and corporate profits, which yielded stock estimates by legal form as a by-product.[5] Although the data used in the Young study have not been kept up to date by the OBE, we did attempt to incorporate the statistical revisions necessary to make the components consistent with revised total stock and investment series. These series embodied both ordinary statistical revisions and the adjustments in the estimates of assets transferred between the

[4] For a recent publication describing the OBE estimates see Robert C. Wasson, John C. Musgrave, and Claudia Harkins, "Alternative Estimates of Fixed Business Capital in the United States," *Survey of Current Business*, April 1970, pp. 18–36.

[5] The allocation between corporate and noncorporate is based on the study reported by Allan Young in "Alternative Estimates of Corporate Depreciation and Profits: Parts I and II," *Survey of Current Business*, April 1968, pp. 17–28, and May 1968, pp. 16–28.

public and private sectors necessitated by a shift from sales price to original cost valuation.[6]

Ordinary statistical revisions were assumed to keep relative shares the same as they were in the Young study. The valuation adjustment for assets transferred between public and private ownership was assumed to be 95 per cent corporate for manufacturing equipment and structures, 90 percent corporate for nonmanufacturing equipment, and 100 percent corporate for nonmanufacturing structures.

Institutional structures were defined to be OBE's "institutional structures" plus one-third of the estimated stock of (or investment in) "social and recreational structures." Institutional investment in equipment was estimated residually by subtracting the construction estimates from the flow of funds series on "nonprofit plant and equipment" expenditures; it was assumed to account for a share in the stock of "nonfarm noncorporate manufacturing equipment" (as well as in the depreciation on that stock) equal to its share in the comparable gross investment estimates.

Estimates for farm nonresidential structures and equipment were taken directly from the OBE. Nonfarm noncorporate plant and equipment were the residuals after subtracting corporate farm and institutional plant and equipment from the total privately owned, incorporating the valuation adjustment on assets transferred from public to private ownership.

The subdivision of corporate investment into its financial corporate and nonfinancial corporate subsectors was largely a judgmental procedure. We assumed that in 1948 the investment of financial corporations was split equally between structures and equipment, and that the share allocated to structures steadily increased during the subsequent years, accounting for 55 percent of the total in 1952 and 72 percent of the total by 1968. (This assumption was based largely on the observed rapid growth in investment in structures by life insurance companies.) The annual percentages were then applied to the flow of funds estimates of financial corporate investment in plant and equipment, to obtain the structures and equipment components separately. Nonfinancial corporate investment in structures and equipment are the residuals. These were then depreciated at rates of 2 percent for structures and 8.3 percent for equipment, assuming a 50-year life for structures and a 12-year life for equipment.

b. Private Residual Structures. The basic investment series are again taken from the national income and product accounts as given in the flow of

---

[6] See Wasson, Musgrave, and Harkins, *op. cit.*, for a discussion of these valuation methods.

funds accounts. Since OBE estimates of the stock of housing were not available at the time at which this report was written, the investment series were depreciated exponentially in order to estimate the net stocks and associated depreciation series.

For 1–4 family nonfarm housing a depreciation rate of 2.0 percent was used; for multifamily housing a rate of 2.4 percent was employed, and for farm housing a depreciation rate of 1 percent was applied. Initial stocks for the end of 1949 were selected from the estimates developed in earlier work by one of the authors.[7] The criterion used in selecting the initial stock and the depreciation rate were first, the consistency with the results of the 1950 Census of Housing, and second, whether its computational assumptions in combination with the gross investment series described above yielded housing stocks consistent with the 1960 Census of Housing.[8]

The stock of multifamily dwellings by sector was based on the flow of funds allocation of such investment between corporate and noncorporate purchasers. The 1949 stock was allocated between the two sectors in the same proportion as in an earlier NBER study.[9]

c. Public Sector Structures

(*1*) *Introduction.* In order to arrive at a total stock figure for public structures by means of a perpetual inventory computation, we need an expenditure estimate and a price index for each year as far back as required by the service life assumption. Our two major categories are federal construction and state and local construction. Each of these is divided into several subcategories, which are listed below.

Federal	*State and Local*
Residential	Residential
Nonresidential	Nonresidential

---

[7] H. S. Tice, "Depreciation, Obsolescence and the Measurement of the Aggregate Capital Stock of the United States," *Review of Income and Wealth*, June 1967, pp. 119–54.

[8] The application of this test is made more complicated by the fact that the Census estimates measure the value of "real estate," and there exists little evidence on how these estimates should be divided between land and structures. Unfortunately we have no independent estimates of the value of residential land. In Appendix II the land underlying multifamily dwellings is included in the IRS-based estimates of the land holdings of business firms; the value of the land underlying 1–4 family structures was derived as a fraction of the value of those structures. The OBE has completed estimates of the housing stock since this report was written. See Allan H. Young, John C. Musgrave, and Claudia Harkins, "Residential Capital in the United States, 1925–70," *Survey of Current Business*, November 1971, pp. 16–27.

[9] R. W. Goldsmith and R. E. Lipsey, *Studies in the National Balance Sheet*, Princeton, Princeton University Press for NBER, 1963, Vol. I, p. 260.

Federal (cont.)	*State and Local* (cont.)
Highway	Highway
Conservation and development	Conservation and development
Military	Public service enterprises
Other	Sewer and water
	Other

The state and local government expenditures include federally aided expenditures. All calculations assume declining balance depreciation. The average service life assumptions are: 50 years for federal civilian and state and local residential structures; 50 years for nonresidential buildings; 30 years for highways; 80 years for conservation and development; 50 years for other federal nonresidential structures; 67 years for sewer and water systems; 50 years for public service enterprises; and 50 years for other state and local nonresidential structures.

(2) *Estimates for 1946–68.* Data on both federal and state and local government expenditures on structures during this time period were taken from unpublished Commerce Department data. There were only two departures from the OBE worksheets. Federal nonresidential expenditures in our system were a combination of their "nonresidential" and "industrial" expenditures. Also, the average of the price indexes of these two categories gave the price index used in our calculations for the overall category, nonresidential.

For state and local governments, between 1963 and 1968, the separation of "other," "sewer and water systems," and "public service enterprises" disappears. In order to compute the stocks, we had to have separate expenditure figures for these years. These were obtained by totaling the three categories for each year over the previous five-year period, and computing the percent share of each in the total. The percentages remained reasonably consistent (within 5 percentage points over this time period), so we extrapolated forward, using the mean percent of the 1958–63 total for each category, i.e.,

	Percent
Sewer and water systems	9.2
Public service enterprises	67.2
Other	23.6

(3) *Estimates for 1915–46.* All figures for expenditures were taken from *Construction Volume and Costs, 1915–1956* (page 10), a statistical supplement to *Construction Review*, by the departments of Commerce and Labor.

The price indexes for this period were derived in two different ways for different time periods: 1915–28 and 1929–46. In the later period, indexes were taken from a supplement to the *Survey of Current Business*, "The National Income and Product Accounts of the U.S., 1929–1965, Statistical Tables," pages 164–65. Indexes in this period are the same for both federal and state and local expenditures.

The indexes for the period from 1915 to 1929 are derived from the above indexes with 1929 as the base year. In R. W. Goldsmith, *A Study of Saving in the United States*, Vol. I, Table R-20, pages 608–609,[10] there are several categories of indexes with base year 1929 = 100. The categories are not as specific as our expenditure data call for, but since they are all that is available, we used the category which was the closest approximation to that needed. We took the 1929 figures from the OBE, and extrapolated backward, basing our work on Goldsmith's indexes in the following way, where the numbers in parentheses refer to columns in Goldsmith, *A Study of Saving*, Table R-20 and the weights are the price indexes for each category in 1929 with the base year equal to 1958. The formula we used is: $X_{1958} = $ Goldsmith index$_{1929} \times$ index for 1929$_{1958}$:

Federal		*State and Local*	
Residential	(4) × .592	Residential	(4) × .592
Nonresidential	(3) × .343	Nonresidential	(3) × .343
Highway	(6) × .475	Highway	(6) × .475
Conservation and development	(3) × .402	Conservation and development	(3) × .402
Military	(7) × .380	Sewer and water	(8) × .403
Other	(8) × .342	Public service	(8) × .403
Total	(8) × .413	Other	(8) × .342
		Total	(8) × .413

The price indexes for 1915 to 1946 are virtually the same for both federal and state and local.

(4) Estimates for 1893–1915. (a) Federal. Figures for these early years were taken from the Census Bureau publication, *Historical Statistics of the United States—1789–1945*, Table H: 27–32, page 169. The only available categories that correspond to the categories we used for later years were:

	Column
Total federal	27
Nonresidential	30
Conservation and development	29
Military	28

[10] Three vols., Princeton, Princeton University Press, 1955–56.

The figures for the overlapping years (i.e., 1915 to 1919) show that the categories are not exactly the same but are close enough to be usable.

The price indexes for these early years were derived from the Goldsmith indexes in the same way as the later figures, described above.

(b) State and local. For state and local expenditures on structures, the only available data were for total expenditures. This "total" number was computed from Goldsmith's *A Study of Saving in the United States*, Vol. I, as the sum of columns (2) and (6), Table G–6, page 1,053, and column (3), Table G–15, page 1,067.

(5) *Federally Aided State and Local Construction Expenditures, 1915–66.* From 1915 to 1956, the expenditure figures come from *Construction Volume and Costs, 1915–1956*, a statistical supplement to *Construction Review*, by the departments of Commerce and Labor.

For 1957–66, expenditure figures are not available by category. There is only a total federal aid figure for each year. We allocated this total among the components on the basis of the 1956 figures that were available from *Construction Review* (see above), using the following proportions: Public service enterprises, 0.014; highways, 0.860; nonresidential, 0.124; and sewer and water systems, 0.002.

The same price indexes were used for the federal aid category as were used for state and local government expenditures.

d. Public Sector Equipment. Equipment stock figures were derived in the way described above for structures. The perpetual inventory method for computing net stocks and depreciation was applied to the investment series. Exponential or declining balance depreciation and a 12-year average life are assumed for all categories.

(1) *Federal Government.* The federal equipment sector is broken down into "civilian" and "military." The military investment series for the early years from 1929 to 1946 come from R. W. Goldsmith, *National Wealth of the United States in the Postwar Period*, Table B–166, column (4), page 394.[11] Data for the later years, 1947–68, come from unpublished data from the OBE. The early civilian series, from 1929 to 1946, comes from Goldsmith's *A Study of Saving in the United States*, Vol. I, Table F–16, column (8), page 1,009. The sum of civilian and military invest ent figures gives the total of federal government equipment.

(2) *State and Local Government.* State and local expenditures for early years, from 1929 to 1946, come from *A Study of Saving in the United States*, Vol. I, Tables G–6, column (5), page 1,053, and G–15, column (3),

---

[11] Princeton, Princeton University Press for NBER, 1962.

TABLE I-1

Assumptions of Service Life and Depreciation Rates of Consumer Durables

	Service Life Assumptions (years)		Flow of Funds Deprecia-tion Rate (percent)
	Goldsmith (1)	Flow of Funds (2)	(3)
Jewelry and watches	15	10	.20
Furniture, including mattresses and bedsprings	15	10	.20
Kitchen and other household appliances	12	8	.25
China, glassware, tableware, and utensils	10	8	.25
Other durable house furnishings	10	8	.25
Ophthalmic products and orthopedic appliances	4	4	.50
New cars and net purchases of used cars	15[a]	8	.25
Tires, tubes, accessories, and parts	5	3.3	.60
Books and maps	6	4.76	.42
Wheel goods, durable toys, sports equipment, boats, and pleasure aircraft	10	8	.25
Radio and television receivers, records, and musical instruments	10	8	.25

SOURCES:
Col. 1.   R. W. Goldsmith, *The National Wealth of the United States in the Postwar Period*, Princeton, Princeton University Press for NBER, 1962, Table B-31, p. 252.
Col. 2 and col. 3. Unpublished worksheets of the Flow of Funds and Savings Section, Board of Governors of the Federal Reserve System.
[a] Nonlinear depreciation over this life.

page 1,067. Expenditure estimates for 1947–68 are unpublished Commerce Department data.

The total of all equipment, federal and state and local, is available as a control total for equipment. This "total" figure can be found in OBE's publication, *The National Income and Product Accounts of the United States, 1929–1965*, and in the *Survey of Current Business*, July issues, Table 1.4, line 5.

e. Private Consumer Durables. The gross investment series in both current and constant prices are taken from the OBE's Tables 2.5 and 2.6, "Personal Consumption Expenditures by Type of Product," published regularly in the *Survey of Current Business* and in its supplements. Since the flow of funds considers this to be capital expenditure rather than consumption, depreciation charges must be imputed to the household sector; stock estimates are a by-product of this calculation although they are not published.

The flow of funds estimates differ both in life assumption and in accounting convention from the earlier Goldsmith estimates. The flow of funds uses double declining balance depreciation, while Goldsmith used straight-line depreciation; he also assumed much longer lives than does the flow of funds. The comparisons are summarized in Table I-1. The flow of funds estimates were used (1) since they were readily available, (2) since they have been incorporated into the set of social accounts used elsewhere in the appendix, and (3) since the rates seem somewhat more typical of our present throw-away economy than do Goldsmith's. Estimates in preparation at OBE were not available, even in preliminary form, in time for inclusion here.

f. Inventories

(1) Private Nonfarm Inventories. Private nonfarm inventories are from the national income and product accounts. The levels are book values; the flows are the inventory change component of GNP and thus include the inventory valuation adjustment. The nonfinancial corporate and noncorporate business components are presumed to account for the total; no attempt was made to estimate inventory holdings for nonprofit institutions, households, and financial corporations.

(2) Farm Inventories. Like the estimates of nonfarm private inventory investment, the change in farm inventories was also obtained from the OBE. Year-end holdings come from the *Balance Sheet of Agriculture*, various issues; this series is the sum of "livestock" and "crops stored on and off farms" less "CCC loans" and "CCC-backed loans" from the flow of funds accounts.

(3) Federal Government Inventories. Federal inventory year-end levels are taken, for recent years, from Treasury Department data. The Treasury *Bulletin* contains a quarterly balance sheet for "corporations and certain other business-type activities." The table ending December 31, which usually appears at the end of the April *Bulletin*, was used for each year. From 1956 to 1968, we took the total inventories for all corporations and subtracted from them inventories of the Defense Department, assets of the Panama Canal Corporation being considered civilian. We then added to this figure Commodity Credit Corporation gross "loans receivable–U.S. dollar loans" and the flow of funds figure for CCC-backed loans. This procedure gives total federal inventory levels for each year.

From 1952 to 1955, this computation is made difficult by the fact that the Treasury Department had a different balance sheet and different categories during these years. Prior to 1956, defense assets are not included in the table, and the "total inventory" figure is far lower than the comparable total in the later years. Even with defense inventories eliminated from the total in 1956, the 1955 "total" is half of the 1956 "total." The difference is attributable in part to the fact that General Service Administration and Defense Department inventories are left out in the early years. Since we did not want to include defense inventories, the addition of GSA inventories was all that remained. The largest component of GSA inventories was the category "strategic stockpiles." Goldsmith's estimates of "strategic stockpiles" [12] seem to correspond with GSA "strategic stockpiles" from the Treasury *Bulletin* for the years after 1955, and were therefore deemed adequate. To the sum of "total inventories" and GSA "strategic stockpiles," we then added both sets of CCC loans to give the total federal inventory figure for 1951–55.

Annual flows are measured by changes in this stock so defined.

(*4*) *State and Local Government Inventories.* No estimates were made of the inventories of state and local governments. Goldsmith's earlier work was based on fragmentary evidence which is now out of date.

C. NEW SECTORS

1. Investment Companies

Although the flow of funds accounts include those open-end investment companies which are members of the Investment Company Institute, other investment companies are treated only implicitly, if at all. Their retained earnings are included in the gross saving of the flow of funds investment company sector, since the national income and product accounts do not make a distinction between open-end and closed-end companies.

The estimates presented in this study distinguish between open-end companies and all other registered investment companies. The general procedure employed was first to develop balance sheets for the various types of companies, using the SEC series on total assets as the basis for universe asset holdings, and then to distribute this total among the various asset categories on the basis of sample data. With the exception of common stock, flows were taken to be the difference in balance sheet values of the

---

[12] R. W. Goldsmith, *The National Wealth of the United States in the Postwar Period,* Princeton, Princeton University Press for NBER, 1962, Table B-175 (6), p. 405.

various assets. For stock, in cases where direct flow estimates were not available, an attempt was made to separate unrealized capital gains from net purchases by means of the Standard and Poor's 500-stock price index. The flows thus derived were used as a first approximation; some of them were later modified to reconcile aggregate information from SEC and national income accounts.

a. Open-End Companies. The Investment Company Institute data form the basis of this sector. In the flow of funds accounts, these ICI members are the only companies included. However, data from the SEC on June 30 assets of active registered open-end companies are somewhat larger than the ICI total. Goldsmith's estimates for those years for which the SEC series is not available indicate the same state of affairs.[13] Therefore estimates for non-ICI open-end companies were made as follows. For years in which the SEC totals were available, the June 30 ICI asset, were subtracted and the non-ICI residual was moved to a December 31 basis, using the assumption that the June-to-June increase in assets for non-ICI members took place over time in the same pattern as did that of ICI members. For earlier years, Goldsmith's estimates of the end of year total were used to derive the non-ICI total. It was further assumed that these non-ICI mutual funds had the same portfolio composition as did the ICI members, and that their net purchases of stock bore the same relationship to the change in their holdings of stock as did the purchases of ICI members.[14]

The balance sheet for all open-end companies appears in Table IA-8; their stock purchases are given in Table IA-22.

b. Other Investment Companies. Separate estimates were made for closed-end companies, face-amount companies, and unit trusts.

Estimates of total assets for closed-end companies were derived by linking the Goldsmith series[15] on total assets to the SEC total asset series whose June 30 observations had been put on an end-of-year basis by interpolation. From this total were subtracted the assets of Christiana Securities and, for the two years in which they existed, the assets of dual-purpose funds.[16] This residual estimate of the assets of closed-end companies other than Christiana and of the dual-purpose funds was distributed among the various classes of assets on the basis of portfolio composition

[13] Goldsmith and Lipsey, *op. cit.*, Vol. II, pp. 168–69.
[14] In the case of portfolio composition and change, the flow of funds breakdowns of the ICI data were used.
[15] Goldsmith and Lipsey, *op. cit.*, pp. 170–71.
[16] These companies were first formed in 1967.

data obtained from a sample of 30 companies;[17] to these estimates were added the assets of Christiana and of the dual-purpose funds. With the exception of stock, net purchases of all assets were taken to be equal to the observed change in the balance sheet over the period; in the case of stock, this change was adjusted to allow for appreciation as measured by the Standard and Poor's 500-stock price index. Stock transactions for Christiana were taken directly from company statistics.

Face-amount companies are dominated by Investors Diversified Services (IDS) and Investors Syndicate of America (ISA). Therefore, the estimates for this group consist of Moody's reports on these two companies blown up slightly to allow for the remaining 5 percent of the assets held by other companies. The flows were derived in the way described above.

In order to estimate the assets of unit trusts, a total asset figure was derived from the SEC June 30 observations. Since the SEC *Annual Report* contains estimates of the fraction of these assets which represent shares in other investment companies, these assets were consolidated out of this sector. The remaining assets were assumed to be either tax-exempt bonds or common stock; a brief survey of the various unit trusts represented in Moody's *Bank and Finance Manual* indicates that these companies exist for the accumulation of mutual fund shares, for the accumulation of specific stock, and for the purchase of tax-exempt securities. Estimates of the net issues of, and security purchases by, tax-exempt bond funds were obtained from the SEC; assets which were neither municipals nor investment company shares were assumed to represent common stock. Net purchases of the latter were estimated as described above for closed-end companies.

Liabilities and share values and issues were estimated in several ways. Open-end companies have only short-term liabilities, and in the ICI data these are netted against cash; the value of mutual fund shares is thus equal to the net asset value of the fund. Closed-end company shares typically trade at a discount (or premium) relative to net asset value. Unit trusts distribute portions of the trust corpus as well as paying out the earnings; the redemption value of units can also vary with the market value of the securities. Prices of shares in IDS and ISA also seem to be less than assets per share. This suggests that in deriving an estimate of the market value of the shares of investment companies other than mutual funds, some write-down of their assets should be made.

---

[17] The data for the sample and for dual-purpose funds were taken from Moody's *Bank and Finance Manual* and from Arthur Weisenberger Co., *Investment Companies*, various issues. Information about Christiana came from Moody's.

The debt of non-open-end companies was taken from Moody's reports on IDS, ISA, and "Closed End Companies with Senior Capital." Total share issues are the SEC's series on net issues of investment company shares; the breakdown by type of company was supplied by the SEC.

The balance sheet for the aggregate of these three investment company sectors is given in Table IA-9; stock purchases for this aggregation appear in Table IA-22.

2. Bank-Administered Personal Trusts and Estates

a. Introduction. The estimates discussed here refer to the amount and composition of the assets held in personal trusts or in estates under bank management. Banks manage other types of accounts, and in fact, these other accounts constitute the more important portion of their business. Data exist on the activities of trust departments as a whole, however, for only a small portion of the period under discussion. The assets of those employee benefit accounts which are bank-managed are presumably covered in the statistics on noninsured pension funds, and the bank has somewhat less freedom in decision-making for agency than for trust accounts.[18]

For the period for which data on activities of the entire department exists, some rough estimates were made of the holdings of employee benefit trusts and of agency accounts. These estimates were used as checks on the reasonableness of the estimates of personal trusts and estates. No attempt was made to derive a time series covering the entire portfolio under bank management.

In section b which follows we discuss the sources of information available at the time the estimates were made. Section c contains a description of the estimating procedure used in the two periods into which the nature of the source material available divides the estimates. In this section data are presented on common trust funds, the only component of personal trusts and estates for which a continuous time series is available for a long period of time.

b. The Nature of the Data. With the exception of the early Federal Reserve surveys of common trust funds, the only observations available are of holdings at a point in time; there are no turnover data other than those for common trust funds from 1954 through 1962. Even the balance

---

[18] On the basis of the IRS tabulations of the 1962 fiduciary income tax returns, banks account for only about one-half of the personal trust and estate business. See Internal Revenue Service, *Statistics of Income—1962, Fiduciary, Gift, and Estate Tax Returns,* Washington, D.C., 1965; and *ibid., 1965,* Washington, D.C., 1967.

sheet data which do exist cannot be put together in a satisfactory way to construct a time series; for they cover a different set of institutions, they cover a different set of accounts within these institutions, and the date of the observations varies from year to year. The available material is as follows:

1. American Bankers Association's Surveys of Personal Trusts.[19] These contain the value of assets on June 30, for the years 1958, 1959, 1960, and 1963. They cover only personal trusts, whereas estates are commingled with the personal trusts in subsequent bodies of data. Furthermore, the sample used in these surveys has been questioned by some researchers.

2. Comptroller of the Currency's Reports of the Trust Assets of National Banks. These surveys, which include all types of accounts, cover the period 1963 through 1968, although portfolio detail by type of account is available for only the last three years of the period. Some estimates of the assets managed by state-chartered banks were made, but they are highly aggregative and impressionistic. These estimates apply to the end of calendar years; some effort was made to adjust the data for valuation date discrepancies.[20]

3. The Patman Report, "Commercial Banks and their Trust Departments." This report provides, for the first time, estimates of the assets managed by the entire trust department for all banks as of the end of 1967. The questionnaire, however, contained too little detail by asset group, by account category, and by a cross classification in these two dimensions to be useful for anything more than a broad check on the estimates derived by other means.[21]

[19] American Bankers Association, Trust Division, "National Survey of Personal Trust Accounts," New York, 1959, 1960, 1961, 1965, mimeographed.

[20] The results of these surveys were published in a series of articles in the *National Banking Review* and in a recent paper by Hanczaryk. For further information the reader should consult Stanley Silverberg, "Bank Trust Investments: Their Size and Significance," *National Banking Review*, June 1964; "Growth and Performance of Common Trust Funds in 1964," *ibid.*, June 1965; "Bank Trust Investments in 1964," *ibid.*, June 1965; and "Bank Trust Investments in 1965," *ibid.*, June 1966. There are some additional papers by Edwin W. Hanczaryk: "Growth and Performance of Common Trust Funds in 1966," *ibid.*, June 1967; and *Bank Trusts: Investments and Performance*, Department of Banking and Economic Research, Office of the Comptroller of the Currency, Washington, D.C., 1970, mimeographed. Mr. Hanczaryk was kind enough to provide us with a copy of the last of these manuscripts before its publication.

[21] U.S. Congress, House Committee on Banking and Currency, *Commercial Banks and Their Trust Activities: Emerging Influence on the American Economy*, 90th Cong., 2nd sess., Washington, D.C., July 1968.

4. Trust Assets of Insured Commercial Banks. This survey, conducted by the three bank regulatory agencies, gives universe estimates for all banks as of the end of 1968, cross-classified by asset and by type of account. The portfolio breakdown, while not very detailed, is much less aggregated than that provided by the Patman report.[22]

5. The Goldsmith estimates reported in Volume II of *Studies in the National Balance Sheet*, consist of a merger of the ABA surveys available at the time and the earlier estimates of R. W. Goldsmith and Eli Shapiro, "An Estimate of Bank Administered Personal Trust Funds," *Journal of Finance*, March 1959. These figures again may be presumed to cover only personal trusts, with no allowance for estates, agency accounts, or employee benefit accounts.

6. Common Trust Funds have been surveyed both by the Federal Reserve and by the Comptroller of the Currency. Although they account for only a small portion of the assets held in personal trusts and estates, time series of balance sheets and of transactions data for these funds from 1954 to 1968 do exist. Some performance data are also available.[23]

7. Fiduciary Income Tax Returns. These triennially tabulated returns give some information on property income by type, on expenses, and the like. There is also information on the fraction of fiduciary income accounted for by estates as opposed to trust accounts, and for 1962 it is possible to ascertain the fraction of fiduciary income accruing on the property managed by banks.

c. Estimating Procedure: Balance Sheets. From the discussion thus far, it is clear that we have two periods with entirely different data sets and capabilities. From 1963 on we have a fair amount of information about the assets managed by national banks; we even have some ideas about the variations in portfolio composition as a function of account type. Given the universe estimates for 1968 and to a limited extent for 1967, it is possible to derive estimates of the portfolios of all bank trust departments by type of account for these years.

Since the longest real time series of annual observations is the series on national banks which has resulted from the surveys of the Comptroller of the Currency, the procedure adopted was first to. fill in the missing

[22] Board of Governors of the Federal Reserve System, Federal Deposit Insurance Corporation, and Office of the Comptroller of the Currency, *Trust Assets of Insured Commercial Banks–1968*, Washington, D.C., October 1969. This survey has been continued on an annual basis.

[23] The estimates appear in the Silverberg and Hanczaryk articles cited previously for 1963–68. Estimates for earlier years are found in articles with the general title, "Survey of Common Trust Funds," which appeared in the *Federal Reserve Bulletin* of June 1957, May 1958, May 1959, May 1960, May 1961, May 1962, and June 1963.

cells on asset types by type of account for the years 1963–65. These figures were then expanded to a total for all banks on the basis of the relationships between state and national banks from the 1968 survey, the Patman study, and some of Silverberg's early estimates.

(*1*) *National Banks, 1963–68.* Available data from 1966 to 1968 frequently take the form of portfolio percentages; late and incomplete responses frequently led to the reporting of total assets in dollars and a percentage distribution of the portfolio which was observed. Since these portfolio coefficients are somewhat easier to interpret than are dollar amounts of assets, these coefficients were estimated directly. The only time series of portfolio coefficients for the entire period is that for all trust accounts, covering both personal and employee benefit accounts. The total value of assets for all types of accounts is also known for the entire period. The task is then to estimate a set of account coefficients such that when they are summed over all types of accounts, the results will not conflict with the portfolio composition given for the entire department.

One might first assume that these coefficients are the same for all accounts and thus use the department portfolio as the model for both personal trusts and estates and for employee benefit accounts. The evidence available for 1966–68, however, indicates that this assumption is not likely to be true. One might also assume that the coefficients for a particular type of account are constant or move in some simple or regular way over time. Again evidence suggests that this is not a very reliable assumption, and these ratios seem far from predictable on the basis of the brief bit of history we have at our disposal. Finally, we can look for some consistency in an accounts' share in the department's holding of a particular asset. These ratios did in fact prove stable, and this extrapolation was used to produce initial estimates of these account-specific coefficients.

This method in effect assumes that overall investment policy is set for the department, and that the managers of specific classes of accounts attempt to maintain some relative share of total departmental holdings of the asset in question. Any further adjustments in these portfolio coefficients were made in order to meet the accounting constraints in ways which were most consistent with external evidence and with notions of reasonable portfolio policy dictated by the subsequent development of the accounts involved. In particular, employee benefit trusts were adjusted on the basis of some relationships observed between employee benefit trusts and existing data on private noninsured pension funds, which are largely managed by banks. These considerations constrained the estimates for personal trusts and estates sufficiently to permit making the final estimates for national bank portfolio coefficients shown in Table IA-10.

(2) *All Bank Estimates, 1963–68.* Currently (1970), the only detailed portfolio estimates by type of account are for 1968. The Patman data for 1967 are too aggregated to be of much use in the particular task of estimating the portfolio composition of personal trusts and estates. The early Silverberg estimates relied a bit too heavily on inferences from the portfolios of private noninsured pension funds. For those years, data on portfolio composition by account type are not available even for national banks. We have decided, by default, to accept the time series from these sources on the total assets under management by type of account for all insured banks; but, with the exception of 1968, the earlier estimates of the portfolio composition of these totals were used as checks on our results rather than taken as given. Final estimates were obtained by stepping up the national bank portfolio coefficients by factors derived as the 1968 ratios of all bank to national-bank coefficients. These factors were weighted so as to allow for differences over time in the relative shares of personal trusts and estates in total trust assets for the two sets of banks. The coefficients which result are shown in Table IA-11.

(3) *Estimates Before 1963.* Before 1963 nothing is known explicitly about the employee benefit accounts managed by banks. Existing personal trust estimates refer only to that category of account; thus, the series before and after 1963 are not really comparable, since it is impossible to separate out estates completely from the latter numbers. There is also the problem of converting June 30 data to a year-end basis. Evidence in recent years suggests that most accounts are reviewed during the last quarter of the year; therefore, giving the option of reporting assets at market value as of the last review date before June 30 would tend to produce estimates of the market value of holdings as of the end of the preceding year.

The ABA data also show "units of participation in common trust funds" as a separate asset category, while the questionnaires of the later period ask that the assets held by the common trust fund be distributed among the appropriate categories. Since the valuation date for the common trust fund is somewhat more likely to have occurred on June 30 than is the valuation date for the other accounts in the personal trust category, we first netted out common trust funds from the ABA reports. Subsequently, the time series of end-of-year observations on common trust funds covering the bulk of this early period is added to the end-of-year estimates of the other personal trust accounts.

The estimates for the period before 1963 were based in large measure on the previous work of Goldsmith. His series on personal trusts other than common trust funds was used through 1957; his procedures were then used in interpolating between the ABA surveys, most of which were not available to Goldsmith at the time his estimates were prepared. In this procedure, one assumes that the ABA's reported values of assets other than corporate stock are an adequate measure of the value of these assets on December 31 of the previous year. Holdings of corporate stock were estimated by assuming that net purchases occurred at a uniform rate over the period in question, and that the pattern of the change in holdings not so accounted for followed the time path of the Standard and Poor's 500-stock price index.

Efforts to apply this method of allowing for price movements in other assets proved less successful; the results for common trust funds did not recapitulate known net acquisitions for these funds. The difficulties of using the existing bond price indexes; the lack of detail on the characteristics of the bond portfolios of these funds, which made it difficult to select among the price indexes and the poor results with the common trust funds, made it seem unwise to attempt to account for any but the most obvious effects of security price movements, i.e. those involved with common stock. The results of these manipulations are shown in Table IA-12, panel A.

In order to make this series comparable with the estimates for later years, three further steps were necessary. First, the series had to be adjusted upward to include estates as well as trusts; this was accomplished by stepping up trust assets by a factor derived from IRS statistics of fiduciary income. This factor is the reciprocal of the share of income from trusts in total income paid by fiduciaries, adjusted for differences in bank fiduciaries' shares of the income from trusts and from estates. Allowance was made for differences in portfolio composition between trusts and trusts and estates on the basis of the relationships prevailing in 1968, the year for which such data by type of account existed. The results of this process are shown in Table IA-12, panel B.

The second step involved adding in the series on common trust funds taken from the Federal Reserve Board's surveys for all but the first two years; these are from Goldsmith's estimates. This series and the results of the addition are shown in Table IA-12, panels C and D. Finally, the large "other assets" category was allocated among time deposits, real estate, and miscellaneous on the basis of the average contribution of these three components to this sum in the years for which the breakdown was available.

The final time series, covering the entire period 1951–68, is given in Table IA-14. The flows were taken to be equal to the first differences in this balance sheet for all assets except corporate stock. The problems of measuring net purchases of stock will be discussed for all the new sectors together in a later section of this appendix.

3. Selected Nonprofit Institutions

This sector is constructed out of several independent elements. The estimates of income, fixed investment, and consumption expenditures of nonprofit institutions are those appearing in the OBE's national income and product accounts. Appendix III's estimates of the income, outlay, and balance sheets of foundations, colleges, and universities provided estimates of the financial assets of these institutions; these were supplemented by the estimates of the financial assets of labor unions in Appendix IV in order to yield the estimates of financial assets for the entire sector. Flow of funds accounts estimates of the debt of nonprofit institutions were used on the liabilities side. Finally, the estimate in Appendix II was used for institutional land.

Thus, the estimates grouped under the label "selected nonprofit institutions" do not provide a reliable picture of the role of nonprofit institutions in the economy, nor of the size of their assets. Presumably, the estimates of tangible assets, of income, and of consumption cover all nonprofit institutions. The estimates of financial assets cover only three institutional groups, however; religious organizations and hospitals are obviously major exclusions. To assume that this collection of estimates constitutes a valid approximation of the nonprofit sector is to assert that the holdings of the excluded institutions would make relatively little contribution to the total financial assets of all nonprofit institutions.

It is therefore preferable to consider the aggregates listed under "selected nonprofit institutions" as an attempt to collect known elements of assets, liabilities, and transactions which do pertain to nonprofit institutions, and which belong neither to households proper nor to any other sector in the present scheme of things.

The financial assets in the balance sheet were taken from the work of Nelson and of Troy as reported in Appendixes III and IV of this report. In the case of foundations, estimates began only in 1953; for colleges and universities, estimates were available only for 1953–66. Since the transactions estimates were based on first differences in the balance sheets, a time series covering the years 1951–68 was necessary; and we extrapolated

Nelson's estimates after consultation with him on the appropriate methodology. Troy's time series on total assets and total liabilities were used, the portfolio composition was taken to be the same as that reported for the more limited aggregates, and the 1962 breakdown was used for earlier years.

We have already pointed out that the estimates of the transactions in financial assets were derived from the change in balance sheet holdings. This is true for all assets with the exception of corporate stock; here an adjustment was made to allow for price movements, details of which are given below in section D2. No such adjustment was made for the assets of labor unions, since the reported holdings are valued at cost rather than at market.

4. *Assets of Fraternal Life Insurance Companies, 1951–68*

The assets of fraternal life insurance companies in Table IA-15 are derived from accompanying Tables IA-16 and IA-17. Table IA-17 shows the percentages allocated to each asset in a given year by the ten largest fraternal life insurance companies.[24] Total assets for all fraternal life insurance companies, shown in column 2 of Table IA-16, come from the *Life Insurance Fact Book*. Table IA-16 also shows the percentage which the assets of the ten largest companies comprise of total assets of all companies (column 3). In Table IA-15, the percentages from Table IA-17 are applied to the total assets of all fraternal insurance companies (Table IA-16, column 2) to arrive at the comprehensive breakdown of assets for all companies for the entire period.

The sector accounts for fraternal insurance presented in Appendix I are based on these data. The composition of the bond account was estimated for 1951 and 1952 in order to derive both flows and balance sheets for 1952. Throughout the period covered, the "unallocated bonds" were assumed to be an addition to "corporate and foreign bonds" held by the sector. Other assets were placed in the "unallocated" category. By analogy with the flow of funds treatment of private insurance and pension funds, their liability for policy reserves was taken to be equal to the value of their assets.

With the exception of corporate stock, the flows are taken to be equal to the change in the holdings as shown on the balance sheet. For stocks, an attempt was made to allow for the appreciation shown by the Dow-Jones Industrial Index in defining net purchases.

[24] The figures for these ten largest companies come from survey reports and from *Best's Life Insurance Report*.

5. Mortgage Bankers

These institutions are included in the finance company sector of the flow of funds accounts; thus nothing else in the system is changed by their inclusion or exclusion from explicit consideration. Such stockholdings as they may have are negligible. The data which are given in Table IA-18, therefore, appear here only for the sake of completeness.

From 1951 to 1954, the estimates are those appearing in Saul B. Klaman, *The Postwar Rise of Mortgage Companies*, New York, NBER, 1959. The estimates for 1955 to 1968 are those of the Mortgage Bankers Association; they appear in various issues of *Mortgage Banking*.

D. CORPORATE SECURITIES

1. Value of Corporate Bonds Outstanding

The present flow of funds series consists of Hickman's estimate of the par value of corporate bonds outstanding[25] increased each year by the SEC's estimates of net change in corporate debt securities outstanding.[26] Meiselman and Shapiro derived similar series for several industrial groups of corporations, as well as for the aggregate of nonfinancial corporations.[27] The latter differs from the flow of funds series by amounts which vary from year to year. Since the Meiselman and Shapiro series ends in 1958 and its divergence from the present flow of funds series seems to be the result of statistical revisions for the most part, the flow of funds estimates must be used by default.

Unfortunately, the inclusion of the new institutional sectors for purposes of this study adds reported institutional bond holdings for some years in excess of the residually estimated flow of funds "household" bond holdings. Clearly the bond holdings of these new sectors may be overstated. It is also the case, however, that the SEC net change series has not been checked against a benchmark, since none has been available; and questions have been raised about the completeness of the net change series for many years.

We therefore attempted to provide such a benchmark for 1966 and then to adjust the annual flows in such a way as to account for the change

---

[25] W. Braddock Hickman, *The Volume of Corporate Bond Financing Since 1900*, Princeton, Princeton University Press for NBER, 1953, p. 251.

[26] SEC, *Net Change in Corporate Securities Outstanding*, Washington, D.C., 1966, and SEC, *Statistical Bulletin*, various issues.

[27] David Meiselman and Eli Shapiro, *The Measurement of Corporate Sources and Uses of Funds*, Technical Paper 18, New York, NBER, 1964.

in the par value of corporate bonds between the Hickman study and 1966. The new series is given in Table IA-19.

The resulting series is a par value series, as is the flow of funds series which it replaces. It consists of the published series on the outstanding debt of railroads and utilities, the flow of funds estimates of the outstanding debt of financial institutions, and an estimate of industrial bonds and notes consistent with the totals derived from summing individual company data for all relevant companies in Moody's *1967 Industrial Manual*. Each of these components is described below.

a. Regulated Industries. Data on long-term debt oustanding were taken from statistical reports of regulatory agencies and trade associations.

1. Railroads: Data are those of the Interstate Commerce Commission, *Statistics of Class I railroads*, as reported in Moody's *Transportation Manual* 1969, pages a49 and a50. The sum of "funded debt unmatured," "equipment obligations," and "long-term debt in default" was adjusted upward to allow for switching and terminal companies and other differences between Hickman's estimates and the ICC series.

2. Electric Utilities: Data were taken from the Federal Power Commission's *Statistics of Privately Owned Electric Utilities in the United States*, various years. The series used was "bonds less bonds reacquired" for class A and B electric utilities.

3. Gas Utilities: Data were found in the American Gas Association's *Historical Statistics of the Gas Industry*, 1963, and *Gas Facts*, various issues. The series used covers bonds and debentures of all investor-owned firms in the gas utility and pipeline industries.

4. Telephone and Telegraph: Data were obtained from the Federal Communications Commission's *Statistics of Communications Common Carriers*, various years. Telephone bonds consist of "mortgage bonds," "debentures," and "other funded debt" of annually reporting Bell companies, annually reporting non-Bell companies, and "selected large telephone carriers not subject to the reporting requirements of the commission." Telegraph bonds cover funded debt of both domestic and overseas carriers.

b. Industrial Bonds and Notes. A 1966 benchmark was obtained by summing the long-term debt exclusive of mortgages (bonds and notes including private placements) for all domestic corporations listed in the 1967 edition of Moody's *Industrial Manual*, with some adjustment for the fact that end-of-year data were not available for certain companies. In addition, a similar estimate was derived for nonrail transport, since such companies have issued bonds and their debt was reportedly included in Hickman's benchmark for utilities in 1943. From this total was subtracted Hickman's estimate for "industrial bonds" for 1947, augmented by the difference between Hickman's "utility" estimate and the sum of the utilities estimates described above. The SEC series on net change in industrial and nonrail transport debt outstanding was then stepped up by a factor defined as the ratio of the benchmark difference to the sum of cumulated net change from 1948 through 1966; and a series on outstandings was derived by the same method employed in the flow of funds estimate, using this revised investment series. No revision was made in the net change series for 1967 and 1968.

c. Finance. This series is taken directly from the flow of funds. It consists of the bonds of banks and finance companies.

2. *Corporate Stock*

The value of outstanding domestic stock other than investment company shares shown in Table IA-20 is the series given in Appendix VI of this report with minor modifications occasioned by the substitution of a more refined estimate of investment company shares elsewhere in the system. The estimates of foreign stock held by U.S. residents come from the balance of payments statistics and are incorporated into the flow of funds accounts.

The domestic total was allocated between the stock of nonfinancial corporations and of all financial corporations on the basis of the data on the industrial composition of outstanding stock appearing in Appendix VI. The estimate of financial stock outstanding was interpolated and extrapolated by the finance component of the NYSE stock price index. Net issues are the sum of investment company net issues and the bank issues from the flow of funds. The estimates for nonfinancial corporations were then derived residually.

The net issue series all come from the SEC series "net change in corporate stock outstanding," and these are shown in Table IA-22. The net purchases were taken from the flow of funds accounts, with the exception of households, nonprofit institutions, and the newly created financial institutions.

For all but households, the estimates of Table IA-22 were derived from the holdings data of Table IA-21 and the indicated price index, using the relationship

$$A_t = \left(A_{t-1}\frac{P_A}{P_{t-1}} + N_t\right)\frac{P_t}{P_A}$$

where:

A_t = holdings at the end of year t

P_t = price index at the end of year t

P_A = midyear price during year t, and

N_t = net purchases during year t.

The resulting series are quite noisy; however, the attempt to use a confidential SEC series on net purchases by all investment companies produced an even more peculiar series for nonmutual funds when the open-end purchases were netted out.

TABLE IA-1

Replacement Cost of Consumer Durables and Estimates of Land Values Not Appearing in Appendix II

(*$million*)

| | Consumer Durables | Land | | |
		Farms	Financial Institutions	Nonfinancial Corporate
1952	90,253	67,254	564	21,190
1953	95,603	65,227	659	25,395
1954	99,050	67,562	969	26,564
1955	107,890	70,616	1,044	32,173
1956	117,298	76,084	1,268	37,115
1957	126,533	80,582	1,632	42,123
1958	129,143	87,856	1,710	46,810
1959	136,447	92,540	1,863	53,054
1960	140,845	92,880	2,250	55,883
1961	143,292	98,684	2,681	61,313
1962	150,257	103,940	3,188	66,448
1963	158,569	111,313	3,787	72,332
1964	169,771	119,168	4,412	78,252
1965	183,205	129,002	5,087	83,591
1966	196,879	136,483	6,287	90,190
1967	211,475	144,758	6,727	96,536
1968	233,817	152,599	7,171	102,878

SOURCE: See text.

TABLE IA-2

Replacement Cost of the Stock of Residential Structures, 1952–68

(*$million*)

	1952	1953	1954	1955	1956	1957	1958	1959
All sector total	289,514	301,341	317,300	346,681	373,932	391,757	412,021	439,165
Total public	7,562	8,193	8,586	8,852	9,111	9,506	10,345	11,343
Federal government	3,530	3,694	3,789	3,715	3,657	3,737	4,075	4,580
State and local governments	4,032	4,499	4,797	5,137	5,454	5,769	6,270	6,763
Total private	281,952	293,148	308,714	337,821	364,821	382,251	401,676	427,822
Households	237,260	247,402	261,634	288,085	312,253	327,707	344,411	366,483
Farm	18,433	19,076	19,581	20,614	21,833	22,500	23,179	24,100
Nonfarm noncorporate	14,807	14,964	15,348	16,184	17,001	17,649	18,655	20,217
Corporate nonfinancial	11,449	11,702	12,147	12,941	13,727	14,413	15,447	17,019

	1960	1961	1962	1963	1964	1965	1966	1967	1968
All sector total	457,723	476,723	502,157	532,296	561,620	590,704	627,501	673,240	715,569
Total public	11,943	12,662	13,580	14,106	14,832	15,624	16,689	18,274	19,368
Federal government	4,828	5,059	5,242	5,353	5,531	5,698	5,914	6,303	6,518
State and local governments	7,115	7,603	8,338	8,753	9,301	9,926	10,775	11,971	12,850
Total private	445,780	464,061	488,577	518,190	546,788	575,080	610,812	654,966	696,201
Households	381,204	395,480	413,697	435,499	455,888	475,936	502,130	536,130	567,055
Farm	24,640	24,943	25,549	26,311	26,911	28,108	29,886	31,609	32,860
Nonfarm noncorporate	21,684	23,837	27,387	32,028	27,357	42,762	48,441	54,344	60,987
Corporate nonfinancial	18,279	19,795	21,939	24,345	26,623	28,493	30,575	32,933	35,527

SOURCE: See text.

TABLE IA-3

Replacement Cost of the Stock of Nonresidential Structures, 1952–68

(*$million*)

	1952	1953	1954	1955	1956	1957	1958	1959
All sector total	286,743	299,952	314,471	342,234	378,428	405,220	425,242	445,774
Total public	145,207	153,029	161,766	176,522	195,185	209,735	222,559	235,995
Federal government	44,579	47,872	50,716	53,614	56,925	59,483	61,683	63,983
State and local governments	100,628	105,157	111,050	122,908	138,260	150,252	160,876	172,012
Total private	141,536	146,923	152,705	165,712	183,243	195,485	202,683	209,779
Institutional	15,035	15,844	16,869	18,709	21,025	22,781	24,155	25,530
Farm	10,848	10,735	11,029	11,704	12,505	12,852	13,358	13,529
Nonfarm noncorporate	8,426	8,934	9,487	10,764	12,598	13,745	14,352	15,659
Corporate financial	2,496	2,695	2,991	3,414	3,890	4,347	4,750	5,236
Corporate nonfinancial	104,731	108,715	112,329	121,121	133,225	141,760	146,068	149,825

	1960	1961	1962	1963	1964	1965	1966	1967	1968
All sector total	466,709	493,634	525,140	557,603	594,320	642,981	701,880	762,306	821,453
Total public	249,245	266,539	286,877	308,833	332,764	361,839	395,752	431,548	459,832
Federal government	65,831	68,395	71,791	75,401	79,308	82,694	87,329	93,438	96,898
State and local governments	183,414	198,144	215,086	233,432	253,456	279,145	308,423	338,110	362,934
Total private	217,464	227,095	238,263	248,770	261,556	281,142	306,128	330,758	361,621
Institutional	27,158	29,370	32,019	34,742	37,785	41,498	45,833	50,297	55,741
Farm	14,232	14,329	14,345	14,497	14,863	15,422	16,087	16,706	17,178
Nonfarm noncorporate	16,162	17,508	19,486	21,386	23,628	27,040	30,926	34,846	39,438
Corporate financial	5,577	6,069	6,544	7,298	8,067	8,913	9,961	11,128	12,330
Corporate nonfinancial	154,335	159,819	165,869	170,847	177,213	188,269	203,321	217,781	236,934

SOURCE: See text.

Institutional Investors

TABLE IA-4

Replacement Cost of the Stock of Producer Durables, 1952–68

(*$million*)

	1952	1953	1954	1955	1956	1957	1958	1959
All sector total	138,507	147,919	155,595	170,044	189,057	204,492	212,077	220,232
Total public	12,404	14,557	15,974	17,627	20,170	22,187	23,896	25,414
Federal government	5,755	7,249	7,814	8,300	9,387	10,038	10,571	11,047
State and local governments	6,649	7,308	8,160	9,327	10,783	12,149	13,325	14,367
Total private	126,103	133,362	139,621	152,417	168,887	182,305	188,181	194,818
Institutional	1,708	1,778	1,854	2,023	2,261	2,396	2,474	2,532
Farm	18,430	19,484	20,065	20,996	21,781	22,583	23,623	24,215
Nonfarm noncorporate	25,934	27,032	28,139	30,722	34,240	36,290	37,426	38,272
Corporate financial	2,043	2,269	2,592	3,044	3,575	4,099	4,551	4,995
Corporate nonfinancial	77,988	82,799	86,971	95,632	107,030	116,937	120,107	124,804

	1960	1961	1962	1963	1964	1965	1966	1967	1968
All sector total	227,447	232,566	240,139	249,735	264,133	285,134	314,277	345,085	376,982
Total public	27,051	29,231	30,936	32,636	34,213	36,674	39,710	43,514	47,329
Federal government	11,667	12,814	13,481	13,764	13,783	14,372	14,866	15,455	15,796
State and local governments	15,384	16,417	17,457	18,872	20,430	22,302	24,844	28,059	31,533
Total private	200,396	203,335	209,251	217,099	229,920	248,460	274,567	301,571	329,653
Institutional	2,556	2,549	2,534	2,531	2,577	2,671	2,849	3,065	3,278
Farm	24,052	24,139	24,419	25,263	25,983	27,402	29,412	31,695	34,069
Nonfarm noncorporate	38,667	38,541	38,316	38,264	38,950	40,495	43,301	46,536	50,024
Corporate financial	5,271	5,623	5,938	6,353	6,738	7,178	7,766	8,365	8,974
Corporate nonfinancial	129,850	132,483	138,044	144,688	155,672	170,714	191,239	211,910	233,308

SOURCE: See text.

TABLE IA-5

Inventories, 1952–68

(*$million*)

	All Sector Total	Federal Government	Total Private	Farm	Nonfarm Non-corporate	Corporate
1952	110,867	7,475	103,392	23,174	14,116	66,102
1953	114,042	12,945	101,097	18,647	14,539	67,911
1954	114,645	15,495	99,150	18,462	14,386	66,302
1955	123,258	17,291	105,967	17,859	15,143	72,965
1956	130,036	15,144	114,892	18,514	15,836	80,542
1957	135,045	15,002	120,043	21,193	16,259	82,591
1958	140,662	17,641	123,021	26,199	16,513	80,309
1959	142,852	17,912	124,940	22,748	17,272	84,920
1960	146,954	18,637	128,317	22,962	17,596	87,759
1961	148,983	17,561	131,422	24,305	17,785	89,332
1962	155,833	18,208	137,625	25,487	18,372	93,766
1963	160,719	17,734	142,985	24,888	18,407	99,690
1964	165,247	16,903	148,344	23,159	19,061	106,124
1965	178,575	15,945	162,630	26,667	20,178	115,785
1966	194,397	12,927	181,470	28,373	21,155	131,942
1967	200,690	12,925	187,765	26,476	21,786	139,503
1968	216,173	14,029	202,144	29,451	23,403	149,290

SOURCE: See text.

TABLE IA-6

Extension of Goldsmith Wealth Estimates: Private Sector, 1952–68

(millions of 1958 dollars)

	1952	1953	1954	1955	1956	1957	1958	1959	1960
1. Total residential structures	308,340	321,626	336,794	354,960	369,891	382,557	395,547	412,139	425,597
2. 1–4 family nonfarm	259,585	271,722	285,627	302,770	316,687	328,036	339,155	353,067	363,918
3. Multifamily nonfarm	28,730	29,292	30,021	30,615	31,172	32,077	33,566	35,876	38,156
4. Noncorporate	16,201	16,436	16,756	17,009	17,243	17,667	18,371	19,471	20,701
5. Corporate	12,527	12,853	13,261	13,601	13,922	14,428	15,212	16,396	17,451
6. Farm residential structures	20,025	20,612	21,146	21,575	22,032	22,444	22,826	23,196	23,523
7. Total nonresidential structures	156,438	162,155	168,052	175,003	183,763	192,164	198,863	205,248	212,813
8. Institutions	16,971	17,844	18,962	20,111	21,347	22,692	24,180	25,660	27,324
9. Noncorporate nonfarm	13,424	13,379	13,655	14,611	15,789	16,269	16,749	17,428	18,318
10. Corporate	114,825	119,346	123,518	128,102	134,147	140,472	144,971	149,010	153,864
11. Farm	11,218	11,586	11,917	12,179	12,480	12,731	12,963	13,150	13,307
12. Total producers' durables	147,259	154,214	159,149	166,433	173,784	180,449	182,424	186,766	192,123
13. Institutions	1,914	2,005	2,069	2,164	2,259	2,346	2,372	2,428	2,498
14. Noncorporate nonfarm	36,347	37,067	37,203	37,854	38,757	39,072	39,326	39,597	39,869
15. Corporate	87,766	92,837	97,081	103,188	109,658	116,029	117,481	121,398	126,801
16. Farm	21,232	22,305	22,796	23,227	23,110	23,002	23,245	23,343	22,955
17. Total consumer durables	94,605	101,382	106,620	117,399	123,602	128,590	129,143	134,563	139,589
18. Total inventories	117,453	114,315	110,162	116,862	122,245	125,107	127,495	128,912	124,358
19. Noncorporate	15,500	15,900	15,700	16,300	16,500	16,700	16,600	17,300	17,600
20. Corporate	77,300	78,300	76,000	81,400	86,500	87,000	84,800	89,000	91,900
21. Farm	24,653	20,115	18,462	19,162	19,245	21,407	26,095	22,612	14,858

Institutional Investors

	1961	1962	1963	1964	1965	1966	1967	1968
1. Total residential structures	438,489	453,265	468,744	483,281	496,970	508,119	517,980	530,566
2. 1–4 family nonfarm	373,447	383,408	393,405	402,195	410,821	417,572	423,957	431,878
3. Multifamily nonfarm	41,207	45,720	50,931	56,453	61,318	65,527	68,816	73,333
4. Noncorporate	22,509	25,382	28,933	32,958	36,912	40,284	42,960	46,449
5. Corporate	18,693	20,333	21,992	23,488	24,595	25,427	26,034	27,058
6. Farm residential structures	23,835	24,137	24,408	24,633	24,831	25,020	25,207	25,355
7. Total nonresidential structures	220,265	227,896	235,221	243,547	255,046	267,937	278,862	289,565
8. Institutions	29,109	31,098	32,902	34,923	37,220	39,554	41,639	43,584
9. Noncorporate nonfarm	19,558	20,959	22,786	24,795	27,166	29,779	31,832	33,769
10. Corporate	158,150	162,262	165,831	169,996	176,747	184,609	191,299	198,062
11. Farm	13,448	13,577	13,702	13,833	13,913	13,995	14,092	14,150
12. Total producers' durables	195,203	201,142	208,355	218,978	233,243	251,448	268,309	284,956
13. Institutions	2,538	2,414	2,500	2,409	2,566	2,514	2,683	2,850
14. Noncorporate nonfarm	39,649	39,538	39,369	39,758	40,244	41,836	43,637	45,672
15. Corporate	130,200	136,374	143,140	153,066	165,834	181,294	195,061	208,588
16. Farm	22,816	22,816	23,346	23,745	24,619	25,804	26,928	27,846
17. Total consumer durables	142,437	149,064	157,937	169,095	183,941	199,270	210,632	227,007
18. Total inventories	135,532	141,835	146,312	151,044	162,117	176,892	176,054	190,994
19. Noncorporate	17,800	18,400	18,300	18,900	19,600	20,000	20,200	20,700
20. Corporate	93,500	98,100	103,200	109,100	116,500	130,100	130,900	143,200
21. Farm	24,232	25,335	24,812	23,044	26,017	26,792	24,954	27,094

SOURCE: See text.

TABLE IA-7

Public Sector Wealth Estimates, 1952–68

(millions of 1958 dollars)

	1952	1953	1954	1955	1956	1957	1958	1959	1960
Federal civilian structures	58,220	60,567	62,328	62,920	63,285	63,903	64,769	65,824	66,796
Residential	3,918	3,862	3,789	3,715	3,657	3,737	4,015	4,402	4,585
Nonresidential	54,302	56,705	58,539	59,205	59,628	60,166	60,754	61,422	62,211
Buildings	30,388	32,011	33,261	33,497	33,441	33,373	33,306	33,278	33,314
Highways	1,090	1,119	1,153	1,193	1,230	1,284	1,352	1,403	1,498
Conservation and development	21,810	22,574	23,134	23,533	23,981	24,539	25,124	25,747	26,363
Other	1,014	1,001	991	982	976	970	972	994	1,036
Federal equipment (civilian)	6,938	8,656	9,194	9,321	9,902	10,160	10,467	10,820	11,422
Federal inventories	7,952	13,964	16,679	18,553	15,742	15,154	17,571	17,805	18,507
State and local structures	119,495	125,304	132,396	140,103	147,947	156,595	166,786	177,671	187,721
Residential	4,468	4,959	5,220	5,394	5,564	5,802	6,169	6,498	6,771
Nonresidential	115,027	120,345	127,176	134,709	142,333	150,793	160,617	171,173	180,950
Buildings	37,993	40,266	42,978	46,015	48,916	52,071	55,292	58,203	61,091
Highways	47,714	49,738	52,752	56,023	59,266	62,991	68,039	73,990	79,169
Sewer and water systems	17,940	18,786	19,685	20,637	21,725	22,811	23,872	24,935	25,958
Conservation and development	1,733	1,787	1,846	1,939	2,078	2,211	2,316	2,428	2,553
Public service enterprises	6,527	6,618	6,717	6,865	7,138	7,409	7,734	8,147	8,622
Other	3,120	3,150	3,198	3,230	3,260	3,300	3,364	3,470	3,557
State and local equipment	8,016	8,726	9,601	10,474	11,375	12,297	13,194	14,072	15,061

	1961	1962	1963	1964	1965	1966	1967	1968
Federal civilian structures	67,973	69,193	70,418	71,743	73,131	74,388	75,213	75,815
Residential	4,764	4,854	4,810	4,804	4,831	4,801	4,725	4,673
Nonresidential	63,209	64,339	65,608	66,939	68,300	69,587	70,488	71,142
Buildings	33,407	33,554	33,853	34,279	34,693	34,440	34,172	33,947
Highways	1,587	1,694	1,822	1,930	2,023	2,129	2,219	2,311
Conservation and development	27,145	27,958	28,757	29,535	30,375	31,278	32,043	32,643
Other	1,070	1,133	1,176	1,195	1,209	1,740	2,054	2,241
Federal equipment (civilian)	12,539	13,185	13,403	13,311	13,682	13,810	13,981	14,104
Federal inventories	17,508	18,099	17,681	16,819	15,556	12,207	12,182	12,906
State and local structures	198,475	209,284	221,208	233,791	246,610	259,874	270,606	281,782
Residential	7,153	7,689	7,890	8,138	8,363	8,659	9,015	9,326
Nonresidential	191,323	201,595	213,318	225,653	238,247	251,215	261,591	272,456
Buildings	64,113	66,914	70,156	73,598	77,362	81,657	86,198	90,628
Highways	84,674	90,315	96,731	103,203	109,348	115,505	118,713	122,088
Sewer and water systems	27,045	28,209	29,444	30,927	32,519	34,007	35,563	37,439
Conservation and development	2,689	2,856	3,125	3,382	3,748	4,103	4,506	4,868
Public service enterprises	9,043	9,364	9,782	10,288	10,825	11,323	11,807	12,402
Other	3,759	3,937	4,080	4,255	4,445	4,620	4,804	5,031
State and local equipment	16,064	17,073	18,376	19,730	21,230	23,079	25,382	28,155

SOURCE: See text.

TABLE IA-8

All Open-End Investment Companies, 1952–68

(*$million*)

	Total Assets	Cash	U.S. Government Securities	Corporate and Foreign Bonds	Corporate Shares	Commercial Paper
1952	3,990	135	132	347	3,376	—
1953	4,290	161	133	352	3,644	—
1954	6,251	159	158	449	5,485	—
1955	7,989	121	260	482	7,061	65
1956	9,170	140	280	676	7,995	79
1957	8,831	135	281	790	7,510	115
1958	13,399	204	406	946	11,812	31
1959	16,479	251	579	1,136	14,447	66
1960	17,804	271	647	1,304	15,482	100
1961	24,054	365	723	1,668	21,297	1
1962	22,706	346	787	1,726	19,576	271
1963	27,022	412	780	1,916	23,670	244
1964	29,584	483	835	2,341	25,797	128
1965	37,959	578	874	2,754	33,262	491
1966	37,460	570	1,545	3,136	31,130	1,079
1967	49,034	748	924	3,251	43,051	1,060
1968	57,725	880	1,254	3,736	50,494	1,361

SOURCE: See text.

TABLE IA-9

All Other Investment Companies, 1952–68

(*$million*)

	1952	1953	1954	1955	1956	1957	1958	1959	1960
Cash	20	15	16	35	30	41	34	37	46
U.S. government securities	128	127	123	203	179	177	147	110	216
State and local government securities	—	—	—	—	—	—	—	—	—
Corporate and foreign bonds	85	95	161	180	222	292	311	366	479
Corporate shares	3,165	3,251	4,725	5,677	5,237	4,839	5,642	5,925	5,866
Commercial paper	—	—	—	—	—	—	—	—	—
Mortgages	363	376	372	361	348	328	294	263	247
Miscellaneous assets	32	36	35	46	46	53	57	56	95
Total assets	3,793	3,900	5,432	6,502	6,062	5,730	6,485	6,757	6,949
Total liabilities	49	58	68	85	110	123	133	161	149
Bonds	15	15	15	15	23	24	17	17	19
Short-term loans	7	7	7	7	7	6	6	6	7
Miscellaneous liabilities	27	36	46	63	80	93	110	138	123
Net worth	3,744	3,842	5,364	6,417	5,952	5,607	6,352	6,596	6,800

	1961	1962	1963	1964	1965	1966	1967	1968
Cash	73	108	24	74	44	72	97	150
U.S. government securities	170	168	264	229	153	252	353	569
State and local government securities	20	55	82	137	238	292	329	362
Corporate and foreign bonds	452	492	513	544	338	443	605	540
Corporate shares	6,640	6,469	7,601	7,757	6,941	6,499	8,675	9,422
Commercial paper	—	27	3	44	38	7	6	8
Mortgages	242	239	268	289	301	317	330	312
Miscellaneous assets	115	139	146	154	164	160	187	207
Total assets	7,712	7,697	8,901	9,228	8,217	8,042	10,582	11,570
Total liabilities	195	218	237	255	272	296	306	311
Bonds	23	16	21	25	4	25	24	20
Short-term loans	6	7	7	8	20	21	21	21
Miscellaneous liabilities	166	195	209	222	248	250	261	270
Net worth	7,517	7,479	8,664	8,973	7,945	7,746	10,276	11,259

SOURCE: See text.

TABLE IA-10

Portfolio Composition of Personal Trusts and Estates Managed by National Banks, 1963–68

(*percent*)

Asset Category	1963	1964	1965	1966	1967	1968
I. Bonds and notes	28.02	26.01	24.75	23.97	22.76	22.12
A. U.S. government and agency issues	9.29	8.63	8.31	8.40	7.68	6.59
B. State and local government issues	10.54	10.34	9.66	9.77	8.77	9.43
C. Other bonds and notes	8.19	7.04	6.78	5.80	6.31	6.10
II. Corporate stock	59.92	62.46	63.64	63.47	64.89	65.97
A. Common	58.12	60.59	62.05	61.91	63.40	64.11
B. Preferred	1.80	1.87	1.59	1.56	1.49	1.86
III. Real estate and mortgages	6.72	5.91	6.40	7.80	7.40	7.04
A. Mortgages	2.01	1.33	1.75	2.14	2.17	2.13
B. Real estate	4.71	4.58	4.65	5.66	5.23	4.91
IV. Cash and deposits	3.74	3.80	3.38	3.36	3.42	3.26
A. Time and savings deposits	2.01	2.31	2.25	2.09	2.11	1.90
1. Savings and loan shares	0.37	0.38	0.40	0.36	0.33	0.30
2. Time deposits	1.64	1.93	1.85	1.73	1.78	1.60
a. Own bank	1.16	1.43	1.34	1.07	1.27	1.20
b. Other banks	0.48	0.50	0.51	0.66	0.51	0.40
B. Cash and demand deposits	1.73	1.49	1.13	1.27	1.31	1.36
V. Miscellaneous assets	1.72	1.73	1.64	1.43	1.49	1.59
Total (percent)	100.00	100.00	100.00	100.00	100.00	100.00
Total assets ($million)	47,932	54,443	60,952	54,272	62,217	71,987

SOURCE: See text.

TABLE IA-11

Portfolio Composition of Personal Trusts and Estates Managed
by All Insured Banks, 1963–68

(*percent*)

Asset Category	1963	1964	1965	1966	1967	1968
I. Bonds and notes	23.00	22.31	21.99	23.30	22.15	21.64
A. U.S. government and agency issues	7.84	7.42	7.21	7.23	6.62	5.72
B. State and local government issues	10.82	10.52	9.69	10.08	9.03	9.67
C. Other bonds and notes	4.34	4.37	5.09	5.99	6.50	6.25
II. Corporate stock	68.07	68.76	69.17	67.28	68.58	69.30
A. Common	65.84	66.91	67.44	65.65	67.02	67.37
B. Preferred	2.23	1.85	1.73	1.63	1.56	1.93
III. Real estate and mortgages	4.47	4.38	4.66	5.52	5.32	5.11
A. Mortgages	1.01	0.94	1.21	1.50	1.54	1.53
B. Real estate	3.46	3.44	3.45	4.02	3.78	3.58
IV. Cash and deposits	3.24	3.30	2.96	2.89	2.90	2.80
A. Time and savings deposits	1.77	2.02	1.97	1.85	1.83	1.67
1. Savings and loan shares	0.46	0.46	0.48	0.43	0.39	0.35
2. Time deposits	1.31	1.56	1.49	1.42	1.44	1.31
a. Own bank	0.88	1.11	1.05	0.82	0.98	0.94
b. Other banks	0.43	0.45	0.46	0.60	0.46	0.37
B. Cash and demand deposits	1.47	1.28	0.99	1.04	1.07	1.13
V. Miscellaneous assets	1.20	1.24	1.20	1.01	1.06	1.15
Total (percent)	100.00	100.00	100.00	100.00	100.00	100.00
Total assets ($million)	101,200	105,443	114,952	113,000	126,223	138,368

SOURCE: See text.

TABLE IA-12

Personal Trusts and Estates: Balance Sheets, 1951–62

(*$million*)

	Total Assets [a]	Common Stock	Preferred Stock	State and Local Government	Corporate Bonds	U.S. Government Securities	Mortgages	Cash	Other Assets [a]
A. Personal Trusts Other than Common Trust Funds									
1951	34,590	16,420	1,500	4,600	1,800	7,000	690	640	1,940
1952	34,880	17,850	1,470	5,260	1,390	5,590	710	690	1,920
1953	34,290	17,290	1,390	5,400	2,150	4,770	810	580	1,900
1954	42,080	23,740	1,680	6,100	2,650	4,860	930	410	1,890
1955	48,000	28,510	1,610	6,620	2,580	4,860	980	970	1,870
1956	48,860	30,650	1,450	7,210	2,460	3,690	830	680	1,890
1957	44,103	27,210	1,291	7,791	2,335	2,513	671	385	1,907
1958	53,355	36,017	1,274	7,787	2,589	2,552	738	475	1,923
1959	59,351	40,018	1,235	9,098	2,604	2,794	772	496	2,334
1960	60,723	40,873	1,244	9,182	2,717	2,932	831	530	2,414
1961	72,592	52,059	1,296	10,064	2,880	2,256	886	536	2,615
1962	72,975	49,499	1,316	11,644	3,033	2,773	942	552	3,216
B. Personal Trusts and Estates Other than Common Trust Funds									
1951	38,326	17,020	1,556	4,762	1,808	8,992	794	828	2,566
1952	38,647	18,686	1,541	5,500	1,410	7,252	793	899	2,566
1953	37,822	18,123	1,459	5,654	2,184	6,196	906	757	2,543
1954	46,246	25,059	1,775	6,431	2,711	6,123	1,048	539	2,560
1955	53,136	30,359	1,717	7,041	2,663	6,414	1,114	1,286	2,542
1956	54,528	33,156	1,571	7,791	2,579	4,948	958	916	2,610
1957	49,660	29,833	1,417	8,533	2,482	3,415	786	526	2,669

Year								
1958	2,729	657	876	3,516	8,646	1,418	40,034	60,665
1959	3,313	687	916	3,849	10,104	1,375	44,491	67,541
1960	3,425	734	985	4,038	10,192	1,384	45,420	69,103
1961	3,700	739	1,048	3,099	11,142	1,438	57,697	81,956
1962	4,493	752	1,100	3,761	12,727	1,442	54,167	81,659

C. Common Trust Funds

Year									
1951	b	10	10	290	90	b	110	310	820
1952	b	10	10	340	130	10	130	410	1,040
1953	3	10	10	331	220	10	160	546	1,290
1954	b	10	14	318	289	26	190	748	1,596
1955	1	11	20	322	358	31	214	911	1,869
1956	1	17	27	278	417	39	209	985	1,974
1957	b	14	30	211	526	44	205	936	1,965
1958	1	19	33	174	647	47	221	1,292	2,434
1959	b	18	38	210	710	42	211	1,437	2,668
1960	1	22	46	220	810	45	215	1,454	2,812
1961	1	22	52	219	955	84	232	1,986	3,551
1962	3	24	59	258	1,090	152	239	1,753	3,576

D. All Personal Trusts and Estates

Year									
1951	2,566	838	804	9,282	1,898	4,762	1,666	17,330	39,146
1952	2,566	909	803	7,592	1,540	5,510	1,671	19,096	39,687
1953	2,543	767	916	6,526	2,404	5,664	1,619	18,663	39,112
1954	2,560	549	1,062	6,441	3,000	6,457	1,965	25,807	47,841
1955	2,543	1,297	1,134	6,736	3,021	7,072	1,931	31,270	55,005
1956	2,611	933	985	5,226	2,996	7,830	1,780	34,141	56,502
1957	2,669	540	816	3,626	3,008	8,577	1,622	30,769	51,625
1958	2,730	676	909	3,690	3,435	8,693	1,639	41,326	63,099
1959	3,313	705	954	4,059	3,516	10,146	1,586	45,928	70,209
1960	3,426	756	1,031	4,258	3,736	10,237	1,599	46,874	71,915
1961	3,701	761	1,100	3,318	4,048	11,226	1,670	59,684	85,507
1962	4,496	776	1,159	4,019	4,307	12,879	1,681	55,920	85,235

SOURCE: See text.
a Includes real estate.
b Less than $0.5 million.

TABLE IA-13

Asset Composition of all Common Trust Funds—End of Year, 1954–68

(*percent*)

	1954	1955	1956	1957	1958	1959	1960
Total assets ($million)	1,595.7	1,868.7	1,974.4	1,965.5	2,434.4	2,666.7	2,812.6
	%	%	%	%	%	%	%
Cash	0.7	0.6	0.9	0.7	0.8	0.7	0.8
U.S. government securities	19.9	17.2	14.1	10.8	7.1	7.9	7.9
Marketable: ≤1 year	0.2	0.3	0.3	0.7	0.5	0.8	0.7
Marketable: >1 year	7.7	7.2	5.8	4.9	4.3	5.9	6.6
Other nonmarketable	12.0	9.8	8.0	5.2	2.4	1.1	0.5
State and local government securities	1.6	1.7	2.0	2.2	1.9	1.6	1.6
Corporate and foreign bonds	18.1	19.2	21.1	26.7	26.5	26.6	28.8
Domestic corporate	17.1	18.1	19.8	24.7	24.5	23.4	25.0
Other	1.0	1.1	1.3	2.0	2.0	3.2	3.8
Private placements	n.a.	n.a.	n.a.	n.a.	n.a.	n.a.	n.a.
Mortgages	0.9	1.1	1.4	1.5	1.4	1.4	1.6
Preferred stock	11.9	11.5	10.6	10.4	9.1	7.9	7.6
Common stock	46.9	48.7	49.9	47.7	53.1	53.9	51.7
Bank and finance	5.4	5.0	4.6	4.5	5.2	5.2	5.1
Utility	9.9	10.1	10.2	10.6	11.8	·11.4	12.6
Other	31.6	33.6	35.1	32.6	36.1	37.3	34.0
Savings accounts	a	a	a	a	a	a	a
Other assets	—	—	—	—	—	—	—

	1961	1962	1963	1964	1965	1966	1967	1968
Total assets ($million)	3,550.9	3,577.7	4,539.8	5,819.7	7,529.1	7,612.0	8,347.5	9,553.5
	%	%	%	%	%	%	%	%
Cash	0.6	0.7	0.8	0.7	1.0	0.9	1.0	1.3
U.S. government securities	6.2	7.2	11.0	10.9	9.2	8.9	6.2	5.2
Marketable: ≤ 1 year	0.6	0.8	1.6	1.1	1.0	1.1	0.8	1.3
Marketable: > 1 year	5.3	6.2	9.4	9.8	8.2	7.8	5.4	3.9
Other nonmarketable	0.3	0.2						
State and local government securities	2.4	4.2	7.6	12.1	14.9	17.8	17.7	16.3
Corporate and foreign bonds	26.9	30.5	24.1	23.1	25.0	26.3	25.6	23.9
Domestic corporate	23.0	26.0	24.1	23.1	21.4	21.5	21.7	20.5
Other	3.9	4.5			3.6	4.8	3.9	3.4
Private placements	n.a.	n.a.	n.a.	n.a.	n.a.	n.a.	n.a.	n.a.
Mortgages	1.5	1.6	2.0	2.3	2.4	2.7	2.6	2.4
Preferred stock	6.5	6.7	4.9	3.7	2.9	2.3	2.2	2.6
Common stock	56.0	49.0	49.4	47.0	44.2	40.5	44.3	47.7
Bank and finance	6.6	5.6	5.0	4.2	3.6	3.5	3.3	4.0
Utility	13.7	12.7	11.6	10.6	8.9	8.2	7.0	7.2
Other	35.7	30.7	32.8	32.2	31.6	28.8	33.9	36.5
Savings accounts	a	0.1	0.2	0.2	0.4	0.5	0.4	0.6
Other assets	—							

Notes to Table IA-13.

n.a. = not available.

SOURCES:

1954: *Federal Reserve Bulletin*, August 1956, p. 801.

1955–56: *ibid.*, June 1957, p. 623.

1957: *ibid.*, May 1958, p. 536.

1958: *ibid.*, May 1959, p. 478.

1959: *ibid.*, May 1960, p. 480.

1960: *ibid.*, May 1961, p. 527.

1961: *ibid.*, May 1962, p. 530.

1962: *ibid.*, June 1963, p. 776.

1963: Stanley Silverberg, *National Banking Review*, May 1965, p. 365.

1965: Edwin W. Hanczaryk, *ibid.*, June 1967, p. 442.

1966–68: Hanczaryk, unpublished manuscript.

[a] Less than 0.5 percent.

TABLE IA-14

Assets of Personal Trusts and Estates, 1951–68

(*$million*)

	1951	1952	1953	1954	1955	1956	1957	1958	1959
Total assets	39,146	39,687	39,112	47,842	55,005	56,502	51,625	63,089	70,209
Cash	838	909	767	549	1,297	933	540	676	705
U.S. government securities	9,282	7,592	6,526	6,441	6,736	5,226	3,626	3,690	4,059
State and local government securities	4,762	5,510	5,664	6,457	7,072	7,830	8,577	8,693	10,146
Corporate bonds	1,898	1,540	2,404	3,000	3,021	2,996	3,008	3,435	3,516
Mortgages	804	803	916	1,062	1,134	985	816	909	954
Preferred stock	1,666	1,671	1,619	1,965	1,931	1,780	1,622	1,639	1,586
Common stock	17,330	19,096	18,663	25,807	31,270	34,141	30,769	41,326	45,928
Total, other assets	2,566	2,566	2,543	2,560	2,543	2,611	2,669	2,730	3,313
Real estate	1,403	1,403	1,390	1,399	1,390	1,428	1,459	1,492	1,811
Time deposits	720	720	713	718	713	732	749	766	929
Miscellaneous	443	443	440	443	440	451	461	472	573

	1960	1961	1962	1963	1964	1965	1966	1967	1968
Total assets	71,915	85,507	85,235	101,200	105,443	114,952	113,000	126,223	138,368
Cash	756	761	776	1,491	1,347	1,143	1,170	1,354	1,560
U.S. government securities	4,258	3,318	4,019	7,930	7,829	8,292	8,166	8,358	7,910
State and local government securities	10,237	11,226	12,879	10,953	11,092	11,142	11,395	11,396	13,377
Corporate bonds	3,736	4,048	4,307	4,390	4,610	5,851	6,764	8,199	8,654
Mortgages	1,031	1,100	1,159	1,027	995	1,386	1,698	1,939	2,123
Preferred stock	1,599	1,670	1,681	2,258	1,948	1,986	1,844	1,963	2,676
Common stock	46,874	59,684	55,920	66,626	70,353	77,518	74,184	84,594	93,220
Total, other assets	3,426	3,701	4,496	6,524	7,069	7,633	7,778	8,422	8,847
Real estate	1,873	2,023	2,458	3,506	3,622	3,967	4,548	4,767	4,955
Time deposits	961	1,038	1,261	1,802	2,137	2,292	2,091	2,317	2,298
Miscellaneous	592	640	777	1,216	1,310	1,374	1,139	1,338	1,594

SOURCE: See text.

TABLE IA-15

Portfolio of Fraternal Life Insurance Companies, 1951–68

(*$million*)

Assets	1951	1952	1953	1954	1955	1956	1957	1958	1959
Mortgages	385.1	423.0	452.6	493.5	595.7	651.1	677.3	716.6	738.4
Corporate stocks	97.0	103.6	94.0	102.9	99.5	98.1	92.2	118.8	132.7
Total bonds	1,570.5	1,606.0	1,628.2	1,665.1	1,694.8	1,730.3	1,700.4	1,743.8	1,834.4
Corporate	938.0	959.0	923.2	1,008.2	1,025.1	1,058.6	1,060.3	1,107.8	1,173.0
State and local governments	392.0	401.0	376.4	424.6	432.3	445.1	436.4	438.4	451.2
U.S. government	174.5	178.0	171.0	192.5	196.6	183.5	162.1	155.9	168.3
Unallocated	66.0	68.0	157.6	39.8	40.8	43.1	41.6	41.7	42.0
Real estate	56.0	68.9	79.4	86.8	93.3	93.7	105.6	110.3	115.9
Certified loans	86.3	88.7	92.6	98.8	105.4	110.4	113.2	119.7	127.2
Time and savings deposits	0.2	0.2	0.2	0.3	0.3	0.3	0.3	0.3	0.3
Cash and bank deposits	30.1	28.3	35.6	39.8	28.7	21.7	25.4	26.3	26.4
Other	34.6	40.3	53.3	65.9	64.1	74.5	79.9	82.9	89.2
Total	2,260.0	2,359.0	2,436.0	2,553.0	2,682.0	2,780.0	2,794.0	2,919.0	3,065.0

Institutional Investors

Assets	1960	1961	1962	1963	1964	1965	1966	1967	1968
Mortgages	726.1	810.1	829.2	857.0	884.8	917.1	1,035.3	1,112.1	1,061.0
Corporate stocks	142.3	148.7	152.2	180.7	210.0	214.7	220.6	244.9	259.3
Total bonds	1,951.3	1,852.4	1,940.6	2,030.2	2,101.6	2,158.9	2,315.7	2,394.9	2,435.9
Corporate	1,336.0	1,312.3	1,429.7	1,536.8	1,614.0	1,742.5	1,916.8	2,010.5	2,051.9
State and local governments	460.4	379.6	306.8	275.1	276.4	257.4	259.9	256.1	229.0
U.S. government	154.9	122.9	166.0	179.3	168.0	159.1	139.0	127.8	110.0
Unallocated	—	37.7	38.1	39.1	43.1	—	—	0.4	45.0
Real estate	125.9	133.5	152.2	170.0	168.0	175.1	171.0	190.0	202.2
Certified loans	141.4	141.3	147.9	158.7	164.4	174.4	192.7	210.8	210.0
Time and savings deposits	1.0	0.6	0.7	0.7	0.7	0.8	0.4	0.4	0.9
Cash and bank deposits	25.4	30.3	25.6	33.0	35.0	33.5	23.8	23.3	24.7
Other	99.3	108.0	119.2	119.6	121.2	132.9	139.8	142.5	135.1
Total	3,213.0	3,225.0	3,368.0	3,550.0	3,685.0	3,807.0	4,100.0	4,319.0	4,329.0

SOURCE: See text.

TABLE IA-16

Assets of Fraternal Life Insurance Companies, 1951–68

(*$million*)

	Total Assets		Ratio: Ten Largest
	Ten Largest	All	to All (percent)
1951	$ 990.38	$2,260.00	43.8
1952	1,052.08	2,359.00	44.6
1953	1,101.02	2,436.00	45.2
1954	1,164.49	2,553.00	45.6
1955	1,220.93	2,682.00	45.5
1956	1,289.20	2,780.00	46.4
1957	1,359.47	2,794.00	48.7
1958	1,447.36	2,919.00	49.6
1959	1,536.29	3,065.00	50.1
1960	1,582.59	3,213.00	49.3
1961	1,732.64	3,225.00	53.7
1962	1,830.74	3,368.00	54.4
1963	1,968.52	3,550.00	55.5
1964	2,106.06	3,685.00	57.2
1965	2,275.99	3,807.00	59.8
1966	2,417.25	4,100.00	59.0
1967	2,530.79	4,319.00	58.6
1968	2,775.63	4,329.00	64.1

SOURCE: See text.

TABLE IA-17

Percentage Breakdown of Assets of Ten of the Largest Fraternal Life Insurance Companies, 1951–68

	1951	1952	1953	1954	1955	1956	1957	1958	1959
Mortgages	17.04	17.93	18.58	19.33	22.21	23.42	24.24	24.55	24.09
Corporate stocks	4.29	4.39	3.86	4.03	3.71	3.53	3.30	4.07	4.33
Total bonds	69.49	68.08	66.84	65.22	63.19	62.24	60.86	59.74	59.85
Corporate	41.50	40.67	37.90	39.49	38.22	38.08	37.95	37.95	38.27
State and local governments	17.35	16.99	15.45	16.63	16.12	16.01	15.62	15.02	14.72
U.S. government	7.69	7.53	7.02	7.54	7.33	6.60	5.80	5.34	5.49
Unallocated	2.94	2.88	6.47	1.56	1.52	1.55	1.49	1.43	1.37
Real estate	2.48	2.92	3.26	3.40	3.48	3.37	3.78	3.78	3.78
Certified loans	3.82	3.76	3.80	3.87	3.93	3.97	4.05	4.10	4.15
Time and savings deposits	0.01	0.01	0.01	0.01	0.01	0.01	0.01	0.01	0.01
Cash and bank deposits	1.33	1.20	1.46	1.56	1.07	0.78	0.91	0.90	0.86
Other	1.53	1.71	2.19	2.58	2.39	2.68	2.86	2.84	2.91
Total	100.00	100.00	100.00	100.00	100.00	100.00	100.00	100.00	100.00

	1960	1961	1962	1963	1964	1965	1966	1967	1968
Mortgages	22.60	25.12	24.62	24.14	24.01	24.09	25.25	25.75	24.51
Corporate stocks	4.43	4.61	4.52	5.09	5.70	5.64	5.38	5.67	5.99
Total bonds	60.73	57.44	57.62	57.19	57.03	56.71	56.48	55.45	56.27
Corporate	41.58	40.69	42.45	43.29	43.80	45.77	46.75	46.55	47.40
State and local governments	14.33	11.77	9.11	7.75	7.50	6.76	6.34	5.93	5.29
U.S. government	4.82	3.81	4.93	5.05	4.56	4.18	3.39	2.96	2.54
Unallocated	—	1.17	1.13	1.10	1.17	—	—	0.01	1.04
Real estate	3.92	4.14	4.52	4.79	4.56	4.60	4.17	4.40	4.67
Certified loans	4.40	4.38	4.39	4.47	4.46	4.58	4.70	4.88	4.85
Time and savings deposits	0.03	0.02	0.02	0.02	0.02	0.02	0.01	0.01	0.02
Cash and bank deposits	0.79	0.94	0.76	0.93	0.95	0.88	0.58	0.54	0.57
Other	3.09	3.35	3.54	3.37	3.29	3.49	3.41	3.30	3.12
Total	100.00	100.00	100.00	100.00	100.00	100.00	100.00	100.00	100.00

SOURCE: See text.

TABLE IA-18

Balance Sheet of Mortgage Banking, 1951–68

(*$million*)

	1951	1952	1953	1954	1955	1956	1957	1958	1959
Total assets	692.6	861.1	955.9	1,202.5	1,447.3	1,541.7	1,501.8	1,870.6	2,259.9
Cash (including escrow)	113.7	127.8	151.3	157.5	169.7	185.3	208.3	246.3	289.1
Mortgage and construction loans	454.1	597.8	623.6	882.6	1,113.6	1,155.2	1,045.9	1,333.5	1,615.4
Mortgage loans	—	490.5	501.0	713.0	878.0	944.4	861.0	1,069.5	1,287.2
Construction	—	107.3	122.6	169.6	235.6	210.8	184.9	264.0	328.2
Notes and accounts receivable	33.8	34.7	54.8	30.2	41.7	47.1	53.3	43.8	55.1
Title I and other small loans	2.5	3.7	3.4	1.2	3.9	4.4	9.7	15.0	13.1
Other current assets	17.8	18.1	20.0	34.2	33.3	37.2	47.1	34.3	40.0
Noncurrent assets	70.7	79.1	102.8	96.8	85.1	112.5	137.5	197.7	247.2
Total liabilities	692.6	861.1	955.9	1,202.5	1,447.3	1,541.7	1,501.8	1,870.6	2,259.9
Escrows	69.3	82.0	95.5	101.2	108.4	121.1	133.0	166.9	191.9
Notes payable	383.3	485.9	544.1	738.1	970.0	998.6	907.8	1,157.4	1,439.9
To banks	364.1	466.5	522.3	n.a.	n.a.	n.a.	n.a.	n.a.	n.a.
To others	19.2	19.4	21.8	n.a.	n.a.	n.a.	n.a.	n.a.	n.a.
Accounts payable	20.5	19.7	20.5	22.3	29.6	28.9	28.0	30.3	38.3
Undisbursed mortgage loans	25.5	53.7	52.2	49.0	36.8	28.2	26.0	58.7	50.8
Other current liabilities	22.8	23.0	22.2	44.5	55.9	57.6	55.7	69.4	70.1
Noncurrent liabilities	19.1	27.2	34.1	36.7	34.7	76.6	86.2	89.8	119.9
Net worth	152.1	169.5	187.3	210.7	211.9	230.7	265.1	298.1	349.0

	1960	1961	1962	1963	1964	1965	1966	1967	1968
Total assets	2,360.2	2,884.5	3,262.5	4,474.2	4,686.6	5,226.4	4,535.8	4,543.1	4,371.5
Cash (including escrow)	316.2	366.9	398.4	716.7	850.5	791.6	838.9	890.2	971.8
Mortgage and construction loans	1,615.0	1,972.1	2,216.0	3,117.5	3,172.1	3,683.4	2,904.7	2,829.5	3,315.1
Mortgage loans	1,227.6	1,513.0	1,638.2	2,255.2	2,382.8	2,744.1	2,155.5	2,135.2	2,369.1
Construction	387.4	459.1	577.8	862.3	789.3	939.3	749.2	694.3	946.0
Notes and accounts receivable	71.3	87.5	117.1	100.8	142.3	152.8	111.2	126.0	113.8
Title I and other small loans	18.9	15.4	28.7	89.0	113.7	89.2	107.0	114.0	137.9
Other current assets	57.8	55.8	83.3	140.3	134.4	130.2	143.2	160.9	202.5
Noncurrent assets	281.0	386.8	419.0	309.9	273.6	379.2	430.8	422.5	474.6
Total liabilities	2,360.2	2,884.5	3,262.5	4,474.2	4,686.6	5,226.4	4,535.8	4,543.1	4,371.5
Escrows	217.3	255.8	281.2	623.4	734.0	684.6	733.6	770.6	844.3
Notes payable	1,450.3	1,754.9	2,012.1	2,982.5	3,144.6	3,642.1	2,854.9	2,774.5	3,223.3
To banks	n.a.	n.a.	n.a.	2,877.0	3,014.1	3,522.8	2,722.8	2,656.7	3,064.0
To others	n.a.	n.a.	n.a.	105.5	130.5	119.3	132.1	117.8	159.3
Accounts payable	39.9	42.7	50.6	78.2	71.3	96.4	64.8	77.4	95.0
Undisbursed mortgage loans	53.9	62.2	68.6	n.a.	n.a.	n.a.	n.a.	n.a.	n.a.
Other current liabilities	82.9	90.4	91.0	139.6	95.4	79.8	97.6	104.3	153.7
Noncurrent liabilities	132.8	195.6	233.4	157.7	156.5	219.5	276.3	277.3	293.9
Net worth	383.1	482.9	525.6	492.8	484.8	504.0	508.6	539.0	605.7

n.a. = not available.
SOURCES: See text.

TABLE IA-19

Par Value of Corporate Bonds Outstanding, 1947–68

(*$million*)

	Railroad	Utility	Industrial	Finance [a]	Total
1947	9,630	10,667	6,853	548	27,698
1948	9,698	12,689	8,698	973	32,058
1949	9,896	14,081	9,832	1,403	35,212
1950	9,990	15,176	10,314	1,778	37,258
1951	10,332	16,632	12,332	1,946	41,242
1952	10,587	18,222	15,441	2,176	46,426
1953	10,798	20,601	16,938	3,418	51,755
1954	10,666	22,108	18,884	3,682	55,340
1955	10,719	23,792	20,101	4,852	59,464
1956	10,845	25,298	22,053	5,983	64,179
1957	10,975	29,193	24,264	6,978	71,410
1958	10,972	31,902	27,305	7,184	77,363
1959	10,739	34,059	28,348	8,178	81,324
1960	10,565	36,537	29,316	9,750	86,168
1961	10,395	38,253	32,126	10,525	91,299
1962	10,297	40,515	33,831	11,358	96,001
1963	10,281	42,278	36,315	13,164	102,038
1964	10,386	45,081	38,458	15,808	109,733
1965	10,630	46,031	42,047	18,515	117,223
1966	11,217	50,220	47,975	19,379	128,791
1967	11,480	55,138	57,668	20,681	144,967
1968	10,770	59,893	65,434	21,750	157,847

SOURCE: See text.

[a] Includes insurance and real estate.

TABLE IA-20

Corporate Stock Outstanding, 1952–68

(*$million*)

	Total Out-standing	Invest-ment Company	Other Domestic	Foreign	Domestic Non-financial	Domestic Financial[a]
1952	189,682	7,199	180,235	2,248	152,834	34,600
1953	186,182	7,569	176,565	2,048	151,234	32,900
1954	256,191	10,976	242,809	2,406	213,685	40,100
1955	306,125	13,632	289,672	2,821	257,904	45,400
1956	308,426	14,301	291,103	3,022	259,204	46,200
1957	278,990	13,797	262,500	2,693	221,997	54,300
1958	395,017	19,232	372,095	3,690	318,527	72,800
1959	444,506	22,503	417,774	4,229	351,277	89,000
1960	445,935	23,858	417,410	4,667	348,368	92,900
1961	590,860	31,172	554,086	5,602	444,458	140,800
1962	506,890	29,701	472,475	4,714	390,376	111,800
1963	637,801	34,955	597,701	5,145	396,856	135,800
1964	721,504	39,498	676,736	5,270	567,934	147,300
1965	811,817	45,163	761,606	5,048	616,569	190,200
1966	741,954	44,299	693,331	4,324	566,830	170,800
1967	948,075	58,481	884,356	5,238	738,187	204,650
1968	1,126,238	68,569	1,051,205	6,464	828,874	290,900

SOURCE: See text.
[a] Includes investment company shares.

TABLE IA-21

Corporate Stock Outstanding, 1952–68

(*$million*)

	1952	1953	1954	1955	1956	1957	1958	1959	1960
Total outstanding:	189,682	186,182	256,191	306,125	308,426	278,990	395,017	444,506	445,935
Investment company	7,199	7,569	10,976	13,632	14,301	13,797	19,232	22,503	23,858
Other domestic	180,235	176,565	242,809	289,672	291,103	262,500	372,095	417,774	417,410
Foreign	2,248	2,048	2,406	2,821	3,022	2,693	3,690	4,229	4,667
Memo:									
Domestic nonfinancial	152,834	151,234	213,685	257,904	259,204	221,997	318,527	351,277	348,368
Domestic financial (including investment companies)	34,600	32,900	40,100	45,400	46,200	54,300	72,800	89,000	92,900
Held by:									
Households	142,772	138,382	191,130	225,244	222,040	198,811	288,670	323,612	320,874
Investment company shares	7,199	7,569	10,976	13,632	14,301	13,797	19,232	22,503	23,858
Other	135,573	130,813	180,154	211,612	207,739	185,014	269,438	301,109	297,016
Foundations	4,433	4,569	5,508	6,916	7,510	6,894	7,855	9,287	8,964
Colleges and universities	1,770	1,808	2,478	3,064	3,354	3,098	4,014	4,294	4,165
Personal trusts	20,767	20,282	27,772	33,201	35,921	32,391	42,965	47,514	48,473
Mutual savings banks	336	431	571	655	705	767	862	813	829
Life insurance companies	2,446	2,573	3,268	3,633	3,503	3,391	4,109	4,561	4,981
Property and casualty insurance companies	4,326	4,459	5,942	6,930	7,219	6,664	8,374	9,149	9,372

	1961	1962	1963	1964	1965	1966	1967	1968
Fraternal insurance companies	104	94	103	100	98	92	133	142
Private pension funds	1,843	2,392	3,154	6,085	7,065	7,489	14,525	16,545
State and local government pension funds	56	75	99	127	161	212	345	431
Open-end investment companies	3,376	3,644	5,485	7,061	7,995	7,510	14,447	15,482
Other investment companies	3,165	3,251	4,725	5,677	5,237	4,839	5,925	5,866
Brokers and dealers	583	572	702	857	657	741	538	509
Rest of the world	3,705	3,650	5,254	6,575	6,961	6,091	9,363	9,302

	1961	1962	1963	1964	1965	1966	1967	1968
Total outstanding:	590,860	506,890	637,801	721,504	811,817	741,954	948,075	1,126,238
Investment company	31,172	29,701	34,955	39,498	45,163	44,299	58,481	68,569
Other domestic	554,086	472,475	597,701	676,736	761,606	693,331	884,356	1,051,205
Foreign	5,602	4,714	5,145	5,270	5,048	4,324	5,238	6,464
Memo:								
Domestic financial	444,458	390,376	496,856	567,934	616,569	566,830	738,187	828,874
Domestic financial (including investment companies)	140,800	111,800	135,800	148,300	190,200	170,800	204,650	290,900
Held by:								
Households	431,314	356,844	458,105	522,874	587,617	529,867	686,624	827,978
Investment company shares	31,172	29,701	34,955	39,498	45,163	44,299	58,481	68,569
Other	400,142	327,143	423,150	483,376	542,454	485,568	628,143	759,409
Foundations	10,623	9,760	10,922	13,124	14,924	14,127	15,621	17,472
Colleges and universities	5,003	4,564	5,488	6,207	7,012	6,282	7,754	8,143
Personal trusts	61,354	57,601	68,884	72,501	79,567	76,028	86,557	95,896

(continued)

TABLE IA-21 (*concluded*)

	1961	1962	1963	1964	1965	1966	1967	1968
Held by (cont.):								
Mutual savings banks	894	1,043	1,158	1,259	1,426	1,467	1,686	1,937
Life insurance companies	6,258	6,302	7,135	7,938	9,126	8,755	11,779	13,230
Property and casualty insurance companies	11,755	11,124	12,955	14,745	15,304	13,759	17,709	18,114
Fraternal insurance companies	149	152	180	210	215	221	245	259
Private pension funds	22,856	21,895	27,670	33,527	39,692	38,509	49,491	59,577
State and local government pension funds	583	780	989	1,262	1,614	2,102	2,772	4,051
Open-end investment companies	21,297	19,576	23,670	25,797	33,262	31,130	43,051	50,494
Other investment companies	6,640	6,469	7,601	7,757	6,941	6,499	8,675	9,422
Brokers and dealers	326	444	559	468	518	565	600	137
Rest of the world	11,808	10,336	12,485	13,835	14,599	12,643	15,511	19,528

SOURCE: See text.

TABLE IA-22

Issues and Purchases of Corporate Stock, 1952–68

(*$million*)

	1952	1953	1954	1955	1956	1957	1958	1959	1960
Total issues:	3,149	2,400	2,650	3,001	3,890	3,993	4,292	4,617	3,633
Investment company	648	519	592	935	1,231	1,245	1,833	2,046	1,851
Other domestic	2,441	1,932	1,802	1,893	2,548	2,713	2,127	2,376	1,696
Foreign	60	-51	256	173	111	35	332	195	86
Memo:									
Total domestic issues	3,089	2,451	2,394	2,828	3,779	3,958	3,960	4,422	3,547
Domestic nonfinancial	2,302	1,818	1,574	1,944	2,281	2,440	2,073	2,244	1,574
Domestic financial (including investment companies)	787	633	820	884	1,498	1,518	1,887	2,178	1,973
Purchased by:									
Households	-409	171	2,612	1,084	-791	181	3,212	3,380	-6,920
Investment company shares	648	519	592	935	1,231	1,245	1,833	2,046	1,851
Other	-1,057	-348	2,020	149	-2,022	-1,064	1,379	1,334	-8,771
Foundations [a]	180	298	-883	239	479	329	-1,164	134	545
Colleges and universities [a]	142	103	-103	64	239	168	66	-352	273
Personal trusts [a]	1,766	293	-1,178	-309	2,169	936	-359	-2,323	5,401
Mutual savings banks	109	95	140	84	50	62	95	-49	16

(*continued*)

TABLE IA-22 (*concluded*)

	1952	1953	1954	1955	1956	1957	1958	1959	1960	1961	1962	1963	1964	1965	1966	1967	1968
Purchased by (cont.)																	
Life insurance companies	164	93	270	65	−2	43	78	192	352								
Property and casualty insurance companies	181	190	163	163	136	125	134	267	264								
Fraternal insurance companies a	0	−6	−27	−22	−4	7	−4	−5	21								
Private pension funds	478	545	709	739	941	1,135	1,381	1,743	1,946								
State and local government pension funds	15	19	24	28	34	51	58	75	86								
Open-end investment companies	473	563	297	511	560	815	987	1,295	1,021								
Other investment companies b	0	−9	360	73	23	−90	146	−170	452								
Brokers and dealers	49	−10	131	155	−200	84	−284	79	−27								
Rest of the world	1	55	135	127	256	147	−54	351	203								
Total issues:										6,194	3,170	1,364	3,738	3,309	5,569	6,984	5,273
Investment company										3,219	2,381	1,673	2,513	3,639	4,653	4,671	5,999
Other domestic										2,650	688	−249	1,431	−37	1,169	2,267	−900
Foreign										325	101	−60	−206	−293	−253	46	174
Memo:																	
Total domestic issues										5,869	3,069	1,424	3,944	3,602	5,822	6,938	5,099
Domestic nonfinancial										2,472	592	−300	1,386	25	1,180	2,304	−843
Domestic financial (including investment companies)										3,397	2,477	1,724	2,558	3,577	4,642	4,634	5,942

Purchased by:								
Households	−1,974	−4,374	−4,314	5,299	−1,191	−16,413	−3,335	−13,593
Investment company shares	3,219	2,381	1,673	2,513	3,639	4,653	4,671	5,999
Other	−5,193	−6,755	−5,987	2,786	−4,830	−21,066	−8,006	−19,592
Foundations a	−17	280	−462	579	349	2,234	−636	1,134
Colleges and universities a	55	100	138	−76	122	605	504	56
Personal trusts a	3,604	2,824	1,386	−6,087	−832	12,747	−999	5,406
Mutual savings banks	65	149	115	101	167	41	219	251
Life insurance companies	465	433	246	546	708	268	1,064	1,427
Property and casualty insurance companies	260	248	156	103	87	391	588	1,071
Fraternal insurance companies a	−19	19	2	4	−17	51	−9	3
Private pension funds	2,258	2,198	2,170	2,212	3,124	3,676	4,991	4,713
State and local government pension funds	152	197	209	273	352	488	670	1,279
Open-end investment companies	1,131	909	759	1,131	1,237	1,335	2,061	1,653
Other investment companies b	−64	−41	619	39	−448	416	1,129	368
Brokers and dealers	−45	119	115	−94	51	35	37	−463
Rest of the world	323	109	225	−292	−400	−305	700	1,968

SOURCE: See text.
a Assuming price appreciation as in Dow-Jones Industrial Average.
b Assuming price appreciation as in Standard and Poor's Composite Index.

E. SECTOR BALANCE SHEETS

These balance sheets are the result of supplementing the flow of funds accounts with the data discussed in sections B through D of this appendix. The aggregate corporate stock and bond series were replaced by those covered in section D. The estimates of tangibles from section B were added to these modified flow of funds estimates of financial assets and liabilities in order to produce the full balance sheets of Tables IB-1 through IB-9.

The remaining differences between these estimates and the flow of funds accounts come from two sources. One is the difference in sectoring which results from the exclusion of some nonhouseholds from the household sector given here. The other is the differences in asset categories which result from a higher degree of aggregation.

The entries for the NBER finance sector exceed the corresponding flow of funds aggregates by an amount equal to the sum of the holdings of personal trusts and estates, fraternal insurance companies, and those investment companies not members of the Investment Company Institute. The holdings of the NBER's household sector are less than the corresponding household holdings in the flow of funds accounts by the amount of the holdings of these newly created financial institutions; in addition, the portfolios of nonprofit institutions have been subtracted from the flow of funds household account as well. Additional assets in the form of claims on life insurance and personal trusts were given to the remaining household sector by analogy with the treatment of life insurance and pension fund claims in the flow of funds accounts. Finally, since household holdings of corporate bonds and stock are derived residually, the holdings reported in Table IB-2 also reflect the difference between the series on corporate securities outstanding in the two systems.

The asset categories differ from the flow of funds categories in several additional respects. "Monetary reserves" is the sum of the flow of funds categories gold, foreign exchange, and Treasury currency. Currency and demand deposits, time deposits, and short-term U.S. government securities are equivalent in the two systems. "Other short-term claims" consists of bank loans n.e.c., other loans, consumer credit, security credit, trade credit, taxes payable, and interbank items.

The bonds entry in the present accounts covers all U.S. government and agency issues not included in the short-term claims, state and local government securities, and corporate and foreign bonds, the latter modified as described above. Mortgages covers all mortgages in the flow of funds system; claims on life insurance, pension and personal trusts consists of the flow of funds items life insurance reserves and pension fund reserves plus the total assets of fraternal insurance and of bank-administered personal trusts.

The estimate of corporate shares is the total discussed above in section D2. Equity in unincorporated business is equal to the sum of the net worth of farm and nonfarm noncorporate business. Miscellaneous assets and liabilities are taken directly from the flow of funds accounts; thus the category includes direct investment, other identifiable claims, and various floats and unallocated items.

The totals shown here are those for all domestic sectors. In addition to the discrepancy for any instrument between total assets and total liabilities introduced by removing the rest of the world sector from the flow of funds accounts, there are other discrepancies in the system as well. Bank and holder records differ on currency and demand deposits; the trade credit and miscellaneous accounts both show discrepancies in the flow of funds. These have been preserved in the balance sheet tables appearing below.

TABLE IB-1

Balance Sheet, All Domestic Sectors, 1952, 1960, and 1968

(*$billion*)

	1952	1960	1968
Tangible assets	1,115.3	1,851.3	3,079.5
Land	199.4	411.7	715.4
Reproducible tangible assets	915.9	1,439.6	2,364.1
Structures	576.2	924.4	1,537.1
Durables	228.8	368.2	610.8
Inventories	110.9	147.0	216.2
Financial assets	1,398.2	2,291.8	4,348.7
Monetary reserves	29.5	25.1	22.5
Currency and demand deposits	136.4	150.9	208.6
Short-term claims	335.2	564.1	1,136.0
Time deposits	82.6	173.3	402.6
Short-term U.S. government securities	61.0	80.5	112.6
Other short-term claims	191.6	310.3	620.9
Long-term claims	464.0	771.2	1,342.5
Bonds	237.5	313.4	479.4
Mortgages	91.4	206.8	397.5
Claims on life insurance, pensions, and personal trusts	135.2	251.0	465.6
Corporate shares	186.0	436.6	1,106.7
Equity in unincorporated business	210.3	269.2	392.2
Miscellaneous assets	36.8	74.7	140.2
Total assets	2,513.5	4,143.1	7,428.2
Total liabilities	971.8	1,555.5	2,791.2
Monetary reserves	2.4	2.7	5.1
Currency and demand deposits	137.4	152.2	211.1
Short-term debt	319.0	535.6	1,060.5
Time deposits	84.9	176.8	412.1
Short-term U.S. government securities	63.9	88.2	119.4
Other short-term debt	170.2	270.6	529.0
Long-term debt	462.3	769.1	1,337.3
Bonds	235.7	311.3	474.2
Mortgages	91.4	206.8	397.5
Claims on life insurance, pensions, and personal trusts	135.2	251.0	465.6
Miscellaneous liabilities	50.7	95.9	177.2
Net worth	1,541.7	2,587.6	4,637.0

SOURCE: See text.

TABLE IB-2

Balance Sheet, Households, 1952, 1960, and 1968

(*$billion*)

	1952	1960	1968
Tangible assets	386.3	670.6	1,051.8
Land	58.7	148.6	250.9
Reproducible tangible assets	327.6	522.0	800.9
Structures	237.3	381.2	567.1
Consumer durables	90.3	140.8	233.8
Inventories	—	—	—
Financial assets	716.9	1,196.7	2,312.0
Monetary reserves	—	—	—
Currency and demand deposits	59.3	63.9	107.4
Short-term claims	84.4	173.1	374.7
Time deposits	78.5	164.4	355.1
Short-term U.S. government securities	5.2	7.6	16.3
Other short-term claims	0.7	1.1	3.3
Long-term claims	211.0	358.5	593.8
Bonds	58.6	78.0	93.6
Mortgages	17.3	29.6	34.5
Claims on life insurance, pensions, and personal trusts	135.2	251.0	465.6
Corporate shares	142.8	320.9	828.0
Equity in unincorporated business	210.3	269.2	392.2
Miscellaneous assets	9.1	11.1	15.9
Total assets	1,103.2	1,867.3	3,363.8
Total liabilities	95.4	216.6	409.8
Monetary reserves	—	—	—
Currency and demand deposits	—	—	—
Short-term debt	38.1	77.4	161.4
Time deposits	—	—	—
Short-term U.S. government securities	—	—	—
Other short-term debt	38.1	77.4	161.4
Long-term debt	56.1	136.8	244.1
Bonds	—	—	—
Mortgages	56.1	136.8	244.1
Claims on life insurance, pensions, and personal trusts	—	—	—
Miscellaneous liabilities	1.2	2.4	4.3
Net worth	1,007.8	1,650.7	2,954.0

SOURCE: See text.

TABLE IB-3

Balance Sheet, Selected Nonprofit Institutions, 1952, 1960, and 1968

(*$billion*)

	1952	1960	1968
Tangible assets	23.0	44.7	87.6
Land	6.3	14.9	28.6
Reproducible tangible assets	16.7	29.8	59.0
Structures	15.0	27.2	55.7
Producer durables	1.7	2.6	3.3
Inventories	—	—	—
Financial assets	10.1	20.4	37.0
Monetary reserves	—	—	—
Currency and demand deposits	0.1	0.2	0.5
Short-term claims	—	—	—
Time deposits	—	—	—
Short-term U.S. government securities	—	—	—
Other short-term claims	—	—	—
Long-term claims	3.2	5.5	7.1
Bonds	3.1	5.2	6.6
Mortgages	0.1	0.3	0.4
Claims on life insurance, pensions, and personal trusts	—	—	—
Corporate shares	6.2	13.1	25.7
Equity in unincorporated business	—	—	—
Miscellaneous assets	0.6	1.6	3.8
Total assets	33.1	65.1	124.6
Total liabilities	3.4	9.8	20.7
Monetary reserves	—	—	—
Currency and demand deposits	—	—	—
Short-term debt	a	0.6	2.9
Time deposits	—	—	—
Short-term U.S. government securities	—	—	—
Other short-term debt	a	0.6	2.9
Long-term debt	3.4	9.2	17.8
Bonds	—	—	—
Mortgages	3.4	9.2	17.8
Claims on life insurance, pensions, and personal trusts	—	—	—
Miscellaneous liabilities	—	—	—
Net worth	29.7	55.3	103.9

SOURCE: See text.
a Less than $50 million.

TABLE IB-4

Balance Sheet, Nonfinancial Corporations, 1952, 1960, and 1968

(*$billion*)

	1952	1960	1968
Tangible assets	281.4	446.2	757.9
Land	21.2	55.9	102.9
Reproducible tangible assets	260.2	390.3	655.0
Structures	116.1	172.6	272.4
Producer durables	78.0	129.9	233.3
Inventories	66.1	87.8	149.3
Financial assets	126.3	206.7	357.3
Monetary reserves	—	—	—
Currency and demand deposits	28.8	32.2	28.1
Short-term claims	70.6	129.2	247.9
Time deposits	0.9	2.8	24.8
Short-term U.S. government securities	10.7	15.1	9.8
Other short-term claims	59.0	111.3	213.3
Long-term claims	9.9	6.8	8.7
Bonds	9.9	6.8	8.7
Mortgages	—	—	—
Claims on life insurance, pensions, and personal trusts	—	—	—
Corporate shares	—	—	—
Equity in unincorporated business	—	—	—
Miscellaneous assets	17.0	38.5	72.6
Total assets	407.7	652.9	1,115.2
Total liabilities	165.6	275.0	499.9
Monetary reserves	—	—	—
Currency and demand deposits	—	—	—
Short-term debt	82.0	120.0	222.1
Time deposits	—	—	—
Short-term U.S. government securities	—	—	—
Other short-term debt	82.0	120.0	222.1
Long-term debt	60.2	108.3	204.1
Bonds	44.1	76.3	136.8
Mortgages	16.1	32.0	67.3
Claims on life insurance, pensions, and personal trusts	—	—	—
Miscellaneous liabilities	23.4	46.6	73.8
Net worth	242.1	377.9	615.3

SOURCE: See text.

TABLE IB-5

Balance Sheet, Farm Business, 1952, 1960, and 1968

(*$billion*)

	1952	1960	1968
Tangible assets	138.1	178.8	266.2
Land	67.3	92.9	152.6
Reproducible tangible assets	70.8	85.9	113.6
Structures	29.2	38.8	50.1
Producer durables	18.4	24.1	34.1
Inventories	23.2	23.0	29.4
Financial assets	8.3	7.6	9.4
Monetary reserves	—	—	—
Currency and demand deposits	7.1	5.8	6.1
Short-term claims	—	—	—
Time deposits	—	—	—
Short-term U.S. government securities	—	—	—
Other short-term claims	—	—	—
Long-term claims	—	—	—
Bonds	—	—	—
Mortgages	—	—	—
Claims on life insurance, pensions, and personal trusts	—	—	—
Corporate shares	—	—	—
Equity in unincorporated business	—	—	—
Miscellaneous assets	1.2	1.8	3.3
Total assets	146.4	186.4	275.6
Total liabilities	13.9	23.6	51.4
Monetary reserves	—	—	—
Currency and demand deposits	—	—	—
Short-term debt	6.7	10.9	23.8
Time deposits	—	—	—
Short-term U.S. government securities	—	—	—
Other short-term debt	6.7	10.9	23.8
Long-term debt	7.2	12.8	27.5
Bonds	—	—	—
Mortgages	7.2	12.8	27.5
Claims on life insurance, pensions, and personal trusts	—	—	—
Miscellaneous liabilities	—	—	—
Net worth	132.5	162.8	224.2

SOURCE: See text.

TABLE IB-6

Balance Sheet, Nonfarm Noncorporate Business, 1952, 1960, and 1968

(*$billion*)

	1952	1960	1968
Tangible assets	74.0	112.4	202.8
Land	10.8	18.2	29.0
Reproducible tangible assets	63.2	94.2	173.8
Structures	23.2	37.9	100.4
Producer durables	25.9	38.7	50.0
Inventories	14.1	17.6	23.4
Financial assets	16.2	20.8	26.6
Monetary reserves	—	—	—
Currency and demand deposits	10.4	12.4	12.5
Short-term claims	4.0	5.3	8.8
Time deposits	—	—	—
Short-term U.S. government securities	—	—	—
Other short-term claims	4.0	5.3	8.8
Long-term claims	—	—	—
Bonds	—	—	—
Mortgages	—	—	—
Claims on life insurance, pensions, and personal trusts	—	—	—
Corporate shares	—	—	—
Equity in unincorporated business	—	—	—
Miscellaneous assets	1.7	3.0	5.3
Total assets	90.2	133.2	229.4
Total liabilities	12.4	26.8	61.4
Monetary reserves	—	—	—
Currency and demand deposits	—	—	—
Short-term debt	4.3	13.2	24.8
Time deposits	—	—	—
Short-term U.S. government securities	—	—	—
Other short-term debt	4.3	13.2	24.8
Long-term debt	8.0	13.6	36.6
Bonds	—	—	—
Mortgages	8.0	13.6	36.6
Claims on life insurance, pensions, and personal trusts	—	—	—
Miscellaneous liabilities	—	—	—
Net worth	77.8	106.4	168.0

SOURCE: See text.

TABLE IB-7

Balance Sheet, Federal Government, 1952, 1960, and 1968

(*$billion*)

	1952	1960	1968
Tangible assets	72.0	119.3	166.7
Land	10.8	18.4	33.5
Reproducible tangible assets	61.2	100.9	133.2
Structures	48.1	70.6	103.4
Producer durables	5.6	11.7	15.8
Inventories	7.5	18.6	14.0
Financial assets	50.0	55.9	91.5
Monetary reserves	1.6	1.7	3.3
Currency and demand deposits	7.4	7.2	6.6
Short-term claims	37.0	37.2	67.7
Time deposits	0.4	0.3	0.4
Short-term U.S. government securities	—	—	—
Other short-term claims	36.6	36.9	67.3
Long-term claims	2.9	5.7	9.8
Bonds	a	a	1.4
Mortgages	2.9	5.7	8.4
Claims on life insurance, pensions, and personal trusts	—	—	—
Corporate shares	—	—	—
Equity in unincorporated business	—	—	—
Miscellaneous assets	1.2	4.1	4.1
Total assets	122.0	175.2	258.2
Total liabilities	243.6	263.4	333.2
Monetary reserves	2.4	2.7	5.1
Currency and demand deposits	—	—	—
Short-term debt	66.7	91.3	124.5
Time deposits	—	—	—
Short-term U.S. government securities	63.9	88.2	119.4
Other short-term debt	2.8	3.1	5.1
Long-term debt	171.6	168.1	203.6
Bonds	157.0	146.3	171.1
Mortgages	—	1.3	1.7
Claims on life insurance, pensions, and personal trusts	14.6	20.5	30.8
Miscellaneous liabilities	2.9	1.2	a
Net worth	−121.7	−88.2	−75.0

Source: See text.
a Less than $50 million.

TABLE IB-8

Balance Sheet, State and Local Governments, 1952, 1960, and 1968

(*$billion*)

	1952	1960	1968
Tangible assets	135.0	266.5	518.0
Land	23.7	60.6	110.7
Reproducible tangible assets	111.3	205.9	407.3
Structures	104.6	190.5	375.8
Producer durables	6.7	15.4	31.5
Inventories	—	—	—
Financial assets	20.9	30.8	62.3
Monetary reserves	—	—	—
Currency and demand deposits	7.4	6.4	10.0
Short-term claims	4.0	12.3	31.4
Time deposits	1.6	4.6	19.1
Short-term U.S. government securities	1.5	6.8	10.0
Other short-term claims	0.9	0.9	2.3
Long-term claims	9.5	12.1	20.8
Bonds	9.1	10.8	18.5
Mortgages	0.4	1.3	2.3
Claims on life insurance, pensions, and personal trusts	—	—	—
Corporate shares	—	—	—
Equity in unincorporated business	—	—	—
Miscellaneous assets	—	—	—
Total assets	155.9	297.3	580.3
Total liabilities	32.7	74.5	132.8
Monetary reserves	—	—	—
Currency and demand deposits	—	—	—
Short-term debt	2.5	3.7	9.2
Time deposits	—	—	—
Short-term U.S. government securities	—	—	—
Other short-term debt	2.5	3.7	9.2
Long-term debt	30.2	70.8	123.7
Bonds	30.2	70.8	123.7
Mortgages	—	—	—
Claims on life insurance, pensions, and personal trusts	—	—	—
Miscellaneous liabilities	—	—	—
Net worth	123.2	222.8	447.5

SOURCE: See text.

TABLE IB-9

Balance Sheet, Financial Institutions, 1952, 1960, and 1968

(*$billion*)

	1952	1960	1968
Tangible assets	5.1	13.2	28.5
Land	0.6	2.3	7.2
Reproducible tangible assets	4.5	10.9	21.3
Structures	2.5	5.6	12.3
Producer durables	2.0	5.3	9.0
Inventories	—	—	—
Financial assets	441.7	741.3	1,432.3
Monetary reserves	27.9	22.9	19.2
Currency and demand deposits	7.9	11.2	17.0
Short-term claims	135.4	206.9	405.6
Time deposits	1.2	1.3	3.2
Short-term U.S. government securities	43.7	50.8	76.5
Other short-term claims	90.5	154.8	325.9
Long-term claims	227.6	382.9	702.4
Bonds	156.9	212.9	350.7
Mortgages	70.7	169.9	351.8
Claims on life insurance, pensions, and personal trusts	—	—	—
Corporate shares	37.0	102.6	253.0
Equity in unincorporated business	—	—	—
Miscellaneous assets	6.0	14.6	35.2
Total assets	446.8	754.5	1,460.8
Total liabilities	404.8	666.1	1,282.2
Monetary reserves	—	—	—
Currency and demand deposits	137.4	152.2	211.1
Short-term debt	118.7	218.5	491.8
Time deposits	84.9	176.8	412.1
Short-term U.S. government securities	—	—	—
Other short-term debt	33.8	41.7	79.7
Long-term debt	125.5	249.4	479.8
Bonds	4.4	17.8	42.6
Mortgages	0.5	1.2	2.4
Claims on life insurance, pensions, and personal trusts	120.6	230.4	434.8
Miscellaneous liabilities	23.2	46.0	99.2
Net worth	42.0	88.4	178.6

SOURCE: See text.

Appendix II

Estimates of the Value of Land in the United States Held by Various Sectors of the Economy, Annually, 1952 to 1968

GRACE MILGRAM

COLUMBIA UNIVERSITY

1. TRENDS, 1952 TO 1968

In this paper I attempt to develop a time series of the market value of land, exclusive of improvements, in the United States from 1952 to 1968, ascribing these values to major sectors of the economy, as part of a balance sheet of the nation's wealth. The final results of this effort indicate that the total land value in 1952 was estimated at $201 billion (Table II-1). By 1968, it had increased by three and a half times in current dollars to $726 billion, at an average annual rate of increase somewhat over 8.3 percent. Privately held land increased at the slightly lower average rate of 8.1 percent each year.

NOTE: The preparation of this estimate has been made possible by the cooperation of a number of people, who not only made available published and unpublished data from their files, but who also contributed their advice and thought in a complex field where counsel is essential. I would like to express my gratitude particularly to Albert Balk, author of "*The Free List*": *Property without Taxes*, Russell Sage Foundation/Basic Books, 1970; Daniel Creamer, National Industrial Conference Board; Maurice Criz and David McNelis, Governments Division, Bureau of the Census; Samuel J. Dennis, and his associates, Construction Statistics Division, Bureau of the Census; Jean Dubois, Bureau of Land Management, Department of Interior; Earl Johnson, Appraisal Section, General Services Administration; G. T. Lawrence, Investment Vice-President, Real Estate Financing, Metropolitan Life Insurance Company; Arthur A. Lenroot, Jr., Vice-President, Mortgage Guaranty Insurance Corporation; Allan Manvel, Advisory Commission on Intergovernmental Relations; Catherine E. Martini, Director of Research, National Association of Real Estate Boards; Alfred Schimmel, Vice-President, Douglas Elliman & Co.; William H. Scofield, Economic Research Service, Department of Agriculture; Allan F. Thornton, Director, Division of Research and Statistics, and William F. Shaw, Chief,

(*continued*)

TABLE II-1

Estimated Value of Land by Sector, 1952–68

(*$billion*)

Year End	All Sectors	Nonfarm Households[a]	Nonprofit Institutions	Unincorporated Business	Agriculture	Nonfarm Corporations	State and Local Governments	Federal Government
1952	201.3	58.7	6.3	10.8	69.2	21.8	23.7	10.8
1953	218.2	64.9	7.3	12.5	68.5	26.1	28.2	10.8
1954	233.9	72.7	7.9	12.6	71.4	27.5	30.2	11.5
1955	265.0	84.9	9.1	14.0	75.6	33.2	35.9	12.2
1956	297.8	97.3	10.3	15.9	81.9	38.4	40.6	13.4
1957	329.2	108.9	11.2	17.5	86.8	43.8	46.5	14.4
1958	362.4	121.9	12.5	18.7	94.1	48.5	51.4	15.2
1959	398.8	140.0	13.9	17.8	99.3	54.9	56.4	16.6
1960	420.4	148.6	14.9	18.2	101.6	58.1	60.6	18.4
1961	455.8	161.9	16.4	19.4	107.2	64.0	66.3	20.6
1962	454.9	172.9	17.8	21.5	112.8	69.6	71.9	22.1
1963	524.3	184.8	19.4	21.9	120.2	76.1	78.0	23.9
1964	563.1	198.0	21.1	23.1	128.0	82.7	84.6	25.5
1965	603.4	212.7	22.9	23.7	138.1	88.7	90.1	27.3
1966	645.9	224.5	24.8	26.2	146.6	96.5	97.9	29.5
1967	687.0	237.7	26.9	27.6	155.7	103.3	104.3	31.5
1968	726.5	250.9	28.6	29.0	163.7	110.0	110.7	33.5

SOURCE: See text.

[a] Including land under 1- to 4-family structures, vacant lots, and acreage.

At the same time, the ownership of land shifted dramatically among institutional sectors. This is particularly notable in farmland and household holdings of land underlying 1- to 4-family residential structures, vacant lots, and acreage (Table II-2). The farm holdings dropped from 34 to 23 percent, while the other three items together increased from 29 to 35 percent of the value of all American land. Nonfarm corporate-held land also showed a great relative increase, rising from 11 to 15 percent, although total business land, including that held by partnerships and proprietorships, increased more slowly, going from 16 to 19 percent of the total.

The major part of these shifts occurred in the earlier years from 1952 to 1960, rather than from 1960 to 1968. Indeed, the proportion of total value held by households decreased slightly in the second half of the period, because the increasing proportion of value held in land underlying residences and in vacant lots was not great enough to counterbalance the absolute drop in the value of acreage. It is, of course, no accident that the drop in the proportion held as farmland is close to the increased proportion in residential and business land. The conversion of farmland to urban use, although not necessarily a direct and immediate transformation in the case of any individual piece of land withdrawn from agriculture, has been a pervasive process throughout the country during the past two decades. State and local governmental holdings also rose sharply, from 12 to 15 percent of all land, while the federal share dropped by a percentage point to 4 percent in the midperiod but recovered slightly by the end of 1968.

2. COMPARISON WITH PREVIOUS STUDIES

These estimates are based upon a variety of sources of data and assumptions. One would expect that the importance of land, which represents

(*Note, continued*)

Statistics Section, FHA; Arthur Young and his staff, Housing Division, Bureau of the Census; John Ullman, Department of Management, Marketing, and Business Statistics, Hofstra University; and Roy Wenzlick, Wenzlick Research Corporation. Raymond W. Goldsmith, Director of the study of which this is a part, and Helen Stone Tice of the Federal Reserve System provided most helpful assistance. Robert M. Fisher, Leo Grebler, John R. Meyer, Max Neutze, and William H. Scofield reviewed a draft of the manuscript and offered valuable suggestions for its improvement. My thanks go as well to Chester Rapkin, Director of the Institute of Urban Environment, for his thoughtful comments at all stages of the work.

I am also grateful to Harvey Goldstein and Peter Whalley, who served as research assistants, and to Bernadette Douai, whose patient, careful typing of the manuscript is much appreciated.

roughly a fifth of the wealth of the country, would have resulted in a large body of carefully derived information, but this is not the case. Instead, the data available are fragmentary and unsatisfactory in quality.

The studies of land prices that have been made in the past fall into three general classes: empirical investigations, estimates based on a perpetual inventory of national wealth, and estimates derived from real-property-tax assessment data. The empirical investigations are typically concerned with small areas, and within these, with land in particular uses. Many are cross-sectional, reporting differences in value of land in various uses or locations at a particular time, rather than over a period of time. They frequently report price changes of assessment parcels of land, for sites of buildings, or for other shifting size classifications, without indicating any means of transforming the values into a price for a constant amount of land, whether square foot or acre. If they do present data on price changes for a unit size, the geographical or land-use restrictions may be too narrow to permit expansion of the findings to broader regions of either the metropolitan area or the nation. Any effort to estimate national land values solely on the basis of empirical data relating to market transactions would require a massive new research effort, not the compilation or further analysis of an already existing body of information.

Because of these deficiencies in past efforts to collect direct valuations,

TABLE II-2

Percentage Distribution of Land Value Among Sectors,
1952, 1960, and 1968

Sector	1952	1960	1968
All sectors	100.0	100.0	100.0
Nonfarm households	29.2	35.4	34.6
Institutions	3.1	3.5	3.9
Unincorporated business	5.4	4.3	4.0
Agriculture	34.3	24.2	22.5
Nonfarm corporations	10.8	13.8	15.1
State and local governments	11.8	14.4	15.2
Federal government	5.4	4.4	4.6

SOURCE: See text.

the land components of national wealth have been estimated primarily by means of the perpetual inventory method, developed largely by Raymond W. Goldsmith and carried forward by John W. Kendrick.[1] Here the value of real property is established for a benchmark year, then the value of new construction is added annually, and estimated depreciation of buildings and withdrawals from the existing stock are subtracted. The land value is then estimated as a ratio of net structure value. Obviously, these estimates are only as valid as the construction estimates and the depreciation and land-structure ratios, no one of which is without some question.

An alternative source of estimate lies in the assessment data collected by American cities for the real property tax, the major source of municipal revenues. Since 1956 the ratio of assessed values to market value has been estimated at five-year intervals by the Bureau of the Census on the basis of a sample survey of actual sales during a six-month period. Allan Manvel has used the Census of Governments data to prepare an estimate of land values, making assumptions as to the relation of the assessed value of land to its true market value, as compared with the census-derived estimate of the ratio of the assessed value to the market value of the total property, and making further assumptions as to the proportion of market value of real property ascribable to the land component.[2] Manuel Gottlieb has subjected this study to a critical review, pointing out the statistically inadequate basis for estimates of national average rates which were used in some of the categories.[3] Manvel has made it clear that he himself is aware of the tentative nature of his estimates, but Gottlieb's work serves to point out once again the absence of solid information and the unfortunate necessity of drawing general conclusions from incomplete data if any estimates at all are to be derived.

It is encouraging that some comparability exists between estimates derived by the perpetual inventory method and those based on the Census of Governments data. It is difficult to make a direct comparison, since the types of land included are not precisely the same. A discussion of the

---

[1] Raymond W. Goldsmith, *The National Wealth of the United States in the Postwar Period*, Princeton, Princeton University Press for NBER, 1962. The estimates contained in this work were carried forward to 1966 by John W. Kendrick, "The Wealth of the United States," *Finance*, January 1967, p. 10 ff.

[2] Allan D. Manvel, "Trends in the Value of Real Estate and Land, 1956 to 1966," in *Three Land Research Studies*, Research Report No. 12, National Commission on Urban Problems, Washington, D.C., 1968.

[3] Manuel Gottlieb, "Did USA Land Values Double Between 1956–1966—A Critique of the Douglas Report," Milwaukee, University of Wisconsin Economics Department, 1969, mimeographed.

sources, and their differences and discrepancies, is included in *U.S. Land Prices—Directions and Dynamics*.[4] Table II-3 of this study, taken from that work, summarizes the conclusions and is presented here to indicate the order of magnitude involved.

In the estimates which follow, major reliance will be placed on a third source of data, reports of the book value, or acquisition cost, of land. That held by corporations is reported to the Internal Revenue Service,[5] and "cost" of federal land is reported by the General Services Administration.[6] The Census of Governments issues reports on state and local governmental finances, which show capital outlay for "land and existing structures."[7] Daniel Creamer made use of the IRS data to estimate the value of land held by manufacturing firms. Creamer applied the ratio between book value of land and depreciated value of structures to an estimate of annual investment in real property developed by Patrick Huntley.[8] This produced an annual estimate of additional investment in land, which he added to the book value of the stock, adjusted by an inflation factor to obtain an annual estimate of the value of land holdings.

In the current study, use of the ratio of land to structure value is avoided for the most part, and the value of the stock of land is raised by price indexes developed directly for land, rather than by a general price index. Some of the assumptions underlying the computations are heroic, and averages are drawn from small, and possibly unrepresentative, samples. Yet none of the crucial assumptions duplicates any of those necessary in making estimates by means of a perpetual inventory or of assessment data, both of which employ an estimate of the land to structure-value ratio. Hence, despite its deficiencies, an independent estimate of total land values is produced. The only categories for which this is not true are farmland, vacant lots, and household ownership of residential land and acreage. For the first, the estimates of the Department of Agriculture were adopted; for lots and acreage, those of Manvel, drawn from the Census of Governments, were used; residential land value is based on a land-structure ratio applied

---

[4] Grace Milgram, *U.S. Land Prices—Directions and Dynamics*, Research Report No. 13, National Commission on Urban Problems, Washington, D.C., 1968.

[5] Treasury Department, Internal Revenue Service, *Statistics of Income*, Washington, D.C., published annually.

[6] General Services Administration, *Inventory Report on Real Property Leased to the United States Throughout the World*, Washington, D.C., published annually beginning 1956.

[7] Department of Commerce, Bureau of the Census, *Government Finances*, Washington, D.C., published annually.

[8] Dr. Creamer kindly made his and Patrick Huntley's unpublished estimates available for this study.

TABLE II-3

Comparative Estimates of Total Private, Noninstitutional Land Value and Average Annual Percent Change, Selected Years, 1922–66

	A. Absolute Values in Current Prices ($billion)					
Estimate	1922	1930	1938	1945	1956	1966
1. Keiper et al.	95	112	94	—	244	—
2. Goldsmith–Kendrick	—	—	—	121[a]	207	354
					(228)[b]	
3. Manvel	—	—	—	—	282[b]	549

	B. Average Annual Percent Change				
	1922– 1930	1930– 1938	1945– 1956	1938– 1956	1956– 1966
1. Keiper et al.	2.1	−2.1	—	5.4	—
2. Goldsmith–Kendrick	—	—	5.0	—	5.5
			(5.9)		(4.5)
3. Manvel	—	—	—	—	6.9
					(6.0)[c]

SOURCES: Line 1: Joseph S. Keiper, Ernest Kurnow, Clifford D. Clark, and Harvey H. Siegel, *Theory and Measurement of Rent*, Philadelphia, Chilton, 1961, Chapter II. Line 2: Raymond W. Goldsmith, *The National Wealth of the United States in the Postwar Period*, Princeton, Princeton University Press for NBER, 1962, Table II, pp. 86–87; and John W. Kendrick, "The Wealth of the United States," *Finance*, January 1967, p. 10 ff. Line 3: Allan D. Manvel, "Trends in the Value of Real Estate and Land, 1956 to 1966," Research Report No. 12, Washington, D.C., National Commission on Urban Problems, 1968, p. 16.

[a] Taken from Goldsmith, *op. cit.*, Table II, p. 55, col. 4.

[b] The categories of land included in the three estimates vary slightly, primarily in the exclusion, or inclusion, of land owned by public utilities. Keiper excluded public utilities. Goldsmith himself reports that for land included in Keiper's estimate, his figure would approximate $207 billion, whereas Manvel estimates comparable land as reported by Goldsmith as valued at $228 billion. He has adjusted the figures estimated from Census of Governments reports to include publicly held and state-assessed properties based on constant land-value proportion. A similar adjustment has been made by the authors of this report in the 1966 figure.

[c] These percentages are based on the unadjusted estimates made by Manvel. The lower estimate (in parentheses) is the percentage change if it is assumed that there is no increase in the proportion of land in all real property values. The higher figure, preferred by Manvel, assumes an increasing proportion of value ascribable to land.

TABLE II-4

Comparative Estimates of Total Private, Noninstitutional Land Value
and Average Annual Percent Change, 1956–66

Estimate	1956 ($billion)	1966 ($billion)	Annual Rate of Change (percent)
Goldsmith–Kendrick	207	354	5.5
Manvel	282	549	6.9
Milgram	234	494	7.8

Sources: Tables II-1 and II-3.

to a perpetual inventory estimate of the structure value. If this estimate approaches the others, it can only serve to increase our confidence in the essential reliability of the figures.

Because of the time periods to which other studies apply, the most appropriate comparisons for the estimates made here are those prepared by Allan Manvel and by Goldsmith and Kendrick for 1956 and 1966. These estimates, adjusted to cover all privately held land, are given in Table II-4. The current estimate falls between those of Goldsmith and Kendrick, which are low, and those of Manvel, which are considerably higher. Since our study has, in essence, accepted Goldsmith's 1952 estimates as a base from which to begin, it is not surprising that our result is closer to Goldsmith's figure in 1956. The rate of increase, however, is higher than that of the other series, so that it is much closer to Manvel's estimate by 1966. The range in these estimates is large, with the highest in 1966 over 50 percent greater than the lowest. Yet, in view of the data gaps which have been spanned by simplifying assumptions in each of these estimates, it is indeed gratifying that they are as close as they are.

3. METHODS OF ESTIMATION

Although the general approach in the derivation of this estimate was the use of reported book value of holdings, book value data are not available for all sectors. Thus, it was necessary to employ different bases of estimation to obtain the desired aggregates. The methods used for each sector are described in the following sections.

A. Book Values

In reporting to the Internal Revenue Service, businesses divide their assets among those that are depreciable, depletable, and nondepreciable, in order to take advantage of the tax benefits to be gained from depreciating capital assets. For corporations, complete data are available from their balance sheets. Regulations applicable to partnerships and proprietorships do not require the same information to be filed, and data are uneven. In the case of vacant land, the reported book value is the price in the year of acquisition, carried forward without change from year to year. In the case of newly acquired property which consists of both land and structure, the acquisition price is normally divided between the two types of assets in accordance with the ratio of land and structure in the assessed value if the site is within a local taxing jurisdiction which makes a separate determination, or through some other appraisal method. Once again, this figure is carried forward as the book value of the land. No adjustments are made for changes in its market value so long as the land remains in the same ownership.

Ideally, to determine the market value at any given time from the book value, we should have a land price index by which to adjust the value of the stock of land continuing in the same ownership; a distribution of book values by date of acquisition or a benchmark estimate of total market value at a given year; and a record of the former and newly adjusted book value of land transacted during the year so that any sold could be subtracted from the stock before the stock's value has been changed by application of the price index, and added at market value after the stock adjustment. In fact, we have none of these figures, and a large part of this work, therefore, consists of deriving estimates of these items.

B. Land Price Indexes

There are a number of data sources from which a rudimentary index can be derived for different types of land, at least to 1966 (Table II-5). Chief among these is the series on value of farmland prepared by the U.S. Department of Agriculture.[9] It is the only published series in which values are reported on a per acre basis, thus lending itself directly to the preparation of an index for farmland.

Unfortunately, the series refers only to land in farm use, excluding that which has been converted from farm to nonagricultural use during the

[9] For 1950 to 1967, a summary table is presented in Department of Agriculture, Economic Research Service, *Farm Real Estate Market Developments*, CD-70, April 1968, Table 21, p. 27. For later years the estimate is based on unpublished data from ERS.

TABLE II-5

Land Price Indexes for Nonmetropolitan, Metropolitan Ring, and
Central City Areas, 1952–66

(*1952 = 100*)

Year	Nonmetropolitan (1)	Metropolitan Ring of SMSA [a] (2)	Central City (3)
1952	100	100	100
1953	99	135	117
1954	104	143	123
1955	111	180	145
1956	121	200	160
1957	129	230	180
1958	141	250	195
1959	149	270	209
1960	153	290	220
1961	162	310	236
1962	170	325	250
1963	182	345	265
1964	195	360	280
1965	211	370	290
1966	225	390	309

SOURCES: Col. 1 computed from data of col. 5, Table 21, p. 27, Economic Research
Service, Department of Agriculture, *Farm Real Estate Market Developments*, CD-70, April
1968. Col. 2, Table II-6. Col. 3, see text.
[a] Standard Metropolitan Statistical Area.

year. The land undergoing urbanization is undoubtedly that with the most
rapidly increasing price. In fact, farmland in nonmetropolitan counties,
although at a lower price, shows a greater increase than that in metropolitan counties, primarily because of the greater diversion of land to
urban use in the latter.[10] Hence, an index based on land continuing in farm
use will tend to underestimate changes in national land prices, though the
degree of underestimation cannot be determined. The estimated farm

[10] Department of Agriculture, Economic Research Service, unpublished memorandum
by William H. Scofield, December 1967.

value, however, does include some effect of increased demand resulting from urban expansion and speculative activities preceding such expansion, not simply an increased value arising from agricultural activities. The farmland index, consequently, has been taken as representative of all non-metropolitan land, whether in farm or small-city use.

Since 1956, there has also been available an estimate of market value of the public domain managed by the Bureau of Land Management of the Department of the Interior, which gives, in addition, the acreage under its jurisdiction.[11] This estimate is based on appraisals of the value of similar land in the private sector, which is subject to normal market transactions. The Bureau has translated its estimates into a price index, which can be considered appropriate for the type of land in the public domain; that is, land largely devoted to grazing and forests. Although the level of prices is much lower than that of farmland, the rate of increase is slightly greater, supporting the view that the farm index understates rising trends. The Bureau's index has been used in conjunction with others in estimating the value of federal land.

Three sources of price data are available for urbanizing land (Table II-6). One is the FHA series of site prices for new construction financed with FHA-insured mortgages.[12] This is located largely in suburban areas. These data, of course, incorporate not only changes in raw land prices, but also increases in costs of land preparation and changes in the size of sites.

Maisel has estimated that approximately half of the increase from 1950 to 1962 in the San Francisco area arose from increases in land prices and the remaining half from the other two factors.[13] Although San Francisco land prices are not typical of those of the nation as a whole, the discrepancy in factors affecting these changes in price would almost certainly be less than the level of prices. In the absence of similar studies in other places, the annual nationwide average increase in site value was reduced by 50 percent, and the resulting series transformed into an index.

There are also two studies available which report changes in per-acre prices of land over time within a single developing suburban area, one for

---

[11] Unpublished memorandum supplied by Jean Dubois, Bureau of Land Management, Department of the Interior.

[12] Reported in annual issues of Department of Housing and Urban Development, *Statistical Yearbook.* Prior to 1966, the series was issued as part of the Federal Housing and Home Finance Agency's *Annual Report.*

[13] Sherman J. Maisel, "Background Information on Costs of Land for Single-Family Housing," in *Housing in California,* Appendix to Report, Governor's Advisory Commission on Housing Problems, San Francisco, 1963, Table 4, p. 226.

TABLE II-6

Components of Metropolitan Ring Land Price Index, 1952–68

(1952 = 100)

Year	Adjusted FHA Site Prices (1)	Los Angeles Residential Land (2)	Northeast Philadelphia, All Land (3)	Estimated Metropolitan Ring (4)
1952	100	100	100	100
1953	105	124	177	135
1954	110	146	173	143
1955	118	172	250	180
1956	129	202	218	200
1957	137	246	304	230
1958	144	261	355	250
1959	151	280	380	270
1960	155	310	410	290
1961	159	330	440	310
1962	165	350	470	325
1963	176	360	500	345
1964	182	370	520	360
1965	196	380	540	370
1966	204	395	565	390
1967		410	575	410[a]
1968		420	585	430[a]

SOURCES: Col. 1 adjusted for increase in costs of site preparation and size. See text.

Col. 2 curve smoothed graphically and extended from data in Frank G. Mittelbach, "Patterns of Land Utilization and Costs: A Study of Los Angeles," (unpublished), Table VI-4, p. VI-9.

Col. 3 curve smoothed graphically and extended from data in Grace Milgram, *The City Expands*, Washington, D.C., 1968, Table 28, p. 86.

Col. 4 is the average of columns 1 through 3.

[a] Extrapolated.

Los Angeles and one for Philadelphia.[14] These series were smoothed by graphic methods and the curves projected for the years after the conclusion of each study. No other studies could be found in which data were reported in a form permitting their incorporation into a time series. The three series reported above were combined through an unweighted average, and the base converted to 1952 equal to 100. This index was used to compute the price change in land in the metropolitan ring areas.

No aggregate land-price data could be found for central cities, although scattered information which reveals a variety of movements is available for various cities. Studies of urban renewal sites showed an overall increase, although the degree varied among cities.[15] Consultation with a number of realtors and other experts familiar with city development indicated a general belief that, in toto, city values have risen but notso rapidly as those in suburban areas. An index for metropolitan central-city land was constructed, falling halfway between the farmland and suburban indexes already developed. This is imprecise as to level, but not as to position within the major land submarkets.

C. The Stock of Land

It would have been preferable to have an independently derived initial valuation of land at some base period. It was beyond the scope of this study, however, to attempt either a de novo construct of a land value inventory for the 1950's, or to carry back the price indexes for a long enough period so that the value of the beginning stock of land would prove unimportant when considered in relation to newly purchased land over the whole period. As a consequence, Goldsmith's valuation was employed as a starting point in the estimates for all sectors except agriculture and individual households (Table II-7).[16] For smaller sectors than those reported in Goldsmith's table, proportions were taken in the same ratio as the book value of the subsector to the book value of the larger sector reported.

For corporations and local and state governments, the 1952 estimates were used as the base year. For federal government lands, the series of acquisitions begins in 1956; so that year was taken as the base and the

[14] Frank G. Mittelbach, "Patterns of Land Utilization and Costs: A Study of Los Angeles," University of California, Los Angeles, unpublished; Grace Milgram, *The City Expands*, Washington, D.C., 1968.
[15] For example, see Neil N. Gold and Paul Davidoff, "The Supply and Availability of Land for Housing for Low and Moderate-Income Families," in *Technical Studies*, Report of the President's Committee on Urban Housing, Washington, D.C., 1969, Vol. II, Table 76, p. 373.
[16] Goldsmith, *op. cit.*, Table A-41, p. 188.

TABLE II-7

Estimated Value of Land Held by Nonfarm Corporations and Governments, 1952

(*$million*)

Corporate holdings	
Total	21,753
Finance	10,080
Manufacturing	4,926
Retail and wholesale	2,751
Services	1,701
Public utilities	872
Mining	297
Contract construction	235
Other	891
Federal government	10,797
State and local governments	23,700

SOURCE: See text.

years from 1952 to 1955 were extrapolated from subsequent trends. Book values for the land holdings of unincorporated businesses, institutions, and households are not available, so other methods not requiring an independent figure for a base year were used to estimate their value. In general, book values of sectors in the base year were approximately one-third of the amount reported in 1968.

It is obvious that any addition to the stock between successive years is brought in at current market value. These annual differences were computed and assumed to be the value of land at current market price. There is almost certainly some land included in what we call the "stock," which, in fact, was transacted and, hence, already raised to market value. Application of a price index to this part of the stock would thus raise the value of that transacted land twice. There are no data by which to estimate the extent of this overstatement. Mortgages on 1- to 4-family unit properties insured by FHA had a median duration of approximately ten years,[17] indicating a transaction or prepayment rate of approximately

[17] Department of Housing and Urban Development, *Statistical Yearbook, 1966*, FHA Table 72, p. 142.

5 percent each year. In early years, almost all of these are likely to be sales rather than prepayment of a mortgage by the owner. Residential sales, however, are influenced by the great mobility of the American population. There is no reason to suppose that other sectors of the economy transact properties at so high a rate. In a rapidly developing section of Philadelphia subject to speculative forces, the maximum proportion of vacant land acreage transacted was 11 percent, and this steadily decreased over the years until it reached 3 percent of available vacant land.[18] Thus, turnover rates of 4 to 5 percent might be considered normal in number of properties, though possibly not in value of properties. The proportion of real property transacted each year—that is, structure and land—is almost certainly lower than this, particularly in view of the increasing tendency to sell companies through transfers of stock rather than by transfer of real property. Whatever its extent, this overestimate in the stock of land to be increased by the index offsets to some degree the underestimate which may exist because of the downward bias in the nonmetropolitan land index component.

D. Estimate of Value by Sector

Since we have not one index, but three, the land owned by any sector must be divided among the three types before its value is raised by the index. This was done differently for each sector.

(*1*) *Corporations.* For corporations, there is, of course, no inventory of location of types of establishment by size of parcels they occupy, which would permit a direct allocation. Number of establishments and number of employees are reported for the United States, for metropolitan areas in total, and for each individual Standard Metropolitan Statistical Area (SMSA). The same data are also reported for counties, so that it is possible to distinguish between central counties and ring counties in SMSA's. The establishments in central cities have more employees on the average, but presumably are more intensive in their use of land per employee— certainly in area, although not necessarily in dollar value. There is no information to answer the question of whether companies which have located outside of central cities in order to get more space are satisfied merely to achieve additional space, or whether they also want to reduce total land expenditure. On the other hand, each establishment, no matter how small, uses some land. As a result, the sheer number of establishments has some effect. Consequently, land values were divided

[18] Milgram, *The City Expands*, Table 19, p. 69.

TABLE II-8

Allocation of Corporation Land Value by Location and by Subsector,
1952 Stock and Subsequent Purchases

(*percent*)

Location	Manu-facturing	Retail and Whole-sale	Services	Contract Con-struction	Public Utilities	Finance
			1952 Stock			
Nonmetropolitan	30	30	20	20	10	10
Ring	18	29	20	25	25	10
Central city	52	41	60	55	65	80
			Subsequent Purchases			
Nonmetropolitan	30	30	20	20	10	10
Ring	45	35	30	27	30	15
Central city	25	35	50	53	60	75

SOURCE: See text.

among metropolitan and nonmetropolitan areas in accordance with a ratio which took account of both the proportion of employees and of reporting units in their respective areas, using the national totals for the economic sector (Table II-8). One estimate was made based on data for 1963, midway in the time period investigated here, and kept constant for 1952 and subsequent years. Within metropolitan areas, a similar ratio by which to divide the 1952 stock was determined. It was based on the average values of employment and number of establishments in central and ring counties in twelve SMSA's in 1951 (Table II-9).

Since 1952, there has been, of course, a trend toward movement of industrial and commercial establishments away from central cities. Dorothy K. Newman has reported on value of new construction in central cities and ring areas for selected industrial groups.[19] For land not carried in the stock but newly transacted from year to year, in sectors on which she reported, the division between central city and ring was made on the basis of her report (Table II-10). For sectors not given, the proportions

[19] Dorothy K. Newman, "The Decentralization of Jobs," *Monthly Labor Review*, May 1967, pp. 7–13.

TABLE II-9

Percentage of Employees (E) and Establishments (ES) in Central Counties by Subsector, Twelve Selected SMSA's,[a] 1951

Metropolitan Area	Services		Finance		Public Utilities		Construction	
	E	ES	E	ES	E	ES	E	ES
Atlanta	96	91	93	98	98	50	90	86
Boston	60	48	76	56	62	45	43	29
Chicago	93	89	97	97	96	86	89	81
Cleveland	98	97	95	96	97	88	96	93
Dayton	83	85	74	63	88	66	86	78
Detroit	91	88	92	89	90	88	85	81
Indianapolis	91	88	92	86	95	60	92	79
New Orleans	91	90	97	96	87	80	93	90
New York	92	88	96	94	91	87	79	66
St. Louis	78	68	83	71	76	60	61	51
San Francisco	88	83	91	87	89	77	75	68
Washington	84	80	81	80	73	57	58	48
Average	87	83	83	84	88	70	79	70
Weighted average	84	80	88	88	82	66	73	64

SOURCE: See text.
[a] Standard Metropolitan Statistical Area.

used for 1952 were adjusted in favor of suburban values to a small degree.

Values were estimated separately for each of the seven most important industries by application of the appropriate index to each type of land in accordance with the procedure described above (Table II-11). The total values for these industries were then expanded by the proportions their book value bears to total book value of all corporations, minus the industry-class agricultural, forestry, and fishing, to give a total estimate of market value of holdings of nonfarm corporations (Table II-12). The agricultural category was excluded because corporate farm holdings are included by the Department of Agriculture in its estimates of the value of farmland. A very slight undervaluation results from the omission of corporate forestry and fishing land. The IRS reports were available only

TABLE II-10

Percent of New Private Nonresidential Building Outside the Central Cities of SMSA's[a] by Region, 1960–65 and 1954–65[b]

Type of New Nonresidential Building	Percent of Valuation of Permits Authorized for New Nonresidential Building				
	United States	North-east	North Central	South [c]	West [c]
			1960–65		
All types [d]	47	53	49	34	53
Business	47	54	47	33	52
Industrial	62	71	59	46	69
Stores and other mercantile buildings	52	68	57	34	56
Office buildings	27	26	30	22	32
Gasoline and service stations	51	61	52	39	57
Community	45	47	47	33	53
Educational	45	47	46	34	50
Hospital and institutional	35	35	36	20	48
Religious	55	66	57	42	60
Amusement	47	41	60	46	45
			1954–65 [e]		
All types [d]	49	55	51	34	55
Business	46	56	50	33	50
Industrial	63	73	59	47	72
Stores and other mercantile buildings	53	69	55	33	58
Office buildings	27	25	31	20	32
Gasoline and service stations	53	66	54	40	59
Community	45	52	50	33	57
Educational	50	53	54	36	58
Hospital and institutional	36	38	36	21	50
Religious	54	67	55	39	62
Amusement	48	48	51	41	50

SOURCES: Unpublished data of the Bureau of the Census: tabulated at the request of the Bureau of Labor Statistics and based on a sample of over 3,000 permit-issuing places. Dorothy K. Newman, "The Decentralization of Jobs," *Monthly Labor Review* 90 (May 1967), pp. 7–13.

[a] Standard Metropolitan Statistical Area.

[b] Data for groups of years are used to avoid erroneous impressions from erratic year-to-year movements in building construction.

[c] Data for southern and western SMSA's reflect a more significant degree of annexation and area redefinition and are therefore less reliable than figures for other regions.

[d] Includes types not shown separately and excludes major additions and alterations for which type of building is not known.

[e] Excludes data for 1959, for which comparable information is not available.

TABLE II-11

Estimated Value of Land Held by Corporations in Seven Major Industry Groups, 1952–66

(*$million*)

	Total	Manufac- turing	Retail and Wholesale Trade	Mining	Services	Public Utilities	Contract Construction	Finance
1952	20,862	4,926	2,751	297	1,701	872	235	10,080
1953	24,774	5,762	3,200	308	2,031	983	289	12,201
1954	26,322	6,069	3,421	344	2,121	981	317	13,079
1955	31,556	7,474	4,122	374	2,564	1,109	390	15,523
1956	36,617	9,042	4,630	393	2,870	1,254	448	17,980
1957	41,698	10,199	5,185	431	3,319	1,443	528	20,593
1958	46,870	11,378	5,855	495	3,639	1,615	615	23,274
1959	52,885	12,345	6,327	522	4,046	1,741	667	26,034
1960	56,273	13,237	6,806	548	4,269	2,015	763	28,635
1961	62,074	14,556	7,125	636	4,743	2,275	989	31,751
1962	67,477a	15,348	7,954	690	5,138	2,444	1,119	34,784
1963	73,759	16,721	8,704	760	5,587	2,629	1,264	38,094
1964	80,018	18,125	9,485	848	6,093	2,841	1,447	41,180
1965	86,194	19,757	10,211	919	6,517	3,037	1,664	44,090
1966	93,775	21,748	11,155	1,012	7,229	3,308	1,808	47,515

SOURCE: See text.

a Interpolated.

TABLE II-12

Estimated Market Value of Land Held by Nonfarm
Corporations, 1952–66

(*$million*)

	Total Value of Stock (1)	Seven Major Industry Groups			Ratio: Col. 2 to Col. 1 (5)
		Total Stock (2)	Result of Price Rise (3)	Net Addition (4)	
1952	21,754	20,862			95.9
1953	26,054	24,774	24,297	477	95.2
1954	27,533	26,322	25,878	444	95.6
1955	33,217	31,556	30,973	583	95.0
1956	38,383	36,617	35,335	1,282	95.4
1957	43,755	41,698	40,928	770	95.3
1958	48,520	46,870	45,190	1,680	96.6
1959	54,917	52,885	51,331	1,554	96.3
1960	58,133	56,273	54,547	1,726	96.8
1961	63,994	62,074	59,887	2,187	97.0
1962	69,636	67,477 [a]	n.a.	n.a.	96.9
1963	76,119	73,759	69,839	3,920	96.8
1964	82,664	80,018	77,867	2,151	96.8
1965	88,678	86,194	83,369	2,825	97.2
1966	96,477	93,775	91,117	2,658	97.2

n.a. = not available.
SOURCE: See text.
[a] Interpolated.

through 1966 at the time this report was prepared. Estimates for 1967 and 1968 are straight-line extrapolations of the trend of previous years.

It should be noted that the differences in value resulting from the allocation process are marginal. Thus, for corporations, if all land is assumed to be covered by the nonmetropolitan price index, the 1966 valuation differs by $19.2 billion, or 18 percent of the valuation obtained with land allocated among types. Differences resulting from relatively minor variations in allocation among the three types of land would be correspondingly less. Differences would be much greater, of course, if values resulting from an assumption of total nonmetropolitan location were compared with those obtained by an assumption of total location in the metropolitan ring, but the latter assumption is completely unreasonable and, therefore, the degree of difference has not been tested.

(2) *Partnerships and Proprietorships.* Although the Internal Revenue Service has reports for some years for the book value of land held by partnerships and proprietorships, these are incomplete both as to industries and as to years. It can be assumed, however, that in any industry, rentals bear some relatively constant relation to gross receipts, and that rentals, in turn, are a reflection of the value of the land, regardless of the institutional form of the business.

The gross receipts for each type of business are reported by industry. Following the line of reasoning described above, the ratio of gross receipts of partnerships and of proprietorships to corporations was calculated (Table II-13) and applied to the previously estimated land holdings of corporations to derive an estimate of the value of land held by the other types of business (Table II-14). These were totaled and expanded by the same ratios as those used to expand the corporate sector, thus producing the estimates of total value of land held by unincorporated businesses.

(3) *Federal Government.* The process by which federally owned land was evaluated was similar in concept to that used for corporations, but differed in execution because of the difference in available data. Since 1956, the General Services Administration has issued an annual inventory of real property owned by the United States government, classified as urban or rural, as well as by agency, state, predominant usage, and other categories.[20] Acreage of land is given, and the "cost" of land and buildings is entered separately. In the case of property held for some time, cost is the actual acquisition cost to the government, including zero cost for public domain land or gifts. For example, the "cost" of the land obtained in the Louisiana Purchase, or through Seward's Folly in Alaska, has not been adjusted to current values. Current acquisitions, however, are supposed to be reported at actual cost or, if acquired through donation or means other than purchase, at the estimated fair price had the parcel been purchased.[21] As with corporations, the difference in cost between subsequent years produces a net figure on the value of newly acquired ground.

Although each year the acreage is classified as urban or rural, the cost is given only as a total and, of course, it cannot be divided in the same ratio as the acreage. To aid in this allocation, use was made of the values

---

[20] General Services Administration, *Inventory Report on Real Property Owned by the United States throughout the World*, annual publication, beginning 1956.
[21] *Ibid.*, June 1968, p. 3.

TABLE II-13

Gross Receipts of Partnerships (P) and Proprietorships (PR) as a Percent of Corporate Receipts, by Industry, 1952–66

	Manufacturing		Retail and Wholesale Trade		Mining		Services		Utilities		Contract Construction		Finance	
	P	PR	P	PR	P	PR	P	PR	P	PR	P	PR	P	PR
1952	3.98	2.92	33.90	59.97	18.45	8.87	67.26	162.06	1.56 [a]	6.39 [a]	1.56 [a]	6.39 [a]	15.67	15.09
1953	3.70	2.62	31.18	52.17	17.24	9.93	63.86	156.02	1.56 [a]	6.39 [a]	1.56 [a]	6.39 [a]	15.93	15.73
1954	3.42	2.32	28.46	44.37	16.03	10.08	60.46	149.98	1.56 [a]	6.39 [a]	1.56 [a]	6.39 [a]	16.19	16.37
1955	3.13	2.02	25.74	36.58	14.82	10.19	57.06	143.94	1.56 [a]	6.39 [a]	1.56 [a]	6.39 [a]	16.45	17.02
1956	2.85	1.98	33.02	38.28	13.61	10.49	53.67	131.18	1.56 [a]	6.39 [a]	1.56 [a]	6.39 [a]	16.72	16.68
1957	2.57	1.95	20.29	40.19	12.40	10.80	50.27	118.42	1.56 [a]	6.39 [a]	1.56 [a]	6.39 [a]	16.98	16.35
1958	2.47	1.95	19.01	37.72	10.74	13.67	50.32	116.74	1.92	7.21	1.92	7.21	13.56	18.48
1959	2.16	1.88	16.47	36.54	9.67	10.15	43.16	112.06	1.82	6.67	1.82	6.67	11.69	12.22
1960	2.02	1.90	14.70	33.19	9.68	14.42	41.98	105.20	1.56	6.80	1.56	6.80	10.21	13.41
1961	1.85	1.78	14.03	32.14	8.48	10.41	40.65	99.15	1.76	6.18	1.76	6.18	11.34	12.21
1962	1.66	1.68	12.48	30.36	7.63	8.26	39.01	98.01	1.40	5.97	1.40	5.97	12.02	11.17
1963	1.46	1.52	11.66	29.38	7.86	8.00	37.62	94.09	1.38	6.04	1.38	6.04	12.07	10.93
1964	1.45	1.48	10.84	28.40	8.09	7.75	36.22	90.16	1.36	6.12	1.36	6.12	12.12	10.68
1965	1.11	1.44	9.60	27.13	7.28	7.92	34.04	81.51	1.52	6.39	1.52	6.39	11.15	11.44
1966	1.09	1.28	9.28	26.09	6.35	8.04	33.17	77.68	1.31	6.11	1.31	6.11	12.61	12.20

SOURCE: Calculated from U.S. Bureau of Internal Revenue, *Statistics of Income, Tax Returns of Corporations, Partnerships, and Sole Proprietorships.*

[a] Data unavailable; percentage extrapolated.

TABLE II-14

Estimated Value of Land Held by Partnerships and Proprietorships in Seven Major Industry Groups, 1952–66

($million)

	Total	Manufac-turing	Retail and Wholesale Sales	Mining	Services	Public Utilities	Contract Construction	Finance
1952	10,471	340	2,643	81	3,901	70	336	3,100
1953	11,914	366	2,679	84	4,466	78	379	3,862
1954	12,128	368	2,492	90	4,463	78	378	4,259
1955	13,347	366	2,569	93	4,516	88	419	5,296
1956	15,212	437	2,839	95	5,305	100	431	6,005
1957	16,722	461	3,136	101	5,598	115	448	6,863
1958	18,064	503	3,322	101	6,079	147	456	7,456
1959	17,102	499	3,354	101	6,280	148	495	6,225
1960	17,634	520	3,259	132	6,284	168	507	6,764
1961	18,817	529	3,290	120	6,631	181	589	7,477
1962	19,936	513	3,407	110	7,040	180	620	8,066
1963	21,162	498	3,572	121	7,359	195	658	8,759
1964	22,397	532	3,722	135	7,700	213	705	9,390
1965	23,087	505	3,751	140	7,703	240	786	9,962
1966	25,422	515	3,945	145	8,013	226	785	11,793

SOURCE: As for Table II-13.

TABLE II-15

Estimated Average Price per Acre of Rural Federal Land, 1956–67

(*dollars*)

	Public Domain (1)	Farmland (2)	Rural Public Land (3)
1956	5.34	66.14	11.42
1957	4.89	72.13	10.89
1958	4.95	76.98	12.15
1959	5.07	84.03	12.97
1960	6.59	89.05	14.84
1961	8.90	91.20	17.13
1962	9.88	96.47	18.54
1963	10.68	101.74	19.79
1964	11.30	108.67	21.04
1965	12.68	116.26	23.04
1966	14.06	125.85	25.24
1967	15.35	134.20	27.24

SOURCES:
Col. 1. Computed from price index supplied by Jean Dubois, Bureau of Land Management, Department of Interior.
Col. 2. Department of Agriculture, Economic Research Service, *op. cit.*, Table 21, p. 27.
Col. 3. See text for method of derivation from data in columns 1 and 2.

of farmland and of the public domain in the jurisdiction of the Bureau of Land Management. After an examination of the governmental agencies which held the land and the predominant usage within each agency, it was decided that the rural land held by the government could reasonably be valued by a formula which ascribed one-tenth to the farmland value and nine-tenths to the type of land held in the public domain. An estimated average acreage price for rural land held by the government was thus produced (Table II-15). Multiplication of the rural acreage for 1956 by this figure gave an estimated total value of government-held rural land in 1956, which was then subtracted from Goldsmith's governmental estimate of 1956 to produce a benchmark figure for urban land for that year. For each year thereafter, the difference in number of rural acres was multiplied by the average price of rural land and the result subtracted from the difference in cost to obtain the additional urban values (Table II-16). The results for each year were added to the appropriate stock after the value of the urban stock had been raised by the urban price index and that of the rural stock had been raised by the nonmetropolitan index, as described in the section dealing with corporate land. In actual practice, since the value of the public domain is directly reported, its acreage was subtracted from rural acreage at the start of this process, and its value added to the total for each year after all the other calculations were completed. A slight overestimate results from the failure to exclude federal land leased to farmers and grazers, the value of which is also included in the Department of Agriculture estimates. The current value of this land is estimated at $3.8 million, and thus would have no appreciable effect on the figures reported here.[22] The values for 1952 through 1955 were estimated from trends of the nonmetropolitan price index, and those for 1967 and 1968 were estimated by extrapolation of the trend shown in the immediately preceding years.

(4) *State and Local Governments.* As part of its series on governmental finance, the Bureau of the Census issues annually a report on the expenditures of state and local governments for a number of classes, including land and existing buildings. A major, but undeterminate, number of existing structures are purchased to be cleared, and their cost of acquisition can, in fact, be considered a part of the land cost. In the present estimates, the actual amounts reported by the Census were reduced by 10 percent, to adjust both for that part of the acquisition which, in fact, applied to existing structures bought to be used as such, and for any sales of land which may have occurred but which are not reported separately in revenues.[23] These figures then served as the equivalent to the net acquisition to the stock (Table II-17). For the 1952 base value, Goldsmith's estimate of that year was accepted.

No means of separating the land into classes was found. No data exist on the total amount of land owned, or annually acquired, by municipalities inside and outside of metropolitan areas—either by acreage or by

[22] Letter to the author from William H. Scofield, Economic Research Service, Department of Agriculture, May 14, 1970.

[23] In the absence of factual data, there are differing judgments as to the most appropriate adjustments to make. Maurice Criz, assistant chief of the Governments Division, Bureau of the Census, believes that 2 or 3 percent would be more accurate (letter to the author, November 20, 1970). Since the absolute magnitude of land acquisition is low, the differences resulting from use of the lower adjustment rate would affect only the figures after the decimal point in Table II-1, col. 7.

TABLE II-16

Estimated Value of Land Held by the Federal Government in the United States, 1952–68

(*$million*)

| | A. Net Additions | | | | B. Change in Value of Stock | | | | | |
| | | Net Addition to Stock During Year | | | | Increased Value of Standing Stock, by Location | | Addition of New Land, by Location | | Total Value of Public Domain |
	Value of Stock[a]	Total	Rural	Urban	Estimated Total	Rural	Urban	Rural	Urban	
1952					10,797[b]					
1953					10,763[b]					
1954					11,488[b]					
1955	2,463				12,237[b]					
1956	2,512	48	−2	50	13,400			2,621	8,230	2,549
1957	2,552	41	11	30	14,399	2,804	9,218	2,802	9,268	2,329
1958	2,752	198	476	−278	15,218	3,054	10,009	3,065	10,039	2,114
1959	3,146	393	118	205	16,609	3,244	10,742	3,725	10,464	2,420
1960	2,956	157	3	154	18,361	3,837	10,987	4,025	11,192	3,144
1961	3,462	157	3	154	20,559	4,261	11,975	4,270	12,124	4,160
1962	3,765	303	3	300	22,106	4,484	12,857	4,487	13,011	4,608
1963	3,980	215	20	196	23,859	4,801	13,792	4,604	14,092	4,963
1964	4,128	144	18	131	25,541	5,140	14,938	5,160	15,134	5,247
1965	4,393	264	20	244	27,279	5,573	15,739	5,591	15,870	5,818
1966		264	1	263	29,494	5,982	16,822	6,002	17,066	6,426
1967					31,518[b]			6,500[b]	18,000[b]	7,000
1968					33,543[b]			7,000[b]	19,000[b]	7,500

SOURCE: See text.

[a] Excluding public domain administered by Bureau of Land Management, Department of Interior.

[b] Extrapolated.

TABLE II-17

Estimated Market Value of Land Holdings of State and Local
Governments, 1952–68

(*$million*)

	Value of Stock (end of year)	Result of Price Rise	Net Addition
1952	23,700		
1953	28,206	27,729	477
1954	30,233	29,616	617
1955	35,902	35,071	832
1956	40,573	39,492	1,081
1957	46,529	45,442	1,087
1958	51,383	50,252	1,131
1959	56,377	54,980	1,397
1960	60,599	59,195	1,404
1961	66,284	64,841	1,443
1962	71,938	70,261	1,677
1963	77,982	76,254	1,728
1964	84,641	82,661	1,980
1965	90,128	88,037	2,102
1966	97,860	95,526	2,324
1967	104,300 [a]	101,500	2,500
1968	110,700 [a]	108,000	2,700

SOURCE: See text.
[a] Extrapolated.

dollar value. If it were assumed that all land was nonmetropolitan in
character, it would have been valued at $95 billion by the end of 1968.
Since the land is located in all three of the classes, it seemed more reasonable to raise its value by the central-city land index, which fell between
the nonmetropolitan and ring area indexes. This procedure produced
a land value of $110 billion in 1968, 15 percent higher than the first
figure.

As with the other sectors for which data were not available, the estimates
for 1967 and 1968 were extrapolated from trends of the previous years.

(5) *Nonprofit Institutions.* Data which would permit an estimate of land ownership by nonprofit institutions is completely lacking. Some tax jurisdictions do publish reports of the assessed value of real property owned by these institutions. The assessments, however, are made in an even more cursory manner than assessments in general, since no tax payments result from the process. In addition, the jurisdictions involved are scattered and are not notably representative. Only occasionally is an effort made to separate land from other real property. Moreover, the relation of land to structure value is extremely variable, even for a single type of institution. Balance sheets of assets are only rarely available for public perusal.

Under these circumstances, it was assumed that the percentage which institutional holdings formed of all holdings during the 1950's, as reported

TABLE II-18

Estimated Value of Land Held by Institutions, 1952–68

	Nonprofit Institutions as Percentage of Noninstitutional Total	Total Value ($million)
1952	3.24	6,300
1953	3.45	7,277
1954	3.50	7,911
1955	3.55	9,084
1956	3.57	10,263
1957	3.53	11,224
1958	3.56	12,455
1959	3.62	13,935
1960	3.67	14,883
1961	3.73	16,390
1962	3.78	17,802
1963	3.84	19,387
1964	3.89	21,083
1965	3.95	22,928
1966	4.00	24,842
1967	4.08	26,930
1968	4.10	28,612

SOURCE: See text.

by Goldsmith, would continue during the 1960's. The 1950–58 percent-ages were calculated, projected forward, and applied to total holdings, as calculated for other sectors (Table II-18).

(6) Household Property

a. One- to Four-Family Residential Land. The major part of residential property is owned by households for their own use, rather than as an investment. This, of course, is particularly true of single-family structures. Most multifamily structures, which are an increasing part of the inventory, are owned by investors, who report to IRS in the same way as other types of property-holders, either as corporations or as proprietors or partner-ships. Therefore, the value of the land on which they are built is included in either the nonfarm corporations or in the unincorporated business sector. Owner-occupants may report property tax payments and mortgage interest payments, but they have no reason to report either the total value, or land and structure values, of their homes to IRS or to any agency other than the U.S. Census Bureau, which collects this information once a decade. The decennial housing census includes estimates of the value of single-family owner-occupied structures, and of the average value of units in other classes of residential structures. As a result, an estimate of total worth of the residential stock can be developed for 1960. Comparable figures do not exist for 1950, when data were published only for mortgaged structures.

Consequently, for estimates of residential land values, reliance must be placed either on the Census of Governments assessment data or on a perpetual inventory—which is obviously preferable for annual estimates. In order to utilize this method, attention was focused on the rate of depreciation and on the land-structure value ratio, particularly for single-family structures.

In *The National Wealth*, Goldsmith assumed an eighty-year life with straight-line depreciation, or 1.25 percent a year. This is somewhat lower than the compound rate of 2 percent used by Grebler et al. to approximate a straight-line 1.4 percent rate.[24] In developing their formula, Grebler and his colleagues made use of an FHA study which showed an annual average linear rate of depreciation of 1.2 percent. They also allowed for demoli-tions at a variable rate for each decade; that for 1940–53 was estimated at an annual rate of 0.12 percent of the structural value of the stock at the

---

[24] Leo Grebler, David M. Blank, and Louis Winnick, *Capital Formation in Residential Real Estate: Trends and Prospects*, Princeton, Princeton University Press for NBER, 1956, p. 381.

beginning of the year. Goldsmith's depreciation estimate is gross, including demolitions.

In the face of differences between the housing market in 1952–68 and that of the earlier period, FHA records were examined for current valuations of older single-family structures. The records actually available were the error print-outs for all appraisals of single-family homes for which application had been made for mortgage insurance in the last five months of 1968, constituting 2,191 usable records. The entire record for the property is printed, with a notation of the column in which the error occurred. This cannot be considered a random sample, but there is no reason to suppose that a systematic bias is introduced. Entries for which an error occurred in any of the items relevant to this study were, of course, excluded.

The reported sale price, the estimated site value, and the estimated replacement cost were taken for all transactions, classified by year of construction. The transactions were further classified by the four major geographical regions of the country, but no differences emerged, and the final results were analyzed only for the country as a whole. Site value was subtracted from both sale price and replacement cost estimates, and the difference between sale price and replacement cost was calculated for each time-class, in order to obtain the average loss of value of the structures independent of changes in site values (Table II-19). A regression of loss of value against years produced an estimated straight-line annual depreciation rate of 0.6 percent, about half of that shown in the earlier study.

The withdrawal rate, however, seems to have increased. Such a finding is consistent with the increase in demolititions resulting from urban renewal and highway programs in the last two decades, and from an apparent acceleration in the so-called filtration process, marked most vividly by a growing volume of abandoned structures. The report on components of change in the housing stock, 1950 to 1960, showed a loss of 3,716,000 units, or 8 percent of the total 1950 stock of 46,137,000.[25] An examination of the size, condition, and value in 1950 shows that the withdrawn units were smaller, in worse condition, and of lower value than the units remaining in the stock. For owner-occupied units, the median value of the withdrawn units was about two-thirds that of those remaining, and rental values showed the same proportion. The estimated 8 percent loss in numbers is thus equivalent to an approximately 5.3 percent loss in value. In annual terms, this results in an estimated decline

[25] Census of Housing, 1960, *Components of Inventory Change*, Vol. IV, part 1A, Table 3, pp. 46–47.

TABLE II-19

Residential Depreciation Rates,[a] 1901–67

Date of Construction	Depreciation Rates (percent)
1967	7.0
1966	8.5
1965	10.3
1964	16.6
1963	11.2
1962	11.6
1961	16.2
1960	14.5
1959	12.0
1958	16.6
1956–57	14.8
1954–55	15.8
1952–53	17.7
1950–51	19.1
1948–49	18.3
1946–47	21.8
1941–45	21.0
1936–40	27.2
1931–35	32.3
1926–30	30.0
1916–25	42.4
1901–15	42.5
Before 1901	57.0

SOURCE: See text.

[a] Estimated by the loss in value reflected in the difference between sales price and replacement cost taken as a percent of replacement cost. Figures are given by date of construction and cover single-family structures submitted for FHA mortgage insurance in the last quarter of 1968.

of 0.5 percent, for a total decrease from depreciation and withdrawal of 1.1 per year. This rate was applied to the perpetual inventory of residential structures developed in the study and described in Appendix I.

To determine the estimated value of the land, land-structure ratios were applied to the structural values developed by the perpetual inventory, with a combined depreciation and withdrawal rate of 1.1 percent. Computationally, the ratios used are essentially the site-to-value proportions reported for existing single-family housing with FHA-insured mortgages, but reduced in each year by one percentage point.

Structures covered by FHA mortgages are not representative of the whole range of houses in the country. Site-structure ratios from two other sources were compared with them. First, in connection with its efforts to develop a construction cost index, the Census of Housing has prepared a site-to-value estimate for new houses in 1968. Second, on request, the Mortgage Guarantee Insurance Corporation examined the estimated site-to-value ratios for a random sample of mortgages it had insured in 1968, covering both new and existing structures (Table II-20). For new structures, the Census of Housing and MGIC figures were very close, while the FHA figures for the latest available data were over one percentage point higher. For existing housing—again, the latest available FHA data—FHA was one percentage point higher than MGIC. The trend has been toward a higher ratio so it is probable that, were 1968 figures available, the discrepancy would be greater. Moreover, the ratio of new housing is lower than that for existing ones, and though new housing is only a small component of the total housing supply in any one year, it would tend to lower the overall ratio to some degree. Inclusion of 2-to-4-unit structures

TABLE II-20

Average Site-to-Total Value Ratios for Single-Family Structures, 1966 and 1968

(*percent*)

Source of Estimate	Year	Ratio
A. New Construction		
FHA	1966	19.6
Census of Housing	1968	18.1
MGIC	1968	17.9
B. Existing Housing		
FHA	1966	21.2
MGIC	1968	20.2

Sources: See text.

TABLE II-21

Estimated Value of Land Held by Households, 1952–68

(*$million*)

	Total	Underlying 1- to 4-Family Structures	Vacant Lots	Acreage
1952	58,969	36,140	15,949	6,880
1953	66,125	39,147	17,068	9,910
1954	74,849	43,535	18,374	12,940
1955	88,994	52,271	19,773	16,950
1956	101,296	61,096	21,200	19,000
1957	112,106	67,326	22,730	22,050
1958	124,282	74,972	24,260	25,050
1959	141,579	87,669	25,810	28,100
1960	149,372	90,922	27,350	31,100
1961	161,925	98,835	28,940	34,150
1962	172,899	109,569	30,430	32,900
1963	184,843	119,323	33,870	31,650
1964	197,990	130,230	37,310	30,450
1965	212,651	142,701	40,750	29,200
1966	224,494	152,344	44,200	27,950
1967	237,694	163,351	47,643	26,700
1968	250,894	174,358	51,087	25,450

SOURCE: See text.

also tends to lower the ratio. In view of these considerations, the trends shown by the FHA ratios were accepted, but at the slightly lower level.

The value of land so estimated has been ascribed to the household sector (Table II-21). The proportion of structures containing 1 to 4 units that are owned by business enterprises is very small. Their value has already been included in the estimate of business holdings. This double-counting, however, serves as an offset to land underlying multiunit buildings owned by individuals (not included among partnerships or sole proprietorships), for which no estimate has been made.

b. Vacant Lots. The valuations placed upon vacant lots in the Census of Governments reports have been accepted here, with linear interpolation for intermediate years. These values have been included with those of land underlying 1- to 4-family structures in the household sector. The same problem of double-counting of business holdings exists here as in the case of residential land. The extent to which such land is, in fact, owned by businesses rather than by individuals is another unanswered question in land economics; such indications as there are lead to the conclusion that, in general, the proportion is not large.

c. Acreage. There is one remaining type of land which is not reported and whose dimension is difficult to estimate. This is the value of acreage owned by individuals and, hence, not included in any of the other classes of holders. It encompasses recreational land owned by individuals rather than by business concerns; abandoned farmland not put to other business or residential use; and any investment, by individuals not classified as proprietors, in land within or outside of urban areas which has not been legally subdivided and, hence, is not included as lots in the Census of Governments assessment data. Except for ground in areas undergoing development, where prices may increase sharply prior to platting, land in this class would have a low acreage price, and would be of greater importance in estimates of acreage than of value.

The difference between the Census of Governments estimate for acreage and farms, and that of the Department of Agriculture for farmland, ranges from $30 billion in 1956 to $68 billion in 1961 and then drops to $56 billion in 1966 (Table II-22). These amounts would seem to be the maximum values of nonfarm acreage that have been omitted from the estimate. In fact, the omission cannot be this high, since much of the land classified as acreage is owned by business organizations and institutions, or is the site for second homes, whose structural value is included in the perpetual inventory. For purposes of this estimate, the amount of difference has been interpolated on a straight line between the years for which data are available. For 1967 and 1968, the 1961–68 trend was continued. For 1952 to 1955, since there is no Census of Governments estimate prior to 1956, it was assumed that prices of acreage had increased at the same rate as the suburban price index; that the greater increase in value of acreage from 1956 to 1961 over that shown by the index was the result of increased amounts of land; and that land had been added to the inventory from 1952 to 1955 at the same rate as in the next five-year period, 1956 to 1961. The estimated change in valuation of this acreage was then derived from the price index and divided equally among the four years. It was then assumed that in all years, half the calculated amounts were attributable to the household sector.

TABLE II-22

Estimate of Value of Acreage Held by Household Sector, 1952–68

(*$billion*)

	Value of Farmland (1)	Value of Farms and Acreage (2)	Value of Acreage (3)	Household Share of Acreage Value (4)
1952	69.2		13.2	6.6
1953			17.4	8.7
1954			21.6	10.8
1955			25.8	12.9
1956	81.9	111.9	30.0	15.0
1957			37.7	18.9
1958			45.3	22.7
1959			53.0	26.5
1960			60.6	30.3
1961	107.2	175.5	68.3	34.2
1962			65.8	32.9
1963			63.3	31.7
1964			60.9	30.5
1965			58.4	29.2
1966	146.6	202.5	55.9	28.0
1967			53.4	26.7
1968			50.9	25.5

SOURCES:
Col. 1. Table II-1, col. 5.
Col. 2. 1956 and 1966: Manvel, *op. cit.*, Table 1, p. 6; 1961: "Taxable Property Values," *Census of Governments*, 1962, Table 9, p. 41.
Col. 3. 1956, 1961, and 1966, col. 2 minus col. 1. Other years by extrapolation or interpolation.
Col. 4. 50 percent of col. 3. See text.

Appendix III

Estimates of Balance Sheets and Income Statements of Foundations and Colleges and Universities

RALPH L. NELSON

QUEENS COLLEGE, CITY UNIVERSITY OF NEW YORK

FOUNDATIONS

a. Types of Foundations Included

The series relate to foundations that meet F. Emerson Andrews' definition, contained in *The Foundation Directory*, of "a non-governmental, non-profit organization having a principal fund of its own, managed by its own trustees or directors, and established to maintain or aid social, educational, charitable, religious or other activities serving the common welfare."[1]

Not included, therefore, are a number of other kinds of philanthropic agencies though they may contain the term "foundation" in their names. Many are fund raising organizations, distributing their receipts to health and welfare agencies. Others operate institutions such as hospitals, schools, and research institutes. Neither these nor other types hold large endowments or emphasize the making of grants in their programs.

Also excluded from this series are foundations organized to conduct programs of corporation giving, the so-called company-sponsored foundations. Despite assets on the order of $1.7 billion in 1968, most of these foundations serve as reservoirs whose purpose is to smooth corporate contributions flows. Relatively few of them have achieved the status of being fully or even substantially endowed.

[1] New York, Russell Sage Foundation for the Foundation Library Center, 1960, p. ix.

The series thus includes foundations established by individuals and families, many of which are fully endowed. Others are still in the process of forming and developing, serving in part as conduits for personal giving, and awaiting the large endowment transfers that commonly take place on the death of the founder. Also included are community foundations, whose endowment is typically built through small and medium-sized gifts and bequests from many individuals.

b. Sources of Data and Estimation Procedures

Estimates of total income, outlays and assets were based primarily on data presented in the three editions of *The Foundation Directory* and the *Treasury Department Report on Private Foundations*.[2] The directory provided benchmark data for the years centering about 1956, 1960, and 1965, while the Treasury Department Report provided totals for 1962. The first two editions of the directory provided asset data for many foundations in ledger value only; this must be kept in mind when comparing them with market value estimates based on cumulative additions to endowment, adjusted by security price indexes. For 1962 and 1965, the benchmark totals were expressed in market values; so less ambiguous comparisons are possible.

The year 1962 was taken as the base year in developing this series. This was done because the Treasury Department survey of some 6,000 foundations provided market value data for a larger list of foundations than did any other compilation. Moreover, the data for all foundations related to the same year whereas in *The Foundation Directory* the assets of listed foundations may have been those for any of several years. In compiling the directory, the objective was to present the most recent information, insofar as this was feasible; therefore the data for a given foundation may relate to any of three or four years.

The Treasury Department estimate, adjusted to exclude company-sponsored foundations, indicated the total 1962 market value for the assets of all foundations to be $15,085 million. Working forward and backward in time from this point, estimates were made of annual additions to assets, in current dollars, resulting from new endowments. Adjusting for these additions, we were able to provide totals for successively later or earlier years. The cumulative total was, of course, adjusted for changes in securities price levels before continuing the series.

The price index employed for stock prices was the Standard and Poor's

---

[2] Treasury Department, Washington, D.C., 1965.

500-stock index. For bonds, it was the corporate AAA market value index. In both cases 1962 was taken as 100. Stocks were given a weight of 0.75, bonds a weight of 0.25.

The estimates of the annual increase in foundation assets, resulting from factors other than security price changes, were based on data on receipts and outlays of foundations. Here the Treasury Report, Edition 3 of *The Foundation Directory*, and the several Patman reports[3] provided information on receipts of gifts and contributions, on investment income, and on outlays for grants and administrative and project expenses.

For the 1960–65 period, comprehensive tabulations appeared with sufficient frequency to require relatively little interpolation. Before 1960, the problem was more complicated. Derivation of the annual growth in assets from endowment gifts required a detailed examination of the time pattern in the establishment of new foundations and of the dates on which transfers were made, the latter usually coming some time after foundations were initially established. Fortunately, much of this kind of estimation had already been done in preparing *The Investment Policies of Foundations*.[4] With some rudimentary interpolation, it was possible to develop a tolerably defensible series on annual increments to endowment for the period 1953–60. Estimates of annual increments for the period since 1965 are based on extrapolations of the several receipts and outlays series. A relatively orderly pattern of growth for each series was assumed. Analysis of the 1968 estimate, presented below (page 384), suggests that the extrapolations were reasonably accurate.

Comparison of benchmark totals with the series developed by the procedures described above was possible for the 1956–58, 1960–62, and 1964–65 periods, since comprehensive data were presented in the three editions of *The Foundation Directory*. As mentioned above, the presence of ledger value data and the spread of several years in asset data given in each edition of the directory makes direct and precise comparisons impossible. However the rough comparisons, allowing for the effects of these statistical biases, suggest that the estimates probably come close to actual market values.

Having developed the annual series on total market value of foundation assets (see Table III-1), the next step was to estimate the composition of

[3] House Select Committee on Small Business, *Tax Exempt Foundation and Charitable Trusts: Their Impact on Our Economy*, Washington, D.C., December 31, 1962; December 21, 1966; March 26, 1968; and June 30, 1969.

[4] Ralph L. Nelson, *The Investment Policies of Foundations*, New York, Russell Sage Foundation, 1967.

TABLE III-1

Annual Income Statements of Foundations, 1953–68

(*$million*)

	Investment Income	Gifts and Contributions Received	Total Receipts	Administration and Project Expenses	Grants	Total Outlays	Net Increase in Assets
1968	1,040	1,300	2,340	220	1,670	1,890	450
1967	960	1,215	2,175	205	1,520	1,725	450
1966	880	1,135	2,015	195	1,370	1,565	450
1965	805	1,043	1,898	184	1,220	1,404	494
1964	740	952	1,692	170	1,060	1,230	462
1963	670	793	1,463	149	905	1,054	409
1962	601	729	1,330	135	803	938	392
1961	593	567	1,160	130	637	767	393
1960	562	525	1,087	120	557	677	410
1959	518	486	1,004	110	477	587	417
1958	467	447	914	100	448	548	366
1957	423	408	831	90	740	830	1
1956	372	369	741	80	599	679	62
1955	328	330	658	70	283	353	305
1954	277	291	568	60	219	279	289
1953	228	252	480	50	164	214	266

SOURCE: See text.

total assets by type, in as much detail as possible. Here the several Patman reports proved valuable. They contained detailed asset breakdowns for groups of 534 to 647 foundations, including most of the largest ones. The Patman totals accounted for between two-thirds and three-fourths of total estimated assets of all foundations. The Treasury Department Report also provided asset breakdowns. The two sources thus provided direct data for the years 1960, 1962, and 1967.

Asset breakdowns were much more sparse for the period before 1960. Eight foundations could be found that provided market value breakdowns for the years 1954 and 1958. These, then, were used as "benchmark years" and provided the means for interpolation of percentage distributions.

For the whole 1953–68 period, interpolations were made of the percentage distributions of assets as indicated by the available direct data.The interpolation process was guided by such factors as year-to-year movements in stock and debt prices. This meant that the effect of such changes was in a rough way incorporated into the interpolation. Having developed an annual series on the percentage distribution of assets (shown in Table III-2), it was applied to the estimated totals to provide dollar values for each type of asset. The final series (shown in Table III-3), therefore, presents estimates of the market value, in current dollars, of the several types of foundation assets.

A check on the estimate of foundation assets for 1968 has been made possible by the publication, in 1971, of Edition 4 of *The Foundation Directory*. The market value of assets for the 5,454 foundations listed in the directory totaled $25,181 million. This figure is not comparable to the estimate presented here for the following reasons:

1. The directory does not include foundations having less than $500,000 in assets; our estimate includes all size classes.

2. The directory includes company-sponsored foundations; our estimate excludes them.

3. Our estimate reflects 1968 market values only. The directory market value data are based on 1968 data for some foundations and 1969 data for others, the years of record for nearly all the foundations listed. Thus, the 12.4 percent decline in equity prices (Standard and Poor's 500-stock index) and the 15.1 percent decline in AAA bond prices are in part reflected in the directory total.

The accompanying reconciliation of the above-listed differences suggests that our 1968 estimate is a tolerably accurate one.

TABLE III-2

Distribution of Foundation Assets, 1953–68

(percent)

	1953	1954	1955	1956	1957	1958	1959	1960	1961	1962	1963	1964	1965	1966	1967	1968
Cash	1.0	1.0	0.9	0.8	0.7	0.6	0.8	1.3	1.2	2.6	2.2	1.6	1.3	1.2	1.0	1.0
A/R and N/R	1.3	1.2	1.4	1.3	1.4	1.2	1.4	1.4	1.4	1.4	1.4	1.4	1.4	1.3	1.4	1.4
Government obligations																
U.S.	20.6	19.4	16.4	15.2	15.2	10.8	10.6	10.4	8.8	7.8	7.3	6.8	6.4	6.8	5.3	4.9
State and local	0.1	0.1	0.1	0.1	0.1	0.1	0.1	0.2	0.2	0.2	0.2	0.2	0.2	0.2	0.6	0.6
Corporate bonds	7.8	7.3	6.4	7.6	9.6	10.0	9.4	10.3	11.2	16.0	14.6	13.2	11.3	13.7	11.7	9.1
Mortgages	0.6	0.6	0.6	0.6	0.6	0.6	0.6	0.7	0.8	0.9	0.8	0.7	0.7	0.6	0.5	0.5
Corporate stock	67.2	69.2	72.8	72.7	70.6	75.1	75.0	71.6	72.3	64.7	67.5	70.3	73.2	70.7	72.4	75.4
Other investments	0.5	0.4	0.4	0.7	0.8	0.6	0.6	0.9	1.2	3.6	3.4	3.2	3.0	3.1	4.7	4.8
Tangible assets	0.4	0.4	0.5	0.5	0.5	0.5	1.0	2.7	2.2	1.9	1.8	1.8	1.8	1.7	1.8	1.7
Other assets	0.5	0.4	0.5	0.5	0.5	0.5	0.5	0.5	0.7	0.9	0.8	0.8	0.7	0.7	0.6	0.6
Total	100.0	100.0	100.0	100.0	100.0	100.0	100.0	100.0	100.0	100.0	100.0	100.0	100.0	100.0	100.0	100.0

A/R = accounts receivable; N/R = notes receivable.
SOURCE: See text.

	($million)
Total assets, 5,454 foundations of *Foundation Directory*, Edition 4	25,181
Plus: Estimated total assets of 2,000 foundations having between $200,000 and $500,000 in assets[a]	660
Estimated total assets of 18,500 foundations having less than $200,000 in assets[b]	680
Estimated assets, all foundations	26,521
Less: Estimated 1968 assets of company-sponsored foundations not included in our estimate[c]	−1,660
	24,861
Adjustment for 1968 to 1969 decline in securities prices partly reflected in *Foundation Directory* total[d]	−1,626
Adjusted total assets based on *Foundation Directory*	23,235
1968 estimate based on procedures used in this study	23,172

Notes to tabulation

[a] Assumes average assets of $330,000 per foundation.

[b] Based on average assets estimate of $37,000 per foundation presented in *The Foundation Directory*, Edition 3.

[c] Four-year extrapolation of Edition 3 tabulation, recording $1,300 million in assets of company-sponsored foundations for 1964–65. Annual growth estimate of $90 million based on 1964–65 pattern of gifts received, investment income, and expenditures.

[d] Assumes half of *Foundation Directory* assets related to 1968, half to 1969. The 1968 to 1969 decline for total assets was 13.1 percent, the decline in equities being given a weight of 0.75, that in debt a weight of 0.25.

COLLEGES AND UNIVERSITIES

a. Coverage of Colleges and Universities

The series applies to all colleges and universities in the United States, including both privately and publicly controlled institutions. In compiling the data, separate tabulations were made for private and public institutions, and these were combined for purposes of summary totals. The pattern of receipts and outlays differed between the two types of institutions. As would be expected, government support was more important in public institutions, and private tuition and philanthropic receipts were more important in private institutions. The aggregate series does not separate the two types of institutions, nor does it provide breakdowns of receipts by source and objective.

TABLE III-3

Assets of Foundations, 1953–68

(*$million*)

	1953	1954	1955	1956	1957	1958	1959	1960	1961	1962	1963	1964	1965	1966	1967	1968
Cash	68	80	86	83	68	63	99	163	176	392	356	299	265	240	216	232
A/R and N/R	88	96	133	134	138	126	173	175	206	211	227	261	285	260	302	324
Government obligations																
U.S.	1,401	1,544	1,558	1,570	1,484	1,130	1,313	1,302	1,293	1,177	1,181	1,269	1,305	1,359	1,144	1,135
State and local	7	8	10	10	10	10	12	25	29	30	32	37	41	40	129	139
Corporate bonds	530	581	608	785	937	1,046	1,164	1,289	1,646	2,414	2,362	2,464	2,304	2,737	2,524	2,109
Mortgages	41	48	57	62	59	63	74	88	118	136	129	131	143	120	108	116
Corporate stock	4,569	5,508	6,916	7,510	6,894	7,855	9,287	8,964	10,623	9,760	10,922	13,124	14,924	14,127	15,621	17,472
Other investments	34	32	38	72	78	63	74	113	176	543	550	597	612	619	1,014	1,112
Tangible assets	27	32	48	52	49	52	124	338	323	287	291	336	367	340	388	394
Other assets	34	32	48	52	49	52	62	63	103	136	129	149	143	140	129	139
Total	6,799	7,961	9,502	10,330	9,766	10,460	12,383	12,520	14,693	15,086	16,179	18,667	20,389	19,982	21,575	23,172

A/R = accounts receivable; N/R = notes receivable.
Source: See text.

TABLE III-4

Annual Income Statements of Colleges and Universities, Calendar Years 1953–66

(*$million*)

	Total Receipts, All Sources	Total Expenditures for Current Operations	Expenditures on Land, Buildings, and Equipment	New Funds in Endowment	Net Change in Unexpended Plant Funds	Interest on External Debt	"Cash Flow" Deficit Before Financial Transfers	Net Increase in External Debt	Transfers from Endowment	Residual (Implied) Change in Cash Balance
1966	15,930	13,160	3,391	526	(137)	274	(1,284)	1,220	111	47
1965	14,119	11,457	2,835	471	171	205	(1,020)	962	62	4
1964	12,258	9,722	2,432	438	194	162	(690)	644	44	(2)
1963	10,690	8,368	2,313	404	122	132	(649)	654	29	34
1962	9,415	7,395	1,988	360	119	105	(552)	563	19	30
1961	8,286	6,535	1,606	332	112	86	(385)	386	16	17
1960	7,301	5,739	1,415	318	53	72	(296)	337	21	62
1959	6,517	5,200	1,213	304	38	59	(297)	253	20	(24)
1958	5,932	4,633	1,136	280	87	45	(249)	248	13	12
1957	5,637	4,128	1,155	382	171	34	(233)	241	3	11
1956	4,968	3,639	965	379	111	25	(151)	171	(10)	10
1955	4,072	3,248	700	214	39	19	(148)	128	11	(9)
1954	3,613	2,956	624	156	14	15	(152)	104	23	(25)
1953	3,271	2,703	501	137	10	13	(93)	60	17	(16)

NOTE: Numbers in parentheses have negative values.
SOURCE: See text.

b. *Sources of Data and Estimation Procedures*

The basic source for the income statement data was the Biennial Survey of Higher Education[5] for the period 1951–52 through 1963–64. Beginning in 1965–66, the surveys have been taken annually, and the design of the questionnaire has been changed. Thus, data for 1965–66 and 1966–67 (the latest year available) are not wholly comparable to those for earlier years. The differences, however, are minor and do not materially affect the continuity of the series.

As requested in the questionnaire, and presented in the statistical summaries by the Office of Education, the receipts and expenditures data are not organized as corporate income statement and balance sheet data are organized. Emphasis is on the source of moneys by type and objective, and likewise on the expenditure. Double counting occurs in places, and certain categories of receipts and expenditures are omitted. Fortunately, the double counting and omissions account for relatively minor parts of the totals.

Given the characteristics of the data, it was necessary to develop a systematic set of accounting categories into which the data could be put, and which would lead to the development of an aggregate income statement. The test of the success with which the several receipts and expenditure categories were extracted from the Office of Education tabulations, and cast into income statement form, is reflected in the residual. As shown in Table III-4, the residual, for most years, was gratifyingly small relative to the magnitudes of receipts and expenditures.

The basic estimates of income statement categories were based on academic fiscal year data, as provided to the Office of Education. All of the summary income statements were on a July 1–June 30 basis. In the period 1951–52 through 1965–66, where data were available only every other year, linear interpolations provided the estimates for the missing

[5] U.S. Office of Education, *Biennial Survey of Higher Education, Receipts, Expenditures, and Property, 1951–52*, Washington, D.C., 1955. U.S. Office of Education, *Statistics of Higher Education, Receipts, Expenditures, and Property, 1953–54*, Washington, D.C., 1957. *Ibid.*, *1955–56*, 1959. *Ibid.*, *1957–58*, 1961. U.S. Office of Education, *Financial Statistics of Higher Education, 1959–60*, Washington, D.C., 1964. U.S. Office of Education, *Higher Education Finances, 1961–62, 1963–64*, Washington, D.C., 1968. U.S. Office of Education, *Financial Statistics of Institutions of Higher Education: Current Funds, Revenues, and Expenditures, 1965–66*, Washington, D.C., 1969. U.S. Office of Education, *Financial Statistics of Institutions of Higher Education: Property, 1965–66*, Washington, D.C., 1969. U.S. Office of Education, *Financial Statistics of Institutions of Higher Education: Current Funds, Revenues, and Expenditures, 1966–67*, Washington, D.C., 1969. U.S. Office of Education, *Financial Statistics of Institutions of Higher Education: Property, 1966–67*, Washington, D.C., 1969.

years. The only exception to this procedure was in the interpolation for 1956–57. Here, the effects of a very large Ford Foundation grant were included. Part of the grant was reflected in the Biennial Survey of 1955–56, and an adjustment was required, prorating the grant between 1955–56 and 1956–57.

Having developed an annual income statement based on fiscal years ending on June 30, the next step was to convert the series to a calendar year basis. This was done by a simple averaging of successive pairs of academic (June 30) fiscal year totals.

Estimates of the financial assets of colleges and universities were made by cumulating net additions to endowment, beginning with a base year (June 30, 1952) estimate of total market value of $3.2 billion. This was approximately 6 percent above the book value of assets in that year of relatively low stock prices, and roughly accorded with what fragmentary evidence one could find on the market-to-book-value ratio for that year.

	Ratio: Market to Book Value	Weight	
Government bonds	0.83 ×	.20 =	0.166
Nongovernment bonds	0.85 ×	.20 =	0.170
Common stocks	1.27 ×	.51 =	0.648
Preferred stocks	0.86 ×	.09 =	0.077
Total			1.061

The $3.2 billion base value was then increased each year by the addition of new endowments, the accumulated market value up to a given year being adjusted for the yearly changes in the level of securities prices. Two series were developed for total value of endowments, one using the stock price index as the adjustment factor, the other assuming that no change in securities prices had taken place, thus serving as a rough measure of the nonequity component of the trend.

Studies by the Boston Fund showed that, in market value, the percentage of total endowment in equities rose only moderately over the period, from about 53 percent to about 60 percent.[6] Given the strong

---

[6] Values for the early 1950's are from U.S. Office of Education, "College and University Endowments: A Survey," Circular 579, Washington, D.C., 1959. Values for the more recent period are based on data from annual issues of *The Study of College and University Endowment Funds*, Boston Fund, 1956–67.

growth in stock prices, this meant that to keep the share of equity below 60 percent, a persistent portfolio readjustment out of equities and into debt must have occurred. To capture this process roughly, multipliers were selected to adjust the stock-based price totals and debt-based price totals. Using these multipliers, in each year adding to 1.00, the estimated total assets at market value—broken into two categories of debt and equity —were produced. The equity multiplier for 1952–53 was .47, rising by a uniform .01 per year to 1966–67. Thus, the multiplier itself was independent of the stock price levels of any particular year. The equity-debt breakdown, of course, reflected the levels of stock prices as the equity multiplier applied to their fluctuating totals.

The application of the above procedure yielded broad breakdowns between debt and equity that agreed quite well with the distribution found by the Boston Fund in its studies covering from 50 to 60 percent of total college and university endowments. Perhaps most gratifying, the June 30, 1967 market value estimate produced by the above procedure was $12.0 billion. The first market value data developed by the Office of Education survey of all colleges and universities referred to that date. Their figure was $11.9 billion.

Having developed the annual series of total market values, the next step was to separate its distribution into more detailed equity and debt categories. (These may be seen in Table III-5.) The distributions were based upon the detailed breakdowns for the institutions with the largest endowments presented in the annual Boston Fund surveys. They, however, did not provide a breakdown between corporate and government bond holdings. Two Office of Education studies provided such a breakdown for 1948–58 and for 1963, and thus permitted separate estimates of the holdings of the two kinds of bonds.

The following procedures were used to place the endowment series on a December 31 basis. First, for all categories of assets other than common stock, the average of the June 30 values preceding and following the given December 31 was taken as the estimate of the year-end value. This was done on the assumption that market price levels for noncommon stock assets moved in a relatively smooth fashion, not subject to significant short-term fluctuations.

For the common stock December 31 market value series, a somewhat different procedure was followed. As explained above, the market value series was based on accumulations of endowments over academic years. A fairly continuous flow of endowment grants over the year was assumed, and the stock price index used to adjust the series was taken as the average

TABLE III-5

Assets of Colleges and Universities, 1953–67

(*$million*)

	1953	1954	1955	1956	1957	1958	1959	1960	1961	1962	1963	1964	1965	1966	1967
	Dollar Market Value of Endowments as of June 30														
Cash or equivalent	40	44	52	52	81	60	47	30	40	102	143	190	288	254	156
Corporate bonds	584	602	718	979	1,223	1,052	1,217	1,476	1,509	1,745	1,637	1,674	1,847	1,995	2,088
Government bonds	620	551	458	544	516	751	811	989	1,006	1,157	1,082	1,123	1,239	1,338	1,392
Preferred stocks	265	254	259	238	238	204	176	177	144	145	125	110	122	127	180
Common stocks	1,392	1,915	2,573	2,988	2,802	3,568	4,048	3,766	4,955	4,084	4,952	5,833	6,767	5,963	7,020
Other investments	33	36	43	52	58	72	95	103	144	247	250	351	376	277	240
Real estate—leased	73	80	95	104	139	156	189	185	208	238	179	210	243	277	252
Real estate—operated	60	65	78	98	70	66	68	89	56	102	98	90	88	115	120
Mortgages	33	36	48	62	133	132	149	185	200	264	197	251	277	334	336
Other	33	36	43	47	52	48	41	44	64	43	72	200	232	242	300
Total	3,133	3,619	4,367	5,164	5,312	6,109	6,841	7,044	8,326	8,127	8,735	10,032	11,479	10,922	12,084
Physical plant and equipment[a]	7,046	7,560	8,524	8,902	10,126	11,180	12,365	13,588	15,176	16,728	19,079	21,336	23,927	26,917	30,381
External debt	n.a.	539	677	795	1,020	1,276	1,515	1,782	2,190	2,553	3,315	3,862	4,603	5,786	7,487
	Market Value as of December 31														
Cash or equivalent	42	48	52	67	71	54	39	35	71	123	167	239	271	205	
Corporate bonds	593	660	849	1,101	1,138	1,130	1,347	1,493	1,627	1,691	1,656	1,760	1,921	2,042	
Government bonds	586	505	501	530	634	781	900	998	1,082	1,120	1,163	1,181	1,289	1,365	
Preferred stocks	260	257	249	238	221	190	177	161	145	135	118	116	125	154	
Common stocks	1,548	2,221	2,815	3,116	2,877	3,824	4,117	4,004	4,858	4,424	5,370	6,091	6,887	6,128	
Other investments	35	40	48	55	65	84	99	124	196	249	301	364	327	259	
Real estate—leased	77	88	100	122	148	173	187	197	223	209	195	227	260	265	
Real estate—operated	63	72	88	84	68	67	79	73	79	100	94	89	102	118	
Mortgages	35	42	55	98	133	141	167	193	232	231	224	264	306	335	
Other	35	40	45	49	50	45	43	54	54	58	136	216	237	271	
Total	3,274	3,973	4,802	5,460	5,405	6,489	7,155	7,332	8,567	8,340	9,424	10,547	11,725	11,142	

Source: See text.

[a] Book value as of June 30.

of the twelve monthly averages of weekly indexes for the Standard and Poor's 500-stock index. The June 30 values of common stock holdings, thus estimated, were averaged for pairs of successive years to produce preliminary December 31 estimates.

To produce final December 31 estimates, the fluctuating nature of common stock prices had to be recognized. This was done by the use of an adjustment factor which was expressed as the ratio of the 500-stock index for December 31 of a given year to the "monthly average of weekly indexes" used in the initial adjustment for market price trends. In this way, the level of the stock market on the last day of the year was incorporated into the December 31 asset holdings.

Appendix IV

The Assets of Labor Unions

LEO TROY

RUTGERS UNIVERSITY

1. SOURCES AND METHODS

The sources of the statistics on union assets and liabilities are the financial reports of unions, filed annually with the U.S. Department of Labor under provisions of the Labor-Management Reporting and Disclosure Act of 1959, and reports published by individual organizations in journals, newspapers and convention proceedings. The latter source was used to add the financial reports of organizations not subject to the LMRDA of 1959 (primarily unions of government employees) and to fill certain gaps in reports filed with the USDL.

Data are available for 1962–66 and for 1968; 1967 is the average of 1966 and 1968. The figures were adjusted to compensate for variations in the number of unions on the tapes of the Department of Labor.

All figures on total assets, total liabilities and net assets are the sum figure for local unions, intermediate union groups, and regional, national, and international unions.

2. NOTES ON INDIVIDUAL ITEMS IN COMBINED BALANCE SHEET OF LABOR UNIONS

The items shown in Table IV-1, which should be regarded as preliminary, are dated as of the end of the year and are defined as follows:

Cash: Includes cash on hand and in banks and other financial institutions, such as building and loan associations, savings and loan associations, and credit unions, as well as in escrow accounts. Certificates of deposit are also included.

U.S. Treasury Securities: The value reported is original cost.

Mortgage Investments: The total value shown by the union is unrecovered cost. The mortgages were purchased on a block basis from banks or similar institutions. Mortgage-secured loans made by a union are reported under loans receivable.

Other Investments: This item may be regarded as consisting primarily of equity holdings. However, it may also include U.S. government obligations other than Treasury securities, as well as state, municipal, and foreign government securities. The value reported by the union is at cost.

Fixed Assets: Includes land, buildings, automotive equipment, and office furniture and equipment at fair market value or net value, as shown on the unions' books.

Unclassified Assets: This is a residual item devised for this tabulation because of errors on the original USDL tapes.

Total Assets: This is the sum of reported totals.

Total Liabilities: This is the sum of the reported totals.

Net Worth: This is the arithmetic difference between total assets and total liabilities.

TABLE IV-1

Combined Balance Sheet of Labor Unions, 1962–68

(*$million*)

	1962 (1)	1963 (2)	1964 (3)	1965 (4)	1966 (5)	1967 (6)	1968 (7)
Cash	534	615	629	677	755	823	894
U.S. Treasury securities	406	407	379	392	423	444	465
Mortgages	134	147	143	138	144	149	153
Other investments	275	287	324	335	403	450	497
Fixed assets	267	281	302	348	344	377	410
Unclassified assets	155	139	134	135	137	143	151
Total assets	1,772	1,876	1,901	2,025	2,206	2,388	2,570
Liabilities	212	228	241	244	258	287	317
Net worth	1,559	1,648	1,660	1,781	1,948	2,101	2,253

SOURCE: See text.

Appendix V

The Distribution of Assets Among Individuals of Different Age and Wealth

JOHN BOSSONS

UNIVERSITY OF TORONTO AND

NATIONAL BUREAU OF ECONOMIC RESEARCH

THE purpose of this Appendix is to provide estimates of the distribution of the value of different assets over individuals characterized by age and gross wealth (total assets). The contributions of this endeavor are twofold: (1) to provide estimates of the distribution of wealth among individuals of different gross wealth within each of several different age classes, thus providing information on the relative importance of age as a factor determining wealth differentials, and (2) to do so for the entire household sectors. Though some estimates of the composition of asset portfolios for individuals classified by age and gross wealth have been provided in previous studies, these estimates have (through being based on estate tax return data) been limited to top wealth-holders.[1]

The estimates presented in this Appendix are based on data collected in the 1963 Survey of Consumer Finances conducted for the Board of

---

NOTE: The author is indebted to Nahide Craig, Lee Friedman, and Thad Mirer for programming and research assistance provided during the course of this study, and to the Board of Governors of the Federal Reserve System for providing a copy of a tape containing the individual responses to the 1963 Survey of Consumer Finance on which the analysis of this appendix is based.

[1] Recent studies of the distribution of wealth based on estate tax data include Robert J. Lampman, *The Share of Top Wealth-Holders in National Wealth, 1922–1956*, Princeton, Princeton University Press for NBER, 1962; James D. Smith, "Income and Wealth of Top Wealth-Holders in the United States, 1958," Ph.D. dissertation, University of Oklahoma, 1966; Internal Revenue Service, *Statistics of Income—1962, Personal Wealth Estimated from Estate Tax Returns*, Washington, D.C., 1967. For a review of previous studies, see Lampman, *op. cit.*, Chapter 1. For data provided in these studies on the distribution of total assets by age and gross wealth of decedents, cf. *ibid.*, Table 48. Estimates of the distribution of assets by age and net wealth are provided in *Personal Wealth*, Tables 11–14.

Governors of the Federal Reserve System by the Census Bureau.[2] The survey responses were originally analyzed on a family unit basis; to obtain data for individuals, each set of data collected for a family unit was divided among family members, using data on asset components and income shown for individuals within each family. Because a number of assets could not be divided between husband and wife on the basis of data collected from respondents, estimates were obtained using two extreme assumptions and were then compared with estimates obtained from estate tax returns for 1962; the proration basis used (allocating such assets exclusively to the husband) was based on the closer conformity to estate-tax-based wealth estimates thus obtained.

In subsequent sections, the estimates obtained from analysis of the individual responses are presented. The aggregate estimates are compared to corresponding estimates obtained from other sources in section 1. The distribution of assets, corporate stock, and other portfolio components are discussed in the subsequent three sections.

1. COMPARISON OF AGGREGATE WEALTH ESTIMATES FROM DIFFERENT SOURCES

Aggregate assets owned by the household sector are shown in Table V-1, which is derived from two sources, the flow of funds data described in Appendix I of this volume, and estimates obtained by aggregating responses to the Survey of Consumer Finance. Both sources pertain to the value of assets owned by individuals as of the end of 1962.

As is now well known, a number of assets tend to be systematically understated in survey responses.[3] This tendency is clear from the comparison presented in Table V-1, which shows the survey aggregates substantially understating the aggregate value of certain components of household wealth, relative to estimates obtained from aggregate data. The aggregate value of savings accounts, U.S. government securities, state and local bonds, interests in personal trusts, and interests in pension reserves are particularly badly understated. (Certain other assets, notably currency and deposits, are understated because of omission on the survey questionnaire; currency held by respondents was, for example, not ascertained in the survey.)

---

[2] For a description of the survey, see Dorothy S. Projector and Gertrude S. Weiss, *Survey of Financial Characteristics of Consumers,* Washington, D.C., Board of Governors of the Federal Reserve System, 1966, especially pages 45–62.

[3] Cf. Robert Ferber, *The Reliability of Consumer Reports of Financial Assets and Debts,* Studies in Consumer Savings, Number 6, Urbana, Ill., University of Illinois, 1966.

TABLE V-1

Alternative Estimates of Aggregate Value of Household Wealth
Components, 1962

(*$billion*)

	Estimates Based on Flow of Funds		Estimates Based on Survey		Difference Between Estimates
Liquid assets					
Currency and deposits	67.6		23.7		
Savings accounts	204.8		104.8		
Brokerage account credit balances	1.2	273.6	0.6	129.1	144.5
U.S. government securities	62.6		33.3		
State and local bonds	20.0		12.7		
Corporate and foreign bonds	0.0	82.6	5.9	51.9	30.7
Total liquid assets		356.2		181.0	175.2
Other assets					
Stocks		372.6		376.9	−4.3
Mortgages and notes	32.1		44.5		
Life insurance	91.9		77.4		
Annuity interest	—		1.1		
Interest in personal trust	85.3	209.3	54.3	177.3	32.0
Equity in noncorporate business		290.9		172.4	118.5
Principal residence	—		465.9		
Other residence	—		128.3		
Household goods	—	—	58.3	652.4	−652.4
Profit-sharing plans	—		6.9		
Pension reserves	109.5		19.3		
Estates in probate	—		11.5		
Miscellaneous	14.3	123.8	—	37.7	−86.1
Total household assets		1,352.4		1,597.6	−245.2

NOTES: The 1963 Federal Reserve Survey of Financial Characteristics of Consumers included 2,557 respondents who gave data sufficiently complete to tabulate. As part of the survey design, each respondent was given a weight reflecting the number of similar units (with respect to income) in the total population. These weights were accepted in calculating the above and following tables. Further information on the weighting procedure may be found in Dorothy S. Projector and Gertrude S. Weiss, *Survey of Financial Characteristics of Consumers*, Washington, D.C., Board of Governors of the Federal Reserve System, 1966, p. 56.

After reinterviews, there were 556 cases for which some information was missing on wealth and/or income. These cases were accepted as respondents in the survey because in most cases the missing amounts were judged to constitute a negligible portion of the consumer unit's wealth and income. Adjustments for these items were made in the survey editing and processing procedure, generally imputing the mean value based on households with similar age and income characteristics. Further detail may be found in Projector and Weiss, *op. cit.*, pp. 53–56.

Though the survey included information on debt secured by each asset, only the gross values were used here, to facilitate comparison with wealth estimates based on other sources (such as the Internal Revenue Service Estate Tax Returns).

For two assets, life insurance and closely held corporate stock, it was necessary to adjust survey data. To obtain estimates of the equity value of life insurance policies, ratios of equity to face value, by age class, were applied to the survey data on face values. These ratios were obtained from Internal Revenue Service, *Statistics of Income—1962, Personal Wealth Estimated from Estate Tax Returns*, Washington, D.C., 1967, Table J, p. 78.

In the case of closely held corporations, the survey data on book values of businesses in which the family had an active interest were adjusted upward by a factor of two, in order more adequately to reflect market values.

In the case of closely held corporations and unincorporated businesses, book values rather than reported market values were used, reflecting the problems observed by Projector and Weiss, *op. cit.* It should be noted that the book values of unincorporated businesses included in this and other tables in this Appendix are estimates of the value of equity in such businesses and hence may be negative in individual cases. Negative values for components of this item occur in three out of 2,557 cases for active partnerships and in five cases for active sole proprietorships. Such negative values reflect the lack of limited liability for owners of unincorporated businesses. It is interesting to note that in only one case out of 2,557 was the market value of any of these items reported negative.

The effect of most response errors underlying the aggregate understatement of savings accounts, bonds, and beneficial interests is to understate assets of almost all individuals by a relatively small dollar magnitude. That is, a large part of the error is likely to be relatively insignificant in its effect on estimates of the distribution of wealth, merely causing the true distribution of wealth to be dispersed around a slightly higher median than that estimated from the survey data, without materially affecting the dispersion of the distribution around its median. Consequently, it will be assumed in this Appendix that the response bias underlying the understatement of aggregate estimates obtained from the survey responses is not of material importance in analyzing the distribution of these aggregates over individuals in different wealth classes.[4]

[4] Response errors taking the form of deliberate omissions of important assets items by a respondent to the survey undoubtedly account for some of the aggregate understatement; response errors of this form would necessarily affect the dispersion as well as the median of the distribution of assets subject to such error. It is assumed in this Appendix that such deliberate omissions are of second-order importance compared to the effect of widespread omission of minor asset items. The major assets for which this assumption is likely to be invalid are equities in unincorporated businesses, in closely held corporations, or in real estate. In these cases, there may be frequent reporting of investments on the basis of their original cost rather than their current book or fair market values, as well as cases of deliberate understatement.

A number of assets appear to be understated by, or omitted in, estimates of aggregate gross household sector wealth obtained from flow of funds data. In particular, corporate and foreign bonds, and a number of miscellaneous assets appear to be more accurately estimated by aggregating survey responses than by using flow of funds residuals.

The most serious divergencies between the two aggregate estimates shown in Table V-1 (other than for real property) arise in the cases of unincorporated business equity and of pension reserves. It is possible that the first may in many instances arise from the use of book values rather than market values to measure the value of interests in unincorporated businesses. The divergence in the case of pension reserves is indicative of the lack of knowledge among many individuals (particularly younger individuals) of the present value of their future pension rights.

Two estimates of the distribution of total assets over individuals in different wealth classes are summarized in Tables V-2 and V-3. The two estimates are based on polar extreme assumptions concerning the allocation of assets between husband and wife where no data for such allocation is available. In the first case, such assets are allocated exclusively to the husband; in the second case, they are split evenly between husband and wife. Examining the tables in the light of the estimates presented in sections 3 and 4 below, it is evident that the allocation of assets is of material importance in those cases where the distribution of assets is relatively unequal.

A comparison between estimates obtained from estate tax returns and the survey estimates of total assets allocable to individuals with total assets of more than $60,000 is presented in Table V-3. This table indicates that for most assets other than corporate stocks, it is apparently more accurate to allocate assets of husbands and wives exclusively to husbands than to split such assets among spouses. For corporate stocks, this particularly seems to be the case, since estate-tax-based estimates of corporate stock are likely to be understated as a result of liquidations made in contemplation of death.

Comparing Table V-3 with Table V-1, it appears that most of the understatement in the survey responses evident from Table V-1 is concentrated among individuals with total assets of less than $60,000. The estate tax return estimates of liquid assets (cash and bonds) shown in Table V-3 are roughly $50 million greater than the corresponding estimates obtained from the Survey of Consumer Finances. However, much of this understatement is likely to reflect liquidation of corporate stock and of unincorporated business assets to avoid liquidity problems at death. It would

TABLE V-2

Aggregate Value of Components of Assets in Household Sector for Individuals with Assets of Less than $60,000

(*$billion*)

	Unallocated Wealth of Husband and Wife Allocated Entirely to Husband				Unallocated Wealth of Husband and Wife Split Evenly			
	Below $15,000	$15,000 to $30,000	$30,000 to $60,000	Total Under $60,000	Below $15,000	$15,000 to $30,000	$30,000 to $60,000	Total Under $60,000
Currency, deposits and savings accounts	37.4	24.4	29.4	91.2	39.8	30.9	23.3	94.0
U.S. government securities	6.3	5.1	7.5	18.9	6.9	6.7	6.4	20.0
State and local bonds	—	—	0.1	0.1	—	—	0.2	0.2
Corporate and foreign bonds	0.1	0.9	1.6	2.6	1.1	0.4	1.5	3.0
Stocks	3.6	10.3	27.0	40.9	9.4	22.4	37.6	69.4
Mortgages and notes	2.8	3.2	7.9	13.9	4.1	6.7	6.7	17.5
Life insurance equities	32.5	15.7	12.1	60.3	41.4	15.0	9.3	65.7
Real estate	126.6	183.0	130.6	440.2	259.8	143.3	74.9	477.9
Other	48.0	43.9	64.0	155.9	79.1	62.1	45.2	186.4
Total	251.5	286.5	280.2	824.0	441.6	287.5	205.1	934.2

Notes to Table V-2.

Figures may not add to totals due to rounding.

The basic wealth-holding unit for purposes of the survey consists of families and unrelated individuals, as defined by the Bureau of the Census. It was necessary for purposes of this table to decompose the survey family data into individual data.

All wealth and income components in the survey were recorded in one of three ways: a single entry representing the total family wealth; two entries representing first the share of the husband and wife (H & W) and second, the share of the other family members (OFM); three entries, one each for the head, spouse, and all OFM. We may list the components by the way in which they were recorded. Note that a component may appear on more than one list if its subcomponents are recorded in different ways.

Single Entry	Double Entry	Triple Entry
Credit-brokerage account	Income (all times)	Checking accounts
Other federal securities		Savings deposits
State and local bonds		Federal savings bonds
Corporate and foreign bonds		Mortgages and notes (some types)
Stock (all types)		Life insurance (face)
Mortgages and notes (some types)		Annuities
Trust assets		
Noncorporate business assets		
Principal residence		
Other real estate		
Household goods		
Profit-sharing plans		
Retirement plans		
Estates in probate		

Wealth was allocated in the following manner: in all cases wealth to OFM was split evenly among all adults other than head and spouse. If there were no such adults, OFM wealth was split evenly among the children.

For triple-entry components, wealth was assigned as recorded (and OFM was split by the above procedures). For single-entry items, the share allocable to husband and wife is estimated by distributing the total family holdings of such assets between husband and wife together and other family members together in proportion to the distribution among them of incomes from that asset. If no income was reported, the wealth was divided evenly among wealth-holders in the family. (One exception to this occurs when there is no wife present. The head then receives a double share.) The share to OFM was computed as a residual in both cases. The H & W share was divided in two ways (applicable also to double-entry items); first, all H & W wealth was assigned to the husband; second, the wealth was evenly split between head and spouse. Wealth aggregates were estimated separately for each assumption.

For additional information see notes to Table V-1.

SOURCE: Analysis of individual responses to 1963 Survey of Consumer Finances.

TABLE V-3

Comparison of Household Survey Estimates with Estimates Obtained from Estate Tax Returns, 1962

(*$billion*)

| | Household Survey Estimates | | | | | | Estimates Based on Estate Tax Returns (individuals with assets over $60,000) |
| | Unallocated Wealth of Husband and Wife Allocated Entirely to Husband | | | Unallocated Wealth of Husband and Wife Split Evenly Between Husband and Wife | | | |
	Total from Survey	Assets Under $60,000	Assets Over $60,000	Total from Survey	Assets Under $60,000	Assets Over $60,000	
Cash	129.0	91.2	37.7	129.0	94.0	35.1	70.7
Bonds	51.8	21.6	30.2	51.8	23.2	28.6	47.9
Stocks	376.9	40.9	336.0	376.9	69.4	307.5	325.8
Mortgages and notes	44.5	13.9	30.6	44.5	17.5	26.8	30.4
Life insurance equity	77.4	60.3	17.1	77.4	65.7	11.6	15.6
Real estate	594.2	440.2	154.0	594.2	483.7	110.5	188.0
Other assets	323.8	155.9	170.7	323.8	186.4	137.4	73.6
Total	1,597.6	824.0	795.6	1,597.6	940.0	657.6	752.0

NOTES: Figures may not add to totals due to rounding. Other notes are as in Table V-2.
SOURCES: Survey estimates are tabulated from individual responses. Estate tax estimates are obtained from Internal Revenue Service, *Statistics of Income—1962.*

accordingly seem safe to assume that less than one-tenth of the $175 million understatement of liquid assets shown in Table V-1 is allocable to top wealthholders.

There is a substantial understatement of equity in unincorporated businesses in estimates based on estate tax return data. (Equity in unincorporated business is not shown separately in the aggregated estate tax return data and is therefore included in "other assets" in Tables V-2 and V-3.) Such understatement is undoubtedly due to liquidation of interests in such businesses in contemplation of death, though mortality losses due to the decedent's having been a principal in such firms may also be a factor. The understatement of this item shown in Table V-3 is itself understated by the fact that such assets have been measured in terms of book value in the case of the survey responses, but are presumably measured at closer to market value on estate tax returns.

Holdings of real estate by individuals with assets of more than $60,000 would appear to be significantly understated in survey responses, as seen when one compares the survey estimates shown in Table V-3 with the corresponding estate-tax-based estimates. It is possible that this may be due largely to reporting of values closer to original costs than to current market values, the latter presumably being the basis for valuation on estate tax returns.

2. DISTRIBUTION OF TOTAL ASSETS

The distribution of total wealth among individuals in different age and asset classes is shown in Table V-4. In these and all subsequent tables in this Appendix, wealth components of husbands and wives which were not obtained separately in the survey interviews have been allocated exclusively to the husband.[5] Allied estimates of the number of individuals in different age and wealth classes are presented in Table V-5.

The number of individuals with little wealth is pronounced, as is implied by the figures shown in Table V-5. Their importance in the distribution of wealth is shown in Table V-4. Though more than five-sixths of all individuals had less than $15,000 in total assets, such individuals accounted for less than one-sixth of the total wealth of the household sector. Moreover, approximately 20 percent of the wealth owned by such individuals was attributable to individuals more than 64 years old.

---

[5] For a description of the procedure used to decompose family data into estimates on an individual basis, see the notes to Table V-2.

TABLE V-4

Distribution of Household Assets Among Individuals Classified by Age and Total Assets, 1962

Total Assets Owned by Individual	Age of Individual						
	Under 25	25 to 34	35 to 44	45 to 54	55 to 64	Over 64	All Ages
A. Total Assets Owned by All Individuals in Each Class ($billion)							
Less than $15,000	15.0	32.6	52.0	63.3	48.0	46.3	257.3
$15,000–$30,000	3.5	41.3	62.3	75.1	54.5	49.9	286.5
30,000– 60,000	1.1	23.5	55.4	68.5	80.5	51.3	280.2
60,000–100,000	0.9	4.1	21.5	29.8	37.7	45.4	139.3
100,000–200,000	2.6	1.3	40.0	23.4	48.0	21.4	136.7
200,000–500,000	0.6	8.2	15.2	31.8	44.8	56.9	157.5
500,000–1,000,000	2.1	2.3	15.6	15.1	27.8	38.2	101.0
Over $1,000,000	—	25.3	24.8	63.4	60.0	65.5	239.0
All individuals	25.8	138.6	286.7	370.2	401.3	374.9	1,597.6
B. Percentage Distribution (percent of total wealth)							
Less than $15,000	0.9	2.0	3.3	4.0	3.0	2.9	15.8
$15,000–$30,000	0.2	2.6	3.9	4.7	3.4	3.1	17.9
30,000– 60,000	0.1	1.5	3.5	4.3	5.1	3.2	17.5
60,000–100,000	0.1	0.3	1.4	1.9	2.4	2.9	8.8
100,000–200,000	0.2	0.1	2.5	1.5	3.0	1.3	8.6
200,000–500,000	—	0.5	1.0	2.0	2.8	3.6	9.9
500,000–1,000,000	0.1	0.1	1.0	0.9	1.7	2.4	6.3
Over $1,000,000	—	1.6	1.6	4.0	3.8	4.1	15.0
All individuals	1.6	8.7	17.9	23.2	25.1	23.5	100.0

NOTE: Figures may not add to totals due to rounding.
SOURCES: Tables V-13 to V-19. Individual responses to 1963 Federal Reserve Board Survey of Financial Characteristics of Consumers.

By contrast, individuals with total assets worth more than $200,000 accounted for virtually one-third of the total assets of the household sector, even though comprising only 0.5 percent of the tabulated population. These individuals were heavily concentrated in higher age classes, with individuals more than 54 years old accounting for close to 60 percent of total assets held by members of these wealth classes.

The increasingly unequal distribution of wealth as age increases is to be expected on several grounds. The principal reason for this result is, of course, that lifetime incomes are distributed unequally (partly because of the incidence of bequests), and that human capital is ignored in the assets tabulated in this Appendix. Were differences in human capital the

TABLE V-5

Distribution of Number of Individuals Classified by Age and Total Assets, 1962

Total Assets Owned by Individual	Under 25	25 to 34	35 to 44	45 to 54	55 to 64	Over 64	All Ages
					Age of Individual		

Total Assets Owned by Individual	Under 25	25 to 34	35 to 44	45 to 54	55 to 64	Over 64	All Ages
A. Number of Individuals (millions)							
Less than $15,000	57.1	22.0	23.4	21.7	16.0	14.4	154.6
$15,000–$30,000	0.2	1.9	3.0	3.5	2.5	2.3	13.3
30,000– 60,000	—	0.6	1.4	1.7	1.9	1.3	6.8
60,000–100,000	—	0.1	0.3	0.4	0.5	0.6	1.9
100,000–200,000	—	—	0.3	0.2	0.4	0.2	1.0
200,000–500,000	—	—	0.1	0.1	0.2	0.2	0.5
500,000–1,000,000	—	—	—	—	—	0.1	0.2
Over $1,000,000	—	—	—	—	—	—	0.1
All individuals	57.3	24.7	28.4	27.5	21.4	19.0	178.4
B. Percentage Distribution (percent of grand total)							
Less than $15,000	32.0	12.4	13.1	12.1	8.9	8.1	86.6
$15,000–$30,000	0.1	1.1	1.7	1.9	1.4	1.3	7.5
30,000– 60,000	—	0.3	0.8	1.0	1.1	0.7	3.8
60,000–100,000	—	—	0.2	0.2	0.3	0.3	1.0
100,000–200,000	—	—	0.2	0.1	0.2	0.1	0.6
200,000–500,000	—	—	—	0.1	0.1	0.1	0.3
500,000–1,000,000	—	—	—	—	—	—	0.1
Over $1,000,000	—	—	—	—	—	—	0.1
All individuals	32.1	13.8	15.9	15.4	12.0	10.7	100.0

NOTE: Figures may not add to totals due to rounding.
SOURCE: Individual responses to 1963 Federal Reserve Board Survey of Financial Characteristics of Consumers.

only source of differences in lifetime income, financial wealth would be determined partly by variations in rates of return realized on invested capital and partly by variations in the cumulative amount of previous saving by each household, with the latter being the dominant factor accounting for systematic variations in wealth across age groups. Were consumption a constant fraction of lifetime income and were current income a constant fraction of lifetime income (regardless of age), then average wealth would increase with age and the distribution of wealth would become more unequal as age increased. Taking the normal lifetime profile of income into account would change this conclusion only marginally. Both variations in rates of return on capital and variations in lifetime income on human capital would result in an increasingly unequal distribution of wealth as age increases.[6]

To the extent that variations in rates of return on capital are in part attributable to rents on scarce types of human capital, we may expect the rate of increase of wealth with age to depend in part upon the fraction of total assets invested in corporate stock (since most of the variance in rates of return is attributable to returns on such assets).

3. DISTRIBUTION OF SHAREHOLDINGS

The ownership of common and preferred shares is heavily concentrated among older individuals and among individuals with large wealth. The total value of corporate stocks owned by individuals in different age and asset classes is shown in the first part of Table V-6; the share of household sector ownership of stocks allocable to individuals in each age and asset class is shown in the second half of this table. A comparison of Table V-6 with Table V-4 provides some interesting insights into the extent to which stock ownership is concentrated among upper age and asset classes.

While 72 percent of total assets in the household sector is owned by individuals more than 45 years old, 83 per cent of corporate stock is owned by individuals older than 45. The effect of age becomes more pronounced as age increases. For individuals aged 45 to 54, their share of the aggregate value of stocks owned by the household sector is almost identical to their share of total assets in the household sector. Individuals aged 55 to 64 account for 28 percent of corporate stocks owned by the household sector and 25 percent of total assets. Individuals more than 64 years old account for 32 percent of the value of the stocks owned by all individuals, while accounting for only 23.5 percent of total assets.

Among individuals more than 45 years old, the relative importance of corporate stocks rises as total assets of the individual rise. Individuals in this age group with over $200,000 of assets account for 63 percent of total stock owned by the household sector, while accounting for only 25 percent of total assets. Individuals more than 45 years old with assets above $1 million account for more than one-third of total corporate stock held by the household sector and for only one-eighth of total household-sector wealth.

---

[6] For a brief review of sources of income and wealth differentials, see J. E. Stiglitz, "The Distribution of Income and Wealth among Individuals," *Econometrica*, July 1969, pp. 382–97.

TABLE V-6

Distribution of Household-Owned Corporate Equities Among Individuals Classified by Age and Total Assets, 1962

Total Assets Owned by Individual	Age of Individual						
	Under 25	25 to 34	35 to 44	45 to 54	55 to 64	Over 64	All Ages
A. Total Amount of Corporate Equities Owned by All Individuals in Each Class ($billion)							
Less than $15,000	0.6	0.5	0.3	0.7	0.9	0.6	3.6
$15,000–$30,000	0.2	0.8	1.8	1.3	3.6	2.6	10.3
30,000– 60,000	0.1	4.7	3.4	7.0	5.6	6.3	27.0
60,000–100,000	0.5	3.3	2.8	4.3	11.8	6.4	29.1
100,000–200,000	0.4	0.5	11.8	6.5	11.8	7.1	38.1
200,000–500,000	0.1	1.1	4.3	13.8	14.7	35.1	69.2
500,000–1,000,000	1.3	1.7	1.8	6.1	17.8	18.1	46.9
Over $1,000,000	—	1.0	19.5	47.0	39.8	45.6	152.8
All individuals	3.2	13.6	45.7	86.7	106.0	121.8	377.0
B. Percentage Distribution (percent of grand total)							
Less than $15,000	0.2	0.1	0.1	0.2	0.2	0.2	0.9
$15,000–$30,000	—	0.2	0.5	0.4	1.0	0.7	2.7
30,000– 60,000	—	1.2	0.9	1.9	1.5	1.7	7.2
60,000–100,000	0.1	0.9	0.7	1.1	3.1	1.7	7.7
100,000–200,000	0.1	0.1	3.1	1.7	3.1	1.9	10.1
200,000–500,000	—	0.3	1.1	3.7	3.9	9.3	18.4
500,000–1,000,000	0.4	0.5	0.5	1.6	4.7	4.8	12.4
Over $1,000,000	—	0.3	5.2	12.5	10.5	12.1	40.5
All individuals	0.9	3.6	12.1	23.0	28.1	32.3	100.0

NOTE: Figures may not add to totals due to rounding.
SOURCES: Tables V-13 to V-19.

The average ratio of the value of corporate stock to the value of assets owned by each individual in different age and asset classes is shown in Table V-7. Because of the relatively small sample size in each one of the cells, it would be erroneous to assign too much weight to specific numbers in this table. Moreover, because of the relatively small number of large-wealth owners who are young, it is necessary to be particularly wary of estimates shown for individuals below 45 years of age. The relatively high variance in the ratios of traded stock to total stock for individuals between 25 and 44 years old with wealth greater than $60,000 reflects a predictably high variance in the relative importance of investments in closely held companies. In part, this variance may be due to the incidence of bequests consisting of interests in closely held companies. In part, the high variance

TABLE V-7

Average Ratio of Value of Stocks to Total Assets for Individuals Classified by Age and Size of Total Assets, 1962

(percentage of total assets)

Total Assets Owned by Individual	Age of Individual						
	Under 25	25 to 34	35 to 44	45 to 54	55 to 64	Over 64	All Ages
Less than $15,000	6.2	1.4	0.6	1.1	1.8	1.3	1.4
$15,000–$30,000	4.9	2.0	2.8	1.8	6.7	5.2	3.6
30,000– 60,000	11.2	19.8	6.1	10.3	6.9	12.2	9.6
60,000–100,000	62.1	80.2	13.1	14.3	31.3	14.1	20.9
100,000–200,000	14.5	36.9	29.5	27.9	24.5	33.2	27.8
200,000–500,000	21.7	13.4	28.5	43.4	32.8	61.7	43.9
500,000–1,000,000	63.8	74.0	11.2	40.7	64.2	47.5	46.4
Over $1,000,000	—	3.8	78.5	74.2	66.3	69.6	63.9
All individuals	16.2	9.7	15.9	23.5	26.4	32.5	23.7

SOURCES: Tables V-13 to V-19.

TABLE V-8

Ratio of Value of Traded Stocks to Total Stocks Owned by Individuals Classified by Age and Total Assets, 1962

(percentage of total stocks)

Total Assets Owned by Individual	Age of Individual						
	Under 25	25 to 34	35 to 44	45 to 54	55 to 64	Over 64	All Ages
Less than $15,000	100.0	94.2	98.3	99.9	82.6	99.9	94.7
$15,000–$30,000	94.5	71.3	69.4	68.7	90.7	92.1	83.1
30,000– 60,000	96.2	10.0	34.4	86.8	88.2	84.2	66.7
60,000–100,000	73.3	100.0	38.3	89.3	94.6	100.0	89.8
100,000–200,000	100.0	11.9	23.3	67.2	84.7	64.2	58.1
200,000–500,000	99.8	14.3	41.2	35.0	75.8	93.5	73.6
500,000–1,000,000	100.0	2.3	65.5	21.7	45.8	71.1	53.1
Over $1,000,000	—	75.5	21.7	23.9	53.5	59.0	42.1
All individuals	95.2	42.7	30.0	38.4	66.7	75.4	57.9

SOURCES: Tables V-13 to V-19.

may be due simply to the relative infrequency with which individuals less than 45 years old become proprietors of successful new corporations.

Average ratios of the value of traded stock to the value of total stock owned by individuals classified by age and gross wealth are shown in Table V-8.

4. DISTRIBUTION OF OTHER ASSETS

Estimates of the different components of wealth owned by individuals in different age and asset classes are shown in Tables V-13 through V-18. (A summary table showing the components of wealth for individuals in all age classes combined is presented in Table V-19.) These tables provide substantial detail on the composition of wealth in different age and asset classes.

The relative importance of liquid assets and investments in real estate and household durables is shown in Tables V-9 and V-10. As these tables indicate, the importance of both types of assets is highest for individuals with small amounts of wealth. As Table V-9 indicates, the combined importance of cash and bonds is particularly high for individuals over 64, compared with individuals in all wealth classes combined in different age classes. In addition, the importance of liquid assets is enhanced in higher wealth classes by the importance in such classes of investments in state and local bonds, which because of their tax-exempt status are attractive to individuals whose marginal tax rate is higher than that of the marginal investor in the state and local bond market. State and local bonds are a significant fraction of liquid assets for individuals with more than $500,000 in total assets.

The relative importance of real property, shown in the tabulations presented in Table V-10, is particularly pronounced in low wealth classes. As wealth increases, the relative importance of real property declines. A similar decline in the relative importance of real property (though not as precipitous) may be observed as the age of the individual increases.

Among other assets, the distribution of unincorporated business assets is particularly interesting. The relative importance of these assets in different age and wealth classes is shown in Table V-11. Such assets are of particularly large relative importance for wealth holders with assets between $30,000 and $500,000, almost without regard to the age of the wealth-holder. As a result, the relative importance of unincorporated business assets for all individuals in an age class is almost entirely un-affected by age in the top four age classes. (In the bottom two age classes, the paucity of individuals with wealth above $60,000 dominates the result.)

TABLE V-9

Relative Importance of Cash and Bonds Among Asset Holdings for Individuals Classified by Age and Total Assets, 1962

(percentage of total assets)

Total Assets Owned by Individual	Age of Individual						
	Under 25	25 to 34	35 to 44	45 to 54	55 to 64	Over 64	All Ages
Less than $15,000	26.0	11.0	13.6	13.7	18.6	25.1	17.0
$15,000–$30,000	3.4	2.9	4.4	9.1	17.5	19.7	10.6
30,000– 60,000	3.5	5.1	8.1	11.1	15.0	25.8	13.8
60,000–100,000	5.8	0.9	4.4	11.1	15.8	15.5	12.4
100,000–200,000	29.9	2.1	7.5	5.9	12.0	23.6	11.7
200,000–500,000	2.5	1.4	6.8	5.0	4.8	9.0	6.4
500,000–1,000,000	0.2	1.9	0.4	3.5	5.4	13.6	7.3
Over $1,000,000	—	1.0	3.1	2.9	9.5	13.0	7.2
All individuals	19.1	4.6	7.0	8.6	12.9	17.6	11.3

SOURCES: Tables V-13 to V-19.

TABLE V-10

Relative Importance of Real Property Among Asset Holdings of Individuals Classified by Age and Total Assets, 1962

(percentage of total assets)

Total Assets Owned by Individual	Age of Individual						
	Under 25	25 to 34	35 to 44	45 to 54	55 to 64	Over 64	All Ages
Less than $15,000	5.5	61.1	59.2	71.6	57.2	56.5	49.2
$15,000–$30,000	77.8	78.4	80.2	71.0	59.6	53.1	68.9
30,000– 60,000	0.8	60.9	52.3	49.3	50.7	43.9	50.1
60,000–100,000	8.7	14.0	59.5	39.5	35.4	32.8	38.4
100,000–200,000	—	53.2	41.7	40.3	27.8	24.1	33.1
200,000–500,000	—	15.7	35.8	26.4	12.6	11.7	17.4
500,000–1,000,000	3.2	7.1	4.2	24.6	16.9	22.0	17.5
Over $1,000,000	—	1.1	4.5	11.3	9.6	8.9	8.4
All individuals	15.5	50.2	51.1	46.7	35.8	31.0	37.2

SOURCES: Tables V-13 to V-19.

Over all individuals, the relative importance of unincorporated business assets is approximately 5 percent for individuals with assets of less than $30,000 or assets of greater than $500,000 and is approximately between 15 and 20 percent for individuals with assets between $30,000 and $500,000.

The estimates shown for the relative importance of most other variables are relatively low and deserve little comment. The one exception consists of the high values shown for the relative importance of equity in life insurance in the low wealth classes, a phenomenon which may in part be due to an overstatement of the ratio of life insurance equity to life insurance face value for individuals in the bottom age classes. The relative importance of bequests as a source of wealth is shown by the relative importance of estates in probate compared to total assets for individuals in higher wealth classes who are less than 35 years old.

5. ASSET-HOLDING PATTERN FOR INDEPENDENT INDIVIDUALS LESS THAN 25 YEARS OLD

In the preceding analysis, all individuals less than 25 years old have been aggregated together. In this section, individuals in this age group who are heads of households or living in independent establishments are segregated out and examined separately. Such persons account for 7.5 million individuals out of the 57.3 million individuals included in the under-25 age group. (Most of the remaining 49.8 million individuals are dependent children.)

Estimated asset-holdings for such individuals are presented in Table V-12. By comparing the estimates shown in this table with the results of previous analyses reported above, it can be seen that independent individuals under 25 years of age are much more like individuals in higher age groups than like dependent children in the pattern of their asset holdings. Of particular interest is the almost complete absence of investments in common stocks and in equity interests in unincorporated businesses. Consequently, it may be assumed that the magnitude of investments in such assets shown earlier is the result of distribution of such equities to dependent children by parents in order to avoid estate taxes and to reduce current personal income taxes on income from the business. Since de facto control of such equity interests would in most such instances continue to reside in the parents, the figures presented on the distribution of asset ownership by age class present a biased estimate of the distribution of the control of wealth by age class.

Further data on independent individuals less than 25 years old are presented in Table V-20.

TABLE V-11

Relative Importance of Equity in Unincorporated Business Among Asset Holdings for Individuals Classified by Age and Total Assets, 1962

(*percentage of total assets*)

Total Assets Owned by Individual	Age of Individual						
	Under 25	25 to 34	35 to 44	45 to 54	55 to 64	Over 64	All Ages
Less than $15,000	21.2	6.4	8.4	1.2	7.3	2.5	5.8
$15,000–$30,000	9.3	7.3	3.5	7.4	7.5	15.3	7.9
30,000– 60,000	22.5	2.9	23.1	15.8	17.2	11.5	15.8
60,000–100,000	5.2	—	11.6	24.9	7.2	30.8	19.1
100,000–200,000	55.5	—	11.7	4.3	20.0	14.4	14.5
200,000–500,000	45.0	—	20.1	16.9	35.9	8.1	18.7
500,000–1,000,000	3.2	—	0.5	26.3	1.3	4.1	6.0
Over $1,000,000	—	—	0.5	4.5	4.9	3.9	3.5
All individuals	21.7	4.2	10.4	10.2	13.2	10.8	10.8

SOURCES: Tables V-13 to V-19.

TABLE V-12

Estimated Asset-Holdings for Individuals Less than 25 Years Old in Independent Households, 1962

Asset Class of Individual	Total Assets Owned by Individuals in Class ($ billion)	Number of Individuals (million)	Relative Importance of Assets (percentage of total assets):			
			Cash and Bonds	Corporate Equities	Unincorporated Businesses	Real Property
Less than $15,000	5.7	7.3	11.9	0.7	0.5	52.9
$15,000–$30,000	3.1	0.2	2.7	1.7	2.3	88.1
30,000– 60,000	0.6	—	0.4	—	—	1.3
60,000–100,000	0.1	—	0.6	17.9	13.2	68.3
100,000–200,000	—	—	—	—	—	—
200,000–500,000	—	—	—	—	—	—
500,000–1,000,000	—	—	—	—	—	—
Over $1,000,000	—	—	—	—	—	—
All individuals	9.5	7.5	8.0	1.2	1.2	61.1

Source: Individual responses to 1963 Survey of Financial Characteristics of Consumers.
Notes: Figures may not add to total because of rounding. For other notes, see notes to Tables V-1 and V-2.

TABLE V-13

Components of Wealth for All Individuals Less than 25 Years Old, Classified by Wealth

(*$million*)

	Wealth Class ($thousand)								
	Below 15	15–30	30–60	60–100	100–200	200–500	500–1,000	Over 1,000	Total
Checking accounts	218.21	33.40	2.72	12.14	0.00	0.79	0.00	0.00	267.26
Savings deposits	2,967.52	77.95	7.33	2.33	347.73	7.03	0.69	0.00	3,410.58
Credit balance of brokerage accounts	0.00	5.35	0.03	0.16	2.83	1.29	0.00	0.00	9.67
Total cash	3,185.73	116.70	10.08	14.64	350.56	9.11	0.69	0.00	3,687.51
Federal savings bonds	730.64	2.50	0.00	22.79	9.61	0.00	0.00	0.00	765.53
Other federal securities	0.00	0.00	28.08	0.00	125.19	6.23	0.00	0.00	159.51
State and local government bonds	0.00	0.00	0.00	12.64	43.57	0.00	0.00	0.00	56.21
Corporate and foreign bonds	0.00	0.00	0.00	0.03	250.99	0.00	5.06	0.00	256.08
Total bonds	730.64	2.50	28.08	35.46	429.36	6.23	5.06	0.00	1,237.33
Traded stock	577.78	161.77	114.92	390.18	377.34	130.91	1,322.70	0.00	3,075.60
Closely held stock	0.00	9.35	0.00	142.15	0.00	0.00	0.00	0.00	151.50
Stock, type unavailable	0.00	0.00	0.00	0.00	0.00	0.00	0.00	0.00	0.00
Investment clubs	0.00	0.00	4.58	0.00	0.00	0.27	0.00	0.00	4.86
Total stocks	577.78	171.12	119.50	532.33	377.34	131.19	1,322.70	0.00	3,231.96

(*continued*)

TABLE V-13 (*concluded*)

| | Wealth Class ($thousand) | | | | | | | | |
	Below 15	15–30	30–60	60–100	100–200	200–500	500–1,000	Over 1,000	Total
Mortgages and notes	95.55	8.60	0.00	0.00	0.00	0.00	0.00	0.00	104.15
Equity life insurance	5,368.08	141.23	18.31	0.02	2.33	0.00	0.00	0.00	5,529.97
Annuities	0.00	0.00	0.00	0.00	0.00	0.00	0.00	0.00	0.00
Trust assets	631.73	0.00	36.19	155.51	0.00	186.09	284.37	0.00	1,293.89
Noncorporate business assets	3,186.54	328.34	240.49	44.57	1,448.72	272.27	67.21	0.00	5,588.15
Total other financial assets	9,281.90	478.17	295.00	200.10	1,451.05	458.37	351.58	0.00	12,516.16
Principal residence	0.00	2,363.83	0.00	67.27	0.00	0.00	0.00	0.00	2,431.10
Other real estate	134.46	232.37	0.00	0.00	0.00	0.00	67.29	0.00	434.12
Household goods	968.14	137.89	8.11	7.21	0.00	0.00	0.00	0.00	1,121.34
Total real property	833.68	2,734.09	8.11	74.48	0.00	0.00	67.29	0.00	3,986.56
Profit-sharing plans	19.59	12.74	0.00	0.00	0.00	0.00	0.00	0.00	32.33
Retirement plans	146.67	0.00	0.45	0.00	0.00	0.00	0.00	0.00	147.11
Estates in probate	0.00	0.00	608.23	0.00	0.00	0.00	325.61	0.00	933.84
Total miscellaneous assets	166.25	12.74	608.68	0.00	0.00	0.00	325.61	0.00	1,113.29
Total assets	15,044.90	3,515.32	1,069.45	857.00	2,608.31	604.89	2,072.93	0.00	25,772.81

NOTES: Figures may not add to totals because of rounding. For other notes, see notes to Tables V-1 and V-3.
SOURCE: Individual responses to 1963 Federal Reserve Board Survey of Financial Characteristics of Consumers.

TABLE V-14

Components of Wealth for Individuals Aged 25 to 34, Classified by Wealth

(*$million*)

	Wealth Class ($thousand)								
	Below 15	15–30	30–60	60–100	100–200	200–500	500–1,000	Over 1,000	Total
Checking accounts	731.57	273.80	274.07	28.96	2.56	17.38	21.77	3.82	1,353.93
Savings deposits	2,145.26	829.74	839.96	7.95	11.02	80.23	12.02	0.72	3,926.89
Credit balance of brokerage accounts	0.00	0.02	0.00	0.00	0.03	11.89	0.00	26.44	38.37
Total cash	2,876.83	1,103.56	1,114.03	36.90	13.61	109.50	33.79	30.98	5,319.20
Federal savings bonds	640.94	94.68	84.26	0.01	7.62	7.62	10.86	0.27	846.26
Other federal securities	0.00	0.00	0.00	0.00	0.00	0.00	0.00	89.88	89.88
State and local government bonds	0.00	0.00	0.00	0.00	0.00	0.00	0.00	130.77	130.77
Corporate and foreign bonds	63.05	0.00	4.61	0.00	5.08	0.00	0.00	0.74	73.49
Total bonds	704.00	94.68	88.87	0.01	12.70	7.62	10.86	221.67	1,140.40
Traded stock	440.57	577.51	466.88	3,303.72	56.02	156.51	39.21	724.08	5,764.50
Closely held stock	0.01	226.64	4,197.26	0.00	409.53	938.68	1,688.52	234.64	7,695.28
Stock, type unavailable	0.00	0.00	0.00	0.00	0.00	0.00	0.00	0.16	0.16
Investment clubs	27.27	6.30	0.00	0.00	3.75	0.00	0.00	0.00	37.32
Total stocks	467.85	810.45	4,664.14	3,303.72	469.30	1,095.19	1,727.73	958.88	13,497.26

(*continued*)

TABLE V-14 (concluded)

	Wealth Class ($thousand)								
	Below 15	15–30	30–60	60–100	100–200	200–500	500–1,000	Over 1,000	Total
Mortgages and notes	85.38	565.20	381.53	69.45	5.03	21.06	59.70	15.56	1,202.91
Equity life insurance	5,443.57	2,941.89	1,551.87	131.34	34.62	55.95	17.52	9.11	10,185.87
Annuities	0.00	0.00	0.00	0.00	0.00	0.00	0.00	0.00	00.0
Trust assets	49.10	0.00	436.66	0.00	0.00	717.70	317.66	23,709.86	25,230.99
Noncorporate business assets	2,101.37	3,025.36	691.37	0.00	0.12	0.00	0.00	0.00	5,818.22
Total other financial assets	7,679.42	6,532.46	3,061.43	200.79	39.76	794.72	394.87	23,734.53	42,437.98
Principal residence	13,386.40	28,485.08	11,854.36	212.88	202.11	562.99	156.18	252.37	55,112.37
Other real estate	370.44	1,184.14	1,307.68	221.59	461.36	681.32	0.00	29.15	4,255.68
Household goods	6,164.09	2,687.17	1,149.17	141.08	13.30	37.73	10.42	4.00	10,206.96
Total real property	19,920.93	32,356.40	14,311.21	575.55	676.77	1,282.05	166.60	285.52	69,575.02
Profit-sharing plans	149.46	84.59	38.53	0.00	48.62	18.29	0.00	0.81	340.30
Retirement plans	793.29	290.78	234.61	0.00	11.24	0.00	0.00	0.00	1,329.92
Estates in probate	3.24	0.00	0.00	0.00	0.00	4,865.92	0.00	75.13	4,944.30
Total miscellaneous assets	945.99	375.37	273.14	0.00	59.86	4,884.21	0.00	75.94	6,614.52
Total assets	32,595.02	41,272.92	23,512.82	4,116.97	1,272.00	8,173.29	2,333.85	25,307.52	138,584.38

NOTES and SOURCES: As for Table V-13.

TABLE V-15

Components of Wealth for Individuals Aged 35 to 44, Classified by Wealth

(*$million*)

| | Wealth Class ($thousand) | | | | | | | | |
	Below 15	15–30	30–60	60–100	100–200	200–500	500–1,000	Over 1,000	Total
Checking accounts	1,013.83	620.96	760.07	331.32	475.60	179.47	21.15	66.80	3,469.20
Savings deposits	4,692.28	1,744.57	2,992.37	597.22	2,299.44	719.72	11.38	27.67	13,084.64
Credit balance of brokerage accounts	0.00	0.00	98.71	2.94	0.66	0.97	0.00	1.24	104.53
Total cash	5,706.11	2,365.52	3,851.14	931.48	2,775.71	900.16	32.53	95.71	16,658.36
Federal savings bonds	1,370.05	317.89	384.66	22.42	156.50	45.68	2.50	5.50	2,305.21
Other federal securities	0.00	50.35	67.73	0.00	25.69	20.68	7.47	136.22	308.13
State and local government bonds	0.00	0.00	0.00	0.00	26.91	57.71	13.08	515.11	612.81
Corporate and foreign bonds	6.77	29.38	140.39	2.19	15.93	7.43	8.29	19.01	229.39
Total bonds	1,376.83	397.62	592.78	24.61	225.03	131.49	31.34	675.83	3,455.54
Traded stock	306.47	1,228.16	1,168.89	1,078.50	2,756.20	1,786.76	1,148.45	4,230.87	13,704.31
Closely held stock	5.21	539.62	2,062.79	1,670.82	9,026.45	2,492.90	604.44	15,221.50	31,623.74
Stock, type unavailable	0.00	0.64	146.88	48.54	34.98	51.02	0.00	0.00	282.05
Investment clubs	0.00	0.00	19.50	18.27	0.00	3.49	0.00	0.66	41.92
Total stocks	311.68	1,768.41	3,398.06	2,816.13	11,817.63	4,334.18	1,752.90	19,453.03	45,652.02

(*continued*)

TABLE V-15 *(concluded)*

	Wealth Class ($thousand)								
	Below 15	15–30	30–60	60–100	100–200	200–500	500–1,000	Over 1,000	Total
Mortgages and notes	844.31	389.50	1,106.77	1,201.07	1,715.48	384.93	47.59	222.05	5,911.70
Equity life insurance	5,507.48	3,124.47	2,976.85	1,038.67	938.42	351.49	88.71	83.10	14,109.18
Annuities	12.92	35.33	1.38	3.44	201.92	0.00	0.00	0.00	254.99
Trust assets	268.61	42.47	155.89	21.96	282.91	550.62	12,745.51	2,922.63	16,990.60
Noncorporate business assets	4,354.64	2,160.43	12,804.78	2,500.56	4,665.06	3,057.58	77.83	134.35	29,755.23
Total other financial assets	10,987.96	5,752.20	17,045.67	4,765.70	7,803.78	4,344.62	12,959.64	3,362.13	67,021.70
Principal residence	23,043.36	44,413.06	21,967.62	7,305.44	7,675.01	2,015.20	189.21	573.03	107,181.92
Other real estate	1,055.91	1,835.99	4,469.19	4,846.73	8,389.99	3,209.69	306.06	498.93	24,612.48
Household goods	6,686.54	3,707.34	2,517.65	653.70	640.45	208.73	155.01	52.67	14,622.09
Total real property	30,785.81	49,956.39	28,954.46	12,805.87	16,705.44	5,433.61	650.28	1,124.63	146,416.48
Profit-sharing plans	261.48	681.94	691.18	2.49	195.92	35.36	115.65	21.57	2,005.58
Retirement plans	2,535.82	1,290.20	828.81	183.04	63.22	5.92	21.31	49.34	4,977.65
Estates in probate	27.23	41.09	0.83	1.88	456.21	1.83	24.96	0.00	554.03
Total miscellaneous assets	2,824.53	2,013.23	1,520.82	187.40	715.35	43.12	161.92	70.90	7,537.27
Total assets	51,992.92	62,253.37	55,362.91	21,531.19	40,042.95	15,187.18	15,588.60	24,782.24	286,741.36

NOTES and SOURCES: As for Table V-13.

TABLE V-16

Components of Wealth for Individuals Aged 45 to 54, Classified by Wealth

($million)

	Wealth Class ($thousand)								
	Below 15	15–30	30–60	60–100	100–200	200–500	500–1,000	Over 1,000	Total
Checking accounts	1,322.32	950.58	997.95	334.53	309.98	448.62	117.06	202.72	4,683.76
Savings deposits	6,489.42	4,732.21	4,971.15	1,726.86	852.50	623.57	221.59	417.90	20,035.19
Credit balance of brokerage accounts	0.00	0.00	287.79	0.00	1.85	7.92	0.11	36.34	334.00
Total cash	7,811.74	5,682.79	6,256.88	2,061.38	1,164.33	1,080.10	338.76	656.97	25,052.95
Federal savings bonds	832.10	1,122.17	1,205.43	966.64	151.52	256.45	24.42	2.07	4,560.80
Other federal securities	0.00	0.00	0.00	0.00	1.83	8.23	2.04	90.61	102.72
State and local government bonds	0.00	0.00	0.00	36.20	42.36	82.37	162.38	667.72	991.04
Corporate and foreign bonds	48.64	0.00	156.28	243.16	3.48	152.37	10.26	458.61	1,072.80
Total bonds	880.74	1,122.17	1,361.71	1,246.00	199.19	499.43	199.11	1,219.01	6,727.35
Traded stock	707.25	915.19	6,104.57	3,811.44	4,371.12	4,836.16	1,328.71	11,261.80	33,336.24
Closely held stock	0.00	415.48	817.35	431.12	2,023.10	8,877.26	4,806.28	35,770.91	53,141.50
Stock, type unavailable	0.00	0.00	0.00	0.00	109.15	93.63	0.00	0.00	202.78
Investment clubs	0.82	0.96	109.28	27.51	3.45	2.77	0.31	0.26	145.37
Total stocks	708.07	1,331.63	7,031.21	4,270.07	6,506.81	13,809.82	6,135.30	47,032.97	86,825.88

(continued)

TABLE V-16 *(concluded)*

	Wealth Class ($thousand)								
	Below 15	15–30	30–60	60–100	100–200	200–500	500–1,000	Over 1,000	Total
Mortgages and notes	207.56	1,541.70	1,902.72	799.10	3,310.43	1,343.91	100.48	1,458.91	10,664.81
Equity life insurance	4,990.57	3,419.02	2,717.06	880.05	864.91	784.56	191.42	277.20	14,124.80
Annuities	28.63	82.21	38.20	2.48	0.00	0.00	0.00	11.49	163.00
Trust assets	93.96	10.16	383.56	152.33	0.00	18.36	315.77	1,682.34	2,656.47
Noncorporate business assets	741.85	5,542.70	10,814.53	7,410.08	996.96	5,386.87	3,959.08	2,855.01	37,707.09
Total other financial assets	6,062.57	10,595.78	15,856.08	9,244.03	5,172.31	7,533.71	4,566.74	6,284.95	65,316.17
Principal residence	37,999.42	42,344.00	25,247.92	7,063.04	5,630.51	3,751.50	1,028.07	1,006.89	124,071.36
Other real estate	1,384.54	6,519.09	5,358.80	3,915.87	3,127.72	2,616.86	2,636.26	5,270.67	30,829.81
Household goods	5,959.60	4,416.16	3,128.83	774.26	653.01	2,032.06	50.01	870.01	17,883.94
Total real property	45,343.56	53,279.25	33,735.55	11,753.17	9,411.24	8,400.43	3,714.34	7,147.57	172,785.11
Profit-sharing plans	444.18	411.64	623.24	200.84	200.81	106.61	52.47	111.28	2,151.07
Retirement plans	2,005.59	2,670.58	1,495.32	982.52	701.84	366.77	41.15	30.22	8,293.99
Estates in probate	34.39	0.00	2,121.85	0.00	7.12	0.00	33.42	878.08	3,074.86
Total miscellaneous assets	2,484.16	3,082.22	4,240.41	1,183.36	909.77	473.38	127.04	1,019.58	13,519.92
Total assets	63,290.85	75,093.84	68,481.84	29,758.02	23,363.65	31,796.87	15,081.30	63,361.03	370,227.38

NOTES and SOURCES: As for Table V-13.

TABLE V-17

Components of Wealth for Individuals Aged 55 to 64, Classified by Wealth

($million)

	Wealth Class ($thousand)								
	Below 15	15–30	30–60	60–100	100–200	200–500	500–1,000	Over 1,000	Total
Checking accounts	1,630.24	768.75	1,166.41	585.82	1,023.50	417.49	280.26	530.75	6,403.23
Savings deposits	6,103.02	6,113.38	7,691.49	3,222.31	3,482.3	834.66	563.22	667.54	28,677.74
Credit balance of brokerage accounts	0.00	0.26	0.00	0.10	0.71	51.88	3.63	20.83	77.41
Total cash	7,733.27	6,882.39	8,857.90	3,808.22	4,506.54	1,304.02	847.12	1,219.12	35,158.38
Federal savings bonds	1,184.07	1,752.25	3,114.07	1,445.74	1,034.43	565.81	178.61	126.19	9,401.17
Other federal securities	5.46	51.13	119.54	1.81	94.58	28.61	11.09	839.88	1,152.09
State and local government bonds	0.00	0.00	0.00	475.40	35.12	42.46	323.27	3,192.58	4,068.83
Corporate and foreign bonds	16.55	879.62	14.06	258.96	87.50	202.75	127.43	355.97	1,943.23
Total bonds	1,206.08	2,682.99	3,247.66	2,181.91	1,252.03	839.63	640.40	4,514.61	16,565.32
Traded stock	734.22	3,298.49	4,896.77	11,143.40	9,977.53	11,131.92	8,153.40	21,255.28	70,591.47
Closely held stock	152.18	1.09	654.57	537.94	1,797.02	3,373.84	9,590.50	18,501.47	34,608.60
Stock, type unavailable	0.00	336.87	0.00	92.21	4.48	187.96	32.01	0.00	653.53
Investment clubs	2.22	0.00	0.54	1.64	0.00	0.62	41.64	2.78	49.45
Total stocks	888.63	3,636.45	5,551.88	11,775.19	11,779.47	14,694.35	17,817.55	39,759.53	105,903.05

(continued)

TABLE V-17 (concluded)

	Wealth Class ($thousand)								
	Below 15	15–30	30–60	60–100	100–200	200–500	500–1,000	Over 1,000	Total
Mortgages and notes	510.60	186.59	3,394.65	1,243.98	2,693.80	4,987.95	1,162.29	1,183.53	15,363.41
Equity life insurance	5,806.46	3,423.44	2,990.23	1,430.81	2,482.23	753.68	866.49	626.61	18,379.95
Annuities	0.00	101.03	130.08	86.20	77.04	22.98	2.41	12.37	432.10
Trust assets	50.53	22.28	846.73	0.00	842.19	146.32	135.54	3,144.97	5,188.56
Noncorporate business assets	3,492.02	4,092.73	13,851.88	2,714.30	9,616.86	16,073.37	363.35	2,918.35	53,122.86
Total other financial assets	9,859.61	7,826.08	21,213.57	5,475.29	15,712.12	21,984.30	2,530.08	7,885.84	92,486.88
Principal residence	23,238.79	28,844.78	25,958.76	8,261.94	5,651.13	2,251.81	2,388.57	1,541.20	98,136.98
Other real estate	1,171.61	1,483.41	12,625.26	4,321.31	6,965.31	2,897.05	2,149.85	3,980.33	35,594.13
Household goods	3,072.89	2,173.21	2,211.60	752.56	747.20	487.34	140.48	256.48	9,841.76
Total real property	27,483.30	32,501.40	40,795.61	13,335.81	13,363.65	5,636.20	4,678.90	5,778.01	143,572.86
Profit-sharing plans	195.93	154.39	138.67	300.80	687.71	64.76	389.75	176.23	2,108.25
Retirement plans	665.52	796.66	575.99	648.73	466.67	38.37	310.52	141.63	3,644.09
Estates in probate	10.92	25.01	86.73	142.62	272.92	263.54	542.88	530.89	1,875.50
Total miscellaneous assets	872.37	976.07	801.39	1,092.15	1,427.30	366.67	1,243.15	848.75	7,627.84
Total assets	48,043.24	54,505.38	80,468.01	37,668.58	48,040.90	44,825.17	27,757.19	60,005.86	401,314.32

NOTES and SOURCES: As for Table V-13.

TABLE V-18

Components of Wealth for Individuals Over 64 Years Old, Classified by Wealth

($million)

	Wealth Class ($thousand)								
	Below 15	15–30	30–60	60–100	100–200	200–500	500–1,000	Over 1,000	Total
Checking accounts	1,572.08	1,188.98	513.57	404.39	859.12	1,297.47	723.53	931.75	7,490.89
Savings deposits	8,547.51	7,015.50	8,779.57	4,777.20	3,334.91	1,896.69	1,017.45	260.04	35,628.87
Credit balance of brokerage accounts	0.00	0.00	0.00	0.00	0.32	9.56	0.25	2.23	12.35
Total cash	10,119.58	8,204.48	9,293.14	5,181.59	4,194.35	3,203.73	1,741.22	1,194.01	43,132.10
Federal savings bonds	1,532.93	1,661.77	2,472.11	1,593.30	630.46	265.81	355.35	160.13	8,671.87
Other federal securities	0.00	0.00	0.00	116.27	223.75	745.49	810.60	3,039.86	4,935.98
State and local government bonds	0.00	0.00	139.42	81.39	7.77	734.55	2,245.22	3,622.77	6,831.12
Corporate and foreign bonds	0.00	0.00	1,331.69	81.45	0.00	217.17	14.43	638.30	2,283.04
Total bonds	1,532.93	1,661.77	3,943.22	1,872.41	861.98	1,963.02	3,425.61	7,461.06	22,722.01
Traded stock	623.05	2,377.38	5,280.01	6,412.23	4,560.55	32,842.31	12,901.16	26,892.10	91,888.78
Closely held stock	0.00	204.48	991.02	0.00	2,540.30	2,271.34	3,911.59	17,526.06	27,444.79
Stock, type unavailable	0.00	0.00	0.00	0.00	0.00	0.00	1,334.59	1,157.55	2,492.14
Investment clubs	0.84	0.00	0.00	0.00	0.00	0.00	0.00	0.00	0.84
Total stocks	623.88	2,581.87	6,271.03	6,412.23	7,100.85	35,113.65	18,147.33	45,575.71	121,826.55

(continued)

TABLE V-18 (concluded)

| | Wealth Class ($thousand) | | | | | | | | |
	Below 15	15–30	30–60	60–100	100–200	200–500	500–1,000	Over 1,000	Total
Mortgages and notes	1,101.02	521.56	1,066.18	1,676.03	191.89	2,372.79	3,252.70	1,033.71	11,215.89
Equity life insurance	5,393.34	2,678.87	1,878.65	865.50	547.63	1,588.54	1,486.20	623.34	15,062.07
Annuities	43.79	70.13	0.00	0.00	51.64	10.61	0.00	56.57	232.75
Trust assets	0.00	0.00	0.00	455.99	200.90	1,205.37	76.69	972.24	2,911.19
Noncorporate business assets	1,158.62	7,615.21	5,900.67	13,968.57	3,066.63	4,599.70	1,574.87	2,553.73	40,437.99
Total other financial assets	7,696.77	10,885.77	8,845.51	16,966.08	4,058.69	9,777.01	6,390.46	5,239.58	69,859.88
Principal residence	22,414.81	22,721.99	15,500.67	7,214.69	3,377.56	3,301.17	3,107.96	1,342.19	78,981.05
Other real estate	2,355.66	2,593.99	6,315.98	7,096.64	1,565.70	3,162.76	5,068.86	4,367.20	32,526.81
Household goods	1,421.33	1,163.91	704.27	589.85	199.49	186.78	215.08	112.51	4,593.22
Total real property	26,191.80	26,479.89	22,520.92	14,901.19	5,142.75	6,650.71	8,391.90	5,821.90	116,101.07
Profit-sharing plans	9.95	5.99	0.00	0.00	0.00	93.95	6.37	179.73	295.99
Retirement plans	157.93	60.13	400.43	82.91	0.00	123.76	47.05	42.41	914.62
Estates in probate	0.00	0.00	25.49	0.00	0.00	15.57	52.55	0.00	93.61
Total miscellaneous assets	167.88	66.12	425.92	82.91	0.00	233.27	105.98	222.14	1,304.22
Total assets	46,332.86	49,879.91	51,299.75	45,416.41	21,358.62	56,941.39	38,202.51	65,514.41	374,945.83

Notes and Sources: As for Table V-13.

TABLE V-19

Components of Wealth for Individuals Classified by Wealth

(*$million*)

	Wealth Class ($thousand)								
	Below 15	15–30	30–60	60–100	100–200	200–500	500–1,000	Over 1,000	Total
Checking accounts	6,488.25	3,836.47	3,714.80	1,697.15	2,670.77	2,361.22	1,163.78	1,735.84	23,668.27
Savings deposits	30,945.01	20,513.35	25,281.85	10,333.86	10,327.73	4,161.89	1,826.35	1,373.87	104,763.91
Credit balance of brokerage accounts	0.00	5.63	386.52	3.20	6.40	83.51	3.99	87.08	576.33
Total cash	37,433.26	24,355.44	29,383.17	12,034.22	13,004.90	6,606.62	2,994.11	3,196.79	129,008.51
Federal savings bonds	6,290.75	4,951.25	7,260.52	4,050.90	1,990.15	1,141.38	571.72	294.16	26,550.84
Other federal securities	5.46	101.48	215.35	118.08	471.04	809.23	831.22	4,196.45	6,748.31
State and local government bonds	0.00	0.00	139.42	605.63	155.73	917.08	2,743.95	8,128.95	12,690.78
Corporate and foreign bonds	135.02	909.00	1,647.02	585.79	363.38	579.72	165.47	1,472.63	5,858.03
Total bonds	6,431.22	5,961.73	9,262.32	5,360.41	2,980.30	3,447.42	4,312.37	14,092.19	51,847.95
Traded stock	3,389.34	8,558.51	18,032.04	26,139.47	22,099.21	30,884.57	24,893.64	64,364.13	218,360.90
Closely held stock	157.40	1,396.67	8,723.00	2,782.03	15,796.39	17,954.02	20,601.32	87,254.57	154,665.40
Stock, type unavailable	0.00	337.50	146.88	140.75	148.60	332.61	1,366.60	1,157.71	3,630.65
Investment clubs	31.16	7.26	133.90	47.43	7.20	7.16	41.96	3.69	279.76
Total stocks	3,577.90	10,299.94	27,035.81	29,109.67	38,051.40	69,178.37	46,903.52	152,780.11	376,936.71

(*continued*)

TABLE V-19 (concluded)

	Wealth Class ($thousand)								
	Below 15	15–30	30–60	60–100	100–200	200–500	500–1,000	Over 1,000	Total
Mortgages and notes	2,844.42	3,213.16	7,851.85	4,989.63	7,916.63	9,110.64	4,622.77	3,913.77	44,462.85
Equity life insurance	32,509.51	15,728.92	12,132.98	4,346.38	4,870.14	3,534.22	2,650.33	1,619.36	77,391.84
Annuities	85.34	288.70	169.66	92.12	330.60	33.59	2.41	80.42	1,082.84
Trust assets	1,093.93	74.91	1,859.03	785.79	1,326.00	2,824.48	13,875.53	32,432.04	54,271.70
Noncorporate business assets	15,035.04	22,764.77	44,303.73	26,638.07	19,794.35	29,389.80	6,042.35	8,461.44	172,429.54
Total other financial assets	51,568.23	42,070.46	66,317.24	36,851.99	34,237.71	44,892.73	27,193.38	46,507.03	349,638.77
Principal residence	120,082.77	169,172.74	100,529.33	30,125.26	22,536.32	11,882.67	6,870.00	4,715.68	465,714.78
Other real estate	6,472.62	13,848.99	30,076.91	20,402.15	20,510.08	12,567.68	10,228.32	14,146.27	128,253.03
Household goods	24,272.60	14,285.67	9,719.63	2,918.66	2,253.44	2,952.64	570.99	1,295.68	58,269.31
Total real property	150,827.99	197,307.41	140,325.87	53,446.07	45,299.84	27,402.99	17,669.32	20,157.63	652,437.11
Profit-sharing plans	1,080.58	1,351.30	1,491.62	504.13	1,133.06	318.97	564.24	489.61	6,933.52
Retirement plans	6,304.82	5,108.36	3,535.61	1,897.19	1,242.97	534.82	420.03	263.60	19,307.39
Estates in probate	75.78	66.10	2,843.13	144.50	736.25	5,146.86	979.42	1,484.10	11,476.14
Total miscellaneous assets	7,461.18	6,525.76	7,870.36	2,545.82	3,112.28	6,000.65	1,963.69	2,237.32	37,717.05
Total assets	257,299.79	286,520.73	280,194.77	139,348.17	136,686.43	157,528.78	101,036.38	238,971.05	1,597,586.09

NOTES and SOURCES: As for Table V-13.

TABLE V-20

Components of Wealth for Independent Individuals Less than 25 Years Old, Classified by Wealth

($million)

| | Wealth Class ($thousand) | | | | | | | | |
	Below 15	15–30	30–60	60–100	100–200	200–500	500–1,000	Over 1,000	Total
Checking accounts	163.36	33.19	2.56	0.64	0.00	0.00	0.00	0.00	199.75
Savings deposits	370.14	51.35	0.00	0.00	0.00	0.00	0.00	0.00	421.49
Credit balance of brokerage accounts	0.00	0.00	0.00	0.64	0.00	0.00	0.00	0.00	0.64
Total cash	533.49	84.54	2.56	1.28	0.00	0.00	0.00	0.00	621.87
Federal savings bonds	140.56	0.00	0.00	0.00	0.00	0.00	0.00	0.00	140.56
Other federal securities	0.00	0.00	0.00	0.00	0.00	0.00	0.00	0.00	0.00
State and local government bonds	0.00	0.00	0.00	0.00	0.00	0.00	0.00	0.00	0.00
Corporate and foreign bonds	0.00	0.00	0.00	0.00	0.00	0.00	0.00	0.00	0.00
Total bonds	140.56	0.00	0.00	0.00	0.00	0.00	0.00	0.00	140.56
Traded stock	40.53	53.12	0.00	19.46	0.00	0.00	0.00	0.00	113.10
Closely held stock	0.00	0.00	0.00	0.00	0.00	0.00	0.00	0.00	0.00
Stock, type unavailable	0.00	0.00	0.00	0.00	0.00	0.00	0.00	0.00	0.00
Investment clubs	0.00	0.00	0.00	0.00	0.00	0.00	0.00	0.00	0.00
Total stocks	40.53	53.12	0.00	19.46	0.00	0.00	0.00	0.00	113.10

(continued)

TABLE V-20 (*concluded*)

	Wealth Class ($thousand)								
	Below 15	15–30	30–60	60–100	100–200	200–500	500–1,000	Over 1,000	Total
Mortgages and notes	0.81	8.60	0.00	0.00	0.00	0.00	0.00	0.00	9.41
Equity life insurance	1,501.98	139.79	14.11	0.02	0.00	0.00	0.00	0.00	1,655.89
Annuities	0.00	0.00	0.00	0.00	0.00	0.00	0.00	0.00	0.00
Trust assets	383.56	0.00	0.00	0.00	0.00	0.00	0.00	0.00	383.56
Noncorporate business assets	29.85	70.31	0.00	14.42	0.00	0.00	0.00	0.00	114.58
Total other financial assets	1,916.20	218.70	14.11	14.43	0.00	0.00	0.00	0.00	2,163.44
Principal residence	1,231.94	2,363.83	0.00	67.27	0.00	0.00	0.00	0.00	3,663.04
Other real estate	134.46	232.37	0.00	0.00	0.00	0.00	0.00	0.00	366.83
Household goods	1,638.23	137.89	8.11	7.21	0.00	0.00	0.00	0.00	1,791.43
Total real property	3,004.63	2,734.09	8.11	74.48	0.00	0.00	0.00	0.00	5,821.31
Profit-sharing plans	0.00	12.74	0.00	0.00	0.00	0.00	0.00	0.00	12.74
Retirement plans	44.38	0.00	0.41	0.00	0.00	0.00	0.00	0.00	44.78
Estates in probate	0.00	0.00	608.23	0.00	0.00	0.00	0.00	0.00	608.23
Total miscellaneous assets	44.38	12.74	608.64	0.00	0.00	0.00	0.00	0.00	665.76
Total assets	5,679.78	3,103.19	633.42	109.01	0.00	0.00	0.00	0.00	9,525.41

NOTES: As for Tables V-1 and V-3.
SOURCE: Individual responses to 1963 Federal Reserve Board Survey of the Financial Characteristics of Consumers.

Estimates of the Market Value of the Outstanding Corporate Stock of All Domestic Corporations

PETER EILBOTT

QUEENS COLLEGE

1. INTRODUCTION

This appendix discusses the procedure for estimating the market value of all outstanding stock (both common and preferred) of domestic corporations; that is, companies incorporated in the United States. Two sets of data are derived. One represents the value of all outstanding stock, including shares held by other corporations. Included in this total, unavoidably, are the shares of some companies which are 100 percent owned by other companies, even though these wholly owned subsidiaries should really be excluded from the compilations. The other set of data represents the value of all outstanding stock exclusive of intercorporate holdings, including 100 percent owned subsidiaries.

Shares of nonprofit corporations are excluded from the totals, as are shares issued by investment companies (defined as all companies registered under the Investment Company Act of 1940). The market value of the outstanding shares of investment companies listed on exchanges is included in the totals for the exchanges, however; and the market value of the outstanding shares of unlisted investment companies is included in the value of privately held stock, though the value of all of these shares is excluded from the overall totals.

2. THE MARKET VALUE OF ALL OUTSTANDING STOCK

Table VI-1 shows the estimated market-value totals and their components. Briefly, the procedure used to derive the estimates involves the summation of the following values, which are obtained separately; the

TABLE VI-1

The Market Value of the Outstanding Stock of Domestic Corporations

(*all values year-end, $billion*)

	Companies Listed on the New York Stock Exchange (1)	Companies Listed on the American Exchange (2)	Companies Listed on Other Exchanges (3)	Large Companies Traded Over-the-Counter (4)
1952	118.2	12.5	3.1	28.0
1953	115.3	11.3	2.8	27.3
1954	166.1	16.4	3.6	38.0
1955	203.6	20.1	4.0	45.0
1956	214.5	23.0	3.8	46.0
1957	192.1	19.3	3.1	44.0
1958	271.8	24.1	4.3	59.0
1959	302.6	19.1	4.2	66.0
1960	302.1	18.0	4.1	69.1
1961	381.7	25.4	5.3	105.8
1962	339.9	17.7	4.0	90.1
1963	404.2	18.9	4.3	98.8
1964	465.7	19.9	4.3	120.8
1965	528.5	21.3	4.7	137.3
1966	474.2	19.4	4.0	131.4
1967	595.4	32.5	4.0	172.0
1968	680.1	49.6	5.1	220.7

Source: See text.

resulting totals are then adjusted to eliminate the shares of investment companies:

1. The value of the shares of all domestic corporations listed on United States stock exchanges.

2. The value of the shares of large domestic corporations traded over the counter (OTC), derived basically from SEC data.

Open-End Investment Companies (5)	Investment Companies Registered with SEC (6)	Privately Held Companies and Small Companies Traded Over-the-Counter (7)	All Domestic Corporations (1+2+3+4+ 5−6+7) (8)	All Domestic Corporations Excl. Intercorporate Holdings (9)
3.9	6.5	66.2	225.4	180.8
4.1	6.8	65.5	219.7	177.3
6.1	10.2	78.0	298.0	246.4
7.8	12.9	84.7	352.3	290.3
9.0	14.4	69.5	351.4	291.0
8.7	12.8	59.1	313.5	262.4
13.2	18.8	95.1	448.7	372.4
15.8	22.5	113.9	499.1	417.7
17.0	24.8	109.3	494.8	416.6
22.8	32.0	149.8	658.8	553.4
21.3	32.1	123.3	564.2	470.5
25.2	38.1	185.0	698.3	595.0
29.1	43.4	195.8	792.2	673.4
35.2	49.8	216.3	893.5	757.7
34.8	48.8	196.2	811.2	689.5
44.7	64.1	250.3	1,034.8	879.6
52.7	75.9	297.1	1,229.4	1,045.0

3. The value of the shares of privately held domestic corporations and of small corporations traded OTC. The data are obtained by subtracting estimated dividend payments of listed companies, large OTC companies, and investment companies from total dividend payments of all domestic corporations; the residuals are then blown up on the basis of yield data derived on a sample basis.

A detailed description of the estimating procedure and the sources from which the estimates were derived is presented below.

a. Listed Companies

1. The value of the shares of domestic companies listed on the New York Stock Exchange—Data obtained from the exchange.

2. The value of the shares of domestic companies listed on the American Stock Exchange—Data obtained from the exchange, except for the years 1952 through 1955, when the market value of domestic listed companies was not broken out separately. It was assumed that in these four years, domestic companies accounted for 74 percent of the market value of all listed stock on the ASE (the average percentage throughout the later 1950's and most of the 1960's).

3. The value of the shares of domestic companies listed on other United States stock exchanges—Data obtained from the annual reports of the SEC; they refer only to companies not also listed on another exchange. The SEC broke out the market value of foreign companies listed on other exchanges only after 1959. It was assumed that in previous years the market value of foreign companies accounted for 0.3 percent of the value of all stock listed on other exchanges (the average percentage in the years 1960 through 1963).

b. Large Companies Traded Over the Counter

For the years 1952 through 1963, except for 1953, the SEC in its annual reports published a year-end market value figure for large over-the-counter (OTC) companies. That is, it estimated the market value of all issues (common and preferred) of those companies traded OTC which had more than 300 shareholders of record. Included in the total were industrial companies, banks, insurance companies, public utilities, and real estate and other financial companies. Excluded from the total were stocks admitted to listed or unlisted trading privileges on stock exchanges, Canadian and other foreign companies, and investment companies. About 3,500 companies were included in the SEC total in 1952, and the number increased to over 4,100 by 1963. The OTC market value data derived here represent the SEC totals in the years between 1952 and 1963, except for 1953. The 1953 figure was obtained by interpolating between the 1952 and 1954 SEC data on the basis of the changes in the National Quotation Bureau's index of 35 industrial stocks during the two years.

No SEC data are available after 1963, since the tabulations were then discontinued. A 1964 figure was obtained from the New York Stock

Exchange Census of Shareowners,[1] which provides an estimate of the market value of the outstanding stock of 4,150 large OTC companies at the end of 1964. The NYSE total was adjusted upward on the basis of the relationship between the 1961 SEC figure and the 1962 NYSE Census figure[2] (giving an estimate of the market value of the outstanding stock of about 3,675 large OTC companies at the end of 1961). That is, the 1961 SEC total was 4 percent larger than the 1961 NYSE total; therefore, the 1964 NYSE market-value estimate was increased by 4 percent.

Data for 1965 through 1968 were obtained on the basis of changes in the NQB industrial index, Moody's bank stock index, and Moody's two insurance stock indexes (life, and fire and casualty) during these years. For the period 1957 through 1963, in which the SEC reported not only a total OTC value, but also broke it down into three components (banks, insurance companies, and industrials and all other), each year's values were projected to the end of the following year in two ways:

1. The total market-value estimate was projected on the basis of the percentage change in the NQB index.

2. The three components of the total were projected on the basis of the change in the relevant index, and the projections were then summed. The average percentage change in the insurance sector was obtained by weighting the two insurance indexes on the basis of market values in the two sectors. These values were obtained by blowing up Internal Revenue Service data on the amount of dividends paid by life insurance stock companies and by other insurance companies on the basis of Moody's data on yields of life insurance companies and fire and casualty companies.[3] This procedure assumes that OTC issues with more than 300 shareholders of record accounted for the same proportion of the total outstanding stock of both types of insurance company.

The projected totals came close to the actual SEC (or adjusted NYSE) value in most cases: 9 of the 14 projections were within 5 percent of the actual value; and 13 of the 14 were within 8 percent of the reported total. The results were slightly better using three indexes instead of one, though

---

[1] *Shareownership USA: The 1965 Census of Shareowners*, New York, New York Stock Exchange, 1965.

[2] *The 17 Million: The 1962 Census of Shareowners*, New York, New York Stock Exchange, 1962.

[3] Between 1966 and 1968, when no IRS data were available, it was assumed that the market value of life insurance companies was 50 percent greater than that of fire and casualty companies (on the basis of the relationship in previous years).

the differences were small. In 8 of the 14 cases, the projected values were smaller than the actual values, and errors of understatement were larger than errors of overstatement. The slight downward bias resulting from use of the indexes presumably reflects the fact that the number of companies covered by the SEC increased by about 600 during the period.

Since the component projection method is more logical—and also performed slightly better—it was employed to project market values for 1965 through 1968. (While an overall 1964 OTC value was available from the NYSE, no industry data were reported. Therefore, the 1963 SEC industry totals were projected by the index method, and the resulting values were adjusted upward so that their sum equaled the overall OTC value derived from the NYSE.)

The projected value of large OTC companies at the end of 1968 was $220.7 billion (based on about 4,100 companies). The NYSE reported that the actual market value of about 7,450 large OTC companies was $366 billion at the end of 1969.[4] The projections, therefore, proved to be reasonably accurate, since the actual value was based on about 80 percent more companies than the projected one, and there was a moderate decline in the various OTC indexes between the end of 1968 and the end of 1969.

c. *Investment Companies*

To eliminate the market value of investment companies from the total estimated value of all outstanding stock, the value of open-end companies which are members of the Investment Company Institute (ICI) is added to the value of all other stock (listed, OTC, and privately held), and the value of all investment companies registered with the SEC is then subtracted from the resulting total. Investment companies which are registered with the SEC, but which are not ICI members, are either listed on exchanges, and therefore included in the exchange market-value totals (these are primarily closed-ends), or they are included in the estimates of the value of privately held stock. ICI members, on the other hand, while registered with the SEC, are neither listed nor in the privately held total.

Year-end data on the market value of ICI members are obtained from the ICI. Data on the market values of investment companies registered with the SEC, as of June 30, are obtained from the SEC Annual Reports. These data are adjusted to year-end totals by interpolating between June 30 values for ICI members. For example, the value of ICI open-ends

---

[4] *Shareownership—1970: The 1970 Census of Shareowners*, New York, New York Stock Exchange, 1970.

increased by 15.8 percent between June 30, 1962 and December 31, 1962, and by 28.8 percent between June 30, 1962 and June 30, 1963; the value of investment companies registered with the SEC increased by 31.9 percent between June 30, 1962 and June 30, 1963. Therefore, the value of investment companies registered with the SEC is assumed to have increased by $(15.8/28.8) \times 31.9$ percent between June 30, 1962 and December 31, 1962.

For the years 1952 through 1954, in which June 30 data were not available from the ICI, year-end market values of investment companies registered with the SEC were obtained by extrapolating the 1955 year-end SEC total (obtained by the method discussed in the previous paragraph) backward on the basis of the year-end to year-end changes in the value of ICI open-ends.

d. Privately Held and Small Over-the-Counter Companies

The market value of privately held companies (all domestic corporations which are not listed, not traded OTC, and not members of the ICI)[5] and of small OTC companies is derived by blowing up their estimated total dividend payments on the basis of yield data obtained primarily from a sample of ASE stocks. Dividend payments are obtained by subtracting dividends paid by listed companies, large OTC companies, and investment companies from total dividends paid by all U.S. corporations. The errors contained in the resulting market-value totals are discussed following the explanation of the procedure.

Method of Calculation

(*1*) *Total dividends paid by all U.S. corporations.* Data obtained from the IRS *Statistics of Income, Corporation Tax Returns.* Dividends paid include distributions in cash and other assets—but not in their own stock—by all U.S. corporations. Liquidating dividends and capital gains distributions are included in the data.

Minus (*2*) *Dividends paid by domestic corporations listed on the NYSE.* Data obtained from the exchange. They represent total cash distributions, including liquidating dividends and capital gains distributions. Before 1966, the exchange reported the amount of dividends paid by all listed companies, as well as dividend payments by listed foreign companies; the amount of dividends paid by domestic companies could therefore be

---

[5] As previously indicated, the total value of privately held companies unavoidably includes the value of some wholly owned subsidiaries, though these companies are eliminated when a total market-value figure, net of intercorporate holdings, is derived.

obtained directly. Dividend payments by foreign listed companies have not been reported since 1965, though the market value of these companies is reported. Since there was relatively little difference, in most years before 1965, between the yield on all listed stock and the yield on foreign listed stock, dividend payments by foreign companies after 1965 were estimated by applying the yield on all listed stock to the average yearly market value of listed foreign stock.

Minus (3) Dividends paid by domestic corporations listed on the ASE and on other exchanges. Since dividend data are not reported by these exchanges, dividend payments were estimated on a sample basis. For each year between 1952 and 1968, the percentage of ASE stocks which were dividend-paying, as well as the average yield on dividend-paying stocks, was estimated on the basis of a sample of about one hundred stocks. The high and low prices for the year, as well as the amount of dividends paid (if any), were determined for each of these stocks every year. Foreign issues and issues of investment companies were excluded from the sample.

About 25 percent of the stocks in the sample were non-dividend-payers in 1952, and the percentage increased fairly steadily to over 50 percent by 1968. Non-dividend-paying stocks were concentrated in the lower price ranges; therefore, a weighting procedure was used to determine what percentage of the total *market value* of all ASE stocks they accounted for. Each year's sample was broken up into different average-price categories: $0–$10, $10–$20, and so on; for example, a stock whose high price for the year was $37, and whose low price was $18, fell into the $20–$30 category. The number of non-dividend-paying stocks in each price category was multiplied by the average price in that category, the total was summed, and the sum was expressed as a percentage of the sum of the total number of stocks in each price category multiplied by the average price in that category. On the basis of this weighting procedure, the percentage of the total market value of all ASE stocks accounted for by non-dividend-paying stocks increased from about 10 percent in 1952 to about 44 percent in 1968.[6]

The increase apparently reflects the fact that a substantial number of old, established companies, which tended to be dividend-payers, were listed on the ASE in the 1940's and early 1950's. Many of these companies

[6] This weighting procedure is accurate only if the higher-priced stocks have as many shares outstanding as the lower-priced ones. On the basis of a small sample of stocks that was checked in one year, this seemed to be a reasonable assumption, but there was not enough time to engage in a more thorough verification.

have since been listed on the NYSE. Their place has been taken, for the most part, by smaller and newer companies, which concentrate on growth and tend to follow a policy of retaining all earnings.

The average yield on each dividend-paying stock was obtained by dividing its yearly dividend payment by the average of its high and low price for the year. The weighting procedure previously employed was then used to determine the average yield for all dividend-paying stocks; that is, the average yield of dividend-paying stocks in the various price categories was weighted on the basis of the number of such stocks and the average price in each of the categories. The data indicate that during the period 1952–68, average yields of dividend-paying stocks on the ASE corresponded fairly closely to average yields of dividend-paying stocks listed on the NYSE, and to those contained in the NQB index (though the percentage of stocks which were non-dividend-payers was much higher than on the NYSE).

The average market value of domestic stocks listed on the ASE and on other exchanges was then derived by averaging the market values at the beginning and end of each year. For example, the market value of domestic stocks listed on the ASE and on other exchanges was $26.8 billion at the end of 1956, and $22.4 billion at the end of 1957; the average market value during 1957 was, therefore, assumed to be $24.6 billion. Each year's average market-value was then multiplied by the percentage of market value estimated to be dividend-paying, and the resultant total was multiplied by the average yield on dividend-paying stocks in order to obtain the estimates of dividend payments by stocks listed on the ASE and on other exchanges.

The data, as shown in Table VI-2, indicate an increase in dividend payments through 1956, followed by a decline through 1967. This pattern is explained by the fact that the rise in market values between 1952 and 1956 overcame the effect of falling yields. Between 1956 and 1967, the continued fall in yields, combined by relative stability in market values, resulted in a decline in estimated dividend-payments. The failure of market values to rise after 1956 (until 1967) must have been the result of the same factor which apparently caused non-dividend-payers to increase in importance—the replacement of older, well-established companies by newer and smaller ones.

Minus (4) Dividends paid by large industrial companies traded OTC. In 1952, and between 1957 and 1963, as previously indicated, the SEC broke down its OTC total, and an estimate of the market value of industrial stocks was, therefore, available. From 1963 on, market-value estimates were

TABLE VI-2

Estimated Dividends, American Stock Exchange and Other Exchanges,
1952–68

	Yield[a] (percent) (1)	Percent of Market Value Dividend-Paying (2)	Average Market Value in Year ($million) (3)	Dividends (1) × (2) × (3) ($million) (4)
1952	6.0	90.0	15,480	836
1953	5.9	87.7	14,830	767
1954	5.1	90.2	17,050	784
1955	4.7	89.7	22,430	945
1956	4.6	88.5	25,840	1,052
1957	4.7	86.6	24,610	1,002
1958	4.1	84.4	25,400	879
1959	3.8	74.1	25,830	727
1960	4.3	67.4	22,700	658
1961	3.4	70.0	26,350	627
1962	4.2	65.3	26,200	718
1963	3.6	73.3	22,450	592
1964	3.5	74.0	23,700	614
1965	3.3	69.8	25,100	578
1966	3.2	66.7	24,650	526
1967	2.6	63.5	29,900	495
1968	2.4	55.6	45,580	608

SOURCE: See data description.
[a] Dividend-paying stocks.

obtained (as discussed in the explanation of the derivation of an overall OTC figure) by using the NQB index for extrapolation. Between 1952 and 1957, market-value estimates were obtained by interpolation, using the NQB index. The average market-value of OTC industrial stocks each year was then derived, adopting the same procedure employed for ASE stocks (the average of two year-end values).

Each year's average market value was then multiplied by the percentage of market value estimated to be dividend-paying, using the percentages obtained from the ASE sample (on the assumption that the OTC markets have been characterized by the same trend toward smaller, growth-oriented companies in recent years). The resulting dividend-paying, market-value totals were then multiplied by average-yield values, obtained from a combination of the yield on ASE stocks and the yield on stocks contained in the NQB index, to obtain estimated dividend payments of large industrial companies traded OTC,[7] as shown in Table VI-3.

Minus (5) Dividends paid by banks and insurance companies traded OTC. Data obtained from IRS *Statistics of Income, Corporation Income Tax Returns.* According to the 1959 SEC Annual Report, the 700 banks included in the SEC OTC total accounted for about 75 percent of the assets of all U.S. banks at the end of 1958. At the end of 1968, the 700 largest banks in the country also accounted for about 75 percent of the total assets of all U.S. banks. A few of these banks are now listed, while almost none were in 1958; therefore, the banks which are now traded OTC probably account for less than 75 percent of the assets of all U.S. banks. Nevertheless, as an approximation, 75 percent of the dividends paid each year by all U.S. banks are subtracted. This introduces an error into the residual (because of the listed banks), which is discussed below.

According to the 1958 SEC Annual Report, the 300 insurance companies included in the SEC OTC total had a market value of $11.5 billion at the end of 1957; while 17 insurance companies, with a market value of about $1.6 billion, were then listed on exchanges. There are probably very few privately held insurance companies, and their market value is likely to be very small. Data in Moody's and in the New York State Insurance Reports show that the 150 largest fire and casualty companies write over 95 percent of the insurance written by all fire and casualty companies. According to Moody's, the 150 largest life insurance companies have over 95 percent of the assets of all life insurance companies.

---

[7] The NQB computes a quarterly yield on the stocks in its index, and these were averaged each year to obtain yearly data. Throughout the whole period, the yields conform closely to the yields of stocks contained in the Dow-Jones industrial index. The market value of the 35 stocks in the NQB index represented about 7 percent of the total estimated market value of all OTC industrial stocks (including public utilities) in 1967. In 1950, according to G. Leffler (*The Stock Market*, New York, Ronald Press, 1951), the 35 stocks accounted for about one-sixth of the market value of all OTC industrial stocks (excluding utilities). On the strength of these two bits of information, the ASE and NQB yields each year were weighted on a 90–10 basis, on the assumption that there tends to be some correspondence in quality between ASE stocks and those OTC stocks not included in the NQB index. Since, in most years, there was relatively little difference between the ASE and NQB yields (the ASE yields were generally slightly higher), the particular weights selected would in most cases make very little difference.

TABLE VI-3

Estimated Dividends, Large Over-the-Counter Industrial Stocks, 1952–68

	Yield on 35 Stocks in NQB Index[a] (percent) (1)	Weighted Yield ASE and NQB Stocks[b] (percent) (2)	Percent of Market Value Dividend Paying (3)	Average Market Value in Year ($billion) (4)	Dividends: (2) × (3) × (4) ($million) (5)
1952	5.80	6.00	90.0	16.0[c]	864
1953	5.75	5.90	87.7	15.5	802
1954	5.00	5.10	90.2	18.4	845
1955	4.35	4.60	89.7	24.0	995
1956	4.60	4.60	88.5	26.9	1,095
1957	5.25	4.75	86.6	25.7	1,057
1958	5.00	4.20	84.4	28.2	1,001
1959	3.50	3.75	74.1	34.6	960
1960	3.55	4.20	67.4	37.8	1,070
1961	3.00	3.35	70.0	48.2	1,130
1962	3.25	4.10	65.3	51.6	1,380
1963	3.20	3.55	73.3	46.2	1,202
1964	2.85	3.45	74.0	54.9	1,402
1965	2.80	3.25	69.8	72.5	1,644
1966	3.15	3.20	66.7	81.5	1,740
1967	2.50	2.60	63.5	102.6	1,694
1968	1.90	2.35	55.6	138.2	1,804

SOURCE: See data description.

[a] Average of five quarterly figures, periods ending January 1 through following January 1. Quarterly data are derived from price data at the end of each quarter and from dividends paid during that quarter.

[b] Yield on dividend-paying stocks.

[c] End-of-year value.

(Many of these are not stock companies, but there is no reason to assume that the largest stock companies do not also account for the great bulk of all stock company assets.) As an approximation, 85 percent of the dividends paid by all U.S. insurance companies are subtracted each year; it is implicitly assumed that the remainder represents dividends paid by listed insurance companies and has already been subtracted, and that the privately held total includes no insurance companies.

Minus (6) Capital gains distributions. Total dividends paid by U.S. corporations, as reported by the IRS, include capital gains distributions; these must be subtracted to arrive at a true dividend residual. The totals subtracted here are those reported by the ICI for its member funds. Total capital gains distributions reported in the National Income Supplement in its reconciliation of IRS dividends with National Income dividends are not subtracted; the data include capital gains distributions of listed closed-end funds, and for the most part, these payments had already been removed when NYSE dividends were subtracted.

Minus (7) Dividend payments, open-end mutual funds. Total reported by the ICI. Dividend payments by closed-end funds are not subtracted, since the NYSE dividend total includes payments by listed closed-ends.

Equals (8) Residual. Dividends paid by privately held and small OTC companies. This residual was blown up on the basis of the yield data employed for large OTC industrial stocks; that is, the weighted average of ASE and NQB yields. The use of these yield data represents an attempt to treat privately held and small OTC companies in the same fashion as publicly traded ones. IRS data on the value of privately held stock appearing in estates are not used in the calculations.[8] The IRS tends to value this stock either in terms of book value or, when it tries to determine market value, it apparently uses very conservative price-earnings ratios.

The market-value totals thus derived were increased by 25 percent to take account of non-dividend-paying companies; that is, it was assumed that non-dividend-payers accounted for 20 percent of total market value in the privately held and small OTC sector. The use of this percentage is based on two assumptions. First, that privately held and small publicly traded companies are more likely to be non-dividend-payers than are larger publicly traded companies. Second, that privately held companies (though perhaps not small OTC companies) have not been characterized by the same trend toward a sharp increase in the percentage of non-dividend-payers which has characterized companies listed on the ASE since the late 1950's. The market value of privately held companies is tied, by and large, to book value for estate and for some other purposes though it is treated differently in this analysis; therefore, these companies would not have quite the same incentive as publicly traded ones to retain all of their earnings and to generate a rapid growth of profits, thereby raising the price of their stock and creating capital gains. Consequently, it is arbitrarily assumed that, in the early 1950's, privately held and small OTC companies were more likely to be non-dividend-payers than were listed and large OTC companies, but that the percentage of non-dividend-payers has not changed since.

[8] Internal Revenue Service, *Statistics of Income—1965, Fiduciary, Gift, and Estate Tax Returns*, Washington, D.C., 1967.

The resulting market-value data are yearly averages. They are converted to year-end totals on the basis of the relationship each year between the year-end and the average value of the NYSE composite index. In the years 1966 through 1968, it was assumed that the market value of stock in privately held and small OTC companies accounted for the same percentage of the total market value of all outstanding stock that it accounted for in 1965.

Following are the major problems connected with the estimates of the market value of stock in privately held and small OTC companies (aside from the assumption that 20 percent of the companies are non-dividend-payers).

Evaluation

1. Errors in the size of the residual:

(a) In arriving at a residual, 75 percent of the dividends paid by all U.S. banks have been subtracted since banks traded OTC accounted for 75 percent of the assets of all banks in 1958. Several large banks became listed in the 1960's; therefore, it seems likely that the percentage of total dividends accounted for by OTC banks gradually declined during the decade. Consequently, the amounts subtracted in recent years as dividend payments by OTC banks are too large, and the residuals, therefore, are too small.

(b) In arriving at a residual, 85 percent of the dividends paid by all U.S. insurance companies have been subtracted. The remaining dividends were assumed to represent payments by listed insurance companies, which had already been subtracted. If listed insurance companies increased in importance during the 1960's, the amounts subtracted as dividend payments by OTC insurance companies are too large, and the residuals are too small.

(c) Total dividends paid by all U.S. corporations include liquidating dividends. Liquidating dividends paid by NYSE companies have been deducted but not those paid by other listed, or large OTC, companies. Therefore, too little is being deducted, and the residuals are too large. (This is probably a very small item.)

(d) Total dividends paid by all U.S. corporations include capital gains distributions. Capital gains distributions by investment companies listed on the NYSE, and by open-end companies which are members of the ICI, have been deducted but not those paid by other investment companies. Therefore, too little is being deducted, and the residuals are too large.

(e) It was assumed that non-dividend-payers accounted for the same percentage of both large OTC industrial stocks and ASE stocks. If this assumption is invalid, the amount of dividends paid by large OTC industrial companies is incorrectly estimated and, depending on the direction of the error, the residuals are either too large or too small.

Items (a) and (b) probably outweigh in importance items (c) and (d); in the absence of knowledge of the direction of error in item (e), it seems likely that the dividend residual is too small, and that there is a systematic bias toward underestimating the market value of the stock of privately held and small OTC companies. However, the resulting error is likely to be small. Therefore, mistakes in calculating the size of the dividend residual are unlikely to lead to serious errors in the estimates of the market value of all outstanding stock, unless there is a significant difference between large OTC industrial companies and ASE companies in the importance of non-dividend-payers.

2. Estimates of the market value of privately held and small OTC companies in a particular year may be subject to a fairly sizable error. The total for any year depends crucially not only on the size of the dividend residual, but also on the yield value employed to blow up the residual. Use of a 3.5 percent figure, when the actual yield was 4 percent, would result in an overstatement of market-value totals by one-seventh. Consequently, if the yield data derived from the sample of ASE stocks were unrepresentative, market-value changes in the short run may be considerably distorted. For example, the decline from 1955 to 1956, and the very rapid increases from both 1957 to 1958, and 1962 to 1963, seem unreasonable. For the period 1952–68 as a whole, the yield data seem reasonable. Therefore, if it is appropriate to use these data for the stock of privately held and small OTC companies, the market-value totals over the whole period should tend to be satisfactory, despite shortcomings in the value for any particular year.

3. The estimates of the market value of private held and small OTC companies include the value of open-end investment companies which are not members of the ICI, nonlisted closed-ends, and other types of investment companies, since these companies' dividend payments are in the dividend residual. The value of these companies is not included in the total market value of all stocks, since they are registered with the SEC, and the value of all registered companies has been subtracted in arriving at an overall total. In the same way, listed closed-ends are in the NYSE and in the ASE totals, though they are not in the overall market-value total.

4. The value of wholly owned subsidiaries filing separate tax returns is included in the estimated market value of privately held and small OTC companies. Wholly owned subsidiaries include companies which could file consolidated returns since they are owned 80 percent or more by another company (95 percent before 1954), but which choose to file separate returns. It also includes companies which are completely, or largely, owned by other companies—for example, in the oil industry—but whose ownership is so divided that no one company owns as much as 80 percent of the subsidiary; in this situation, the subsidiary must file a separate return. Dividends paid by subsidiaries filing separate returns are included in total dividends paid by all U.S. corporations and are, therefore, included in the dividend residual, unless the subsidiaries have sufficient public ownership to be listed or traded OTC.

Subsidiaries which have little or no public ownership should really be excluded from the compilations, since they are, for all intents and purposes, part of their parent companies. In the absence of data on the importance of these subsidiaries, there seems to be no way of eliminating them. As discussed below, consolidated filing has increased in importance, so subsidiaries should now account for a smaller percentage of the estimated market value of all outstanding stock than they did in earlier years. In any case, though, these subsidiaries are not included in the estimated market value of all outstanding stock net of intercorporate holdings.

e. Intercorporate Holdings

The total market value of all outstanding stock was reduced each year by the ratio of dividends received by domestic companies from domestic companies to total dividend payments by domestic companies in that year. In computing these ratios, total dividends and capital gains distributions of mutual funds were subtracted from total domestic corporate dividend payments, and dividend income of mutual funds was subtracted from dividend receipts of domestic companies. (The dividend receipts data do not include capital gains income of mutual funds.) This adjustment permits the exclusion of stock held by mutual funds from intercorporate holdings. Data on the dividend income of mutual funds were unavailable; their dividend payouts were used as a proxy (since the funds are required to distribute almost all of their dividend income). In 1966 through 1968, intercorporate holdings were assumed to account for the same percentage of total outstanding stock that they accounted for in the years 1963–65.

The data, as shown in Table VI-4, indicate that the ratio of dividends received to dividends paid declined from a level of about 20 percent in 1952 to a level of about 15 percent in 1963–65. This decline is surprising, considering the extent to which companies have acquired stock in other companies over the last 15 to 20 years. The decline is probably explained, in large part, by an increase in consolidated filings. In 1952, corporations filing consolidated returns accounted for 10 percent of all corporate assets and 17 percent of all dividend payments.[9] In 1965, they accounted for 25 percent of all assets, and 41 percent of all dividend payments.[10] While some of the increase may simply reflect mergers which have occurred during the period (if two previously independent companies merge, they may then file consolidated returns), a large part of the increase probably reflects the fact that subsidiaries which previously filed separate returns are now filing consolidated ones. There were significant changes in the tax laws affecting consolidated returns in both 1954 and 1964; in these two cases, especially in 1964, there was a sharp increase in the number of consolidated returns filed immediately after the law was changed. What has apparently happened, therefore, is that some subsidiaries which used to be in the intercorporate total are no longer recorded as such.

f. Treasury Stock

The market value of stock listed on the NYSE and the ASE includes Treasury stock (shares held in corporate treasuries for stock options, acquisitions, conversions of convertible debentures, and so forth). While the SEC Annual Reports made no specific statements on the subject, it seems likely that the OTC market-value data also included the value of Treasury stock. If stockholdings of the household sector are to be derived as a residual after subtracting all other ownership groups' holdings from the total value of outstanding stock (including Treasury stock), the residual will then be too large. A quick check of a few companies in one year indicated that Treasury stock was insignificant for large companies, but accounted for as much as 10 percent to 20 percent of the total number of outstanding shares of smaller companies.

3. SOURCES OF ERROR IN THE ESTIMATES

Most sources of error in the estimates of the market value of all outstanding stock have already been discussed in the description of the

[9] Internal Revenue Service, *Statistics of Income—1952, Corporation Income Tax Returns*, p. 74.
[10] Internal Revenue Service, *Statistics of Income—1965, Corporation Income Tax Returns*, p. 201.

TABLE VI-4

Dividends Paid and Received by U.S. Corporations, 1952–65

(*$million*)

	Dividends Paid			Dividends Received			Ratio of Dividends Received to Dividends Paid
	All U.S. Corporations[a]	Investment Companies[a]	All U.S. Corporations Except Investment Companies[a]	All U.S. Corporations[b]	Investment Companies[b]	All U.S. Corporations Except Investment Companies[b]	
1952	11,262	280	10,982	2,350	175	2,175	19.8%
1953	11,601	280	11,321	2,389	200	2,189	19.3
1954	11,913	380	11,533	2,332	225	2,107	18.3
1955	13,592	533	13,059	2,572	268	2,304	17.6
1956	14,498	665	13,833	2,688	315	2,373	17.2
1957	14,914	695	14,219	2,681	365	2,316	16.3
1958	14,951	725	14,226	2,829	412	2,417	17.0
1959	16,242	942	15,300	2,948	460	2,488	16.3
1960	17,193	980	16,213	3,084	520	2,564	15.8
1961	18,038	1,135	16,903	3,276	565	2,711	16.0
1962	19,565	1,158	18,407	3,645	595	3,050	16.6
1963	21,105	1,162	19,943	3,592	630	2,962	14.8
1964	23,305	1,355	21,950	4,022	740	3,282	15.0
1965	25,997	1,845	24,152	4,521	845	3,676	15.2

Notes to Table VI-4

SOURCES: Internal Revenue Service, *Statistics of Income—1965, Corporation Income Tax Returns*, Washington, D.C., 1969; Moody's Investors Service, *Moody's Bank and Finance Manual*, New York, 1966.

ᵃ Includes capital gains distributions.

ᵇ Excludes capital gains income. Investment companies' dividend payouts are used as a proxy for their dividend receipts.

---

derivation of the market value of privately held and small OTC companies; errors arising from the assumption that 20 percent of these companies are non-dividend-payers, errors in the size of the dividend residual, and errors arising from the use of the yield data derived from the sample of ASE stocks. There is one additional source of error, arising from a situation the reverse of that caused by the filing of separate tax returns by wholly owned subsidiaries.

A company could be 90 percent, or even 99 percent, owned by another company and file a consolidated return with its parent, while still having enough shareholders to be listed on an exchange, or more probably, to be traded OTC. The total market value of the stock of such a company would be included in the value of listed or OTC stock, but no deduction would be made for that fraction of the company's shares held by its parent corporation, since the IRS would not record either its dividend payments or the dividends received by the parent company from its subsidiary. Western Electric is an example of such a company. Having attained 300 shareholders of record, it was first included in the OTC universe of the SEC in 1960. However, since the company filed a consolidated return with AT&T, that fraction of its shares and market value owned by AT&T (over 98 percent) would not be subtracted in arriving at an estimate of intercorporate holdings.

Under such circumstances, the value of intercorporate holdings is understated, and the market value of all outstanding stock net of intercorporate holdings is overstated. There are not likely to be very many companies which file consolidated returns, but which have a sufficient number of shareholders to be listed or traded OTC; however, there are probably several large companies in this category (including the above mentioned Western Electric and other subsidiaries of AT&T), and they might account for several billion dollars in market value.

4. MARKET VALUES BY INDUSTRY

Table VI-5 shows the industrial distribution of the market value of all outstanding stock. The following procedure was used to obtain these

TABLE VI-5

Market Values of the Outstanding Stock of Domestic Corporations, by Industry, 1952–65

(year-end values; $billion)

Industry	1952	1953	1956	1957	1958	1959	1960	1961	1962	1963	1964	1965
Aircraft	1.6	1.9	4.7	3.2	4.6	4.5	4.4	4.8a	5.7	6.4	8.5	14.7
Amusement	1.8	1.3	1.7a	1.5a	2.4a	1.8	2.4	3.0	2.3	3.1	3.8	4.8
Automotive	11.3	9.8	20.6	15.3	22.6	27.3	20.6	28.7	27.1	36.2	43.7	47.5
Building trades	1.4a	1.3a	3.0a	2.9a	4.5a	4.7a	4.8a	6.0a	4.8a	5.2a	5.6a	6.8
Chemical	24.6	24.7	42.2	38.3	53.0	67.0	62.1	72.9	77.6	90.3	111.0	96.1
Electrical equipment	9.6	10.0	16.3	15.7	22.9	41.6	41.3	52.0	39.8	49.3	50.4	65.5
Financial (incl. investment companies)	34.6	32.9	46.2	54.3	72.8	89.0	92.9	140.8	111.8	135.8	148.3	190.2
Food products	9.7	11.5	11.0	11.3	16.8	17.0	22.7	30.3	25.1	28.3	32.8	38.0
Leather	0.6	0.5	0.6	0.5	0.8	0.9	0.9	0.9	0.9	1.4	1.7	2.1
Machinery and metals	9.4	9.6	16.2	13.3	17.4	27.1	26.4	30.1	22.8	24.8	29.7	42.7
Mining	4.1	3.5	9.5	5.9	9.9	10.4	8.4	9.9	7.6	8.7a	9.6a	12.2a
Office equipment	2.7	2.8	8.0	9.5	13.9	6.3	8.8	17.5	12.3	23.1	23.7	46.1
Paper and publishing	8.6	9.7	16.8	15.0	20.9	20.5	19.1	22.6	17.3	20.6	28.4	31.3
Petroleum and natural gas	34.9	33.6	61.2	46.3	65.0	53.9	53.0	64.8	69.4	95.3	86.7	95.9
Railroads and railroad equipment	8.3	7.2	8.6	5.9	9.0	8.9	7.6	9.2	8.7	10.8	12.6	14.4
Real estate	4.7	4.1	5.2	3.5	7.5	10.2	7.9	10.7	8.6	17.3	16.6	19.8
Retail trade	11.4	12.1	12.5	12.4	19.8	22.4	22.6	35.3	27.4	32.2	48.9	47.8
Rubber	1.9	1.8	3.9	3.7	5.1	7.8	4.5	6.1	4.5	5.4	6.1	6.7
Shipbuilding	0.9	0.9	1.9	1.6	1.6	0.8	1.2	1.1	1.5	1.4	1.8	2.0
Steel and iron	8.0	7.3	17.4	11.5	18.8	20.9	15.8	20.5	13.8	17.8	22.7	25.9
Textile	4.5	3.8	3.7	2.5	4.5	5.1	4.1	6.4	5.8	7.3	11.9	12.9
Tobacco	2.0	2.0	2.1	2.3	3.2	3.6	4.6	7.7	4.2	4.6	4.7	5.4
Utilities	31.4	31.1	47.3	44.6	63.8	68.8	82.1	107.9	96.1	109.9	124.6	111.5
Total	228.0	223.4	360.6	321.0	460.8	520.5	518.2	689.2	595.1	735.2	833.8	940.3

Notes to Table VI-5

SOURCE: See text.
ᵃ New York Stock Exchange market value only.

---

estimates. Limitations of the procedure are discussed following the explanation.

Dividend data by industry for domestic stocks listed on the New York Stock Exchange (encompassing only dividends paid on common stock) were obtained from the exchange. Dividend data for all domestic corporations (representing payments on both common and preferred stock) were obtained from IRS Statistics of Income, and were placed on a basis comparable to that of the NYSE.[11] That is, the IRS does not necessarily assignind ustrial subgroups to the same industries to which they are assigned by the NYSE. Since dividend data by industrial subgroups were available only from the IRS, the IRS industry categories were brought into conformity with those of the NYSE. Table VI-6 shows the IRS industrial subgroups contained within each NYSE industry.

NYSE dividends were then subtracted from IRS dividends in order to obtain estimates of the industrial distribution of non-NYSE dividends.[12] Market value–dividend ratios by industry were then derived for companies listed on the NYSE, using year-end data on industry market values for common stocks. These ratios were applied to the estimates of non-NYSE dividend payments by industry in order to obtain preliminary estimates of the industrial distribution of the market value of stocks not listed on the NYSE.

[11] Dividend data for industrial subgroups were not available from the IRS in 1954 or 1955; therefore, industry totals were not derived in these two years. A small percentage of IRS dividends (less than 8 percent in most years) were not classified by industry; these dividends were contained in an "all other" category, or they represented payments by industrial subgroups for which the appropriate NYSE industry could not be determined. Similarly, before 1959, a small percentage of NYSE dividends (less than 2 percent) were not classified by industry; these dividends were contained in an "all other" category or in a category labeled simply "U.S. companies abroad."

[12] The farm machinery industry was excluded in these calculations. Dividend data for the industry were available from the IRS and the NYSE only through 1958; after 1958, the industry's dividends were included in the machinery and metals category. Totals for the service industry (as reported by the NYSE after 1958) were also excluded, since the comparable IRS industry could not be determined.

TABLE VI-6

Internal Revenue Service Industry Subgroups Contained Within the
New York Stock Exchange Industry Categories

NYSE Industry	IRS Industrial Subgroups Contained in This Industry
Aircraft	Aircraft and parts; air transportation
Amusement	Motion pictures; amusement, except motion pictures
Automotive	Motor vehicles and equipment; urban, suburban, and interurban transport; trucking and warehousing; other motor-vehicle transportation
Building trade	Construction
Chemical	Chemical and allied products; stone, clay, and glass products
Electrical equipment	Electrical machinery and equipment; scientific instruments, photographic equipment, watches
Financial	Finance; insurance; lessors of real property
Food products	Food and kindred products; beverages
Leather	Leather
Machinery and metals	Fabricated metal products; machinery, except transportation and electrical (excluding office equipment and, before 1959, agricultural machinery)
Mining	Mining and quarrying (excluding crude petroleum and natural-gas production)
Office equipment	Office equipment; furniture and fixtures
Paper and publishing	Paper and allied products; printing and publishing; lumber and wood products
Petroleum and natural gas	Crude petroleum and natural gas; petroleum and coal products
Railroad and railroad equipment	Railroad transportation; railroad equipment
Real estate	Real estate, except lessors of real property other than buildings
Retail trade	Retail trade
Rubber	Rubber products
Shipbuilding	Ship and boat building; water transportation
Steel and iron	Primary metal industries
Textile	Textile and mill products; apparel manufacture
Tobacco	Tobacco
Utilities	Communications; electric and gas; other public utilities

These data were then adjusted each year by applying the following ratio (from that year's data) to each industry total:

The total market value of all outstanding stock *minus* the market value of all NYSE stock $\Bigg\}$ The sum of the preliminary estimates of the market values of non-NYSE industries

In these calculations, the total market value of all outstanding stock includes the value of investment companies, since the dividend totals for the financial industry include dividends paid by investment companies. Similarly, the value of investment companies is included in the value of NYSE stock.

This procedure, in a very rough way, adjusts for the fact that price-dividend ratios may not be the same for both NYSE and non-NYSE stocks. It also adjusts, again in a rough way, for the exclusion of IRS dividends in the "all other" category, as discussed below.

The adjusted estimates of the market values, by industry, of the outstanding corporate stock of non-NYSE companies are added to the NYSE industry market-value totals (including both common and preferred stock) in order to obtain the final estimates of the market value of all outstanding corporate stock by industry (including investment companies).[13]

These are the limitations of the procedure employed here:

(a) The NYSE and the IRS may not always assign particular companies to the same industry, since the NYSE does not necessarily follow the Standard Industrial Classification. As a result, there may be a lack of comparability between the IRS industry data and the NYSE industry area. A similar problem arises when the IRS, but not the NYSE, transfers a company from one industry one year to another industry the following year.

---

[13] Because of a few minor adjustments and discrepancies, the sum of the adjusted industry totals is less than the market value of all outstanding stock (including investment companies) throughout the whole period. For example, in one or two cases every year, reported dividend payments by NYSE companies in specific industries exceeded total dividend payments by that industry as reported by the IRS. Market value data for these industries represent only reported NYSE market values. Also, NYSE market values for the "all other," farm machinery, services, and "U.S. companies abroad" industries are excluded from the overall market value totals in the procedure followed here.

(b) The IRS may, on occasion, transfer industry subgroups between industries. The year-to-year comparability of the IRS industry classifications would have to be examined in order to obtain more accurate industry totals.

(c) The IRS data include both common and preferred dividends, while the NYSE data include only common dividends. Since the industrial distribution of common and preferred dividends is likely to differ, an error of unknown magnitude is introduced into the results.

(d) As previously indicated, a small percentage of IRS dividends was in an "all other" category, or was in industrial categories for which the comparable NYSE industries could not be determined. However, NYSE-listed companies which are in these various categories do end up in some industry in the NYSE classification. The procedure used here assumes that the industrial division of the companies contained in these IRS categories corresponds to the industrial division of the preliminary estimates of the market value of non-NYSE companies.

5. COMPARISON WITH OTHER ESTIMATES

The overall market-value totals derived here are slightly larger than the values reported by the SEC between 1952 and 1954, and are smaller between 1955 and 1958 (when the two series are put on a comparable basis by excluding from the SEC series the amount of listed and unlisted foreign stock outstanding in the United States). The values derived here become slightly larger again in 1959, and the difference between the two series becomes steadily more pronounced after 1964. By the end of 1968, the discrepancy amounts to $312 billion, or 42 percent of the SEC total.

The basic reason for the growing discrepancy in the 1960's is the differential price behavior of stocks listed on the NYSE, the ASE, and those traded OTC. The SEC data are obtained by extrapolating a 1960 benchmark figure on the basis of changes in Standard and Poor's 500-Stock Price Index, which includes only stocks listed on the NYSE. However, OTC prices started increasing more rapidly than NYSE prices after 1960, while ASE prices started increasing more rapidly after 1966. Therefore, the use of a price index based solely on NYSE price changes creates a constantly increasing divergency (at least, throughout a good part of the 1960's) from actual market values.

The values derived here are somewhat larger than the values reported by the Federal Reserve Board between 1952 and 1954, and are smaller between 1955 and 1960 (when the two series are placed on a comparable basis). The values derived here become larger again in 1961, and remain larger through 1968, but they are much closer to the FRB totals than to those of the SEC. The Federal Reserve Board data are apparently derived by applying a constant multiplier to the total value of listed stock (that is, it is assumed that the value of OTC and privately held stock increased in proportion to the increase in the value of listed stock). Even though OTC prices increased more rapidly than prices of listed stock during the 1960's, the discrepancy between the two series was apparently kept relatively small by new listings; that is, the increase in the number of companies listed on exchanges in the 1960's caused listed market values to rise considerably more rapidly than the rise shown by exchange price indexes.

The total derived here for 1960 is about $25 billion, or 5 percent larger than the estimate derived by Crockett and Friend[14] (after the two estimates are placed on a comparable basis, since these authors included the value of investment companies as well as the value of foreign stock outstanding in the United States in their total, and used middle of the year, rather than year-end, values). The difference is completely in the OTC and privately held sector, as might be expected. It does not seem to be due to the fact that they estimated OTC market values through a dividend residual method, instead of using the SEC data. A small part of the difference is due to two minor errors made by Crockett and Friend. First, in obtaining a dividend residual to estimate the value of unlisted stock, they subtracted total dividend payments by listed companies from total dividends paid by U.S. corporations. This subtracts too much, since dividend payments by listed companies include payments by Canadian listed companies to their non-U.S. stockholders, though these amounts are not included in total dividend payments of all U.S. corporations. The subtraction of payments by Canadian listed companies to their U.S. stockholders is compensated for by Crockett and Friend when they add total dividend payments by foreign companies to their U.S. stockholders to total dividends paid by U.S. companies in arriving at their dividend residual. Their second error is the subtraction of total capital gains distributions from total U.S. dividend payments in arriving at a dividend residual. Since dividend payments reported by the NYSE include capital gains distributions, there is double counting; and, again, too much is deducted. As a result of these two errors, their dividend residual is too small by about 5 percent, and they underestimate market values by about $5 billion.

[14] Jean Crockett and Irwin Friend, "Characteristics of Stock Ownership," American Statistical Association, *1963 Proceedings of the Business and Economic Statistics Division,* pp. 146–68.

By far the major part of the difference between the two estimates can be attributed to the treatment of non-dividend-paying stock, since Crockett and Friend use almost the same yield figure employed in this analysis to blow up their 1960 dividend residual. They estimated that 9 percent of the market value of OTC stock (except banks and insurance companies) was non-dividend-paying and used this percentage for both OTC industrial stock and for privately held stock. Their estimate was based on a sample of 300 OTC companies drawn from the National Stock Summary.

In this analysis, a 20 percent figure was used for privately held and small OTC companies. Use of a 9 percent figure would reduce the estimate of the market value of these companies by about $12 billion. In addition, in estimating dividends paid by large OTC industrial companies, it was assumed here that 33 percent of the market value of these companies was non-dividend-paying (based on the ASE sample). Use of a 9 percent figure would increase estimated dividend payments by large OTC companies by $370 million. This would reduce the size of the dividend residual by 11 percent, and reduce the estimate of the market value of the stock of privately held and small OTC companies by another $9 billion.

Consequently, not only are the estimates of the market value of privately held and small OTC companies strongly influenced by the yield data employed in the analysis, but they are also affected by the assumed importance of non-dividend-payers. This affects the market-value total directly, and affects it indirectly by influencing the size of the dividend residual.

6. SUGGESTIONS FOR FURTHER RESEARCH

a. *Estimates of the Market Value of Privately Held and Small OTC Companies*

These estimates could be improved in two ways. First, OTC industrial stocks could be sampled each year to determine the importance of non-dividend-paying companies. This would improve the estimates of the amount of dividends paid by large OTC industrial companies, and would improve the accuracy of the dividend residual. Second, unpublished IRS data could be examined, if possible, to determine whether they provide any information on the number of privately held companies paying dividends.

b. *Estimates of the Value of Intercorporate Holdings*

These estimates could be improved if additional information about wholly owned subsidiaries were available from the IRS; that is, dissemination of information, for each of the years covered by the analysis, about the number and importance of subsidiaries which had filed separate returns in the previous year but were now filing consolidated returns. The data show a sharp increase in the importance of corporations filing consolidated returns. Presumably, though, only part of this increase reflects a change in corporate filing practices; a part must reflect new corporate acquisitions during the period. If the two components could be separated, the data on intercorporate holdings could be placed on a fairly consistent basis.

c. Estimates of the Value of Treasury Stock

Estimates of the value of Treasury stock could be obtained by sampling listed and OTC companies in selected years during the period covered by the analysis.

d. Estimates of the Total Value of Outstanding Corporate Stock

As indicated earlier, an error is introduced into the estimates because of wholly owned subsidiaries which file consolidated tax returns, but which have a sufficient number of shareholders to be listed on an exchange, or to be traded OTC. Some attempt could be made to determine the number and importance of those companies which fall into this category.

Appendix VII

The Measurement of Foreign Holdings and Transactions in United States Corporate Stock

LEWIS LIPPNER

BOARD OF GOVERNORS OF THE FEDERAL RESERVE SYSTEM

THE largest variety and most comprehensive collection of data pertaining to portfolio investment is compiled by the U.S. Treasury Department in conjunction with the Federal Reserve System. Primary statistics on the principal types of data and the principal countries or areas involved in these capital transactions are published monthly in the *Treasury Bulletin*, and to a lesser extent in the *Federal Reserve Bulletin*. Pursuant to executive order and various administrative regulations, securities brokers and dealers, banks, and other nonbanking financial institutions (insurance companies, funds, and so on) are directed to report their international security transactions monthly to the Federal Reserve banks. "The existing regulations require that all U.S. residents report transactions in long-term securities with foreigners whether made in their own behalf or on behalf of their customers provided the total of purchases or sales is greater than a monthly average of $100,000 in the six months ending with the reporting date."[1] The S-form data are then consolidated and published by the Treasury. This is the raw material from which the Commerce Department's Office of Business Economics ultimately produces lines 34–36 and line 52 of the U.S. balance of payments account (adjustments to S-form data are discussed below).

In general, data on foreign purchases or sales of securities[2] are reported on the basis of the foreign country or geographic area in which the records of the reporting institutions show the transactor to be domiciled. Transactors are likely to be financial institutions acting as agents for the actual purchaser.

---

[1] Report of review committee for balance of payments statistics to the Bureau of the Budget, *Balance of Payments Statistics, Review & Appraisal*, April 1965, p. 77.

[2] Foreign purchases or sales of foreign securities should be equal to U.S. sales or purchases of foreign securities, respectively.

Because reporting institutions are not expected to go beyond the addresses shown on their records, they may not be aware of the actual country of domicile of their client. Thus, a beneficiary may not be domiciled in the same country as the transacting agent, and geographical classification cannot with certainty be said to reflect the amounts actually purchased by investors purported to be domiciled in a particular country or area. The year-to-year variations in a country's purchases, however, can probably be assumed to reflect the general trend of purchases in each geographical region, with the notable exceptions of transactions reported by agents located in Switzerland, the Bahamas, and Bermuda.[3] Dealings in securities in these countries overwhelmingly represent the interest of clients living elsewhere.

In addition to problems related to the geographical distribution of securities purchases and sales, problems arise from omissions in the data caused by the failure of transacting agents to file the appropriate reports. Most Treasury Department reporting forms are filed by banks, securities brokers and dealers, and major insurance companies. However, the growth of other financial intermediaries in recent years suggests that laxity in report filing may not be uncommon. Many U.S. investment funds, pension funds, or educational institutions may invest directly in foreign assets. Furthermore, transactions in foreign securities by individual U.S. citizens, especially those living abroad, are often made through foreign channels and hence go unrecorded.[4] The actual size of such omissions is not known, nor is there any rough indication of their magnitude. Current OBE estimates of U.S. holdings of foreign securities are calculated by adding the annual flows reported to the Treasury Department, with various adjustments to the benchmark statistics established by a census taken during World War II. Obviously, the accumulation of even small omissions in any direction over this twenty-year period could affect the totals significantly.

Estimation of foreign transactions in U.S. securities presents similar problems although omissions may well be smaller in this case. Until several years ago, foreign citizens purchasing or selling U.S. securities did so almost exclusively through American banks or brokers who were subject to strict reporting requirements. Omissions still occurred, however, when the transaction was executed by a U.S. financial intermediary

[3] See Fred Ruckdeschel, "Prospects for Foreign Purchases of U.S. Stocks," unpublished Federal Reserve study, July 1969.
[4] *Balance of Payments Statistics*.

and the sales agent was unaware that the beneficiary was a foreign resident. Prior to the mid-1960's, the reported annual flow of foreign investments in U.S. corporate securities was relatively small, and the absolute magnitude of possible omissions was probably correspondingly small. The record growth of foreign investment companies dealing largely, or in some cases exclusively, in U.S. securities increases the possibility of omissions inasmuch as these firms are not subject to reporting requirements required of U.S. transacting agents.

Some types of security purchases are inherently difficult to classify. Total long-term portfolio capital movements are entered in the balance of payments as collected by the Treasury Department, apart from adjustments made for reclassification of items that are actually direct investments.

To facilitate explanation of these adjustments, assume that an American company with a Canadian affiliate desires to purchase Canadian securities. This simple purchase can be accomplished in several different ways. It can be carried out as an investment of parent company funds, in which case the transfer is actually a portfolio investment; or the same firm can purchase the same securities as an investment of the foreign branch. In this second case, the acquisition is not to be regarded as an international transaction at all, but is a domestic Canadian investment by a Canadian company. If the same investment is effected through the use of funds transferred from the home office to the foreign branch, the purchase should properly be considered a direct investment by the U.S.-based parent firm. In many instances, the U.S. parent company may have reported the capital transfer in the third case as a direct investment, while the foreign subsidiary reports the same transaction as a portfolio investment. To avoid this double counting, the OBE finds it necessary to deduct this transfer of funds from the portfolio investment amount in the *Treasury Bulletin*.

The Treasury's reporting system covers only cash trading. But let us now assume that a foreign-based company purchases shares of an American enterprise by means of a stock transfer. This assignment of stock was made in lieu of a cash disbursement and will be reported by the U.S. company as a foreign direct investment, provided the foreign company acquires more than 10 percent of the voting stock of the American firm. If the foreign company purchases less than 10 percent of voting equity, it is assumed that the firm will not be participating in decisions affecting the management of the domestic company, and the acquisition will be considered a portfolio investment. Thus, in the latter case, an offsetting entry must be made by the balance of payments division (BPD) to remove this transaction from those direct investments already recorded and add it to those portfolio investments previously reported by the Treasury Department. Lastly, let us assume that a foreign owned U.S. subsidiary floats a new stock issue in the United States. If the foreign firm decides to exercise its rights in the new issue, the issue should appear both in the Treasury's portfolio investment report and in the BPD's Foreign Direct Investment Report. The entry must be dropped from portfolio investment to avoid double counting. These represent the most common adjustments performed by the Commerce Department to eliminate items properly considered direct investments in balance of payments terms from the capital movements data compiled by the U.S. Treasury.[5] To illustrate the extraordinary magnitude of adjustments in some years, the BPD found it necessary, in 1968, to exclude the purchase by Royal Dutch Shell Company, Ltd., of $210 million of stock newly issued by its U.S. subsidiary. The purchase was treated as a direct investment.[6] This is not meant to imply that individual adjustments commonly run into hundreds of millions of dollars. Actually, over the period 1952–66, total adjustments of data for most foreign stock purchases by the United States averaged only slightly more than $20 million per year, and adjustments to figures generated for net purchases by foreigners of U.S. stocks averaged less than $15 million per year.

---

[5] Examples of adjustments are the product of conversations which the author has had with Russel Scholl of the Commerce Department's Office of Business Economics.

[6] U.S. BPD: Second Quarter 1969, *Survey of Current Business*, September 1969.

Author Index

Subject Index